D1548224

INTEGRAL HUMAN DEVELOPMENT

RECENT TITLES FROM THE HELEN KELLOGG INSTITUTE SERIES
ON DEMOCRACY AND DEVELOPMENT

Paolo G. Carozza and Aníbal Pérez-Liñan, *series editors*

The University of Notre Dame Press gratefully thanks the Helen Kellogg Institute for International Studies for its support in the publication of titles in this series.

J. Ricardo Tranjan
Participatory Democracy in Brazil: Socioeconomic and Political Origins (2016)

Tracy Beck Fenwick
Avoiding Governors: Federalism, Democracy, and Poverty Alleviation in Brazil and Argentina (2016)

Alexander Wilde
Religious Responses to Violence: Human Rights in Latin America Past and Present (2016)

Pedro Meira Monteiro
The Other Roots: Wandering Origins in Roots of Brazil *and the Impasses of Modernity in Ibero-America* (2017)

John Aerni-Flessner
Dreams for Lesotho: Independence, Foreign Assistance, and Development (2018)

Roxana Barbulescu
Migrant Integration in a Changing Europe: Migrants, European Citizens, and Co-ethnics in Italy and Spain (2019)

Matthew C. Ingram and Diana Kapiszewski
Beyond High Courts: The Justice Complex in Latin America (2019)

Kenneth P. Serbin
From Revolution to Power in Brazil: How Radical Leftists Embraced Capitalism and Struggled with Leadership (2019)

Manuel Balán and Françoise Montambeault
Legacies of the Left Turn in Latin America: The Promise of Inclusive Citizenship (2020)

Ligia Castaldi
Abortion in Latin America and the Caribbean: The Legal Impact of the American Convention on Human Rights (2020)

Paolo Carozza and Clemens Sedmak
The Practice of Human Development and Dignity (2020)

Amber R. Reed
Nostalgia after Apartheid: Disillusinment, Youth, and Democracy in South Africa (2020)

James J. Sheehan
Making a Modern Political Order: The Problem of the Nation State (2023)

For a complete list of titles from the Helen Kellogg Institute for International Studies, see http://www.undpress.nd.edu.

INTEGRAL HUMAN DEVELOPMENT

CATHOLIC SOCIAL TEACHING AND THE CAPABILITY APPROACH

EDITED BY
SÉVERINE DENEULIN
AND CLEMENS SEDMAK

University of Notre Dame Press
Notre Dame, Indiana

Library of Congress Control Number: 2023937445

ISBN: 978-0-268-20570-6 (Hardback)
ISBN: 978-0-268-20572-0 (WebPDF)
ISBN: 978-0-268-20569-0 (Epub)

*To all those who have shown through their lives
the path to integral human development*

CONTENTS

ACKNOWLEDGMENTS

This book is the fruit of a long journey that would never have seen the light without those who offered support, encouragement, and a listening ear on the way. At the beginning of the project there was a working group on the topic jointly organized by the Center for Social Concerns and the Kellogg Institute for International Studies of the University of Notre Dame in Notre Dame, Indiana. The respective directors, Paul Kollman and Paolo Carozza, have been instrumental in the realization of this project. We want to express our gratitude to Paolo and Paul.

The Kellogg Institute facilitated a visiting fellowship for Séverine Deneulin, without which this book would never have been conceived. The Institute also financed three workshops, two in South Bend and one in Dublin, where some of the contributors to this volume presented their ideas. We owe gratitude to Don Stelluto, executive director of the Kellogg Institute, and to its new director, Aníbal S. Pérez Liñan. We also want to thank Bill Purcell and Kelli Reagan from the Center for Social Concerns, who accompanied the book project.

A lot of water has flowed under the bridge, so to say, since we both sat one spring afternoon of 2018 at an outside table on the Notre Dame campus to discuss a draft table of contents for the book. Séverine went back to England and in autumn 2019 joined the newly created Laudato Si' Research Institute at Campion Hall, University of Oxford. The Institute, whose mission is to build the intellectual foundations for a re-ordering of society centered on care for the earth and for the poor, provided the ground and the motivation for advancing this book project to completion. We hope to show that integral human development is not just a concept, but also a commitment.

That is why it is countless women and men who, through their lives and sometimes their deaths, have inspired us on the journey of trying to frame in our academic settings the process of integral human development. The words of Berta Cáceres in her recipient speech when she was awarded the Goldman Environmental Prize in 2015, a few months before she was murdered for defending the rivers and the Lenca people of Honduras, best summarize what the authors of this book have sought to contribute to in an academic and scholarly way:

> Let us wake up! Let us wake up, humanity! We're out of time. We must shake our conscience free. . . . The Gualcarque River has called upon us, as have other gravely threatened rivers. We must answer their call. Our Mother Earth—militarized, fenced-in, poisoned, a place where basic rights are systematically violated—demands that we take action. Let us build societies that are able to coexist in a dignified way, in a way that protects life.

Séverine Deneulin
Clemens Sedmak

Promoting Integral Human Development

Catholic Social Teaching and the Capability Approach

Séverine Deneulin and Clemens Sedmak

THE SIGNS OF THE TIMES

In October 2018, the Intergovernmental Panel on Climate Change (IPCC) made a final call for "unprecedented changes at all levels of society"—cultural, economic, political, social, technological, ethical—to address the climate emergency and keep temperature rise to 1.5 degrees above pre-industrial levels (IPCC 2018). In its report on biodiversity loss, the Intergovernmental Science-Policy Platform on Biodiversity and Ecosystem Services (IPBES) declared that there must be "transformative changes," which it understood as a "fundamental, system-wide reorganization across technological, economic and social factors, including paradigms, goals and values" (IPBES 2019), if we are to reverse the current levels of deterioration of water, land, air, ecosystems, and extinction of animal and plant species.

In August 2021, the IPCC renewed its alarming call, and renewed it again more urgently in March 2022 in its sixth assessment report (IPCC 2022). Keeping global temperatures 1.5 degrees above pre-industrial levels will require mammoth undertakings at all levels of society, by every individual, every institution. Failing to reach that target will entail an uncertain future for humanity. Extreme weather events have intensified over the past three years globally. To mention a few: the wildfires in Australia in December 2019, the heat wave in Western Canada in June 2021, the wildfires in Greece in August 2021, the floods in Germany in July 2021, the European heat wave of July 2022 and its worst draught ever recorded, the first rains ever in Greenland—and the list of unprecedented extreme weather events could go on and are only intensifying as the years go by. And to this one can add the global coronavirus pandemic linked to the destruction of animal habitats; scientists had for some time warned of the increased risk of zoonotic diseases linked to environmental destruction (UNEP 2020).

The climate emergency, however, is not the only sign that something has gone awry with our global economic model of production and consumption. Inequality has also risen significantly over the last century. There has been massive progress globally in terms of health care, educational achievements, and general living conditions thanks to public investment in water, sanitation, schools, and hospitals (Roslin 2010), but vast inequalities remain, and the global coronavirus pandemic has made these even more manifest, with the poorest and most vulnerable most affected (UNDP 2021).

Already in the late 1980s and early 1990s, United Nations organizations urged the creation of a path of human progress and development that was sustainable and human. In 1987 the World Commission on the Environment and Development, in its report *Our Common Future*, asked for governments to make policy decisions that would not compromise the ability of future generations to fulfil their human needs (WCED 1987). In 1990 the United Nations Development Programme published its first Human Development Report; these reports would provide an annual snapshot of how people were doing, not only how their countries' economies were doing, such as whether their countries had made progress in improving their health, education, and political participation, their social environments and security, their living conditions, and their quality of life in general. Its 2019 report is dedicated to the theme of inequality and discusses how socio-economic vulnerability and greater exposure to environmental risks interact. As the report puts it succinctly, "The effects of climate change deepen existing social and economic fault lines" (UNDP 2019, 17). Its 2020 *Report on Human Development and the Anthropocene* argues further that human and life systems will not be brought back into balance without a radical transformation of power relations and without addressing socio-economic and political inequalities but, most of all, without rethinking what being human means and re-evaluating the meaning of human development when the human is conceived of as embedded into a complex web of life and not separate from ecosystems (UNDP 2020).

Set against the background of such a bleak panorama of the global social and environmental situation, initiatives to redefine what counts as progress or development and to propose a renewed notion of what counts as prosperity or human flourishing have intensified, with not just the UNDP urging for deep reflection on what makes us human and therefore challenging the understanding of what counts as human development or human progress (UNDP 2020, 112). In the UK, a commission was set up in 2009 to rethink sustainable development (Jackson 2016, 2021). The commission's report argued for a shift of our conception of prosperity from income growth to the "quality of our lives, the health of families, satisfaction with work, sense of shared meaning and purpose" (Jackson 2016, 22). That same year the French government also set up a commission to measure economic performance and social progress apart from gross domestic product and consumption indicators, which led to the consideration of new indicators of quality of life (Commission on the Measurement of Economic Performance and Social Progress 2010). The Himalayan kingdom of Bhutan was one of the first countries to move away from assessing progress according to how the economy was doing and toward how people are doing across a number of domains, such as psychological well-being, time use, and ecological diversity and resilience (Ura et al. 2012). In 2015 all the world governments agreed at the United Nations General Assembly to a set of policy goals, the Sustainable Development Goals (SDGs), which cut across a large array of domains, from protecting life underwater to addressing inequality, including gender inequality, ensuring decent employment, providing urban infrastructure, improving living conditions in slums, and many others (UN 2015). Some, however, have expressed doubts as to whether the SDGs are able to inspire the deep structural economic, social, cultural, and moral transformation needed (Sachs 2017).

At the level of civil society, initiatives are also springing up to redirect the economy to serve people and their flourishing. Globally, the social and solidarity economy is gaining strength, and businesses are finding ways to recover their social purpose following Milton Friedman's declaration in the 1970s that a company existed for the sole purpose of making profit, such as the Certified B Corp initiative, which certifies companies' social and environmental performance, and the United Nations Global Compact initiative. University education and curricula are also being re-structured to respond to the climate emergency, and new ways of learning are being tested that link cognitive learning with experiential learning in connection to the land (Renouard et al. 2021). There is an urgency and a seriousness that cannot be denied. What is at stake is fundamentally the future of humanity on the planet, but also questions about the human person and her dignity, her development, and the ecology—the key values of globalized societies.

A CALL TO DIALOGUE AND ACTION

All the above initiatives and searches for new understanding can be seen as "signs of the times," an expression that has become part of Catholic tradition since the Second Vatican Council. Well before the UNDP launched its Human Development Reports in 1990 and argued that the question of development and progress is linked to the question of what it is to be human, the Catholic tradition had been reflecting on these questions for a long time. As an intellectual tradition that seeks to analyze social and economic realities from the perspective of the Christian faith, the social teachings of the Catholic tradition, known as Catholic Social Teaching (CST hereafter), have long been exploring questions of socio-economic development and its ultimate ends, an idea we will develop further shortly. CST offers an interpretative framework, a normative vision for personal and social transformation. The normative vision of CST is rooted in a moral tradition that recognizes "constants in context" (Bevans and Schroeder 2004), universal aspects of the human condition with tangible normative impacts. This tradition is linked to the idea of natural law (Pope 2005) and has been criticized, among other reasons, on the grounds of a suspected fact/value fallacy and an explicit "essentialism" (Pope 2001, 90–92). These criticisms may not share the theoretical assumptions of the tradition and its commitment to moral realism and universalism, but might nonetheless support important aspects of the "practical force of natural law" expressed in the Nuremberg trials, the Universal Declaration of Human Rights, or Martin Luther King, Jr.'s "Letter from a Birmingham Jail" (Pope 2001, 92). The situation we find ourselves in may justify a focus on the practical implications of this normative universal vision rather than the theoretical disagreements. Different approaches may be able to find the concepts of human dignity or integral human development useful, even without a consensus on justification and the fundamental background assumptions.

This volume is intended to offer a dialogue and common ground for action. CST is well prepared for this kind of dialogue because of its non-static nature and its ultimately practical intention of social transformation. CST is a rich tradition that goes beyond a "Western" understanding of development and personhood, as chapter 2 of this volume (by Dana Bates) shows.[1] As this volume illustrates, CST is always in dialogue with the socio-economic, political, and indeed intellectual context in which the Catholic tradition develops its social teachings. CST is dynamic and permeable, shaped and challenged by contemporary developments and open to new "signs of the times." Like any other tradition, it can be seen as an ongoing conversation and engagement with the world.

The dialogue partner of CST presented in this volume is the capability approach, a major ethical framework in contemporary social sciences.[2] The capability approach, not unlike CST with its commitment to questions of values and ultimate values, has shifted the understanding of social and economic progress from how much people have to what they can do and be as human beings, whether they can lead healthy lives, express themselves without fear, pursue knowledge, or enjoy aesthetic beauty. This way of ethical thinking has been pioneered by economist and philosopher Amartya Sen. Most of the initiatives to redefine progress briefly mentioned above do refer in one way or another to Sen's capability approach (hereafter CA). This book engages in an intentional conversation with the CA, an intellectual tradition in which scholars from many disciplines reflect on "development as freedom" and the kinds of practices and policies that enable people to flourish.

As the chapter authors of this volume will discuss, CST, with its emphasis on the human person, can be enriched by a conversation with a versatile and influential approach that owes a lot to Aristotle and his philosophy, which has obviously also shaped the history of CST. At first glance, this conversation could prove to be difficult. The conversation partners are quite different. CST is an expression of a particular faith tradition and part of the teaching office of the Catholic Church. It expresses the social dimension of the Christian faith and is ultimately concerned with discipleship and a pilgrimage toward a transcendent, ultimate goal. The CA belongs within a social-scientific discourse with a special focus on development studies and an emphasis on the individual and her freedoms.

Why would a dialogue between CST and the CA with a focus on "integral development" and "integral ecology" be fruitful? We believe that this dialogue is warranted because of their shared concern with human well-being and the protection of dignity. The common ground for this dialogue is their concern with and commitment to human development in a holistic way. Additionally, both CST and the CA have emerged as normative approaches because of their distinct concern with social exclusion and practices of marginalization. Both normative frameworks have responded to social realities with the goal of social transformation. Both are committed to dealing with very similar questions: What is a good human life? What are reasons to value a particular kind of life? What is an appropriate understanding of human development in the light of these fundamental normative questions? How can we deal with the future of humanity and the planet?

This book's conversation between these two normative frameworks, the CA and CST, is warranted not only because they both have close connections to social practices but because, as many contributors to this book will discuss, they share many common grounds in their understanding of development and socio-economic progress. The two approaches have common grounds (such as the importance of Aristotelian thinking and a focus on the human person) and a shared concern with notions of well-being and fulfilment. This dialogue is also warranted because CST and the CA are open to engaging with many traditions and frameworks. Neither approach is closed off, neither has been developed in isolation, and both reflect their engagement with heterogeneous contexts and sources. That is why we are particularly interested in the "enrichment effect" of this dialogue with a primary focus on CST as a tradition that can easily engage with the CA. Our volume focuses on the questions: What can the social teachings of the Catholic tradition learn from an engagement with the CA? How can CST be enriched through insights and contributions of the CA? Or, more specifically, can CST accommodate the CA in its service to integral human development?

This focus does not rule out, of course, the idea that the CA could benefit from an engagement with CST, especially with the latter's emphasis on the most disadvantaged, flourishing communities, human finitude and limits, and responsibility for creation. The social reality of the matter, however, is that the dialogue is not strictly reciprocal and that there is an asymmetry in the sense that scholars working within CST tend to be more interested in the CA than are scholars of the CA in CST. CST is perceived as a normative framework housed within a particular and rich faith tradition and within a global religious institution. The CA, with its non-denominational roots and its impact on the policy and reporting cultures of many non-governmental organizations (NGOs) and governing bodies, including the United Nations, seems to appeal to a larger audience. We do hope that the contributions of this book might be of interest to scholars of the CA as well; our project is, in any case, intended to be a conversation-starter. We believe that the CA can be inspired by the fundamental questions about values, community, future generations, and the ecology raised in CST.

A word about the terminology: when we talk about CST, we mean the social teachings of the Catholic tradition. We prefer to consider the body of social teachings that are contained in papal encyclicals and the documents of bishops' conferences (known as Catholic Social Teaching) as "tradition" since it is set within the context of a broader dynamic of intellectual contributions and debates, spiritual foundations, and social practices. CST is as much an intellectual and theological tradition as it is a social one. It is more than "head"; it is also "hands" and heart," as we will discuss further below. The non-negotiable core of CST is its commitment to the dignity of the human person, firmly grounded in an understanding of natural law. Pope Francis's encyclical *Laudato Si': On Care for Our Common Home*, has offered a new framework for thinking about development by introducing the concept of "integral ecology" as a new lens through which to assess integral human development (Francis 2015). Our book will draw heavily from this encyclical as a key text from which to understand the signs of the times.

We have conceived this book for an audience that is heterogeneous, both academically and geographically. It is aimed at students, scholars, and practitioners in global affairs, development studies, or the social sciences more widely who seek to better understand the Catholic tradition and its social teachings and what it can offer to address humanity's current socio-environmental challenges. It is also aimed at students and scholars in theology and religious studies and those working in faith-based organizations who seek to understand what the normative framework of the capability approach can contribute to the development of the social teachings of the Catholic tradition in its efforts to interpret situations of social and environmental degradation and transform them in the light of the Christian faith. This book is intended to serve individuals and communities in the global North and the global South and all those concerned with questions of ecology, environmental crises, and the future of humanity on planet Earth. Both the capability approach and the social teachings of the Catholic tradition are "designed" to bridge the gap between theoretical discourse and social transformation. In this sense, the book provides examples of action and change on the ground, such as among women victims of violence in Uganda, migrant children in Austria, indigenous communities in the Amazon, and informal settlement residents in Argentina. Ultimately, we intend the book to be of interest to those who care about Pope Francis's concerns with the cry of the earth and the cry of the poor.

Since we are speaking to a diverse audience, the following sections offer a short primer in what CST and the CA are. We then highlight some points of complementarities and tensions and conclude with a presentation of this edited volume's contributions.

THE CATHOLIC TRADITION AND ITS SOCIAL TEACHINGS

A former archbishop of El Salvador, (now saint) Oscar Romero, was assassinated on Monday, March 24, 1980, while he was celebrating Mass in the chapel of Divine Providence Hospital in San Salvador, where he lived. In his homily—the very last he preached—he quoted an important passage from *Gaudium et Spes* (Joy and Hope), a key document from the Second Vatican Council[3] also entitled the *Pastoral Constitution on the Church in the Modern World*:

> We do not know the time for the consummation of the earth and of humanity, nor do we know how all things will be transformed. As deformed by sin, the shape of this world will pass away; but we are taught that God is preparing a new dwelling place and a new earth where justice will abide, and whose blessedness will answer and surpass all the longings for peace which spring up in the human heart. . . . Therefore, while we are warned that it profits a man nothing if he gain the whole world and lose himself, the expectation of a new earth must not weaken but rather stimulate our concern for cultivating this one. For here grows the body of a new human family, a body which even now is able to give some kind of foreshadowing of the new age. Hence, while earthly progress must be carefully distinguished from the growth of Christ's kingdom, to the extent that the former can contribute to the better ordering of human society, it is of vital concern to the Kingdom of God. (Vatican Council 1965, 39)

A few minutes after completing this short homily and proclaiming these words, he was fatally shot.

This paragraph encapsulates the essence of the interpretative framework the Catholic Church uses to understand the social and economic reality known as Catholic Social Teaching: Whatever we find on this earth is transitional and will not last. There is a promise of a transformation beyond our imagination. This transformation will be a healing of a world deformed by sin. The hope for and expectation of a new earth nourishes the commitment to renew the earth as it is now in order to bring about a new humanity in the Here and Now that is an expression of the Kingdom of God. However, we could also understand these lines as a powerful reminder that the Kingdom of God has a dimension in the "Here" and "Now," it is "among us" (cf. Gospel of Luke, chapter 17, verse 21), and what we build here in love is there to last; working for the Kingdom of God in our days and times engages with the beginning of something that will continue to eternity. This perspective gives even deeper urgency and meaning to our commitments and work.

Admittedly, there is language in this paragraph, as well as in the social teachings of the Catholic tradition more generally, that may not appeal to or make sense to all readers ("sin," "God is preparing," "blessedness," "Christ's kingdom," "Kingdom of God"). However, it seems safe to assume that believers and non-believers alike can understand the call to transformation in *Gaudium et Spes* in the light of acknowledging a transcendent dimension of the human condition. The body of social teachings of the Catholic tradition is concerned with the relationship between "the ultimate" and "the present." It shares many of the ideas about justice and peace that can be found in secular philosophical traditions and in concrete activities on the ground (as the chapter authors of this book will show). But it frames them in a specific way that connects visible actions with intangible realities. The "what" of an action may be the same as in secular traditions (say, reducing child malnutrition), but there is a specific "why," and therefore a specific "how" (taking the spiritual dimension into consideration, for instance).

A lot can be said about paragraph 39 of *Gaudium et Spes*, but even more can be learned from the homilist, who did not simply preach and teach from a pulpit but incarnated CST with his own life. Archbishop Oscar Romero was shot because he was speaking out against the killing by the state and its army of peasants who demanded agrarian reforms. The day before he was killed, he made a special appeal "to the army's enlisted men, and in particular to the ranks of the National Guard and the police." In his Sunday homily, which was radio-broadcast all over El Salvador, he pleaded with the soldiers: "Brothers, you are part of our own people. You are killing your own brother and sister campesinos, and against any order a man may give to kill, God's law must prevail: 'You shall not kill!' (Ex. 20:13). No soldier is obliged to obey an order against the law of God. No one has to observe an immoral law. It is time now for you to reclaim your conscience and to obey your conscience rather than the command to sin" (Romero 1980).

Romero read the reality of his country at his time in the light of the social teachings of the Church, and this became for him a more and more dangerous thing to do. Romero's public reflection on the role of soldiers in the violence in his country signed his own death sentence. Reading the signs of the times in the light of CST and acting on this reading also led to the death of Dorothy Stang, an American-Brazilian religious sister who was killed in the Amazon Basin after having advocated for the rights of the poor and the needs of the environment. She chose not to be silent in the face of the injustice against peasants and indigenous peoples (Global Sisters Report n.d). This is also to say that enacting CST is not harmless; it comes with costs and sacrifice, since it challenges existing power dynamics.

Oscar Romero would interpret the contemporary political agenda of his country with the Scriptures and through the lens of CST, which served him as a way of "seeing the world." He would ponder and evaluate the state's actions in the light of CST's normative criteria, such as "the dignity of the human person" and "the common good." These criteria served as reference points for Romero in making clear political and social judgments about state repression and the legitimacy of the peasants' demands; at the same time, however, CST was not a political philosophy for him but a spirituality, a form of life, an integral part of being a Christian in a specific political context. He would live CST and die because of becoming a witness to this living tradition of social teachings. Oscar Romero's life best exemplifies a first characteristic of CST: a commitment to social (and ecological) justice based on a faith commitment and the hope for a "new world." Dorothy Stang is also a witness who reminds us of the "moral clarity" that can be reached by taking CST and the ecological and social dimensions of the faith seriously. She was shot when she was walking to a community meeting; her way was blocked and, when armed men asked whether she had any weapon on her, she pointed to the Bible as her only "weapon" and quoted the famous line from the Sermon on the Mount: "Blessed are the poor in spirit . . ." Then she was killed. The beatitude she quoted was influential in the early Christian tradition as an expression of the importance of the right attitude toward possessions and the world (Murphy 2007).

CST is an expression of the social dimension of the Christian faith; the 1971 Synod of Bishops on the theme of "Justice in the World" summarized this call thus: "Action on behalf of justice and participation in the transformation of the world fully appear to us as a constitutive dimension of the preaching of the Gospel, or, in other words, of the Church's mission for the redemption of the human race and its liberation from every oppressive situation" (Synod of Bishops 1971, 6).

This statement affirms that one cannot credibly live the Gospel without social and political commitments and engagements. This has traditionally been expressed as the unity between love of God and love of neighbor (Rahner 1969). In his apostolic exhortation *Evangelii Gaudium*, Pope Francis (2013) makes this point forcefully when he writes that "a personal and committed relationship with God . . . at the same time commits us to serving others" (*EG* 91).[4] CST, one could say, is a spirituality rather than a doctrine or set of norms, a *regula* (moral order) to be lived rather than a rule to be followed. It has a theological and not a philosophical foundation, that is, it is ultimately based on an encounter with Jesus, the Messiah (or Christ), and a personal relationship with God. But this relationship cannot be lived without "a turn to the other," as the first letter of John in the New Testament puts it succinctly: "Whoever does not love their brother and sister, whom they have seen, cannot love God, whom they have not seen" (first letter of John, chapter 4, verse 20).

The social dimension of the faith has been an integral part of the Christian tradition from the very beginning. To emphasize the importance of "love of neighbor" as part, expression, and consequence of love of God, an often-quoted Gospel passage in the first six centuries of the Church is from the Gospel of Matthew, chapter 25, verses 31–46, which reads: "Whatever you did for one of these least brothers [and sisters] of mine, you did for me." This again shows the specific Christian framing of the turn to the other (or, to use the later terminology in CST, the framing of "a preferential option for the poor") with its challenge of not instrumentalizing the most disadvantaged for purposes of inner edification.

The first centuries of the Christian era developed a social theology and a clear commitment to paying special attention to the most vulnerable members of society. The teachings of the social dimension of the faith have led to remarkable provocations that can be seen as "thorns in the flesh" of the privileged and the self-righteous (or, one could say, in the flesh of all of us), some of them finding their way into official documents. One example of a provocative prominent teaching is an exhortation from St. Ambrose quoted by Pope Paul VI (1967) in his encyclical *Populorum Progressio*: "You are not making a gift of what is yours to the poor man, but you are giving him back what is his. You have been appropriating things that are meant to be for the common use of everyone. The earth belongs to everyone, not to the rich" (*PP*, 23). There are many more examples—for instance, in the sermons of John Chrysostom or in the writings of the Cappadocian Fathers (Daley 2017). *The Rule of St. Benedict*, a reference for those seeking to live the monastic life till this day, expresses elements of the social tradition. In chapter 31, St. Benedict talks about the Cellarer of the Monastery who has to "provide for the sick, the children, the guests, and the poor, with all care, knowing that, without doubt, he will have to give an account of all these things on judgment day." In chapter 53 (which concerns hospitality and the reception of guests) one reads: "Let the greatest care be taken, especially in the reception of the poor and travelers, because Christ is received more specially in them" (Benedictine Centre, n.d.). These passages illustrate how the transcendental dimension brings concrete behavioral expectations. They could be seen by the modern-day reader as examples of spirituality expressed in social action.

The social teachings of the Christian tradition,[5] however, are not about teaching alone; the New Testament also gives many examples of concrete actions. Beginning with the book of Acts, one reads that among the early Christians "there was no needy person among them" (Acts, chapter 4, verse 34) and that there was a daily distribution for the widows (Acts, chapter 6, verse 1). The year 368 was of special importance in this regard: There was a famine in Cappadocia due to a severe drought, and the moral paradigm at the time was indifference. Basil of Caesarea preached a sermon titled "In Time of Famine and Drought" and organized famine relief activities. He established a *ptochotropheion* (a poor house/hospital) and bought available local grain from wealthy landowners that he distributed to the starving; his whole family was engaged in these relief efforts, motivated by a new way of seeing society as a community and the human person as a being with dignity (Holman 2001). This new way of seeing the person and the community was described by a historian as "a revolution of social imagination" (Brown 2002, 2012).

These actions stretched the imaginations of Basil's contemporaries and continues to do so. The values of dignity and solidarity were translated into practices and institutions along with a new language for talking about community and justice. Thus we have here a second characteristic of CST: it is the expression of the social dimension of the Christian faith, which has been translated into practices, institutions, and the social imagination since the beginnings of Christianity.

This rich and broad tradition of the social practices of the Christian church has been condensed into a more clearly defined body of texts called "Catholic Social Teaching," which is formed from a set of official Church documents, mostly papal encyclicals (i.e., letters to be circulated) that deal with social issues. The first of these so-called social encyclicals was the 1891 document titled *Rerum Novarum* (*RN*), by Pope Leo XIII. He addressed the situation of workers in the aftermath of the Industrial Revolution. *Rerum Novarum* introduced important concepts and topics such as a just wage, the right to private property and its social function, and the universal destination of the goods of the earth.[6] Pope Leo XIII defended labor unions. He also made reference to the social tradition of the early Church, quoting Gregory the Great's exhortation to assume an attitude of service and stewardship (*RN* 22), and he insisted that the Church be a key player in shaping policy debates on social and political matters (*RN* 13). In the document *Rerum Novarum* also anticipated the message of *Gaudium et Spes* 30, quoted above, by underlining the Church's commitment to social transformation: "Neither must it be supposed that the solicitude of the Church is so preoccupied with the spiritual concerns of her children as to neglect their temporal and earthly interests. Her desire is that the poor, for example, should rise above poverty and wretchedness, and better their condition in life; and for this she makes a strong endeavor" (*RN* 28).

Pope Leo XIII took substantial risks by beginning to talk about social issues the way he did—with authority and an explicit reference to his authority on social matters as well. A pope who links matters of faith and revelation to social and political concerns makes himself vulnerable to all kinds of criticism, since there are many stakeholders with strong interests in the social status quo. We can see some aspects of this vulnerability today in Pope Francis, who made powerful statements about different social matters, including "an economy that kills," in *Evangelii Gaudium*

(*EG* 53; Tornielli and Galeazzi 2015; Tornielli 2018). Ever since 1891, the social encyclicals of the Church have dealt with social matters of a changing nature. CST addresses "res novae" ("new things," the "signs of the times"). Key areas of concern are the family, human work, economic life, political community, global realities, the environment, and peace. Environmental concerns have been recognized as major "signs of the times" since near the end of the twentieth century. In the encyclical *Laudato Si'* Pope Francis responded to the unprecedented ecological crisis; it follows the general order of CST but expands it through its explicit focus on the ecological dimension and environmental concerns.[7] CST is based on a clear architecture of society, with the individual person as the foundation, the family as the first school of life and fundamental cell of society, and the community as a place of formation of solidarity on a local and global scale. Community and livelihood are built up by human work with its threefold purpose of self-realization, sustenance, and contribution to the common good. As highlighted earlier, CST is characterized by "constants in context" and continuity, but also by openness to development and change. It provides a theological perspective that is different from an economic or philosophical dimension, especially by connecting all issues with "first things" (creation questions) and "last things" (the afterlife and the purpose of life), that is, with "the ultimate" and the question of what it is that has and gives ultimate value. However, CST appeals to "common sense" and contains some fundamental moral values such as solidarity, subsidiarity (that is, the idea that a central authority should do only what cannot be done at the local level), care for creation, and common good.

Working with CST documents poses certain challenges, since its textual basis is diffuse (Rowlands 2021). Any statement made with official teaching authority within the context of the Church (every statement by a bishop, for instance) is relevant for CST. This means that we are dealing with a vast number of texts; consequently, there has to be some selectivity at play when working with CST documents. Besides, the statements in the documents cannot simply be "copied" but have to be properly contextualized. Furthermore, they leave interesting questions open (e.g., about what is a just wage or the preferred form of government), and there are areas of CST in which message and language are contested, for example, the areas of gender (see the chapter by Dunne in this volume),[8] the concept of family, the appeal to natural law (see the chapter by Russell), and questions of authority and authenticity. The latter questions include the question of the realization of CST principles within the Church in her institutionalized form.

In spite of these difficulties, the basics are clear and simple: at the very core of CST is a commitment to the dignity of the human person, created in the image and likeness of God. This influential approach with its equalizing effect (insisting that all persons are created in the image and likeness of God) can create a powerful story to be brought into public and pluralistic discourse (Waldron 2010),[9] a story that has influenced the human rights language and tradition (Glendon 2013). The *Compendium of the Social Doctrine of the Church*, published by the Pontifical Council of Justice and Peace (PCJP), leaves no room for doubt about the central place of the commitment to human dignity: "The whole of the Church's social doctrine, in fact, develops from the principle that affirms the inviolable dignity of the human person" (PCJP 2005, 107). Acknowledging the dignity of the human person means acknowledging the person in her uniqueness, her mystery, her special place in creation, which cannot be mistaken for a meritocratic or civic understanding of dignity or an understanding of dignity based on particular faculties, such as reasoning skills (Ober 2014; Genuis 2016). Human dignity, according to CST, is based on natural law, which does not close off a discussion but necessitates a constant dialogue with the signs of the times (Van Tongeren 2013).

This commitment to human dignity is also at the center of the two latest documents of CST, Pope Francis's *Laudato Si'*, published in June 2015, and *Fratelli Tutti*, which came out in October 2020. *Laudato Si'* has sometimes been considered the opening of a "third stream within Catholic Social Thought" (after Pope Leo XIII's 1891 encyclical on the situation of workers and Pope Paul VI's 1967 encyclical on development) for its focus on the environment. *Laudato Si'* is indeed about the environment, but it is primarily about human dignity. Paragraph 160 states that "what is at stake is our own dignity." The encyclical is an "appeal to everyone throughout the world not to forget this dignity which is ours" (*LS* 205). It operates with an understanding of dignity as conferred upon a person through the special love of the Creator for each human being (*LS* 65), which is a biblically rooted idea of equality in which "the rich and the poor have equal dignity, for "the Lord is the maker of them all" (Proverbs, chapter 22, verse 2) (*LS* 94). The dire situation of those who live in conditions of poverty and exclusion should not make us forget their "immense dignity" (*LS* 158). In a number of passages of *Laudato Si'* Francis talks about aspects of living with dignity; for example, in the context of water he states that "our world has a grave social debt towards the poor who lack access to drinking water, because *they are denied the right to a life consistent with their inalienable dignity*" (*LS* 30, italics original). Restoring a sense of dignity to the excluded is a moral imperative (*LS* 139). And this focus on dignity is also the foundation of solidarity. It is a crucial normative reference point for a reawakening of a spirit of solidarity. In *Fratelli Tutti* Pope Francis argues that it is "by acknowledging the dignity of each human person [that] we can contribute to the rebirth of a universal aspiration to fraternity" (*FT* 8) (see the chapter by Meghan Clark on dignity and solidarity). The word "dignity" appears sixty-six times in *Fratelli Tutti*.

Environmental degradation has effects on the experience and protection of dignity: "Human beings too are creatures of this world, enjoying a right to life and happiness, and endowed with unique dignity. So we cannot fail to consider the effects on people's lives of environmental deterioration" (*LS* 43). An unjust global system has "effects on human dignity and the natural environment" (*LS* 56). And "we know how unsustainable is the behavior of those who constantly consume and destroy, while others are not yet able to live in a way worthy of their human dignity" (*LS* 193). Based on this prominent notion of dignity, *Laudato Si'* also draws practical conclusions for stewardship and the care of creation: "By virtue of our unique dignity and our gift of intelligence, we are called to respect creation and its inherent laws, for "the Lord by wisdom founded the earth" (Prov. 3:19) (*LS* 69). Every act of cruelty toward any creature is "contrary to human dignity" (*LS* 92). In *Laudato Si'* Pope Francis urges every person on the planet to adopt a lifestyle full of acts of love, which express our own dignity as human beings (*LS* 211). And in *Fratelli Tutti* he takes the Parable of the Good Samaritan as an enactment of the meaning of dignity:

> The parable clearly does not indulge in abstract moralizing, nor is its message merely social and ethical. It speaks to us of an essential and often forgotten aspect of our common humanity: we were created for a fulfilment that can only be found in love. We cannot be

indifferent to suffering; we cannot allow anyone to go through life as an outcast. Instead, we should feel indignant, challenged to emerge from our comfortable isolation and to be changed by our contact with human suffering. That is the meaning of dignity. (*FT* 68)

Thus we have a third characteristic of CST: it is formed from a body of texts that flow from the affirmation of the inviolable dignity of the human person and examine its implications for the areas of human work, economic life, political decision-making, environmental protection, international peace and conflict resolution, family life, and so on. In that regard, CST proposes a specific vision of development based on this inviolable dignity, which it calls "integral human development." *Fratelli Tutti* connects dignity and integral human development explicitly: "Every human being has the right to live with dignity and to develop integrally" (*FT* 107). From this follows a fourth characteristic: CST is a specific interpretative frame for analyzing social and economic realities that connects material and immaterial dimensions of life and emphasizes the role of moral and spiritual values in development processes and outcomes. This is not exclusive to the Catholic social and intellectual tradition, of course, but is a feature of CST nonetheless.

CST brings something unique and attractive to both development discourse and practices. It offers an understanding of what it calls "authentic development," or "integral human development," by linking social and economic change to personal growth (*PP* 6). It seeks the development of the whole person (*PP* 14) by addressing all dimensions of the human person, including the inner dimension. It is a point with which Pope John Paul II started to write in *Sollicitudo Rei Socialis*, the encyclical commemorating the twentieth anniversary of *Populorum Progressio* in 1987 (*SRS* 1). In this encyclical the pope argues that development has a central ethical and cultural dimension (*SRS* 8) and an undeniable moral character (*SRS* 33): "Development which is merely economic is incapable of setting [wo]man free, on the contrary, it will end by enslaving [her] further" (*SRS* 46).

Hence, the documents of CST use moral language in discussing issues of development. They often combine this moral language with discussion of virtues, especially generosity (*PP* 54), which translates into "willing sacrifice" (*PP* 47). There is also moral language in the identification of vices, especially when talking about avarice and pride. In *Populorum Progressio* Pope Paul VI talks, for example, about the dangers of avarice and makes a strong statement: "Avarice, in individuals and in nations, is the most obvious form of stultified moral development" (*PP* 19). This echoes early Christian warnings that avarice is a fundamental and principal fault of the soul, an evil that breeds further evil (see the first letter of Timothy, chapter 6, verse 10). In connection with nations, Paul VI also discusses "pride," even "stubborn pride" (*PP* 53) or "haughty pride" (*PP* 62, 82) and "nationalistic pride" (*PP* 72). We find moral language employed in the category of "jealousy" in discussing the destructive jealousy of and between nations (*PP* 49, 52, 62, 76). Pope Francis uses strong moral language in *Laudato Si'*, too. For example: "When people become self-centred and self-enclosed, their greed increases" (*LS* 204); "he [Orthodox Patriarch Bartholomew] asks us to replace consumption with sacrifice, greed with generosity, wastefulness with a spirit of sharing, an asceticism" (*LS* 9); "Christian spirituality proposes a growth marked by moderation and the capacity to be happy with little" (*LS* 222). One element of *CST* is the "seamless garment" (*LS* 9) that connects the micro-relations between friends and individuals with the macro-relations between communities and nations.

Consonant with CST's commitment to dignity is its reconstruction of the goals of development, as discussed in the opening paragraph of *Populorum Progressio*: to ensure a decent life, which is to say, to escape hunger, poverty, endemic disease, and ignorance; to share in the benefits of civilization; and to improve human qualities and strive for fuller growth (*PP* 1). The goal of a humane and humanely decent life is reached once discrimination has been eliminated, the human person has been liberated from the bonds of servitude, and people are given "the capacity, in the sphere of temporal realities, to improve their lot, to further their moral growth and to develop their spiritual endowments" (*PP* 34). The temporal and material sphere, on the one hand, and the spiritual and immaterial sphere, on the other, are closely linked, so much so that they cannot be separated from one another.

CST insists that issues affecting the human dignity of individuals and peoples cannot be reduced to technical problems, for in this way ethical direction would be lost. The search for solutions to global problems such as poverty, a lack of decent work, or environmental degradation cannot be separated from our understanding of human beings. This is why CST is concerned with what could be called "over-development" or "super-development," defined as "an excessive availability of every kind of material goods for the benefit of certain social groups" (*SRS* 28); if "development" is also about redistribution, then this kind of over-development, often expressed in a throw-away culture (*SRS* 28; *LS* 16, 20–22), is a violation of and hindrance to "integral" human development. In *Laudato Si'* Pope Francis makes this connection between wrong development and environmental degradation very clear. Misleading priorities lead to destructive practices and habits that exploit the environment.

Even if there are important policy implications of a CST-based vision of development, such as special attention to redistributive policies and tax regimes or a greater focus on civic education or education for the common good, CST is not ultimately about influencing policy. A CST-based vision of development invites movement from (rational) decisions to (spiritual) discernment, from a philosophy of justice to a spirituality of justice. This movement is very visible in Pope Francis's encyclical *Laudato Si'*. It offers a two-fold transformation: of technical problems into moral questions and of moral questions into spiritual challenges.

This is why CST describes development work as primarily a vocation, as Pope Benedict XVI wrote in his encyclical *Caritas in Veritate*, published in 2009 (*CV* 11,16): A vocation is a call that requires a free and responsible answer. Integral human development presupposes the responsible freedom of the individual and of peoples: no structure can guarantee this development over and above human responsibility" (*CV* 17). As a vocation, development work calls for nothing less than a conversion (*SRS* 38), a term that Pope Francis has prominently placed in *Laudato Si'* (*LS* 5, 217). Development based on a "spirituality of justice" is an expression of love; love leads to the willingness to make sacrifices (*PP* 47), which are necessary if redistribution is to become real. The readiness to pay higher taxes, for example, can be seen as an expression of love (*PP* 47); educators should inspire young people "with a love for the needy nations" (*PP* 83). Clearly, the (challenging) concept of love emerges as the key notion. As Pope Paul VI wrote: "It is the person who is motivated by genuine love, more than anyone else, who pits his intelligence against the problems of poverty" (*PP* 75); and, according to Benedict XVI: "only in charity, illumined by the light of reason and faith, is it possible to pursue development goals that possess a more humane and humanizing value" (*CV* 9).

Integral human development, as seen through the lens of CST, offers a relational understanding of development and the human person, a consideration of cultural richness, spiritual depth, and the recognition of non-productive aspects of human life, a special consideration of the most disadvantaged and those left behind, the pursuit of first and last questions, questions about intrinsic and final goods. A CST approach to integral human development is not compatible with a neutral understanding of development, a one-dimensional understanding of the human condition (be it materialist or spiritualist), selective approaches that focus on majorities, and what Pope Francis has called a "technocratic paradigm" (*LS* 106–114).

We will see that some of these aspects are nuanced differently in the capability approach. But there is sufficient common ground between the CA and CST: an understanding of development beyond gross domestic product (GDP), an emphasis on dialogue and inclusive process, a notion of development as a value-driven process and concept, and a common focus on human dignity. The dialogue between the tradition of the social teachings of the Catholic Church and the capability approach promises to be fruitful. Before we explore some key aspects of the capability approach, let us summarize the main characteristic features of CST, as this book understands it:

- It is concerned with matters of social (and ecological) justice based on a faith commitment and the hope for "a new world."
- It is the expression of the social dimension of the Christian faith, which has been translated into practices, institutions, and the social imagination since the beginnings of Christianity.
- It is a body of (mostly papal) texts that has streamlined the tradition into an evolving set of principles and topics such as the family, human work, economic life, political community, global realities, the environment, and peace, with the inviolable dignity of the human person as the principle from which the whole of the Church's social thought develops.
- It provides a specific vision of development that pays attention to its immaterial aspects, that is, the intangible infrastructure of

moral and spiritual values. It calls this vision "integral" or "authentic" human development. It emphasizes "the whole person" and "all persons" as the subjects of development—with a critical eye toward those who live in contexts of "superdevelopment."

THE CAPABILITY APPROACH TO DEVELOPMENT

To introduce the capability approach to international postgraduate students, one of us started the class by putting the students in pairs and asked them to discuss whether life was better in the country where they studied than in their country of origin. They were also asked to justify the criteria they had used to make their value judgment. One student from Uganda expressed that life in the United Kingdom was better in the sense that there was universal access to health care and that nobody had to walk for miles, or become indebted, to receive medical care. He also pointed to the freedom to walk along streets that are pedestrian-friendly and free of violence. But he could not understand how a British student counterpart had to make an appointment in advance to meet up with this father. He found the lack of spontaneous social relations difficult to live with. His conclusion was that Uganda was a better country to live in, even if more materially poor, although he recognized that his value judgment was probably conditioned on his not having to worry about securing an adequate income to cover his subsistence and on his having access to health insurance on his return to his country.

This class exercise was used to illustrate what the CA is: a framework to use to make comparative value judgments about states of affairs and to assess whether one state is better than another. It is not a social theory and does not have any explanatory pretensions. All it does is to propose that information about capabilities is more helpful in making comparative value judgments about which situations are better than others than is information about utility, which is prevalent in mainstream economics. In order to assess situations, assessing how people's lives are doing is central to the approach. And in order to assess how much better or worse off people are, the CA argues that one needs to take into account other considerations beyond income and resources, or subjective states such as feelings of happiness or utility. One needs to include information about the actual lives of the affected people and what they can do or be with the resources they possess (what Amartya Sen calls "capabilities"), for instance, whether they are able to live healthy lives, move around freely, pursue knowledge, socialize with others, participate in social and political life, live without fear, be treated with respect, contribute to society through meaningful work, and so on. By shifting the informational basis for evaluating states of affairs from income or utility to capabilities, the CA offers a specific view of what counts as development or progress.

The word "capability" in this context made its début, so to say, in Sen's Tanner Lectures in Human Values, delivered in 1979 (Sen 1980). The CA has now taken on a life of its own. Summarizing the vast amount of literature around it has become impossible. Ingrid Robeyns's open-access book *The Capability Approach Re-Examined* is probably the most authoritative book-length treatment of what the CA is and what it is not (Robeyns 2017). In it Robeyns discusses the many directions in which those working with the approach have taken it over the past three decades (such as poverty and inequality measurement, higher education pedagogies, gender equality, theories of justice, and many others), as well as some of its misunderstandings, such as its so-called individualism and its assimilation with the human development approach put forward by the Human Development Reports of the United Nations Development Programme. Robeyns defines the capability approach as a "conceptual framework for a range of evaluative exercises, including most prominently the following: (1) the assessment of individual levels of achieved well-being and well-being freedom; (2) the evaluation and assessment of social arrangements or institutions; and (3) the design of policies and other forms of social change in society" (Robeyns 2017, 24).

On the basis of this broad definition, she proceeds to present what she calls a modular view of the CA; the first module is a set of propositions that any application or theory based on the approach has to observe. These include the incorporation of functionings and capabilities as key constituents of the evaluative space of states of affairs (see below); the incorporation of conversion factors (see below); the distinction between ends and means; the recognition of the plurality of values; and the consideration of each person as an end. She then establishes a second module, or stage, which involves defining the aim of what one is doing with the approach. Finally, she sets a third stage at which further decisions will have to be made given choices made in the second stage, for example, how to weigh different functionings if the purpose of the use of the CA is to design a composite poverty measure or multidimensional poverty index (Alkire et al. 2015; OPHI 2021). Thus, in some ways one could say that there is not such a thing as "the" capability approach. There is simply an approach in the social sciences to assessing how people's lives are, and, according to this approach, what people are able to do and be should be part of the evaluation of how better or worse their situations are. This approach has come to be known as "the capability approach." But, as Robeyns notes, there are many directions in which the CA has been taken—most notoriously, the direction taken by Martha Nussbaum in seeking to establish a theory of justice based on the CA akin to Rawls's political liberalism (see the chapter by Schulz). But there are other directions, too, such as an approach to assessing poverty (see the chapters by Deneulin and Zampini and by Gainsbauer) or an approach to conceptualizing collective action and social change (see the chapter by Otano Jiménez).

In this section we develop the characteristics that Robeyns enumerates within the context of development theory and practice. We seek to present what the CA is in the context of the discussions on the meaning of the concept of development and progress. And we argue that a capability-based vision of development or progress has six core features—which we will discuss in turn:

1. The inclusion of non-material dimensions (such as considerations about human freedom) in the evaluation of what counts as development or progress.
2. The consideration of people and their flourishing as ultimate ends of development processes and of each person as morally equal.
3. The multidimensional and open-ended nature of human flourishing.
4. The recognition of the interdependence of human life.
5. The centrality of value judgments and the plurality of values.
6. The connection between public reasoning and empathy with the lives of others, along with the promotion of human flourishing.

The CA is born out of Amartya Sen's work in social choice theory and welfare economics (Sen 2017) and is aimed at offering an alternative moral approach to that of utilitarianism in the evaluation of states of affairs. Sen's main concerns were the reduction of the evaluation space of states of affairs to information about utility, the reduction of human action to maximization, and the reduction of human motivation to self-interest (Sen 1977; Sen and Williams 1982). As he put it in his Dewey Lectures of 1984, his aim was "to explore a moral approach that sees persons from two different perspectives: well-being and agency" (Sen 1985, 169). A human being is not a utility maximizer, as economic theory had conceptualized him or her so far, but a free person, someone who is the author of his or her life (agency) and who strives to live well and not just to have more or feel better (well-being).

Sen first used the concept of capability in a public lecture titled "Equality of What?" (Sen 1980). To answer the question of how one's life is going, considerations about incomes and resources may be important but are not good representations of how people actually live. It is important, Sen argues, to evaluate people's lives "in terms of what people are able to be or able to do, rather than in terms of the means or resources they possess" (Sen 2017, 357). This is what he calls functionings, the "beings" and "doings" of people like being in good health, participating in the life of the community, being well nourished, making decisions about one's life, traveling, speaking with others, and so on. A capability is the freedom one has to realize these functionings (Sen 1993). Even if it is the capability rather than the functioning approach that has been adopted as the name for this new moral approach Amartya Sen was introducing in economics, functionings and capabilities belong to the same evaluation space (Sen 1992). An example Sen has often given to illustrate the distinction between functionings and capabilities is that of a starving child and a fasting monk. The latter has the capability to be well nourished but has chosen not to, while the former does not have such a choice. Both individuals have the same level of functionings, but they have different capability sets. Thus we have here a first characteristic of a capability-based view of development: to assess development, one needs to go beyond material considerations about incomes or resources to include non-material considerations such as human freedom.

A second characteristic of a capability-based vision of development is the consideration of people as the ultimate ends of development processes and of each person as a moral equal to every other person. In a seminal article on the concept of development, Sen (1988) refers to Kant's categorical imperative and the centrality in development policy of treating humanity as an end in itself and not a means to other ends. He argues that because human beings are both the main means of production processes and their main beneficiaries, "this dual role of human beings provides a rich ground for confusion of ends and means in planning and policy-making," which "can—and frequently does—take the form of focusing on production and prosperity as the essence of progress, treating people as the means through which that productive progress is brought about (rather than seeing the lives of people as the ultimate concern and treating production and prosperity merely as means to those lives)" (Sen 1988, 41).

A concern for the types of lives that people live was Sen's key motivation for introducing non-material considerations in the informational basis for judging states of affairs. But there he was also concerned for human diversity. To achieve the same level of functioning—say, moving about freely—one person will need a different amount of resources than another given his or her individual social and environmental characteristics, which is called, in the jargon, "conversion factors" (Sen 2017, 26). For example, if a person is visually impaired, she will need a different set of resources than others need to move freely, such as keeping a guide dog, and extra institutional resources, such as street signs and maps in Braille.

This foundation of "each individual person as an end" is also given the name of "ethical individualism" (Robeyns 2008; 2017), for what matters ultimately is not what happens to a group as a whole but what happens to each person in that group. Following Nussbaum (2011), Robeyns (2017) sees ethical individualism as part of treating all human beings as moral equals. Ethical individualism, or seeing each person as an end, does not entail that information about people's lives needs to be confined only to what happens to each person; it can include considerations about structures such as the caste system, political systems, cultural and social norms, and others (e.g., a woman from a scheduled caste in India might not be able to convert the resource of a well in her village into drinking water because she is denied access to the well). According to

Robeyns, whether one extends the evaluation space beyond individual considerations depends on the nature of the evaluative exercise, but it is not a requirement of the CA to undertake in-depth analysis of the structures themselves, such as how the caste system functions to exclude certain groups, how patriarchal social norms prevent girls from pursuing education, or how a "throwaway culture" is destroying ecosystems and affecting people's health. However, the United Nations Development Programme has taken the step of extending the evaluation space of development beyond individual considerations to include "structures of living together" (UNDP 2016, 89–91),[10] such as social values and social norms and the extent to which they enable each person to enjoy a minimum set of valuable functionings/capabilities. However, whether the CA is considered too "individualistic" remains a subject of many debates and continuing diverging opinions, including among the contributors to this book, and the editors also. I (Séverine Deneulin) have changed my view over the years, and the more I have delved into Amartya Sen's writings and their subtleties, it has become clear that relationality and encounters are the building-stones of his body of thought (Deneulin 2021, 44–48; Deneulin and Zampini-Davies 2020). His recent intellectual biography, *Home in the World*, powerfully and movingly illustrates the relational and dialogical evolution of his ideas on social justice and development, not least the importance of life-forming experiences such as the Bengal famine of 1943 and ill health (Sen 2021).

A third characteristic of a capability-based view of development is the multidimensional nature of human well-being, or human flourishing. A person functions in many respects, and there are many activities in which she can participate and many states in which she can be. Sen does not derive the value of capabilities "from one particular 'comprehensive doctrine' demanding one specific way of living" (Sen 1990, 118). This is why he does not define which valuable capabilities should enter the evaluation space. As Robeyns (2017) has noted, the selection of relevant well-being dimensions or relevant capabilities depends on the nature and aim of the evaluation exercise. Sometimes, when discussing "poverty as capability deprivation," which he views as "ultimately a lack of opportunity to lead a minimally acceptable life" (2017, 26), Sen ventures to offer a list of "elementary functionings," such as "being alive, being well-nourished and in good health, moving about freely," and also a list of "more complex functionings," such as "having self-respect and respect for others, taking part in the life of the community" (2017, 357).

It is this multidimensionality that opens up the CA to include other non-material considerations beyond well-being and agency, such as considerations about procedural fairness or non-domination (Robeyns 2017; Sen 2017). It also opens up the approach to the spiritual dimension, with being in relation to a higher source of value or being in relation to ancestors and land and animals as potential valuable functionings. No list can ever exhaust the richness of human life. The specification of the valuable dimensions for a person will often be guided by the objective of the evaluation exercise and data availability.

In the academic literature, some have supported the view of Amartya Sen, that we should leave the approach open-ended and others the view of Martha Nussbaum, who has argued for the need to have a list of ten central human capabilities: to live a life of normal length; to have bodily health; to have bodily integrity; to think and reason (this includes guarantees of freedom of expression); to express emotions; to engage in critical reflection about the planning of one's life; to engage in social interaction and have the social bases of self-respect; to live with concern for the natural environment; to laugh and play; and to control one's environment (this includes participation in political choices that govern one's life and work) (Nussbaum 2011, 33–34). This list approximates what a good human life consists of and forms the basis of constitutional guarantees that all governments are obliged to secure (Nussbaum 2011) (see the chapter by Schulz in this volume). According to Robeyns (2017), this division between Sen and Nussbaum rests more on the different uses of the CA than on versions of it. There is thus not a "Sen version" nor a "Nussbaum version" of the CA. As noted above, Nussbaum's aim is to develop a theory of justice akin to that of John Rawls but to replace his list of primary goods with a list of central human capabilities to inform redistributive principles. Sen's aim is to offer an evaluative framework to use to compare states of affairs as a basis for thinking about questions of justice.

The principle of seeing each person as an end, and each person as morally equal, is central to a capability-based view of development, but the person is not seen in isolation. To be a human being is to interact with others (Sen 2015, 81). Even what counts as a valuable or basic doing or being of a human being is the result of an interactive process of public discussion (Sen 2015, 89). Questioned on how he viewed the individual society relation, he commented that it is a "folly" to separate the individual from the social connections which make the person who she is and that an individual's faculties "to think and value are linked to his or her social existence and connections with each other" (Sen 2019). But, as noted above, there is still disagreement as to how much weight should be placed on the principle that each person is an end and how much should be placed on the principle of relationality and the idea that one exists as a person only in relation to others and the wider web of life. The view that this book adopts is that the CA is not a rigid framework, but a flexible one that can be taken in many directions, and one that opens conversations about how to include indigenous world-views that see all life on earth as an interdependent whole (Deneulin 2021, 50–52).

This interdependence is at the core of the evaluation process, for what people value is the result of their interaction with others. With this comes the recognition of the centrality of values in development and the recognition of value pluralism. One of the reasons for Sen's opposition to drawing a list of valuable human functionings or capabilities is that the same functioning can be valuable in one context, but not in another. Another expression of value pluralism is the CA's openness to multiple sources of values, including those coming from religious traditions. For example, if someone considers fasting a valuable functioning because one belongs to a religious tradition that sees that "doing" as valuable for a set of multiple reasons, the CA can accommodate such values. However, different values do not co-exist alongside each other; they interact and change as a result of interaction and public discussion. The formation of values through public discussion is central to the diagnosis of injustice (Sen 2009, 2017). What one holds as important needs to be critically examined and scrutinized (Sen 2017, 39, 281). Sen gives the example of hunger and environmental degradation to illustrate the role of public discussion in value formation, and in changing people's priorities and views about what should be done. On the latter, he remarks that "the threats that we face call for organized international action as well as changes in national policies particularly for better reflecting social costs in prices and incentives. But they are also dependent on value formation related to public discussions, both for their influence on individual behavior and for bringing about policy changes" (Sen 2017, 40).

This recognition of different sources of values and the interaction of different values coming from different sources is what makes the CA open to religious values and their contribution to public reasoning processes. In an article about why we should preserve the spotted owl, Sen (2004) offers an interesting discussion about the role of public discussion and religious traditions in shaping what is considered valuable. He argues that the spotted owl has no value per se; the value of its survival is only as an outcome of reasoning processes. Some people may value the owl because its very existence gives glory to God, as Pope Francis does in his encyclical *Laudato Si'* when he writes in relation to species extinction that "because of us [humans], thousands of species will no longer give glory to God by their very existence, nor convey their message to us" (*LS* 33). Some may value it because of the owl's place in ecosystems or for other reasons. Interestingly, Sen alludes to his own justification for protecting the spotted owl as a valuable functioning: Buddha's point that "since we are enormously more powerful than other species, we have some responsibility towards them that is linked with this asymmetry" (Sen 2004, 11). In sum, there is a wide range of reasons for which something may be valuable, and this implies that, with reasons interacting, what is valuable is determined through people's interacting with each other, in particular when they interact by trying to put themselves in the shoes of another person.

For Sen, how to decide what is worthy of action is closely connected to our not being indifferent to what is happening to other people. Empathy is central to Sen's account of public reasoning. In the case of hunger, he makes the point that "there is a particular need in this context to examine value formation that results from public discussion of miserable events [famine], in generating sympathy and commitment on the part of citizens to do something to prevent their occurrence" (Sen 2017, 40).

This book follows Sen's invitation to bring our different values into discussion and open ourselves to what is happening to the lives of others, especially those who suffer and lack the opportunity "to lead a minimally acceptable life" (Sen 2017, 26). Given the social and environmental challenges that the world is facing, described at the beginning of this introduction, can the CA on its own give us the interpretative framework necessary to change the current state of affairs? And what is the role and meaning of integral human development, which has been a core concept of CST since the 1960s, in the midst of rising inequalities, global challenges, and new nationalisms? These questions point to the potential fruitfulness of a dialogue between CST and the CA.

CST AND THE CA: A CONVERSATION FOR INTEGRAL HUMAN DEVELOPMENT

Both CST and the CA work with a recognition of the complexity of the human person and a corresponding complexity of development that cannot be reduced to measurable progress, let alone GDP. The CA offers an engagement with human development with an emphasis on non-material aspects such as freedoms. The process of expanding the real freedoms people enjoy has been identified as the key point of development by Amartya Sen (Sen 1999, 4). The CA brings a compelling vision of the connection between resources and capabilities. The approach focuses not primarily on goods but on the ways in which persons can appropriate and make use of goods and transform resources. A CST-inspired understanding of development, as we have seen above, emphasizes a relational understanding of the human person, a normative dimension of development, a consideration of cultural richness, spiritual depth, and a recognition of non-productive aspects of human life. We find a commitment to especially consider the most disadvantaged and those left behind, which puts the CA, as well as CST with its perspectives focused on human dignity and the common good, in contrast to strictly utilitarian approaches.

The question of what people can be and become is central to the CA and is also central to the understanding of integral human development in CST (Deneulin 2021, 21–30). The term "integral human development" was coined by Pope Paul VI in *Populorum Progressio* (*PP* 14). The origin of this idea is indicated with a reference to Lebret (1961). Louis-Joseph Lebret, a French Dominican priest and economist, was inspired to take a closer look at ethical questions of development when he noted that processes of societal advancement that benefit some give rise to the deprivation and suffering of others. In 1929 he came face to face with the dire poverty of French fishermen on the coast of Brittany; he traced the roots of their poverty and found them to stem from global changes and the fact that family fishermen no longer stood a chance of making a decent living when pitted against large-scale commercial fishing (Gasper 2021; Gasper and Keleher 2021). The internationalization and the industrialization of fishing found its victims in village fishing communities and family fisheries. Through participatory research in France and in Latin American communities, Lebret arrived at an understanding of the necessity of human-centered development and invited us to think of development beyond material values. In the words of Denis Goulet, one of Lebret's students: "Societies are more human, or more developed, not when men and women 'have more' but when they are enabled to 'be more.' The main criterion of development is not increased production or material well-being but qualitative human enrichment" (Goulet 1995, 6–7).

This "integral" understanding of development was also inspired, in the Catholic tradition, by the thought of Jacques Maritain, who developed not only an understanding of the common good but also a concept of "integral humanism" in his book *Integral Humanism* (Maritain 1968). He is quoted twice in *Populorum Progressio*, in reference to "a new humanism" (*PP* 20) and to "a full bodied humanism" (*PP* 44). A key dimension of this understanding of "integral" is the recognition of the spiritual dimension of a person and her life. This opens up the horizon for questions of ultimate ends and values, an aspect that has been captured by John Finnis's term "integral human fulfilment" with its orientation toward the lasting and ultimate goal (Finnis, Grisez, and Boyle 1987).

This perspective of ultimate values and "last questions" is an indication of some of the (fruitful) tensions and differences between CST and the CA. CST offers an approach that is, in Joshua Schulz's words, "metaphysically and theologically rich" (Schulz 2016, 29), whereas the CA, especially in Amartya Sen's presentation of it, is more focused on procedures than on ontological commitments. We would like to think of these differences as different "comfort zones" (as Clemens Sedmak spells out in his chapter of this book). Both normative frameworks inhabit certain discursive spaces more effortlessly than others. CST has a strong commitment to the social nature of the person, the necessary role of communities, and the status of responsibilities and duties. It is prepared to use a ("thick") term like "social love" (*LS* 231; Archer 2011). The CA, intellectually closer to political liberalism, will be more at home in discourses that underline the central role of the individual and her rights and legal entitlements. The CA has been criticized for sharing some deficiencies of certain understandings of liberalism—its failing to embrace the constitutive nature of human interdependency, the problematic nature of the public realm, and the exploitative nature of capitalism (Dean 2009).

Obviously, defenders of the CA can always point out that the CA views the human person as a social being and that the CA is not a theory but an open-ended approach to thinking about questions of development and justice from the perspective of the inalienable freedom of each person. "Individual freedom," Sen (1999, 31) writes, "is quintessentially a social product, and there is a two-way relation between (1) social arrangements to expand individual freedoms and (2) the use of individual freedom not only to improve the respective lives but also to make social arrangements more appropriate and effective." There is an undeniable recognition of the community-formed structure of human existence, but it is not accentuated as much as in CST. The same can be said about the concept of human dignity, which is central to CST and based on a clear theological justification—a person is created in the image and likeness of God (PCJP 2005, 144), a justification the CA cannot offer. Similarly, the understanding of agency is nuanced in CST with an explicit consideration of categories such as sin and suffering (see the chapter by Lori Keleher), which are under-developed in the CA. CST works with a theological understanding of the person (PCJP 2005, 34–48), which becomes especially clear in this book in Bates's chapter on personhood in the Orthodox tradition.

These different emphases and even tensions could become fruitful. The CA may serve as a correction of a potential community bias (with its emphasis on each individual person as an end) and a potential responsibility bias (with its emphasis on freedoms, agency, and choices). It can invite conversations about anthropological foundations and give us an understanding of human flourishing (see the chapters by Amy Daughton and Meghan Clark). CST can offer a horizon of normative questions, a sense of spirituality and the importance of faith and faith traditions, a thick understanding of communities, and deep motivations for solidarity (including solidarity with future generations) and care for the planet (see the chapters by Clemens Sedmak, Helmut Gaisbauer, Guillermo Otano Jiménez, and Séverine Deneulin and Augusto Zampini-Davies).

In fact, CST can use a language of sacrifices, which seems necessary in the context of keeping global temperature rise to 1.5 degree Celsius and preventing further biodiversity losses; this language and the motivations to accept restrictions on agency cannot be housed as easily in the CA.

We have divided this book into two parts ("Foundations" and "Common Ground for Action"), with each corresponding to an area of discussion and mutual enrichment between the CA and CST. We have included authors who see more tensions between CST and the CA. In their chapters, Joshua Schulz and Amy Daughton discuss possible conflicting visions of the human good, with Daughton concluding that there is a more favorable complementarity between the two on the basis of Sen's diverse philosophical commitments and Schulz concluding that there is an incompatibility on the basis of Nussbaum's commitment to political liberalism. Katie Dunne highlights a lack of concern for women's lives in CST in contrast to the CA. Other contributors seek to emphasize the common ground between the two. Sedmak places a similar stress on values, freedom, reasoning, and agency, and Lori Keleher similarly stresses agency, relationships, and responsibility. In her chapter Meghan Clark underlines a similar concern for human rights and solidarity; James Bailey, Helmut Gaiesbauer, and Séverine Deneulin and Augusto Zampini-Davies show a similar concern for what happens to the lives of the poor and marginalized; and Guillermo Otano Jiménez demonstrates a similar concern for transformation of unjust structures.

Amy Daughton opens the "Foundations" part of the volume by examining some anthropological differences between Sen's capability-based view of justice and the CST view. She shows that his idea of justice (Sen 2009) is not a discrete theory of justice but is instead intended as a framework within which diverse philosophical commitments might all operate. And she argues that such diversity might, however, be working toward incommensurable visions of the good. She therefore underlines the need to articulate more fully the philosophical commitments implicit in Sen's view of justice and explores what philosophical anthropology may lie beneath it. On the basis of CST's anthropological vision of the human person as an active agent for change and for solidarity who can participate in the shaping of the political community, she advances the idea that Sen's capability-based view of justice has an anthropology that contains implicit normative expectations for human living and inter-subjectivity, calling for a free and active participation in sharing and shaping life together.

Dana Bates continues this anthropological exploration by bringing CA into dialogue with the theological anthropological perspective of Eastern Orthodoxy. In his chapter he focuses on the works of one of the twentieth century's leading Orthodox theologians, Dumitru Staniloae, who articulated a Trinitarian anthropological formula as "persons, in communion, within the medium of a shared nature." Bates argues that this Trinitarian structure of the person, which bears simultaneously on person (agency), communion (solidarity), and nature (structures), can offer some contributions to the development project underpinned by the CA. He contends that this Trinitarian anthropological vision can illuminate the perspective that one cannot meaningfully live without simultaneously enjoying freedoms (agency), communion (solidarity), and the fulfillment of nature's functions (structures). Bates expands on the category of nature to bridge sacred and secular divides and provide a basis for cosmopolitan ethical obligations.

Lori Keleher examines further the conceptual territory of agency and freedom in her chapter. She argues that both CST and the CA can accommodate a broad understanding of agency as "making choices about what one actually does and becomes." After introducing the idea of "authentic freedom," or the freedom to be and do in accordance with one's dignity, she examines the implications of the relational dimension of the human person for the exercise of agency and freedom. Keleher contends that those who wish to promote agency and freedom need to understand and address the structural limitations of agency and authentic freedoms and that not all agency promotion leads to the promotion of authentic freedom.

In his chapter Joshua Schulz argues that the CA, interpreted as a political liberal theory of justice by Martha Nussbaum, and CST understand dignity in very different ways, and this difference impacts their thinking about the nature and norms of community. Schulz critically examines the central claim made by Nussbaum in her capability-based partial theory of justice that the central capabilities she proposes are political entitlements based on a normative account of the relationship between dignity and the human community. He argues that, whereas CST holds that the family and civil society are natural developments of human sociality, implying pre-political norms for practical reason, the CA often defends a liberal-egalitarian model of community. Schulz explores these disagreements by comparing Nussbaum's "intuitive" account of dignity with CST's participative account, highlighting their implications for thinking about the nature of community and the demands of social justice.

The engagement with human dignity continues in Katie Dunne's chapter, in which she argues that CST's conception of the human person is not used to full potential as a resource for confronting injustice against women, despite consistently professing the human dignity of all people. CST's predominant focus on women's relationship to motherhood and the family results in accounts of human flourishing that tend to eclipse the social realities that affect women. In contrast, the CA, especially in Nussbaum's works, has dealt with questions of justice for women by analyzing inequality and deprivation in the space of capabilities, or what each human being can be or do. In her attempt to build a capability-based partial theory of justice, Nussbaum directly asks which capabilities are the most valuable for a woman's life that is worthy of human dignity. In her chapter Dunne proposes a responsible theological anthropology, in dialogue with the CA, that fully affirms women's equality and personhood in CST.

The authors of the last two chapters of the first part, "Foundations," discuss CST's recent incorporation of the concept of integral ecology as a synonym for that of integral human development, as well as its greater emphasis on the interconnection between the flourishing of humans and the good functioning of ecosystems. Cathriona Russell examines our relationships to the environment through the "autonomy approach" in Christian ethics and its relationship to the CA, using political philosophy and creation theology as interpretative categories. She argues that "autonomy implies that morality is not conformity with the norms of society, nor is it found in the teleological structure of nature, but it is rooted in a first-person perspective that acknowledges our likeness to one another as the very condition of our being moral agents." This leads Russell to revisit the concept of the "common inheritance of the earth" as used in CST and to propose an approach to creation theology that "acknowledges the reflexive capacities in human societies to build upon and revise the terms on which they coexist and interact with one another in a finite world."

The idea of sustainable development has been a keyword in the international community to fulfil its responsibilities to nature. In his chapter Clemens Sedmak compares CST and the CA in their view of sustainability. On the basis of three modern topoi—Fukushima, Lampedusa, and Fiji, he highlights differences and common ground between CST and the CA through the lens of responding to the ecological crisis. He argues that, faced with these three topoi, CST provides a language that goes beyond technology and ethics. It is not a social theory but a living tradition and community of discipleship. Another important aspect of CST Sedmak highlights is the theological language of conversion. In contrast, the CA has a less exclusive language and therefore better translates the idea of sustainability into concrete political action. He discusses, to that effect, how the concept of sustainable development has been translated into policy in the Human Development Reports of the UNDP. Though both the CA and CST share common ground, such as placing similar stress on values, freedom, reasoning, and agency, he concludes that CST includes a "mystical" dimension, in the form of silence and contemplation, which has a political dimension that the CA may be able to unpack.

The second part of the book is dedicated to "Common Ground for Action," exploring more practical approaches. One common ground at the level of action is the concept of human dignity. Human dignity is at the core of the United Nations' Human Rights Declaration. In her chapter Meghan Clark argues that the concept of human dignity in the United Nations' founding documents, as well as in CST, has simultaneously an inherent, yet aspirational, character—that is, human rights are already, but not yet, realized at the same time. This paradoxical, and dynamic, character of human dignity is also found in Amartya Sen's understanding of human rights and capabilities. Clark argues that it is in this dynamic aspect of human dignity and human rights—that is, in their dual inherent and aspirational character—that solidarity can be found and the role of the community in promoting human dignity is essential. She concludes that key contributions of CST to larger debates concerning development and human rights are this acceptance of the "already, but not yet" and this emphasis on solidarity and community.

In their chapter Ilaria Schnyder von Wartensee and Elizabeth Hlabse discuss the common ground between CST and the CA from the perspective of women who live with HIV/AIDS in Uganda. On the basis of qualitative research by an organization that provides medical and psychological services and social support to these women, they discuss the critical importance of encounter, that is, of being recognized as a unique person with a unique value, in awakening agency so that the person can become the author of her own life. They analyze the different dimensions of the experience of "encounter," as told by these Ugandan women, and examine some distinct points of emphasis between CST and the CA. They argue that CST goes a step further by giving more substance to the CA's understanding of freedom, which is experienced in relationships.

This responsibility to local communities is explored at a more global level by Guillermo Otano Jiménez, who discusses the mobilization of civil society to end the consumption of mineral resources coming from conflict zones and to improve the labor conditions and health of the workers who extract these resources from the earth. In his chapter Otano Jiménez argues that the literature on collective agency and the CA can offer illuminating insights to illustrate how the idea of "ecological conversion" can be put into practice to transform unjust socio-economic structures and protect our common home. He focuses on the conflict-free technology campaign launched in 2014 by ALBOAN, a Jesuit international non-governmental organization from the Basque Country in Spain, which was framed through the lens of the encyclical *Laudato Si'*. Drawing on the three stages of collective action highlighted by the CA literature—conscientization, conciliation, and collaboration, he discusses how these three elements are central to encouraging ecological conversion at the personal, societal, and institutional levels.

In the next chapter James Bailey examines how the economic structure of private property can be transformed to help children escape poverty in the United States and fulfil their potential. He looks at an initiative to expand the distribution of property (and the privileges that follow from this) in the form of children's savings accounts. And he discusses CST's persistent support for, and defense of, the institution of private property, which it sees as helping not only to alleviate poverty but also to promote human flourishing beyond the merely economic, such as the ability to identify and execute a plan for one's life, which can also be read as a capability for hope in the future. After briefly examining the connection between material well-being and human flourishing in Aristotle and Aquinas, Bailey discusses the magnitude and manifestations of economic inequality in the United States, with a particular focus on wealth inequality and how the latter affects children. He draws some implications of the differential impact of income and assets for human well-being and discusses why introducing children's savings accounts could be one important mechanism for reducing wealth inequality and promoting human dignity.

Child poverty and a special program aimed at addressing it is also the object of the chapter by Helmut Gaisbauer. He analyzes an Austrian initiative, a day-care organization, to provide better conditions for children in Romania to live flourishing lives and escape deep capability deprivation. Gaisbauer demonstrates how the initiative is an illustration of CST's preferential option for the poor and solidarity in practice. He argues that the CA provides a helpful framework to help us identify those who live in poverty and what living in poverty entails, and therefore helps enact CST's preferential option for the poor, especially in child poverty contexts. Gaisbauer describes some concrete ways in which the initiative transforms at the structural level the obstacles and adverse circumstances that prevent children from fully realizing their potential. He highlights that this structural transformation also relies on the dedication and commitment of key individual persons.

The book draws to a close with a chapter by Séverine Deneulin and Augusto Zampini-Davies. They describe the journey so far in bringing the CA and CST into dialogue and advance a methodology for future research on how to combine these two interpretative frameworks so as to better respond to the "cry of the poor and of the earth" (*LS* 49). And they follow CST's inductive method of see-judge-act and combine each stage with the CA, using illustrative examples from Latin American informal settlements and the Amazon basin. In this concluding chapter Deneulin and Zampini-Davies aim to sketch key features of such a combined methodology, which could inform analysis and social action in other contexts so as to promote the development of each person, and the whole person, in relationship with others and the natural world of which she is part.

CONCLUDING REMARKS

This book is intended to open and deepen a dialogue between important and influential normative frameworks. We do not want to gloss over the differences, but want to see these differences as mutually enriching: the capability approach, with its emphasis on values and freedom and its greater attention to the lives of women, can enrich the social teachings of the Catholic tradition with its emphasis on faith and community; conversely, Catholic Social Teaching, with its categories of "structural sin," "the universal destination of goods," and "ecological conversion," can offer conceptual and analytical lenses for the capability approach. In this volume the editors and chapter authors seek to point out the significant common ground that these two traditions (one secular, one faith-based) share—a commitment to an integral understanding of development that is so much needed today as we face an unprecedented challenge of maintaining a functioning common home in which all humanity can flourish. The question posed by Pope Francis in *Laudato Si'* is relevant to both normative frameworks and actually to all of us: "What kind of world do we want to leave to those who come after us, to children who are now growing up?" (*LS* 160)

NOTES

1. In *Laudato Si'*, Pope Francis notes the influence of Patriarch Bartholomew (*LS* 7–9).

2. For other efforts at bringing the Catholic social tradition in dialogue with the social sciences and other approaches in social theory, see Cloutier (2017) and Daly (2021).

3. The Second Vatican Council was an ecumenical council of the Roman Catholic Church that brought all the bishops of the Church together to address over a period of three years (1962–1965) the relationship of the Church with the world and contemporary societies.

4. We follow the CST convention of quoting all papal documents using the initials of their titles, followed by paragraph numbers (e.g., *LS* 7–9).

5. We use "Christian" rather than "Catholic" to indicate that the discussions of the social dimension of the faith in the early centuries were more about "living the Gospel" than about different institutional forms of the Church.

6. The "universal destination of goods" is an important aspect of CST that is based on the belief that God created the earth for all and that the right to private property of individuals has to be balanced with the needs of all. The goods of creation remain destined to the development of the whole person and of all humanity. In this sense, private property has a social dimension: "The fact that God has given the earth for the use and enjoyment of the whole human race can in no way be a bar to the owning of private property. For God has granted the earth to mankind in general, not in the sense that all without distinction can deal with it as they like but rather that no part of it was assigned to any one in particular and that the limits of private possession have been left to be fixed by man's own industry and by the laws of individual races. Moreover, the earth, even though apportioned among private owners, does not cease thereby to minister to the needs of all, inasmuch as there is not one who does not sustain life from what the land produces" (*RN* 8).

7. Notwithstanding its anthropocentric outlook, *Laudato Si'* talks about "the intrinsic dignity of the world" (*LS* 115).

8. For a critical lens on CST and women's reproductive rights, see Beattie (2015, 152–57).

9. Waldron makes the point that the *imago Dei* approach to dignity, even though theologically controversial, has something unique to offer since it talks about the (equal) rank that we hold in creation and the connection to three basic rights, the right to life, welfare rights, and the right not to be subject to degrading treatment.

10. The term comes from Paul Ricoeur's ethics *Oneself as Another*. See Deneulin (2008). Ricoeur's original definition refers to the notion of institution: "By institution, we understand the structure of living together as this belongs to a historical community, a structure irreducible to interpersonal relations and yet bound up with these" (Ricoeur, 1992, 194).

WORKS CITED

Alkire, Sabina, James Foster, Suman Seth, et al. 2015. *Multidimensional Poverty Measurement and Analysis*. Oxford: Oxford University Press.

Archer, Margaret. 2011. "Caritas in Veritate and Social Love." *International Journal of Public Theology* 5: 273–95.

Beattie, Tina. 2015. "Dignity Beyond Rights: Human Development in the Context of the Capabilities Approach and Catholic Social Teaching." *Australian eJournal of Theology* 22, no 3: 150–65.

Benedict XVI. 2009. *Caritas in Veritate: On Integral Human Development in Charity in Truth.* https://www.vatican.va/content/benedict-xvi/en/encyclicals/documents/hf_ben-xvi_enc_20090629_caritas-in-veritate.html.

Benedictine Centre. Not dated. *The Rule of St. Benedict.* https://www.benedictinecenter.org/wp-content/uploads/2018/09/RuleBenedict_scr.pdf.

Bevans, Stephen B., and Roger P. Schroeder. 2004. *Constants in Context: A Theology of Mission for Today.* Maryknoll, NY: Orbis Books.

Brown, Peter. 2002. *Poverty and Leadership in the Later Roman Empire.* Hanover, NH: University Press of New England.

———. 2012. *Through the Eye of the Needle: Wealth, the Fall of Rome, and the Making of Christianity in the West, 350–550 AD.* Princeton, NJ: Princeton University Press.

Cloutier, David. 2017. "What Can Social Science Teach Catholic Social Thought about the Common Good?" In *Empirical Foundations of the Common Good: What Can Theology Learn from Social Science,* edited by Daniel Finn. New York: Oxford University Press, 170–200.

Commission on the Measurement of Economic Performance and Social Progress. 2010. *Report.* https://ec.europa.eu/eurostat/documents/8131721/8131772/Stiglitz-Sen-Fitoussi-Commission-report.pdf.

Daley, Brian. 2017. "The Cappadocian Fathers and the Option for the Poor." In *The Option for the Poor in Christian Theology,* edited by Daniel G. Groody. Notre Dame, IN: University of Notre Dame Press, 77–88.

Daly, Daniel J. 2021. *The Structures of Virtue and Vice.* Washington, DC: Georgetown University Press.

Dean, Hartley. 2009. "Critiquing Capabilities: The Distractions of a Beguiling Concept." *Critical Social Policy* 29, no. 2: 261–78.

Deneulin, Séverine. 2008. "Beyond Individual Freedom and Agency: Structures of Living Together in the Capability Approach." In *The Capability Approach: Concepts, Measures and Applications,* edited by Flavio Comim, Mozaffar Qizilbash, and Sabina Alkire. New York: Cambridge University Press, 105–24.

———. 2021. *Human Development and the Catholic Social Tradition: Towards an Integral Ecology.* Abingdon, UK: Routledge.

———, and Augusto Zampini-Davies, 2020. "Religion and the Capability Approach." In *The Cambridge Handbook of the Capability Approach,* edited by Siddiq Osmani, Mozaffar Qizilbash, and Enrica Chiappero-Martinetti. Cambridge: Cambridge University Press, 686–705.

Finnis, John, Germain Grisez, and Joseph Boyle. 1987. "Practical Principles, Moral Truth, and Ultimate Ends." *American Journal of Jurisprudence* 32: 99–151.

Francis. 2013. *Evangelii Gaudium: The Joy of the Gospel*. Apostolic exhortation. https://www.vatican.va/content/francesco/en/apost_exhortations/documents /papa-francesco_esortazione-ap_20131124_evangelii-gaudium.html.

———. 2015. *Laudato Si': On Care for Our Common Home (LS)*. Encyclical. https://www.vatican.va/content/dam/francesco/pdf/encyclicals/documents /papa-francesco_20150524_enciclica-laudato-si_en.pdf.

———. 2020. *Fratelli Tutti: On Fraternity and Social Friendship*. Encyclical. https://www.vatican.va/content/francesco/en/encyclicals/documents /papa-francesco_20201003_enciclica-fratelli-tutti.html.

Gasper, Des. 2021. "L.-J. Lebret: A Human Development Ethics Grounded in Empirical Social Research and a Global Perspective." *Journal of Global Ethics* 17, no. 2: 146–66.

———, and Lori Keleher. 2021. "Investigating L.-J. Lebret as a Pioneer of Human Development Thinking and Global Development Ethics." *Journal of Global Ethics* 17, no 2: 115–26.

Genuis, Quentin I. T. 2016. "Dignity Reevaluated: A Theological Examination of Human Dignity and the Role of the Church in Bioethics and End-of-Life Care." *Linacre Quarterly* 83, no. 1: 6–14.

Glendon, Mary Ann. 2013. "The Influence of Catholic Social Doctrine on Human Rights." *Journal of Catholic Social Thought* 10, no. 1: 69–84.

Global Sisters Report. Not dated. *Sr. Dorothy Stang Resources*. https://www .globalsistersreport.org/resources/sr-dorothy-stang-resources.

Goulet, Denis. 1995. *Development Ethics: A Guide to Theory and Practice*. London: Zed Books.

Intergovernmental Panel on Climate Change (IPCC). 2018. *Summary for Policymakers of IPCC Special Report on Global Warming of 1.5°C*. https://www .ipcc.ch/2018/10/08/summary-for-policymakers-of-ipcc-special-report -on-global-warming-of-1-5c-approved-by-governments.

———. 2022. *Contributions of Working Group II on Sixth Assessment Report: Climate Change 2022: Impacts, Adaptation and Vulnerability*. https://www .ipcc.ch/report/sixth-assessment-report-working-group-ii.

Intergovernmental Science-Policy Platform on Biodiversity and Ecosystem Services (IPBES). 2019. *Global Assessment Report on Biodiversity and Ecosystem Services*. https://www.un.org/sustainabledevelopment/blog/2019 /05/nature-decline-unprecedented-report.

Jackson, Tim. 2016. *Prosperity without Growth: Foundations for the Economy of Tomorrow.* Revised edition. Abingdon, UK: Routledge.

———. 2021. *Post-Growth: Life after Capitalism.* Cambridge: Polity Press.

John Paul II. 1987. *Sollicitudo Rei Socialis.* Encyclical. https://www.vatican.va/content/john-paul-ii/en/encyclicals/documents/hf_jp-ii_enc_30121987_sollicitudo-rei-socialis.html.

Lebret, Louis-Joseph. 1961. *Dynamique Concrète du Développement.* Paris: Editions Ouvrières.

Leo XIII. 1891. *Rerum Novarum: On Capital and Labor.* Encyclical. https://www.vatican.va/content/leo-xiii/en/encyclicals/documents/hf_l-xiii_enc_15051891_rerum-novarum.html.

Maritain, Jacques. 1968. *Integral Humanism: Temporal and Spiritual Problems of a New Christendom.* Translated by Joseph W. Evans. New York: Charles Scribner's Sons.

Murphy, Roseanne. 2007. *Martyr of the Amazon: The Life of Sister Dorothy Stang.* Maryknoll, NY: Orbis Books.

Nussbaum, Martha. 2011. *Creating Capabilities.* Cambridge, MA: Harvard University Press.

Ober, Josiah. 2014. "Meritocratic and Civic Dignity in Greco-Roman Antiquity." In *The Cambridge Handbook of Human Dignity,* edited by Marcus Düwell et al. Cambridge: Cambridge University Press, 53–63.

Oxford Poverty and Human Development Initiative (OPHI). 2021. *Global Multidimensional Poverty Index.* https://ophi.org.uk/global-mpi-2021.

Paul VI. 1967. *Populorum Progressio: On the Development of Peoples.* Encyclical. https://www.vatican.va/content/paul-vi/en/encyclicals/documents/hf_p-vi_enc_26031967_populorum.html.

Pontifical Council for Justice and Peace (PCJP). 2005. *Compendium of the Social Doctrine of the Church.* https://www.vatican.va/roman_curia/pontifical_councils/justpeace/documents/rc_pc_justpeace_doc_20060526_compendio-dott-soc_en.html.

Pope, Stephen. 2001. "Natural Law and Christian Ethics." In *The Cambridge Companion to Christian Ethics,* edited by R. Gill. Cambridge: Cambridge University Press, 2001, 77–95, here 90–92.

Pope, Stephen J. 2005. "Natural Law in Catholic Social Teachings." In *Modern Catholic Social Teaching: Commentaries and Interpretation,* edited by K. Himes. Washington, DC: Georgetown University Press, 41–71.

Rahner, Karl. 1969. "Reflections on the Unity of Love of Neighbour and Love of God." In *Theological Investigations,* vol. 6, essay 16. https://www.karlrahnersociety.com/resources/.

Renouard, Cécile, Rémi Beau, Christophe Goupil, and Christian Koenig, eds. 2021. *The Great Transition Guide: Principles for a Transformative Education.* https://lori.ccampion.ox.ac.uk/sites/default/files/inline-files/The-Great -Transition-Guide-Principles-for-a-Transformative-Education_0.pdf.

Ricoeur, Paul. 1992. *One Self as Another.* Translated by Kathleen Blamey. Chicago: University of Chicago Press.

Robeyns, Ingrid. 2008. "Sen's Capability Approach and Feminist Concerns." In *The Capability Approach: Concepts, Measures and Applications*, edited by Sabina Alkire, Mozaffar Qizilbash, and Flavio Comim. New York: Cambridge University Press, 82–104.

———. 2017. *Wellbeing, Freedom and Social Justice: The Capability Approach Re-Examined.* Cambridge: Open Book.

Romero, Oscar. 1980. *Homily for the Fifth Sunday of Lent: The Church Serves Personal, Communal, and Transcendent Liberation.* http://www.romerotrust .org.uk/homilies-and-writings/homilies.

Roslin, Hans. 2010. *The Joy of Stats.* https://www.gapminder.org/videos/the-joy -of-stats.

Rowlands, Anna. 2021. *Towards a Politics of Communion: Catholic Social Teaching in Dark Times.* London: T&T Clark.

Sachs, Wolfgang. 2017. "The Sustainable Development Goals and Laudato Si': Varieties of Post-Development?" *Third World Quarterly* 38, no. 12: 2573–88.

Schulz, Joshua. 2016. "The Capabilities Approach and Catholic Social Teaching: An Engagement." *Journal of Global Ethics* 12, no. 1: 29–47.

Sen, Amartya. 1977. "Rational Fools: A Critique of the Behavioural Foundations of Economic Theory." *Philosophy and Public Affairs* 6, no. 4: 317–44.

———. 1980. "Equality of What?" https://www.ophi.org.uk/wp-content /uploads/Sen-1979_Equality-of-What.pdf.

———. 1985. "Well-Being, Agency and Freedom: The Dewey Lectures 1984." *Journal of Philosophy* 82, no. 4: 169–221.

———. 1987. *Ethics and Economics.* Oxford: Clarendon Press.

———. 1988. "The Concept of Development." In *Handbook of Development Economics*, edited by Hollis Chenery and T. N. Srinivasan. Amsterdam: Elsevier, 9–25.

———. 1990. "Justice: Means versus Freedoms." *Philosophy and Public Affairs* 19, no. 2: 111–21.

———. 1992. *Inequality Reexamined.* Oxford: Clarendon Press.

———. 1993. "Capability and Well-Being." In *The Quality of Life*, edited by Martha Nussbaum and Amartya Sen. Oxford: Clarendon Press, 30–53.

———. 1999. *Development as Freedom*. Oxford: Oxford University Press.

———. 2004. "Why Should We Preserve the Spotted Owl?" *London Review of Books* 26, no. 3: 10–11.

———. 2009. *The Idea of Justice*. London: Allen Lane.

———. 2015. *The Country of First Boys and Other Essays*. New Delhi: Oxford University Press.

———. 2017. *Collective Choice and Social Welfare*. London: Allen Lane.

———. 2019. "Connecting Capabilities: Amartya Sen in Conversation with Elaine Unterhalter." Recorded interview, International Conference of the Human Development and Capability Association, September, 9–11, 2019, University of London.

———. 2021. *Home in the World: A Memoir*. London: Allen Lane.

———, and Bernard Williams, eds. 1982. *Utilitarianism and Beyond*. Cambridge: Cambridge University Press.

Synod of Bishops. 1971. *Justice in the World*. https://www.cctwincities.org/wp-content/uploads/2015/10/Justicia-in-Mundo.pdf.

Tornielli, Andrea. 2018. "This Economy Kills: Pope Francis on Capitalism and Social Justice." *International Studies in Catholic Education* 10, no. 2: 233–38.

———, and Giocamo Galeazzi, eds. 2015. *This Economy Kills: Pope Francis on Capitalism and Social Justice*. Collegeville, MN: Liturgical Press.

United Nations (UN). 2015. *The Sustainable Development Goals*. https://sdgs.un.org.

United Nations Development Programme (UNDP). 1990. *Human Development Report: Concept and Measurement of Human Development*. https://hdr.undp.org/en/global-reports.

———. 2016. *Human Development Report: Human Development for Everyone*. https://www.hdr.undp.org/en/global-reports.

———. 2019. *Human Development Report: Beyond Income, Beyond Averages, Beyond Today: Inequalities in Human Development in the 21st Century*. https://www.hdr.undp.org/en/global-reports.

———. 2020. *Human Development Report. The Next Frontier: Human Development and the Anthropocene*. http://hdr.undp.org.

———. 2021. *COVID-19: Socio-Economic Impact*. https://www.undp.org/coronavirus/socio-economic-impact-covid-19.

United Nations Environment Program (UNEP). 2020. *Preventing the Next Pandemic: Zoonotic Diseases and How to Break the Chain of Transmission*. https://www.unep.org/news-and-stories/statements/preventing-next-pandemic-zoonotic-diseases-and-how-break-chain.

Ura, Karma, Sabina Alkire, Tshoki Zangmo, and Karma Wangdi. 2012. *An Extensive Analysis of the Gross National Happiness Index*. https://ophi.org .uk/policy/gross-national-happiness-index.

Van Tongeren, Paul. 2013. "Natural Law, Human Dignity and Catholic Social Teaching." *Religion, State & Society* 41, no. 2: 152–63.

Vatican Council II. 1965. *Gaudium et spes (GS)*. Pastoral constitution. https:// www.vatican.va/archive/hist_councils/ii_vatican_council/documents/vat -ii_const_19651207_gaudium-et-spes_en.html.

Waldron, Jeremy. 2010. "The Image of God: Rights, Reason, and Order." In *Christianity and Human Rights: An Introduction*, edited by John Witte Jr. and Frank Alexander. Cambridge: Cambridge University Press, 216–35.

World Commission on Environment and Development (WCED). 1987. *Report of the World Commission on Environment and Development: Our Common Future*. https://sustainabledevelopment.un.org/content/documents /5987our-common-future.pdf.

PART 1

Foundations

ONE

The Anthropologies of Catholic Social Thought and the Capability Approach

Amy Daughton

ABSTRACT

Amartya Sen's capability approach is designed to be capacious. It can contain practices and interventions that are situated in diverse models of reasoning about justice. This inclusivity is the point: Sen's approach is by way of prioritizing action rather than perfecting the institution and its principles. Nevertheless, it still operates in relation to some moral expectations: that the response to injustice should shape action, that humans should be free to choose lives they have reason to value, and that it is meaningful to talk about injustice at all. There may, then, be an implicit philosophical anthropology at play in the capability approach. For those seeking to use this approach as a vehicle for engaging in social, political, and economic change, uncovering such hidden commitments is crucial. What we will discover is a surprising congruence with Catholic social teaching, rooted in the relational nature of human life understood theologically, where the individual is prized as a constitutive part of the political whole and where public reason itself plays a role in nourishing visions of the good life.

INTRODUCTION

In the wake of Pope Benedict XVI's *Caritas in Veritate* (2009) and, more recently, Pope Francis's *Laudato Si'* (2015), Catholic Social Teaching (CST) has been brought to bear in increasingly public ways on the assumptions underlying concepts of development. This is especially the case in the light of sharply increasing inequality both between and within nations across all the tangled structures of resources, finance, environment, and health care: power in all its forms. While CST has been engaged in its own consideration of development for many years, especially since Pope Paul VI wrote *Populorum Progressio* (1967), these more recent encyclicals have brought Catholic perspectives to the discussion over what is really meant by "development" and what the consequences of its definition might be for visions of how to live well. Powerful examples of other kinds of texts, such as Pope Francis's *Querida Amazonia* (2020a), are part of this picture, centering the agency of the marginalized. The distinctive answers offered by CST are part of a wider landscape of theological voices that have critically questioned "development," including important postcolonial perspectives on the continuing harmful legacy of some forms of development and accompanying theological paradigms (Kwok 2005). Economic, scientific, and social schools of analysis have also been involved in this critical conversation, and the capability approach (CA) represents one such school, which has sought to include ideas of development as freedom or, better, in the words of Amartya Sen, "development as a process of expanding the real freedoms that people enjoy" (Sen 2001, 3). First expressed in Sen's insights, in dialogue with both Indian and "Western" patterns of philosophical thought (Sen 2005), the CA has been taken up in many areas, from the philosophy of justice (Nussbaum 2001) to United Nations indices for data comparison and consequent policy provision (Alkire and Foster 2009).

Certainly, both the CA and CST perspectives meet in a concern for real, seemingly intractable, situations of injustice. For Sen, that is the only way to sensibly discuss the idea of justice: by "examining what emerges in the society, including the kind of lives that people can actually lead" (Sen 2010, 10). Over the 120 years of formal teaching, much CST has similarly developed in response to concrete social circumstances and the "signs of the times."

Yet these are fundamentally different approaches—to respond to injustice rather than to work from an understanding of justice. What is at play here is certainly a difference in methodology: CST represents a practical outworking of a distinct theological understanding of the world, while Sen's philosophical commitments are left implicit. Sen's approach to justice is not a discrete theory, but is instead intended as a framework within which diverse philosophical commitments might all operate for action. As Sen writes: "We can have a strong sense of injustice on many different grounds, and yet not agree on one particular ground as being the dominant reason for the diagnosis of injustice" (Sen 2010, 2). This allows Sen to reflect on the long traditions of reasoning on justice beyond the West but also to conclude that trying to develop a consensus at the conceptual level is unfeasible and redundant (Sen 2010, 9).

Nevertheless, as theologian Stephen Plant has observed: "The very idea of development is conflicted. There are teleological conflicts about what goals development ought to aim at, methodological conflicts about how one achieves development and conflicts about who should be the prime movers in development: states, the market or the poor" (Plant 2009, 849). What is at play in Plant's identification of teleological distinctions goes beyond methodological differences to diverse understandings of what humans are and thus what we are for, let alone how development might contribute to that. For Sen's approach, the "dominant reasons" that motivate work against injustice from different perspectives might well be working toward incommensurable visions of the good, but, at the same time, action on justice could be developing norms about the human person incompatible with some of those visions.

If CST and the CA are to work together constructively, drawing out these distinctions can be of real use. It requires these partners to fully articulate what is at stake in "development" and their motives for engaging in it, thus contributing to the wider enrichment of the public discourse on such questions, itself a significant priority of Sen's. In this chapter, therefore, I seek to first establish the CST perspective, then explore what philosophical anthropology may lie beneath Sen's CA and make sense of it in the light of CST's vision of the human person with a common good. As we shall see, Sen's approach has an anthropology that shapes his implicit normative expectations for human living and inter-subjectivity.

CST: FROM THEOLOGICAL ANTHROPOLOGY TOWARD JUSTICE

There are many threads of Catholic theology that interweave to form the more recent, distinct perspective of CST. The work of Thomas Aquinas strongly marks the pattern of CST in its contemporary forms, especially with respect to the theological anthropology that is its foundation. Ultimately, CST offers a foundation of the value of the individual as an agent for change, understood within a complex political and moral whole.

Imago Dei

The starting point is theological, understanding the human person as fundamentally godly; the human person is created by God in God's own image. Yet, as Ethna Regan has rightly observed in her discussion of the meeting points of theology and human rights, *imago Dei* is not a flat description of various traits but rather "indicative and imperative" (Regan 2010, 65). It is in Aquinas that we find the differentiation within *imago Dei* that further clarifies it as that imperative call to action; he explains it as "a threefold image of 'creation,' of 're-creation,' and of 'likeness'" (Aquinas, *Summa Theologiae* [*ST*] Ia 93.4c). Creation describes our human capacities, re-creation our seeking to fulfill those capacities rightly, and likeness their heavenly perfection. Earlier in the same *questio*, Aquinas establishes those capacities as to know and to love God (Aquinas, *ST* Ia 93.1c).

So, to discuss the nature of the human person in terms of *imago Dei* is both to indicate something about what we are capable of and to name an imperative about our use of those capacities, directed toward God. I want to argue here that this need not introduce a naturalistic fallacy, moving directly from description to prescription: in the words of Regan, "*Imago Dei* is evocative rather than strictly descriptive" and yet "implies an ethical ontology" (Regan 2010, 71). The nature of our existence demands a morally considered exploration of our purpose, which is a continuing task of discovery.

In many respects, CST represents such a search. For example, as Dermot Lane has observed, in *Laudato Si'* (*LS*) Pope Francis made an explicit attempt to tackle environmental issues such as contemporary consumerism by rethinking anthropology: "No amount of talk about ecology will succeed unless and until we come up with what [Pope Francis] calls 'a new way of thinking about human beings'" (Lane 2018, 36, quoting *LS* 215). The shift is to rethink humanity in terms of our creation, embodied, among the rest of creation, with a corresponding responsibility to the world as a gift of God. At the same time, throughout earlier CST and its theological antecedents is a similar emphasis on the human person as the basis from which its principles arise.

This exploration of the human person is intended toward not an isolated individual but rather toward the individual within the community. This is another aspect of the Thomistic heritage, which is that *imago Dei* is tied up with understanding the individual as such and humanity as a moral whole. Knowing and loving God are tasks that are necessarily about others, made in God's image. Aquinas frames this in terms of loving God as imitating God's own loving-relationality, which is also one of the emphases of *Laudato Si'* in Lane's analysis (Lane 2018, 38). In her extended exploration of Karl Rahner's theological anthropology, Regan observes: "There is no individuality without community and no community other than the inter-subjectivity of individuals. Subjectivity stands in tripartite context: the relation of the subject to herself, to God, and to other persons" (Regan 2010, 75). The meaningfulness of our discussion about *imago Dei* is therefore multifold: valuing the human person as such in her universal anthropology, which reflects God; the concrete expression of that reflection in our practices; and ultimately, therefore, about how we treat each other as individuals within a whole, geared toward relationship with God. The theology that nourishes CST thereby has a fundamentally political significance.

It is precisely this political character of anthropology from which CST consistently works, even while the particular shape of the community in question might alter in changing times. We can see such consideration in early formal expressions of CST, such as Pope Leo XIII's 1891 *Rerum Novarum*, concerned with just wage practices but framed in terms of right relationships between employers and workers and between workers through political associations such as guilds and unions. A later example might be found in *Pacem in Terris*, from Pope John XXIII in 1963, which considered the relationships between nations, and within those nations between the organs of the State and the citizens within it, but there are any number of other formal encyclicals to which one could point that are fundamentally concerned with how human persons are to live together in the image of God. Herbert McCabe's commentary on Pope John Paul II's 1993 *Veritatis Splendor* again illustrates the significance of Aquinas's theology on this point, developed from Aristotle's assumptions about political community. According to McCabe, Aquinas "takes Aristotle's political notion of philia (amicitia in his language) as his model for the caritas which is the foundation of the community of the human family as, not merely creatures, but children of God" (McCabe 1994, 65). Here, then, we are natural beings, with corresponding obligations to the rest of creation, as *Laudato Si'* has drawn out so powerfully, but further, we are children of God, seeking to live together in that light.

One outworking of that perspective can be seen in the emphasis on humanity as a politically moral whole in *Caritas in Veritate* (*CV*): "In an increasingly globalized society, the common good and the effort to obtain it cannot fail to assume the dimensions of the whole human family, that is to say, the community of peoples and nations, in such a way as to shape the earthly city in unity and peace, rendering it to some degree an anticipation and a prefiguration of the undivided city of God" (*CV* 7). The unity with which Benedict XVI is here concerned is rendered both as a description of the whole of humanity as the subject of political thought and, again, as an imperative that guides the shape of social and political action toward a shared peace. Yet the end of division is cast as eschatological, happening beyond our world but revealing a teleological purpose for human political life: to attempt such peace in the common good.

I return to the significance that an anthropology of *imago Dei* insists on for the individual within that moral whole, especially as one who acts within that whole to alter it and to pursue her own ends. We see this perhaps most clearly expressed as CST builds from theological anthropology toward principles to guide the establishing of just political communities: solidarity, subsidiarity, and the common good.

The Common Good

Beginning with the common good, already noted above in *Caritas in Veritate* (Benedict XVI 2009) as that which guides the task of political endeavor, CST has repeatedly articulated this principle in the encyclicals of the twentieth century. The documents of the Second Vatican Council give this perennial example, from *Gaudium et Spes*: "the sum of those conditions of social life which allow social groups and their individual members relatively thorough and ready access to their own fulfillment" (Vatican Council II 1965, 26). The Constitutions of the Council continually place the human person at the heart of the collective ecclesial and political task in this way, always in relation to the whole community. So, even when seeking to discuss the "human family," that family's plurality and each individual's agency is explicit and part of the very point made in *Populorum Progressio*: to be "artisans of [our] own destiny" (Paul VI 1967, 65). This further relies on Aquinas's theology, too, as it is Aquinas who places individuals' pursuit of fulfillment within the broader quest for the common good and thus places important limits on their private interests. As he affirms, "no man is entitled to manage things merely for himself, he must do so in the interests of all, so that he is ready to share them with others in case of necessity" (Aquinas, *ST* IIaIIae, 66.2c). Even the protection of the free endeavor of the individual for her own fulfilment locates that as part of a shared duty to each other's fulfilment. Thus, David Hollenbach can expand on the understanding of the common good in terms of "the good realized in the mutual relationships in and through which human beings achieve their well-being" (Hollenbach 2002, 82). In this way, our individual behavior and relationships within the political community are both implicated in the fulfillment of the common good.

This is a distinctly CST perspective, which we might sharply contrast with other expectations of the political encounter. One approach would be the more Hobbesian anticipation that multiple interests lead inevitably to conflict, and another would be that of the utilitarian requirement of the maximum possible good for the maximum possible number. Both of these approaches ultimately rest on a political anthropology that rejects the very possibility of a common good. As Anna Rowlands has astutely noted in her analysis of *Laudato Si'*, "The evil at the root of the ecological crisis is based on a refusal of the substantive good, a turning toward a politics and economics rooted in lack and a consequent *libido dominandi*" (Rowlands 2015, 418). By contrast, seeking the common good from a CST perspective requires attention to individuals' self-striving, without excluding and erasing the interests of vulnerable persons and groups, including them instead as part of the pattern of mutuality. The fear of others' needs that leads to the excessive grasping, hoarding of power, which Rowlands observes *Laudato Si'* critiquing, is distinct from the Thomistic heritage, in which what is mutual and common must respect the particular, right through to the "unrepeatable" individual (John Paul II 1979, 13).

Solidarity and Subsidiarity

The principles of solidarity and subsidiarity both contribute to this reconstruction of CST in terms of the value of the individual, but do so by obliging us to consider the individual always as an actor within the political community. In *Sollicitudo Rei Socialis* (*SRS*) (1987), Pope John Paul II offers perhaps the most comprehensive definition of solidarity in this respect:

> It is above all a question of interdependence, sensed as a system determining relationships in the contemporary world, in its economic, cultural, political and religious elements, and accepted as a moral category. When interdependence becomes recognized in this way, the correlative response as a moral and social attitude, as a "virtue," is solidarity. This then is not a feeling of vague compassion or shallow distress at the misfortunes of so many people, both near and far. On the contrary, it is a firm and persevering determination to commit oneself to the common good; that is to say to the good of all and of each individual, because we are all really responsible for all. (*SRS* 38)

Solidarity requires a political understanding of humankind. The encyclical continues: "Interdependence must be transformed into solidarity, based upon the principle that the goods of creation are meant for all. That which human industry produces . . . must serve equally for the good of all" (*SRS* 39). Such expressions of solidarity have strong resonance with non-theological appropriations of solidarity—interdependence and a sense of mutuality as our goals and work impact each other.

Crucially, though, solidarity works from the anthropological intuition at its heart that consequently summons us and motivates our response, and for CST that anthropology is necessarily always already theological, as Pope John Paul II builds to:

> Solidarity helps us to see the "other"—whether a person, people or nation—not just as some kind of instrument, with a work capacity and physical strength to be exploited at low cost and then discarded when no longer useful, but as our "neighbor," a "helper" (cf. Gen. 2:18–20), to be made a sharer, on a par with ourselves, in the banquet of life to which all are equally invited by God. Hence the importance of reawakening the religious awareness of individuals and peoples. (*SRS* 39)

CST continues to cast this in terms of the image of God as both indicative and imperative: a summons to fulfill that image in our lives and to recognize it in others. This is framed not only in terms of interpersonal obligation, but also increasingly in Christic terms, for example, in Pope Francis's *Evangelii Gaudium* (*EG*) (2013): "True faith in the incarnate Son of God is inseparable from self-giving, from membership in the community, from service, from reconciliation with others. The Son of God, by becoming flesh, summoned us to the revolution of tenderness" (*EG* 88). When Francis claims that "our brothers and sisters are the prolongation of the incarnation for each of us," that is not only a beautiful reflection on the divinization of humankind, but also a radical claim about Christ in humankind and what that calls us to.[1] It is an ancient claim, as we see in Gregory of Nyssa's homily on the love of the poor: "The Lord in His goodness has given them his own countenance in order that it might cause the hard-hearted, those who hate the poor, to blush with shame, just as those being robbed thrust before their attackers the images of their king to shame the enemy with the appearance of the ruler" (translated in Holman 2001, 195). Gregory means that, just as someone being robbed might hold up the face of the king on a coin to shame the thief, so, too, do the poor hold up the face of Christ in their own.

Thus, the *imago Dei* continues to underpin the moral reasoning at play in CST, borne out particularly in its reflections on solidarity, taking us beyond a purely social justice register of obligation. Rowlands again observes this in *Laudato Si'*, where Pope Francis's considerations of justice are not focused on establishing just systems that work mechanically and impersonally. Instead, his "Christian account of reciprocity is rooted in unscripted and noncontrolling forms of reciprocity between citizens and between rich and poor" (Rowlands 2015, 419). In some respects, this approach recalls the "beautiful name of solicitude" (Ricoeur 1994, 180), which itself titles the earlier encyclical that gave us our definition. Solidarity cannot be understood as merely a reaction to the fact of our interdependence through recognizing obligation. Instead, our relationships with others could transform us rather than burden us.

Subsidiarity, too, is fundamentally concerned with right relationships of the individual within the wider schema of social and political life. It calls us to be attentive to the place where a political action can effectively and respectfully respond to any given situation. As Pope Pius XI writes in *Quadregesimo Anno*: "It is gravely wrong to take from individuals what they can accomplish by their own initiative and industry and give it to the community, so also . . . to assign to a greater and higher association what lesser and subordinate organizations can do. For every social activity thought of its very nature to furnish help to the members of the body social, and never destroy or absorb them" (Pius XI 1931, §79). The emphasis in this example is on finding the most local way of acting, which is frequently how subsidiarity is read. That is how subsidiarity appears in the founding Treaty on European Union (1992), for example—to seek to do what can be done locally at the local level. In fact, the principle also requires us to acknowledge that solutions will come from different "levels" and from different spheres. For example, in *Evangelii Gaudium* Pope Francis suggests that "an innate tension also exists between globalization and localization. We need to pay attention to the global so as to avoid narrowness and banality. Yet we also need to look to the local, which keeps our feet on the ground" (*EG* 234).

Crucially, the point of such explorations is to continue to protect the individual within the collective endeavor, a point that Francis was making long before he wrote *Laudato Si'*: "Nor do people who wholeheartedly enter into the life of a community need to lose their individualism or hide their identity; instead, they receive new impulses to personal growth. The global need not stifle, nor the particular prove barren" (*EG* 235). Francis offers an extraordinary image that makes sense of particularity within the ecclesia, as Philip McCosker has observed (2016). This image makes sense of the particular within a political whole:

> Here our model is not the sphere, which is no greater than its parts, where every point is equidistant from the centre, and there are no differences between them. Instead, it is the polyhedron, which reflects the convergence of all its parts, each of which preserves its distinctiveness. Pastoral and political activity alike seek to gather in this polyhedron the best of each. There is a place for the poor and their culture, their aspirations and their potential. Even people who can be considered dubious on account of their errors have something to offer which must not be overlooked. It is the convergence of peoples who, within the universal order, maintain their own individuality; it is the sum total of persons within a society which pursues the common good, which truly has a place for everyone. (*EG* 236)

This image may speak also to our consideration of development—an image that refuses the flat homogeneity of the spherical character of globalization.

I suggest that what we see here is the differentiation that I noted in Aquinas's reconstruction of *imago Dei*. All individuals are called to re-creation of the image of God in their lives, and this is done not through conforming to an identical pattern, but through their particularity, and in relation to particular circumstances. The shape of political community is thereby diversified in Francis's vision.

What I have offered here is a reconstruction of CST, which seeks to emphasize the role of the free individual in communities. That freedom leads, on one side of the coin, to the acknowledgment of plurality of goals, and, on the other, to the recognition of the individual as an active agent for change and for solidarity who can participate in the shaping of the political community that impacts her and others' opportunities. Paul Sigmund, in his work on Thomas Aquinas as a political thinker, understood him as "one of the first to endorse popular participation in government, despite the fact that he was writing before the emergence of national representative institutions" (Sigmund 2002, 328), though of course that participation remains within a structure of inherited hierarchy, as Sigmund himself notes. This leaves us with a picture of the human person as socially and morally bound up with others and called to a free and active participation in sharing and shaping life with those others, underscoring the plurality of how that orientation toward others in community might be worked out together. As we shall see, these are important meeting points with Sen's implicit anthropology.

THE CAPABILITY APPROACH: FROM INJUSTICE TOWARD PHILOSOPHICAL ANTHROPOLOGY?

Like CST, Sen takes an approach to justice that is practically oriented. He identifies his idea of justice with the Sanskrit *nyaya* (justice in realization) in contrast with what he calls "transcendental institutionalism" (2010, ix), or *niti* (principles of justice). In this way, Sen explicitly rejects theories of justice that he sees as primarily concerned with establishing just institutions as abstract thought exercises aimed at perfecting something that does not exist and cannot be agreed upon. Sen associates his own idea of justice with what he calls "comparative" approaches, which are forms of practical reasoning to "address questions of enhancing justice and removing injustice, rather than to offer resolutions of questions about the nature of perfect justice" (Sen 2010, ix). In this way, Sen appears to be offering his idea of justice not as a theory but as a practical attempt at motivating action in the face of recognizable injustice. In contrast with CST, Sen has deliberately held back from articulating a distinct philosophical perspective to make sense of his approach, suspicious of the risk of stagnating in an unwinnable debate about theory.

To follow Paul Ricoeur's distinctions, Sen is beginning from the perspective not of ethical vision or moral norm, but in the conflicts of practical wisdom. Practical wisdom, as Ricoeur casts it, is judgment in situation, a way of responding constructively to moments of conflict between moral norms or between norms and ethical visions—just what Sen is responding to. Practical wisdom offers a "necessary thickness," as Séverine Deneulin has observed (2006, 27), which resources the move from a general approach to the policy-specific in the face of the needs of development. As Ricoeur argued, practical wisdom is not wholly separable from ethical vision, or moral norm, involving "a split, divided, differentiated concept of ethics, the anterior ethic pointing to the root edness of norms in life and desire, the posterior ones aimed at inserting norms into concrete situations" (Ricoeur 2007, 46). It is on the plane of practical wisdom that ethical visions of the good life and the negotiation of moral norms are brought into dialogue with each other as the testing of particular "convictions incorporated in concrete forms of life" (Ricoeur 1994, 289). Sen is creating a framework to identify practical responses that relate back to differing ethical visions, each grounded in a desire for the good life, to use Ricoeur's term, or to use Sen's: a life one has reason to value. That link to "anterior" ethics implied in the practical responses of Sen's ideas for justice and development reveal a certain set of assumptions about the moral anthropology at play in his work that are congruent with those of CST. I will draw out these elements.

Freedom

The first aspect of Sen's anthropology has been clear for decades of his work. Human persons can and should be free. The CA's entire premise is that development work can be done more impactfully by assessing what free choices people's circumstances enable them to make rather than their basic needs, a distinction that Sen characterizes as a "philosophical difference" (Sen 2017, 25). The CA is geared toward the now classic formulation of enabling "people to live the kinds of lives they have reason to value" (Sen 2001, 226). This reveals two important elements. The first is the clear value placed on a person's choices, which is the focus of Sen's own argument. The second is that this reveals what I will later suggest has significance for Sen's work beyond that plane of practical wisdom, at the level of the ethics of the good life, responding to an anthropology of a future-oriented character in humanity. Development, I argue, is concerned with concrete circumstances to enable free choices but is also called upon to nourish the visions of possible lives that human persons might choose.

The first aspect is the obvious value the CA places on a person's choices. As Sen argues, "Different people can have different opportunities for converting income and other primary goods into characteristics of good living and into the kind of freedom valued in human life" (Sen 2010, 254). Attention to such opportunities is a distinctive contribution of the CA, introducing previously "missing dimensions" in analyzing poverty and development (Alkire, 2007). Sen's interest here is in arguing for assessing development by way of capabilities that people gain, but underlying that is an assumption that a person's choices about how to live are important in themselves, even while Sen elsewhere articulates limits on those choices (such as restricting tobacco use in the interest of longer-term well-being). As he observes, "A plausible accounting of opportunities can include having options and it can inter alia include valuing free choice" (Sen 2005, 153).

Sen makes a further distinction between opportunity freedoms and process freedoms. The former are tied up with material needs and circumstances, where, for example, one might be prevented from accessing tertiary education for financial or geographical reasons. These are contrasted with process freedoms, where one is excluded from participation in decision-making about opportunity freedoms. The curtailment of such freedoms can compound each other: the denial of access to education on the basis of gender might implicate both opportunity and process freedoms. Capability requires attention not just to means but to what those means enable a person to do, and this can be impacted by concrete resources, systemic prejudices, or other forms of denials of process. Sen seems to suggest that, as a framework, the CA is intended to address only freedom of opportunity rather than freedom of process: "Capabilities are characteristics of individual advantages, and they fall short of telling us enough about the fairness or equity of the processes involved, or about the freedom of citizens to invoke and utilise procedures that are equitable" (Sen 2005, 156).

In fact, the CA itself relies on process freedoms. This can be seen in the value Sen places on public reasoning as a context required for capabilities to be agreed on or for human rights to be tested for universalizability. It is only through process freedoms that genuinely plural public reasoning can be brought to bear. Even while Sen introduces the limits of the CA for development, he reveals what is needed for debate on justice and consequently what he values for political life, reflective of an anthropology of human freedom. I suggest that in this layered sense of freedom, the CA offers a shift from considering mere material subsistence around people's needs to valuing their decision-making on its own terms while at the same time acknowledging that "the impor-tance of agency does not obliterate the relevance of the outcome" (Sen 2007, 443). This understanding emphasizes the value the CA necessarily places on individual human persons, demonstrated through the atten-tion to their freedom and enabled by concrete resources, circumstance, and participation in decision-making. We might observe resonance here with the way that CST articulates a similar priority for the individual in human dignity and the persistent protection of actors demanded by the principles of solidarity and subsidiarity. This sharpens the sense of a moral intuition in Sen's own approach, as we shall continue to see.

Visions of Living Meaningfully

I want to suggest, however, that Sen's emphasis on freedom to live a life one has reason to value has another level of significance for articulating the anthropology that is at play. I suggest that this can be seen in the human person as future-oriented and capable of narrating meaning. All those with whose development Sen is concerned are not making choices solely around survival but are also seeking meaningfulness for their lives in their ways of living. There is a significant echo here of the way that *Populorum Progressio* articulates what Catholic thinking seeks to enable for people: to become "artisans of their own destiny" (*PP* 65). This is a summons beyond analyzing resources and processes. Instead it implies the need to nourish the visions of possible lives that human persons might choose as well—that ethical desire to live well and meaningfully. It is the role of public reasoning that shapes this element in Sen.

Sen presents public discourse as itself a factor in creating oppor-tunity, but also, I suggest, in enriching our thinking about the kinds of lives we wish to lead. This is indicated in his *Development as Freedom*, in which he argues that public reasoning, grounded in political rights, is formative and "central to the conceptualization of economic needs themselves" (Sen 2001, 154). Sen is suggesting here that our needs are not merely material and logical, nor are they the consequences of arbi-trary preferences, but rather they are grounded in the diverse ways in which the community understands itself and what makes for living well. Consequently, it is public reasoning, supported by "political and civic rights, especially those related to the guaranteeing of open discussion, debate, criticism, and dissent, [that is] central to the processes of generating informed and reflected choices. These processes are crucial to the formation of values and priorities" (Sen 2001, 153). As Deneulin and Augusto Zampini-Davies have noted, however, drawing on United Nations Development Programme observations, the questions about process freedoms for political participation are necessarily sharpened here. For example, "Those with informal and insecure employment have limited capacity to shape the institutions in which they live, and therefore little capacity to build social competences" in order to participate (Deneulin and Zampini-Davies 2016, 4). There have been some important observations on this point with respect to austerity measures in welfare support across Europe (European Parliamentary Assembly 2012). Political and social convictions are shaped by those who have opportunity and the social competences necessary to engage in the public debate, even while it is that discourse and other structures that might shape their opportunities.

Moreover, beyond these questions of value formation it is through public reasoning and encounter with others that we encounter other ways of reasoning and other visions of the good life, thus enriching our thinking about living well and the choices we might make for ourselves. What individuals can imagine for themselves and for others is in part formed by that debate and by their participation in it. Consequently, public discourse can reveal new ways of understanding the world and our roles within it, far beyond the limits of the negotiation of action that Sen intends, thus contributing also to the level of ethical vision on which the CA necessarily rests.

On one hand, this ethical encounter with the other emphasizes the value of a "global examination of each other's position" (Sen 2017, 432), which "need not only be [by] local people, or members of a shared sovereign state" (Sen 2012, 107). That examination includes encountering the real lives of others, discussed further below, but also the contribution of particular cultural forms, which Sen demonstrates in the diverse narratives and resources that he draws on throughout his work, including Arjuna's dilemma in the *Mahabharata*, the teachings of Gautama Buddha in the *Sutta-Nipata*, and the tale of the Good Samaritan in the New Testament.

On the other hand, this also makes room for self-critique, which Sen explores by drawing on Adam Smith, whose impartial spectator is reached by "scrutinising not only the influence of vested interest, but also the impact of entrenched tradition and custom" (Sen 2010, 45). Here, at least, Sen is considering the significance of institutional design, with a striking challenge to institutions that fail to critique their own processes or fail to draw in cultural, religious, and political alternatives, which "leave[s] out perspectives and reasonings presented by anyone whose assessments are relevant, either because their interests are involved, or because their ways of thinking about these issues throw light on particular judgments—a light that might be missed in the absence of giving those perspectives an opportunity to be aired" (Sen 2010, 44).

At the anthropological level, this continues to underscore the contribution of all people to the discussion of justice and action on inequality, another strong echo of subsidiarity that refuses to exclude anyone from the work of transformation. More than that, though, this leaves us with a vision of the human person as fundamentally self-reflective and imaginative, which is seen most clearly in the summons implied in the CA to protect spaces of public reasoning. Finally, then, this exploration of public reasoning underscores that the human person is future-oriented—one who makes sense of her concrete choices in relation to her meaningful end as she understands it, though questions of power asymmetry remain over even the nourishing of our imagination.

Moral Orientation

Most significantly, what builds from this understanding of the human person as a potential contributor within a discursive public sphere is the relationship between persons and to the community. When approaches to political thinking emphasize the individual, it is a usual theological critique that they leave the person atomistic, isolated from moral relationships and characterized only by self-interest (e.g., Cavanaugh 2002, 44). To be sure, Sen does make particular room for ways of reasoning that link self-interest and collective justice, continuing his comparative attempt, rather than designing the perfect institution. For example, Adam Smith's impartial spectator is framed by Sen in terms of good will toward the other by relying on his *Theory of Moral Sentiments*, which calls for spectators to "feel much for others and little for ourselves" (Smith 2003, 30), emphasizing sympathy, generosity, and public spirit as some of the many motivations of human behavior. John Rawls's contractual approach, which protects one's possible social position, nevertheless "takes the form of making the worst-off members of the society as well off as possible" (Sen 2010, 60). Even self-serving decisions can have just outcomes for the vulnerable, such as action to end poverty in order to avoid the discomfort of having to encounter it (Sen 2010, 179).

Sen sees such perspectives as part of a wider plurality of viewpoints that can be drawn on to ensure action against injustice. The CA gives us a way of concentrating "on the informational basis of individual freedoms (not utilities), but incorporates sensitivity to consequences" (Sen 2001, 55), and so can draw on thinking from utilitarianism, libertarianism, and Rawlsian theories of how to identify the just action. Sen does not identify the CA with any one of these approaches, instead understanding it to offer a new set of analytical categories practical wisdom can use to negotiate an action in a situation that brings to bear plural visions of living well. The emphasis that the CA places on public debate over justice takes seriously the ethical imaginations of political communities and the participation of individuals within its formation, which are brought to bear and made sense of in concrete action: "The recognition of evident injustice in preventable deprivation, such as widespread hunger, unnecessary morbidity, premature mortality, grinding poverty, neglect of female children, subjugation of women and phenomena of that kind does not have to await the derivation of some complete ordering over voices that involve finer differences and puny infelicities" (Sen 2001, 254).

Any attempt to theorize about what justice should look like must always be subordinate to acting on what is already agreed upon lest the pursuit of justice itself lose its vigor. As Sen writes, "We may of course be tempted by the idea that we can rank alternatives in terms of their respective closeness to the perfect choice. . . . But that approach does not get us very far" (Sen 2010, 16).[2]

Nevertheless, despite the role retained for self-interest, the CA does ultimately rely on a certain moral intuition, even orientation, toward the other, and perhaps toward the political community. Sen discusses obligation in various ways. One significant example is the obligation of power, which he says is "presented powerfully by Gautama Buddha in *Sutta-Nipata*. Buddha argues there that we have responsibility to animals precisely because of the asymmetry between us, not because of any symmetry that takes us to the need for cooperation" (Sen 2010, 205). The argument offered here is, as Sen puts it, to say that if an action can be performed and it "will create a more just situation in the world (thereby making it justice-enhancing), then that is argument enough for the person to consider seriously what he or she should do" (Sen 2010, 206). Another example, again using religious narrative, is that of the Good Samaritan. Sen highlights the "Good Samaritan" parable as an example of a practical encounter calling one to consider one's conduct in terms of moral interdependence, and in so doing offers a clear connection to the interdependence that summons solidarity in CST. "The Samaritan is linked to the wounded Israelite through the event itself: he found the man, saw the need to help, provided that help and was now in a relationship with the injured person" (Sen 2010, 172). The key moral of the parable for Sen is that no universal duty is identified by Jesus for the Samaritan's actions—it remains on the level of practical engagement rather than theoretical reflection, rooted only in the experienced "force of their mutual connexions" (Sen 2010, 174). This, too, evokes recent CST directly, as the project of Pope Francis's *Fratelli Tutti* (2020b) is framed by this same parable read as a summons to concrete encounter. Philosophically, this could include purely pragmatic acknowledgment of potential mutual benefit and contractarian readings (Sen 2010, 200–204).

It is Sen who introduces the anthropological implication of the force of the encounter between the Samaritan and the Israelite at the very beginning of *The Idea of Justice* (Sen 2010). Sen suggests that human beings have an acute sense of justice insofar as we experience an intuitive indignation in response to injustice, which has historically been sufficient for various figures to insist upon change. Gandhi and Martin Luther King Jr. both acted, Sen argues, from "a sense of manifest injustices that could be overcome" (Sen 2010, vii). There is a strongly optimistic character to this understanding of the human person as oriented toward the other in need. Sen has consequently observed that "there is a particular need in this context to examine value formation that results from public discussion of miserable events, in generating sympathy and commitment on the part of citizens to do something to prevent their occurrence" (Sen 2017, 40). Again, public discourse is key for the CA to work, in this case as a way of engaging one's moral sentiment beyond the direct encounter.

However, these historical examples are somewhat ambiguous, for although they illustrate the struggle in confronting injustice, they are not examples in which all parties intuitively recognize injustices and accordingly act for change. Indeed, it may be that this anthropological aspect to Sen's work includes a moral tension that introduces the possibility that we do all recognize injustice, but that not all of us will act on that recognition or that the incommensurability of goods remains in tension.

I want to return to Ricoeur's commentary here as a way of making sense of the inclusion of the other at the level of the moral intuition. It is a move that is perhaps explained by the philosophical heritage that Sen does not address here, in which indignation as a motive for seeking justice arises in the work of Immanuel Kant (1997, 4.398) and is articulated by Ricoeur: "The desire for justice arises and is developed out of such indignation. . . . It is at the moment when our indignation seeks to justify itself that we really enter into the problem of justice, for indignation remains caught up in the desire to obtain justice for oneself. It lacks the sense of just distance that only our codes, written laws, courts and the like can take in hand" (Ricoeur 2007, 235).

Indignation introduces the question of justice for oneself, and so builds to the idea of obligation to others, which can be established as a moral norm and so legislated for. As Sen's example of sympathy with those undergoing disaster reflects, the desire for the good life also identifies the self as an agent, and consequently as responsible. Thus, the enriching of an ethical vision involves moral sentiments for others as well, which Ricoeur delineates as "self-constancy, solicitude for the neighbour, participation in sovereignty as a citizen" (Ricoeur 2007, 53). I suggest that these commitments are what Sen establishes in his broadly universalizable principle that we should consider acting to "create a more just situation in the world" (Sen 2010, 206).

It is again through public justification that a justice that includes others, mediated by institutions, can be articulated. This is a move that Ricoeur characterizes as a move from the particular, or historical, toward the universal, how we move from cultural forms of justness to actions for justice that can be agreed on and shared. This approach of Ricoeur's may introduce questions over Sen's hesitancy around the institutional elements of justice, as obligation does indeed require the establishing of normative expectations while, practically, the operation of public reasoning also requires certain process freedoms. Still Sen has never denied the importance of the role of institutions in enshrining important principles and justice shaping our values, only stressing that one cannot wait for them to be perfect. Indeed, in *The Idea of Justice* he explores the many institutional forms and practices that shape our understanding of justice, such as the press (Sen 2010, 335–37).

Appropriately, then, what is most valuable to draw from Ricoeur's analysis of indignation at injustice is what it nourishes politically, "rooting our desire for just institutions in a desire for a good life. We can say in this regard that the primitive idea of justice is the unfolding of the desire for a good life at the institutional, communitarian, and dialogical level. This connection between a good life and justice found stable expression, whose emotional and rational strength has not been exhausted, in the idea of a life together" (Ricoeur 2007, 235). The understanding of the good life at the level of the institutional and communal is itself a demand for justice that goes beyond self-interest toward principles of justice that encompass others. It is through their public debate and justification that such intuitions can come to practice (the level at which Sen seeks to operate), but also to articulate and justify, the moral norm that enshrines one's moral obligations toward the vulnerable other. This implicates our behavior toward others in their wider plurality (on which point Ricoeur is following Hannah Arendt; see Ricoeur 2007, 234) at the ethical, moral, and practical levels.

We begin to see, then, implicit in Sen's anterior but unspoken ethics, is an anthropology of the free human person, desiring to live well and envisioning such a future in diverse ways but fundamentally attentive to the moral sentiments implicated in that vision. Sen does not articulate this move from indignation as a revelation of the desire for the good life, brought by the discussion of justice to the institutional or collective level, but he does, as explored above, insist on the role of public reasoning and social institutions themselves in "guiding social choice towards social justice" (Sen 2010, 69). Thus, the morally sensible human person remains dependent on the inter-subjectivity that shapes "the conceptualization of economic needs themselves" (Sen 2001, 154).

CONCLUSION: ARTICULATING THE POSSIBILITIES

There is real congruence between CST and the CA's understandings of the human person. The projects of both CST and the CA are ultimately dependent on a moral anthropology that prizes the individual *qua* the individual while recognizing that she makes sense of the meaningfulness of her life in the light of active relationships to the political community and the end to which her actions are directed. Both rely profoundly on the human person as morally sensible, and thus responsive to injustices that affect herself and others, which indignation recognizes as other selves.

While of course, for CST, the destiny for which we are to be our own artisans is ultimately to be found in God, CST emphasizes that the role of political action (theologically understood or not) is to enable the capabilities of people to actively pursue that end, including resourcing them to assess and value the meaning of their lives. Both the CA and CST, therefore, rely on opportunities for public reasoning that can nourish the individual, in terms both of offering visions of the good life that resource her moral imagination and of supporting the development of her ability to argue for that vision.

Still, there is a point of tension that remains in Sen's methodological emphasis on beginning at pragmatic agreement on action, thus including motivations that ultimately rest in self-interest, despite what I suggest is implicit in the inter-subjective, morally attentive understanding of the human person at play in Sen's own assumptions. The risk that we are left with is that the engagement with divergent reasons for action may have the effect of contradicting the value of the other as another self, and consequently undermining the value of the human person on which Sen fundamentally relies for his project, and which is certainly foundational for CST.

In some ways this concern is likely to be of little interest to Sen, since his stated goal has always been to offer a framework into which otherwise conflicting formulations of justness as an ethic can be reframed to speak to concrete capabilities and consequently to prompt action. His interest is in inciting action, not resolving or even interrogating the tragic incommensurability of the understandings of the good life that lie behind such formulations. Still, while Sen himself may be seeking to avoid establishing a fixed ethics, what his framework insists on is that those who are bringing their diverse convictions to bear on a situation do articulate their reasoning.

As I have suggested above, that reasoning is not only to include capabilities in our practical thinking of how to respond to injustice, but also to recognize the importance of nourishing visions of the good life and the diversity of lives that one might have reason to value. Moreover, the CA does depend on recognizing normative obligations to the other. Therefore, one solution is to respond to the risk of conflicting systems of valuing by more fully articulating the possibilities for just living, attentive to the real consequences for the capabilities of all to pursue a good life, together.

In this way, the CA and CST each challenge the other. The CA's insistence on public justification of one's reasons for acting against injustice may prompt CST to increasingly articulate its vision of human flourishing and how that might shape normative principles of justice. This requires a self-critical consideration of Church practice but also provides an opportunity for CST's particular cultural perspective on living together to enrich the public conversation on justice and the good life. The recent example of *Laudato Si'* addresses this as the responsibility for wider creation. Practices of CST can inculcate the attitudes necessary to sharpen that sense of injustice and strengthen the consequent commitment to solidarity, ultimately shaping a public context in which the CA can operate. At the same time, while I have characterized CST in terms of plurality, that plurality is at the level of diverse creative opportunities for flourishing that subsidiarity requires, all of which remain intertwined with other principles of common good that should protect the individual within the moral whole.

Systems of thinking relying on self-interest risk treating other persons as means rather than also as ends in themselves, and this is at odds with the emphases of the moral anthropologies underlying the CA and CST. At a point in time when forms of racist, anti-Semitic, and otherwise aggressive nationalistic politics are increasingly part of concrete institutions and public discourse, that risk is not a trivial one.[3] As Sen acknowledges, the public discourse also plays a role in cultivating the motivation and reasons to struggle for justice, and so the CA, and the public sphere, sincerely need CST in its articulation of the common good and solidarity as collectively binding and beautiful in their (radical, incarnational) reflection of God. While it is my suggestion that both the

CA and CST leave open the content of the meaning that people find in their lives, both understand the seeking of that meaning to be a fundamentally collective human endeavor bearing moral, inter-subjective implications. What both the CA and CST summon us to, then, is the fulfillment of our human nature in and through those social institutions and political practices. Rather than posit their perfectibility, we are called to shape their transformation.

NOTES

I have used the wording "Catholic social thought" in the title rather than "Catholic Social Teaching" because I will draw on the wider heritage of Catholic social thinking, its sources, and its commentators as I develop my argument. Here I introduce Catholic Social Teaching in the sense of formal Church teaching, for example, in papal encyclicals.

1. There is much to extend thinking on this point in the more recent *Fratelli Tutti* (Francis 2020b), which offers another call to brothers and sisters but frames this in terms of the summons to neighboring.

2. Earlier explored in Sen's *Collective Choice and Social Welfare*, first published in 1971 and re-published in a revised edition in 2017.

3. This, too, is centered in *Fratelli Tutti*, where consideration of the neighbor builds to a discussion of the people and the institutions that mediate encounter. I discuss this directly in relation to populism in my article "Paul Ricoeur and *Fratelli Tutti*: Neighbor, People, Institution" (Daughton 2022).

WORKS CITED

Alkire, Sabina. 2007. "The Missing Dimensions of Poverty Data." *Oxford Development Studies* 35, no. 4: 347–59.

Alkire, Sabina, and James Foster. 2009. "Counting and Multidimensional Poverty Measures." OPHI Working Paper 7. *Oxford Poverty and Human Development Initiative*. University of Oxford, Oxford.

Aquinas, Thomas. 1964 (1485). *Summa Theologiae*. London: Blackfriars with Eyre and Spottiswoode.

Benedict XVI. 2009. *Caritas in Veritate* (*CV*). Encyclical. https://www.vatican.va/content/benedict-xvi/en/encyclicals/documents/hf_ben-xvi_enc_20090629_caritas-in-veritate.html.

Cavanaugh, William. 2002. *Theopolitical Imagination*. London: T&T Clark.

Daughton, Amy. 2022. "Paul Ricoeur and *Fratelli Tutti*: Neighbor, People, Institution." *Journal of Catholic Social Thought* 19, no.1: 71–88.

Denculin, Séverine. 2006. "Necessary Thickening." In *Transforming Unjust Structures: The Capability Approach*, edited by Séverine Deneulin, Mathias Nebel, and Nicholas Sagovsky. New York: Springer.

Deneulin, Séverine, and Augusto Zampini-Davies. 2016. "Theology and Development as Capability Expansion." *Theological Studies* 72, no. 4: 1–9.

European Parliamentary Assembly. 2012. Resolution 1884. *Austerity Measures—A Danger for Democracy and Social Rights*. Brussels: Council of Europe, Assemblée Parliament, June 26, 2012. Originally published as Doc. 12948: Report by the Committee of Social Affairs, Health, and Sustainable Development—Rapporteur, Mr. Andrej Hunko, Germany, Group of the Unified European Left, June 7, 2012.

Francis. 2013. *Evangelii Gaudium* (*EG*). Apostolic exhortation. https://www.vatican.va/content/francesco/en/apost_exhortations/documents/papa-francesco_esortazione-ap_20131124_evangelii-gaudium.html.

———. 2015. *Laudato Si': On Care for Our Common Home* (*LS*). Encyclical. https://www.vatican.va/content/francesco/en/encyclicals/documents/papa-francesco_20150524_enciclica-laudato-si.html.

———. 2020a. *Querida Amazonia: Post-Synodal Apostolic Exhortation for a Church with an Amazonian Face*. https://www.vatican.va/content/francesco/en/apost_exhortations/documents/papa-francesco_esortazione-ap_20200202_querida-amazonia.html.

———. 2020b. *Fratelli Tutti*. Encyclical. https://www.vatican.va/content/francesco/en/encyclicals/documents/papa-francesco_20201003_enciclica-fratelli-tutti.html.

Hollenbach, David. 2002. *The Common Good and Christian Ethics*. Cambridge: Cambridge University Press.

Holman, Susan. 2001. *The Hungry Are Dying: Beggars and Bishops in Roman Cappadocia*. Oxford: Oxford University Press.

John XXIII. 1963. *Pacem in Terris*. Encyclical. https://www.vatican.va/content/john-xxiii/en/encyclicals/documents/hf_j-xxiii_enc_11041963_pacem.html.

John Paul II. 1979. *Redemptor Hominis*. Encyclical. https://www.vatican.va/content/john-paul-ii/en/encyclicals/documents/hf_jp-ii_enc_04031979_redemptor-hominis.html.

———. 1987. *Sollicitudo Rei Socialis* (*SRS*). Encyclical. https://www.vatican.va/content/john-paul-ii/en/encyclicals/documents/hf_jp-ii_enc_30121987_sollicitudo-rei-socialis.html.

———.1993. *Veritatis Splendor (VS)*. Encyclical. https://www.vatican.va/content/john-paul-ii/en/encyclicals/documents/hf_jp-ii_enc_06081993_veritatis-splendor.html.

Kant, Immanuel. 1997 (1785). *The Groundwork of the Metaphysics of Morals*. Translated by M. Gregor. Cambridge: Cambridge University Press.

Kwok Pui-lan. 2005. *Postcolonial Imagination and Feminist Theology*. Louisville, KY: Westminster John Knox Press.

Lane, Dermot. 2018. "Anthropological and Theological Reflections on Laudato Si'." In *Laudato Si', An Irish Response: Essays on the Pope's Letter on the Environment*, edited by S. McDonagh. Dublin: Veritas.

Leo XIII. 1891. *Rerum Novarum*. Encyclical. https://www.vatican.va/content/leo-xiii/en/encyclicals/documents/hf_l-xiii_enc_15051891_rerum-novarum.html.

McCabe, Herbert. 1994. "Manuals and Rule Books." In *Considering Veritatis Splendor*, edited by J. Willkins. Cleveland, OH: Pilgrim Press.

McCosker, Philip. 2016. "From the Joy of the Gospel to the Joy of Christ: Situating and Expanding the Christology of Evangelii Gaudium." *Ecclesiology* 12: 34–45.

Nussbaum, Martha. 2001. *Women and Human Development: The Capabilities Approach*. Cambridge: Cambridge University Press.

Paul VI. 1967. *Populorum Progressio (PP)*. Encyclical. https://www.vatican.va/content/paul-vi/en/encyclicals/documents/hf_p-vi_enc_26031967_populorum.html.

Pius XI. 1931. *Quadregesimo Anno*. Encyclical. https://www.vatican.va/content/pius-xi/en/encyclicals/documents/hf_p-xi_enc_19310515_quadragesimo-anno.html.

Plant, Stephen. 2009. "International Development and Belief in Progress." *Journal of International Development* 21, no. 6: 844–55.

Regan, Ethna. 2010. *Theology and the Boundary Discourse of Human Rights*. Washington, DC: Georgetown University Press.

Ricoeur, Paul. 1994. *Oneself as Another*. Translated by Kathleen Blamey. Chicago: University of Chicago Press.

———. 2007. *Reflections on the Just*. Translated by David Pellauer. Chicago: University of Chicago Press.

Rowlands, Anna. 2015. "Laudato Si': Rethinking Politics." *Political Theology* 16, no. 5: 418–20.

Sen, Amartya. 2001. *Development as Freedom*. Oxford: Oxford University Press.

———. 2005. *The Argumentative Indian: Writings on Indian History, Culture and Identity*. London: Penguin.

———. 2010. *The Idea of Justice*. London: Penguin.

———. 2012. "Values and Justice." *Journal of Economic Methodology* 19, 101–80.

———. 2017. *Collective Choice and Social Welfare: An Expanded Edition*. Revised edition. London: Penguin. First published in 1971.

Sigmund, Paul E. 2002. "Law and Politics." In *Thomas Aquinas: Contemporary Philosophical Perspectives*, edited by Brian Davies. Oxford: Oxford University Press.

Smith, Adam. 2003 (1759). *The Theory of Moral Sentiments*. Translated and edited by K. Haakonssen. Cambridge: Cambridge University Press.

Vatican Council II. 1965. *Gaudium et Spes* (*GS*). Pastoral constitution. https://www.vatican.va/archive/hist_councils/ii_vatican_council/documents/vat-ii_const_19651207_gaudium-et-spes-en.html.

TWO

Orthodox Personhood

Clarifying the Anthropological Presuppositions of Human Development

Dana Bates

ABSTRACT

*In this chapter I explore integral human development from an East-
ern Orthodox perspective in dialogue with the capability approach.
After some introductory remarks about the development-friendly
nature of Eastern Orthodoxy, I examine the human development
implications of the theological anthropology of one of the twentieth century's leading Orthodox theologians, Dumitru Staniloae.
Staniloae consistently articulated the Trinitarian anthropological
formula "persons, in communion, within the medium of a shared
nature." I argue that this Trinitarian structure of the person, focusing simultaneously on person (agency), communion (solidarity), and
nature (structures), clarifies the actual anthropological foundations*

implicit both in Trinitarian theology and in the moral project of human development, as in the capability approach. This approach illuminates the perspective that one cannot meaningfully live without simultaneously enjoying (1) freedoms (agency), (2) communion (solidarity), and (3) the fulfillment of nature's functions (structures). Expanding on the third category of "nature" above, Eastern Orthodoxy's theological anthropology provides four critical insights into the "nature of nature" that, it will be argued, can facilitate its modern retrieval in a way that will motivate human development concerns for both theology and the secular social sciences.

INTRODUCTION

For many Western observers who are concerned with how theology can empower and inform social justice and human development concerns, Eastern Orthodoxy (EO) is a black (-robed) box at best. Often considered overly mystical and concerned only with the liturgy in the temple, EO is often dismissed as a potential dialogue partner and motivating framework for such concerns. In fact, however, EO has very profound justice and human development concerns. Her theology should be fundamentally understood as striving to live the dual commandment of love, which is reflected in the two liturgies: the liturgy in the temple (Love of God) and the liturgy or service in the world (Love of Neighbor). And Orthodox theology is, by its very nature, a "practical theology," attempting not merely to give equal emphasis to both but to synergize these two dimensions. However, not only is there a practical emphasis on living one's theology through loving praxis; Orthodox theology and particularly her anthropology also reflect profound human development concerns.

In this chapter I demonstrate this thesis by exploring integral human development concerns within EO in dialogue with the capability approach (CA). After some introductory remarks about the development-friendly nature of EO, I examine the human development implications of the theological anthropology of one of the twentieth century's leading Orthodox theologians, Dumitru Staniloae. Staniloae consistently articulated the Trinitarian anthropological formula "persons, in communion, within the medium of a shared nature."[1] I argue that this Trinitarian structure of the person, focusing simultaneously on person (agency), communion (solidarity), and nature (structures), clarifies the actual anthropological foundations implicit both in Trinitarian theology and in the moral project of human development, as in the CA. This approach illuminates the perspective that one cannot meaningfully live without simultaneously enjoying (1) freedoms (agency), (2) communion (solidarity), and (3) the fulfillment of nature's functions (structures).

Expanding on the third category of "nature" above, Eastern Orthodoxy's theological anthropology provides four critical insights into the "nature of nature" that can facilitate its modern retrieval in a way that will motivate human development concerns for both theology and the secular social sciences. These are (a) the aforementioned notion of nature as a set of diverse natural human functions or capabilities ("logoi") requiring fulfilment (as in Nussbaum's list of ten central capabilities; Nussbaum 2011, 33–34); (b) the idea of shared human nature understood as an explicit basis for cosmopolitan ethical obligations—the Samaritan ethic; (c) human nature as in continuity (solidarity) with non-human nature (non-human nature has intrinsic, not merely instrumental, value); and (d) nature as a dynamic framework in which the order of creation is not viewed as static/"Platonic" but is responsive to and even partially constituted through human effort and creativity. These four insights provide an approach to nature that creates an ethic of global human solidarity; gives specific moral content to that ethic—that is, fulfillment of universal human functions; and conceptualizes human nature as in solidarity with non-human nature—key to an ecological ethic. Finally, nature itself is (at least partially) advanced and constructed through human effort and intentionality. I close by resituating the category of nature back within the overall Trinitarian anthropological framework of freedom (person) and communion (solidarity).

HUMAN DEVELOPMENT: NATURAL THEOLOGY IN EASTERN ORTHODOXY

EO has its own contribution to make toward clarifying the means and ends of human development (HD). However, before explaining how EO can integrate with HD, it is important to explain how faith and reason in general correlate within the EO moral vision. This involves EO's distinctive sense of natural theology, or the idea that the common apprehensions of humanity have theological value. This can be seen clearly in the thought of the Cappadocian Fathers, who have a normative status in Orthodoxy. Basil the Great (330–79) notes that "We . . . must first, if the glory of the good is to abide with us indelible for all time, be instructed by these outside means, and then we shall understand the sacred and mystical teachings" (cited in Pelikan 1993, 27).

Notice the word "first," which gives a certain priority to philosophy ("these outside means") over, or at least temporally prior to, theology. Gregory of Nyssa (335–95) identified "two ways of joining man to God: true doctrine and clear reasoning, both of which came from God and each of which needed the other to be complete" (cited in Pelikan 1993, 187). Basil the Great argued that there was a "natural rationality implanted in us, telling us to identify ourselves with the good and to avoid everything harmful" and that the Apostle "Paul teaches us nothing new, but only tightens the links of nature" (cited in Pelikan 1993, 31). Dumitru Staniloae's very first sentence of his Dogmatics confirms the centrality of this insight for EO: "The Orthodox Church makes no separation between natural and supernatural revelation" (Staniloae 1994, 1). However, supernatural revelation does "tighten the links of nature"; revelation helps natural human existence and aspirations be understood more fully—even on its own terms—as will be demonstrated by showing how the Trinity can clarify the presuppositions inherent in the moral project HD.

EO's approach to natural theology, unlike most Western approaches, however, is experiential, including but going beyond mere rationality and emphasizing participation in communion, especially the moral obligation for human development. As Staniloae writes, "We experience God through our fellow humans and in the love we have for them, or we test our experience of him by means of the fully responsible love we have for them . . . we recognize Him as a source of supreme personal love who gives us strength to rise higher and higher in our love for one another (Staniloae 2000, 199).

Natural theology in EO is thus related less to intellectual proofs and more to the human experience of responsible love, of efforts to love one's (Samaritan) neighbor as oneself. Natural theology has to do with "man who is endowed with reason, with conscience, and with freedom" and "a tendency of right development" (Staniloae 1994, 1–2). This means that the academic discipline called "development studies," which is concerned with "change for the better" (Sumner 2006) but especially with removing obstacles that afflict the most vulnerable in the world, is an expression, and arguably the most sublime, of natural theology in EO terms. Development studies, which employs all of the human sciences, expresses in a paradigmatic way humanity's reason, conscience, and freedom put to its highest ends—not merely studying but advancing the well-being of all—and the CA offers a normative framework we can use to assess human development, that is, how the well-being of humans has been advanced.

THE TRINITY AND HUMAN DEVELOPMENT

Undergirding this "development-friendly" approach to Orthodox theology is the surprising dogma of the Trinity. All of creation bears marks of this pattern of a unity in diversity, as Plato discussed in his *Parmenides* (a pagan intuition of the Trinitarian structure of reality), but this pattern is most sublimely discerned in the human community. Its importance is, as Bishop Kallistos Ware writes, that the "Trinity constitutes the model and paradigm of all human relationships" (cited in Staniloae 1994, xx). Humans are imago Trinitas, a unity in diversity as the family of humanity.

As is well known in theological circles, there is a wide-ranging "Trinitarian revival," and the Eastern view has been a generative force here (Peters 1993; Rahner 1998; Reid 2000). What might this mean for bringing theology closer to human development concerns? Potentially not much. This is because there is a real danger in how the Trinity is currently interpreted—a misinterpretation that, if not corrected, will leave theology trapped in a form of sectarian or communitarianism. Similar to what is found in communitarian arguments, there is a rush in the Trinitarian discussions to embrace theological notions of "community/relationality," which is indeed noble and an important part of the human condition, but there is a dangerous neglect of both the category of shared human nature (Cunningham 1998, 26) and human agency in notions of personhood. This emphasis on communion to the neglect of other dimensions can lead to a form of theological tribalism and is inimical to a theological ethic relevant to human development.

Especially clear, however, in the Eastern tradition (especially among certain thinkers, such as Staniloae and Maximus the Confessor), the Trinity is not just about communion (*koinonia*) but involves a theological anthropology with three distinct dimensions that help clarify the anthropological foundations of HD. Dumitru Staniloae's formula, and arguably the genuine patristic formula, is precisely this: "persons, in communion, *within the medium of a shared nature*" (Staniloae 1994, emphasis mine; see also Turcescu 2002, 2005). Almost nowhere in the social sciences are persons conceptualized along these lines, where each of these dimensions is intrinsically valuable,[2] but what is even more conspicuous is that within the field of theology, almost all current Trinitarian discussions consistently omit this third dimension of a commonly shared nature (*ousia*). Person (hypostasis), and especially communion (*koinonia*), are emphasized, but this notion of shared nature as a linking factor among all members of humanity is elided. This is disastrous not simply because it does not adhere to an ancient formula but also because it means there has been a lack of reflection on (1) shared human nature as an anthropological basis for human solidarity and (2) the shared creational structures or functions (i.e., nutrition, literacy, sociability) that demand fulfilment for well-being. This neglect of the principle of shared humanity, or "concrete essence,"[3] contributes to the deformation of the mission of the Church as a narrow sectarianism.

Bringing the category of shared nature—one that Dumitru Staniloae (and Maximus the Confessor) consistently emphasized—back into the Trinity can put theology in touch with the questions of the human sciences and especially development studies, concerned as it is with all that goes into the promotion of human well-being qua species. A retrieval of the notion of shared nature, interpreted as an ethical imperative, can also provide benefits for social sciences, especially the CA, which presupposes a vigorous cosmopolitan ethic. More specifically, the neglect of shared nature as a moral category in the ontology of the CA means that there is no clear ethical bridge for moving beyond individual capabilities inasmuch as the CA downplays both communitarian values and shared nature for fear of "organicism" (Nussbaum 2000). Later I will show how EO provides the precise categories for rehabilitating "shared nature" as a moral category in a way that lays bare and clarifies many of the hidden moral presuppositions of secular human development as well as addresses many fears in retrieving the notion of "nature" for a modern set of concerns.

TRINITARIAN ANTHROPOLOGY: AGENCY, SOLIDARITY, AND STRUCTURES

At this point, in order to deepen the dialogue between EO and the CA on the basis of these three categories of the Trinity, I postulate a correlation that brings Trinitarian theology into direct dialogue with fundamental categories in the social/human sciences. The hypothesis is that the Trinitarian picture of personhood (person-communion-nature) not only mirrors but brings into coherence and harmony three inchoate concepts already widely employed in the human/social sciences. The correlation posited is this:

> Agency = Person
> Solidarity = Communion
> Structures = Nature

It is necessary to briefly extrapolate upon each of these categories, showing their separate relevance for human development, as well as their profound interconnections.

- Person—This category points to the sphere of agency, of action, of human freedom. It is the category that seeks to signal and safeguard the dignity of persons, taken separately, and the irreducible originality of every human being. "Person does not exist for anything else, but all things exist for him" (Staniloae 1994, 130). Some tendencies in Western theology have been suspicious of human agency, especially Augustinian-inspired versions.[4] Orthodoxy is "pro-agency," such that one of the most famous quotes of EO is this: "God becomes powerless before human freedom; He cannot violate it since it flows from his own omnipotence" (Lossky 1978,

73). Orthodoxy also gives a certain priority to this category of personhood, even above communion and nature (with the caveat that personhood is inconceivable without communion and shared nature).[5] Western liberalism rightly perceives the importance of this moral category of personhood but neglects others through which individual agency operates, including the two following, communion and shared nature.[6]

- Communion—This is a recognition of the relational nature of all reality and of the need to, in the words of Irish poet John O'Donohue, be in a "circle of belonging" (O'Donohue 1997, 3). Aristotle called the human being the "zoon politikon," the political or social animal. Many, including Staniloae, argue that the Trinity is about communion, or *perichorisis*, the "dance" of community and mutual indwelling, and, as mentioned above, this dimension is receiving interest in modern theology (Cunningham 1998). This is not entirely wrong—but communion does not fully comprehend the moral goods implied in human development.[7] However, as mentioned, the CA tends to downplay this communion dimension out of an understandable set of fears, such as that of intra-group cohesion leading to the dominance of outsiders.[8]

- Shared nature—Both communion and personal freedom operate through a shared human essence that is not a mere abstraction but a set of concrete properties and essential features (one of which is communion, above). There are important universal features of the shared human essence—biological, psychological, and sociological norms and faculties—that require cultivation for human flourishing (e.g., those on Nussbaum's list of ten central capabilities as described in the introduction to this book, p. 1–47, and others; see Alkire 2002a and 2002b). Furthermore, this dimension of shared nature may, in certain views of the human person, provide the basis for cosmopolitanism and what most of the ancient philosophers never understood—the fundamental moral and spiritual duty to care for all humans, not just for those of one's polis—even if it is recognized that humans are indeed political/communal beings and must enjoy particular relations.[9] Fundamental in EO is that "The common nature is the basis for its aspiration towards unity in love" (Staniloae 1994, 69).

While the "nature of nature" will be discussed in further detail below, the argument here is that an adequate conceptualization of the moral task of human development as implied in the CA requires this picture of the human condition, where each of these three dimensions (person-communion-nature) is treated as intrinsically valuable and as mutually enriching. Rarely are these three dimensions ever brought into harmony, where each is deemed intrinsically valuable and interdependent. If this is the true picture of the human condition, then an imbalance in any one or more of these can produce great human misery.

One important point to make at this point of the argument is that cosmopolitan values (human development values par excellence)—even if it is argued that they can be grounded in an empirically shared nature—are not "naturally" or automatically perceived as a moral/spiritual basis for cosmopolitanism and require a community of interpretation and cultivation for their realization. Cosmopolitanism, understood as an ethical obligation for general humanity, must be socialized in a concrete "communitarian" fashion; appealing to individual reason simpliciter, as Sen tends to do, is inadequate. It is, or should be, the precise role of religious narratives and communities to foster this, to counteract the all too human tendency to form selective reciprocities and closed if not predatory identities that create negative externalities. The Church father Chrysostom sought to institutionalize this "communitarian cosmopolitanism" principle by arguing that the key educational role of the family (the most fundamental institution of humankind, which shapes all others), with the mother as the chief pedagogue, was to instill a universal and inclusive love of humankind, of agape, versus a more exclusive love of similar persons, eros (Spidlik 1986, 162).[10] The main point here for the CA is that cosmopolitanism will not magically emerge when communitarian values are done away with, and potentially the opposite; only when a new vision (*theoria* in its original Greek sense) of "communitarian cosmopolitanism" emerges will these values take hold. This involves a spiritual sociology in which these concerns are cultivated in "communities of character" (Thomas 2004, 2005) that instill in a "learn-by-doing" process the virtues of and sacrifices required for universal human development and these values are accorded a sense of "ultimacy" that only religion can, in good faith, offer. A central moral challenge for human development today is how our variegated communal identities, whether they be family, clan, nation, or Church, can internalize a "bonding for bridging" ethic, the formation of communities of belonging that look after the "capability development" of each of their members within, but also bridge outward, and seek a universal, cosmopolitan ethical orientation. The argument here is that the moral vision of EO, particularly its Trinitarian theological anthropology, can inspire this task.

RETRIEVING NATURE: FOUR INSIGHTS FROM EO

Because it is critical to the persuasiveness of this argument, we must return to that especially important issue of clarifying the conditions for retrieving the problematic notion of human nature. It is well known that slavery and gender subordination have been viewed as part of the unchanging "natural" order of things. Modernity, in response to these misuses, is the rejection of a "natural" and unchanging moral order that has indeed often been used to justify oppression (Taylor 1989; Toulmin 1990). This blanket rejection of nature, however, is today having tragic consequences, including dismembering the human "family" sharing this one nature, as well as severing persons' connection with the natural environment.

Orthodoxy, however, provides four critical insights into the "nature of nature" that can facilitate its modern retrieval for both theology and development studies/social sciences. These are seeing (1) nature understood as a set of diverse natural human functions or capabilities ("logoi")[11] requiring fulfilment (like those on Nussbaum's list);[12] (2) human nature "interpreted" as an explicit basis for cosmopolitan ethical obligations—the Samaritan ethic; (3) human nature as in continuity (solidarity) with non-human nature (as non-human nature has intrinsic, and not merely instrumental, value); and (4) nature as a dynamic framework in which the order of creation is not viewed as static/"Platonic" but is responsive to, and even partially constituted and extended through, human effort and creativity. This latter feature of the EO view of nature (not mentioned before) as dynamic—not of an unchanging, timeless order—has a special name in EO, *epektasis*, and merits brief commentary. As Staniloae notes, "The world is not so rigid as is sometimes claimed; on the contrary it too is open to the transforming power of man. Liberty is no abstract quality, continually unverified and uncreative; it grows stronger and proves itself in dialogue with the world and in the affirmation of those creative acts which introduce beneficial changes into the world, society and human relations" (Staniloae 1980, 114).

This is important because Nussbaum derives her list of central human functional capabilities (i.e., a picture of shared human nature) from a characteristically modern approach called "self-hermeneutics" (Maris, Jacobs, and de Ville 2012) and rejects "nature" as an explicit basis for ethics. In this section I aim to show that while this approach has some justification, given modern suspicions about "nature," it also faces important limitations.

It is important to mention again modernity's rejection of natural law or the "cosmic order" (the "order of nature") as a basis for ethical norms. In the West and even before Christianity, traditional natural law theories posited an unchanging sacred order that was often used to justify indifference or various forms of discrimination. This "Platonic" natural order (often called metaphysical realism) understands moral norms and structures apart from human interpretation, intervention, or shaping (Nussbaum 1994, 29). Neo-scholasticism is a modern theological expression of this. Scholasticism was focused on the sphere of the invariable (episteme), the timeless and unchanging "universal," not on history and experience, which are the realm of the variable (phronesis), the realm of action and change. All of this was considered to be founded securely on the teaching of Thomas Aquinas. Garrigou-Lagrange was considered the model Thomist, and his contention was that "action, practice, experience, can never be the first criterion of what is true"; what is true is based on the necessary and unchanging laws of being (Kerr 2007, 12–16).

Nussbaum, on the other hand, proposes a set of natural norms but derives these from an exercise of self-hermeneutics through which the various dimensions of the human good (nature) can be discerned solely through the exercise of individual practical reason.[13] Nussbaum is not naïve regarding the obvious dangers here of perversions of desire ("preference deformation") and subscribes to an "informed desire" approach, or what would be approved by a mature agent who is rational and critically scrutinizes her desires (Jaggar 2006). Nussbaum also occasionally mentions the idea of a therapeutic community as the context for the proper formation of preferences (Nussbaum 2001), but no nurturing community (including family) has a normative, intrinsic moral status given her singular commitment to the principle of each person's capability.

It is clear, though, that Nussbaum's approach, even on its own terms, cannot be adequately theorized on this "self-hermeneutical" basis. In fact, Nussbaum often explicitly (and everywhere implicitly) appeals to another fundamentum. This is the principle of a shared human nature as a basis for moral obligation: "Compassion requires the recognition of a shared humanity" (Nussbaum 1992, 239) within which self-hermeneutics must take place.[14] The contention here is that shared human nature is a tacit moral presupposition of the CA, but its liberalism and almost exclusive preoccupation with individual capabilities means that its own ethical foundations are under-theorized and will lack conviction. This is perhaps why some argue that Nussbaum lacks a theory of moral obligations as mentioned above (Gasper 2004, 187). Relevant here is the insight of Catholic ethicist Lisa Cahill: "Stipulating human characteristics and naming the goods fundamentally important for human flourishing is not nearly as difficult, however, as arguing that all persons are entitled, in principle, to equal access to basic goods" (Cahill 2013, 260). Nussbaum's approach stipulates the human characteristics but cannot accomplish the harder part. The EO understanding of "shared nature," however, provides the moral "argument" for equality; it interprets shared human nature in a way that creates a sense of moral duty for humanity as such.

It is important, however, that the rationale for Nussbaum's and modernity's suspicion of nature as a type of "transcendent" order does not make sense within EO. Nature, in EO, is not conceived as a Platonic unchanging order—which (according to Nussbaum) was carried over into Western ethics through Augustine (Nussbaum 1994, 18).[15] Rather, due to the priority of persons in Orthodoxy, as well as its view of nature as a dynamic order, in EO it is "human agency [that] discovers and achieves new applications of nature's laws in pursuit of more and more useful results" for the development of humankind (Staniloae 2000, 25ff). This point of a malleable ontological/natural order responsive to human agency is fundamental in EO:

> In the human person alone does the rationality of nature's undefined possibilities acquire meaning or a purpose.... As a consciously rational being whose knowledge of the rationality of nature and its

meanings keeps on improving, only the human person himself becomes more rational through nature. [Nature] is made complete by the rationality of the human subject who is also conscious of an inexhaustible wealth that is no monotonous repetition. (Staniloae 2000, 26, 29)

The ontological order is thus advanced to higher stages through human agency and creativity. In the view of EO, God intentionally created nature as an underspecified order that requires human creativity and ingenuity for its ongoing perfection. However, EO, unlike modernity and Nussbaum, regards the natural order, even if incomplete, as having intrinsic or sacred value. Nature, both non-human but especially our shared humanity, has intrinsic worth whether or not a particular practical reasoning agent ascribes it such worth.

In EO, a normative self-hermeneutics is possible, but it requires the self to be embedded in a community committed to these human development ideals and cultivating these social virtues (Harakas 1983). Staniloae notes that justice might have been derived from human experience, however: "If sin [EO understands sin less juridically as an offense against God and more as selfishness, irrationality, or preference deformation] had not in part covered over our authentic human reality, we should not ourselves have to start from an idea of justice but we could begin from the reality of justice that is given within our own equality" (Staniloae 1994, 216).

Deirdre McCloskey notes that for Nussbaum's approach to work, it must more explicitly incorporate the moral virtues—it must start from the idea of justice—and not merely rely on individual practical reason as the starting point (McCloskey 2006; see also Gasper 2006). EO corrects this fault by including the Samaritan commandment ("shared nature" is the ethical correlate to this command in terms of philosophical anthropology) as a fundamental guideline for phronesis, not merely relying on prudential (or instrumental) reasoning. This is important because determining "what is good or bad for humans" cannot reliably be done through an exercise in self-hermeneutics simpliciter, but rather through a hermeneutic of practical reason already committed to working for human development for all. As Aristotle said, "Only the good man's pleasures are real and truly human" (Aristotle 2004, 267).

CONCLUSION: THE HOLY TRINITY'S ILLUMINATION OF THE ANTHROPOLOGICAL VALUES IMPLICIT IN HUMAN DEVELOPMENT

To summarize, the EO Trinitarian analysis makes explicit three dimensions required of human development: person/agency, communion/solidarity, and structures/nature. It has also noted that the latter category of nature can be retrieved for modern concerns because it is viewed in a dynamic fashion, as a basis for cosmopolitan ethical obligations, as the foundation for the various human functions demanding development, and as a basis for ecology. A careful analysis of the theory and practice of human development demands this fuller picture of persons—as individual agents with irreducible value, as simultaneously communal beings, and also and at all times as sharing a common human nature that demands ("cries out to heaven" for) healing in those places where it is wounded and broken. This is a picture of human development that is brought into full relief by the Eastern understanding of the Trinity. In this way, theology places natural moral experience in a clearer light by clarifying the goods involved in human development as well as providing a more secure motivational basis for these commitments. This approach has wide plausibility, bridging sacred and secular divides, inasmuch as it is rooted in the soil (humus) of our shared human nature.

NOTES

1. This "persons in communion within the medium of a shared nature" is a compression of Staniloae's formula, which is variably expressed. For example, Staniloae writes, "Hypostasis [person] cannot be understood emptied of nature, nor separated from relationship" (1994, 100) and "The person without communion is not a person, while communion is conditioned by a common nature" (Staniloae 1994, 70). Or "More or less close relations can certainly be established among all men on the bases of their common origin, and these relations rest ultimately on the basis of a common nature" (Staniloae 1980, 35) and "Each hypostasis is linked ontologically with the other and this bond finds expression in the need they all have to be in relation" (Staniloae 1994, 253).

2. The single exception encountered is this lapidary statement by Des Gasper: "A range of personal, social, and species programmes are at work" (Gasper 2004, 147) in human development.

3. In EO, the shared essence is not an abstraction but rather those genuinely shared "concrete" features (conspecifics) that provide a unity to the human species.

4. EO rejects Augustinianism. Under St. Vincent of Lerins in the Orthodox liturgical calendar, it reads: "Without identifying by name Augustine, Bishop of Hippo, Saint Vincent condemns his doctrine of Grace and predestination, calling it heresy to teach of 'a certain great and special and altogether personal grace of God [which is given] without any labour, without any effort, without any industry, even though they neither ask, nor seek, nor knock" (Sanidopoulos 2009).

5. The very "Filioque" controversy (the Western insertion of the phrase "and the Son" into the Nicene Creed) is related to this, whereby the Eastern Church has seen in the West a tendency to elevate the unity of nature "at the expense of a true distinction of persons among the persons of the Trinity" (Harakas 1983, 27) and thus as distorting the picture of human good in a way that overemphasizes "structure" and underemphasizes free moral agency.

6. Scholars argue that it was Christianity itself that honored the dignity of the individual vis-à-vis the Greek priority of the *polis* (Dumont 1982; Kolakowski 1990).

7. But Lisa Cahill rightly points out a certain compensatory role for relationships when other goods remain unfulfilled: "Relationships among persons and in community are the most fitting and effective response to evil and suffering that we cannot directly alleviate" (Cahill 2013, 73).

8. This is evident when Nussbaum writes that the "family has no moral standing" (Nussbaum 2000, 251).

9. Alexandre de Tocqueville, who noted that "unbelief is an accident; faith is the only permanent state of mankind," was one of the few Western social scientists not hostile to religion. Concerning this issue of the origin of the cosmopolitan position as a moral program (unlike the Stoic version), he correctly noted: "The deepest and most eclectic minds in Rome and Greece were unable to reach this most general and yet most simple of generalizations, that men were alike and that all of them had equal rights. . . . Their minds, although broadened in several directions, were limited in this one and Jesus Christ had to come into the world to reveal that all members of the human race were similar and equal by nature" (Tocqueville 2003, 506–7).

10. This can perhaps help explain why the Apostle James argued that pure religion is to care for orphans and widows. Creation, especially familial relations, provides a form of "grace" or support for well-being or adequate human functioning. The role of the Church and faith is to be those graces for those for whom these creational supports have failed. The idea that grace is

in nature, particularly in the family as a vehicle for well-being, makes sense of this.

11. *Logoi* is one of the most important terms in EO. Vladimir Lossky calls these "norms of existence" (Lossky 1978, 1991); Maximus calls them the divine intentions. Key here is that these norms of nature include the biological and sensible realm and not merely the intelligible; they are the shared principles of existence. *Logoi* is a polyvalent term that also includes virtues and commands. The two Great commands (called *logoi*) correspond to the fundamental functions of human nature, and that is communion with both God and (wo)man. The virtues are also *logoi* in that they structure human agency to live a truly natural life, which is to say, according to God's intentions. The Latin translation of *logoi* is *rationes*.

12. It is noteworthy that Nussbaum (2000, 2011) gives an architectonic role to two capabilities: practical reason and relationality/sociability. This corresponds with the EO picture, which is, however, completed even further if one regards Nussbaum's list as a "picture" of the universal dimension of shared human nature.

13. Other theories, including that of John Finnis, adopt a similar approach as a response to neo-scholasticism (Alkire 2002a; Alkire 2002b; Alkire and Black 1997; Finnis 1980).

14. Similarly, Amartya Sen appeals to the same *fundamentum*: "It is not so much a matter of having exact rules about how precisely we ought to behave, as of recognizing the relevance of our shared humanity in making the choices we face" (Sen 1999, 283).

15. David Bradshaw writes: "The most striking feature of Augustine's conception of being . . . is its static character" (Bradshaw 2004, 224).

WORKS CITED

Alkire, Sabina. 2002a. "Dimensions of Human Development." *World Development* 30, no. 2: 181–205.

———. 2002b. *Valuing Freedoms: Sen's Capability Approach and Poverty Reduction*. Oxford: Oxford University Press.

Alkire, Sabina, and Rufus Black. 1997. "A Practical Reasoning Theory of Development Ethics: Furthering the Capabilities Approach." *Journal of International Development* 9, no. 2: 263–79.

Aristotle. 2004 (350 BCE). *The Nichomachean Ethics*. New York: Penguin.

Bradshaw, David. 2004. *Aristotle East and West: Metaphysics and the Division of Christendom*. Cambridge: Cambridge University Press.

Cahill, Lisa S. 2013. *Global Justice, Christology, and Christian Ethics*. Cambridge: Cambridge University Press.

Cunningham, David S. 1998. *These Three Are One: The Practice of Trinitarian Theology*. Oxford: Blackwell.

Dumont, Louis. 1982. "A Modified View of Our Origins: On the Christian Beginnings of Modern Individualism." *Religion* 12: 1–27.

Finnis, John. 1980. *Natural Law and Natural Rights*. Oxford: Clarendon.

Gasper, Des. 2004. *The Ethics of Development*. Edinburgh: Edinburgh University Press.

———. 2006. "Cosmopolitan Presumptions? On Martha Nussbaum and Her Commentators." *Development and Change* 37, no. 6: 1227–46.

Harakas, Stanley S. 1983. *Toward Transfigured Life: The Theoria of Eastern Orthodox Ethics*. Minneapolis: Light and Life.

Jaggar, Alison M. 2006. "Reasoning about Well–Being: Nussbaum's Methods of Justifying the Capabilities." *Journal of Political Philosophy* 14, no. 3: 301–22.

Kerr, Fergus. 2007. *Twentieth-Century Catholic Theologians: From Neoscholasticism to Nuptial Mysticism*. Oxford: Blackwell.

Kolakowski, Leszek. 1990. *Modernity on Endless Trial*. Chicago: University of Chicago Press.

Lossky, Vladimir. 1978. *Orthodox Theology: An Introduction*. Crestwood, NY: St. Vladimir's Seminary Press.

———. 1991. *The Mystical Theology of the Eastern Church*. Crestwood, NY: St. Vladimir's Seminary Press.

Maris, Cees, Frans Jacobs, and Jacques de Ville, eds. 2012. *Law, Order and Freedom: A Historical Introduction to Legal Philosophy*. Dordrecht: Springer.

McCloskey, Deirdre. 2006. "Hobbes, Nussbaum, and All Seven of the Virtues." *Development and Change* 37, no 6: 1309–12.

Nussbaum, Martha. 1992. "Human Functioning and Social Justice: In Defense of Aristotelian Essentialism." *Political Theory* 20, no 2: 202–46.

———. 1994. *The Therapy of Desire*. Princeton, NJ: Princeton University Press.

———. 2000. *Women and Human Development: The Capabilities Approach*. New York: Cambridge University Press.

———. 2001. *Upheavals of Thought: The Intelligence of Emotions*. Cambridge: Cambridge University Press.

———. 2011. *Creating Capabilities: The Human Development Approach*. Cambridge, MA: Harvard University Press.

O'Donohue, John, 1997. *Anam Cara: A Book of Celtic Wisdom*. New York: HarperCollins.

Pelikan, Jaroslav. 1993. *Christianity and Classical Culture.* New Haven, CT: Yale University Press.

Peters, Ted. 1993. *God as Trinity.* Louisville: Westminster John Knox Press.

Rahner, Karl. 1998. *The Trinity.* New York: Crossroad.

Reid, Duncan. 2000. *Energies of the Spirit: Trinitarian Models in Eastern Ortho-dox and Western Theology.* Oxford: Oxford University Press.

Sanidopoulos, John. 2009. *Saints John Cassian, Vincent of Lerins and Faustus of Riez: Readings and Lives of the Saints for Sunday, May 24, 2009.* https://www.johnsanidopoulos.com/2009/05/saints-vincent-of-lerins-and-john.html.

Sen, Amartya. 1999. *Development as Freedom.* Oxford: Oxford University Press.

Spidlik, Tomas. 1986. *The Spirituality of the Christian East: A Systematic Hand-book.* Kalamazoo, MI: Cistercian Publications.

Staniloae, Dumitru. 1980. *Theology and the Church.* Crestwood, NY: St. Vladi-mir's Seminary Press.

———. 1994. *The Experience of God.* Vol. 1: *Revelation and Knowledge of the Triune God.* Brookline, MA: Holy Cross Orthodox Press.

———. 2000. *The Experience of God.* Vol. 2: *The World: Creation and Deification.* Brookline, MA: Holy Cross Orthodox Press.

Sumner, Andy. 2006. "What Is Development Studies." *Development in Practice* 16, no. 6: 644–50.

Taylor, Charles. 1989. *Sources of the Self: The Making of the Modern Identity.* Cambridge, MA: Harvard University Press.

Thomas, Scott. 2004. "Building Communities of Character: Foreign Aid Policy and Faith-Based Organizations." *SAIS Review* 24, no 2: 133–48.

———. 2005. *The Global Resurgence of Religion and the Transformation of Inter-national Relations.* New York: Palgrave Macmillan.

Tocqueville, Alexandre de. 2003. *Democracy in America.* London: Penguin Classics.

Toulmin, Stephen. 1990. *Cosmopolis.* Chicago: University of Chicago Press.

Turcescu, Lucian. 2002. "'Person' versus 'Individual' and Other Modern Mis-readings of Gregory of Nyssa." *Modern Theology* 18, no. 4: 527–39.

———. 2005. *Gregory of Nyssa and the Concept of Divine Persons.* Oxford: Oxford University Press.

THREE

Freedom and Agency

A Conceptual Exploration within Catholic Social Teaching and the Capability Approach

Lori Keleher

ABSTRACT

The concepts of freedom and agency play essential, yet broad and varied, roles within the many articulations of both Catholic Social Teaching (CST) and the capability approach (CA) and, in turn, within the development efforts grounded in these frameworks. I argue that understanding agency as making choices about what one actually does and becomes, and seeing freedom as the freedom to be and do in accordance with dignity, are conceptually compatible with both CST and the CA. I submit that these philosophical under-pinnings will be valuable to anyone interested in using the CA in a manner consistent with CST. I argue further that this under-standing implies that we (all) ought to focus on promoting those capabilities that allow individuals to act in accordance with dignity. I then explain that the promotion of such capabilities is an unavoidably social process that must recognize and strive to eliminate what CST calls sin, both personal and structural. However, the language of sin is problematic in deliberations within, across, and beyond faith traditions. I demonstrate how the relevant aspects of personal and structural sin found in CST can be helpfully captured using the universal (non-religious) language of personal dignity failure and structural injustice. I then propose that we avoid the language of sin and use this universal language instead.

Until we are all free, we are none of us free.
            —Emma Lazarus, Jewish poet, *An Epistle to the Hebrews*

There can be no progress toward the complete development of
man without the simultaneous development of all humanity in
the spirit of solidarity.
                                                    —Paul VI, *Populorum Progressio*

INTRODUCTION

The concepts of freedom and agency play essential, yet broad and varied, roles within the many articulations of both Catholic Social Teaching (CST) and the capability approach (CA) and, in turn, within the development efforts grounded in these frameworks. My goal in this chapter is not the overly ambitious task of surveying and analyzing each of the many roles of freedom and agency. Instead, I focus on identifying and clarifying the concepts as they might be most interesting and useful to those who wish to understand and promote these values in a way that is consistent with both CST and the CA.

In what follows, I strive to identify, sketch, and explore the concepts of freedom and agency from within the conceptual territory shared by CST and the CA. I begin by explaining why I focus on individual agency, even as we recognize that individuals are relational beings (see section just below). I argue that both CST and the CA can accommodate a broad understanding of agency as "making choices about what one actually does and becomes." Or, to use the language of the CA, making choices about which functionings one achieves. I then argue that this shared conceptual territory will reflect CST's concept of freedom understood as being free to do what we ought to do. I explain how freedom to do what we ought to do is substantially different from freedom to do what we might simply desire to do. To mark this distinction, I call the relevant sort of freedom authentic freedom, which I define as the freedom to be and do in accordance with dignity.

Both CST and the CA understand the individual to be the ultimate unit of moral concern. For this reason, I focus on identifying the agency and freedom of individual human persons. Yet both frameworks also recognize that individuals are relational beings situated in space and time, such that personal relationships as well as economic, social, juridic, political, and cultural structures bear on the agency and freedom of individual human persons in meaningful ways. As the epigraphs to this chapter suggest, there is an ontological dependence between the freedom and development of one and the freedom and development of all. It follows that those who wish to promote the sort of agency and freedom identified in this chapter need to understand and address the structural limitations of agency and authentic freedoms.

Many working within CST already reflect upon what is called structural sin, social sin, or sins of structure that prevent people from being authentically free. I argue that we ought to consider avoiding the language of sin in favor of the nonreligious language of structural injustice and dignity failure. Doing so supports the CST goal of communication and cooperation beyond Catholic circles with those who might not be comfortable using the religious language of sin. As the *Compendium of the Social Doctrine of the Church* (PCJP 2006, 10) puts it: "[T]he text is proposed as an incentive for dialogue with *all* who sincerely desire the good of mankind" (emphasis mine).

Practical efforts to promote and protect agency and freedom ought to be grounded in sound concepts. In this chapter I do the abstract work of conceptual analysis required to provide philosophical underpinnings for understanding and making practical decisions about agency and freedom. I strive to put forward an account that is consistent with both CST and the CA. Because the CA is open to various interpretations in a way that CST is not, the result can be considered one possible Catholic version of the CA. In other words, the account is consistent with Catholic teaching. However, throughout the chapter I explain how many of the valuable insights at work in this CST-informed version of the CA, including the concepts of agency and authentic freedom, need not be understood as uniquely or exclusively Catholic concepts but can be confidently accepted and embraced by non-Catholic and non-religious scholars and practitioners.

RELATIONAL INDIVIDUALS

Ethical individualism is an essential aspect of the CA (Robeyns 2017). Ethical individualism is the principle that individual persons are ultimate units of moral concern. In accordance with this principle, when using the CA Martha Nussbaum says that we must consider "each and every person, taken one by one, respecting each of them as an end" (Nussbaum 2000, 50). This notion is consistent with CST. This framework recognizes not only that each human being is intrinsically valuable as an ultimate end of moral concern but also that each human being is equal in moral value to every other human being (PCJP 2006, 144).

It does not follow from the fact that individual people are recognized as ultimate units of moral concern that individuals are not recognized as social beings with significant relationships and roles within families, communities, teams, and so on. Human beings can also be recognized as having valuable relationships beyond humanity—for example, relationships with other species, nature, or the planet. Nor does ethical individualism's focus on individuals as the ultimate units of moral concern entail the view that individual agents act only in egoistic self-interest, never with a concern for other individuals, justice, or the common good. On the contrary, CST and the CA both recognize individuals as the ultimate units of moral concern and understand individual human persons to be relational beings. Persons are inherently social beings capable of concern for others. They impact and are impacted by their relationships with other individuals, groups, and their situations within social structures.

At least half the items on Martha Nussbaum's list of ten central capabilities (Nussbaum 2011, 33–34, as described in the introduction to this book, p. 1–47) are explicitly relational capabilities (including bodily integrity, senses, imagination, thought, emotions, other species, control over one's environment). The relational capability of affiliation plays a special role in Nussbaum's approach[1] (see Katie Dunne's chapter in this volume); along with practical reason, it is said to "organize and suffuse all others, making their pursuit truly human" (Nussbaum 2000, 82). Likewise, CST is concerned with "not only the individual person but also the social relations existing between [people]" (PCJP 2006, 52). CST holds that, while each person is unique and "unrepeatable in his individuality, every person is a being who is open to relationships with others in society. Life together in society, in the network of relationships linking individuals, families and intermediate groups by encounter, communication and exchange, ensures a higher quality of living" (PCJP 2006, 61).

Both CST and the CA recognize that relationships and groups are not only valuable but necessary for human flourishing. Participation in groups allows individuals to be a part of something bigger than themselves and to bring about certain achievements (functionings) that are simply not possible for individuals to achieve alone, for example, playing in an orchestra, living in community, running for public office, or being a mother. Moreover, relationships and participation in groups allow us to be the relational beings that we are, and therefore, truly and fully human. Thus, a concern for individual human beings necessarily entails concern for groups and relationships.

Yet the fact remains that groups cannot exist without individuals (that is, individuals are conceptually and ontologically prior to groups). Furthermore, although individuals can both derive benefits from and make sacrifices for the good of the group, an individual must never be seen as *merely* a member of a group, nor as one who is expected to sacrifice her genuine human needs for the benefit of the group. A woman may be a mother and/or a wife—and these relationships and roles are valuable—but in addition to being an important part of a family, she is also an individual human being, that is, an agent worthy of human flourishing, in her own right. Being a member of a family might be an integral part of an individual's flourishing. But each member of the family (and of every other group) must always be respected as an end within herself. Women must never be expected to sacrifice, for example, their nutritional needs, while the men in the household eat, in order to be considered "good" wives, mothers, or daughters. Thus, it makes sense to insist that, while relationships and groups are very important, both in themselves and for the good of individuals, individuals are the ultimate (not the only) units of moral concern. For this reason, my focus here is on the agency and freedom of individual human persons (as relational beings).[2]

AGENCY

Agency is a much-discussed and -debated topic within the CA literature. Amartya Sen identifies various agency concepts (including control freedom, instrumental agency success, effective freedom, and realized agency success). At the heart of Sen's approach are two cross-cutting distinctions between (1) agency and well-being and (2) freedom and achievement (Sen 1992, 1999). Nussbaum recognizes that "the concepts introduced by these distinctions are important," but she does not endorse the distinctions. Instead, she holds that "all the important distinctions can be captured as aspects of the capability/function distinction" (Nussbaum 2000, 14). For Nussbaum, the very important concept of agency is already a part of capability. If one has the capability to achieve functioning x, then one can act as an agent with regard to achieving x. Thus (as I argue in detail elsewhere),[3] agency plays a central role in both Sen's and Nussbaum's versions of the CA.

Ingrid Robeyns (2017) has skillfully explained the difference between the capability approach, as a general conceptual framework with several essential features, and particular capability theories and applications that realize the essential features of the approach in various ways. Nussbaum's incomplete theory of justice and Sen's use of capabilities are just two particular applications of the general conceptual framework that is the CA. Robeyns argues persuasively: "Applications of the Capability Approach should endorse some account of agency" but that "the concept of 'agency' can be fleshed out in many different ways" (Robeyns 2017, 64). Thus, agency plays an essential, yet multiple and realizable, role within the theoretical framework of the CA. It follows that there is significant leeway in identifying or constructing a concept of agency that is coherent with the conceptual core of the CA. Therefore, any concept of agency found in CST will be acceptable for use within the CA so long as it does not preclude the other essential aspects of the CA.[4]

For our present purposes, I propose that an individual's agency is exercised any time she makes choices about what she does and becomes. Agency is not an all-or-nothing concept. Instead, agency applies more-or-less to our various choices. In this view, some form and some degree of agency is exercised whenever one makes a choice, even when she is (a) making a relatively trivial choice; (b) choosing not to choose (e.g., by avoiding considering options, just letting things happen, or refraining from acting); (c) choosing from a set of undesirable options or from a diminished capability set; or (d) experiencing conflicting desires. It should be understood that—other things being equal—acting deliber-ately, in accordance with deeply held desires and valued central goals,[5] in ways that have a significant impact in the world, is a thicker, or more robust, exercise of agency. In contrast, making relatively trivial choices (that is, choices that neither stem from deeply held desires nor have significant impact in the world); unreflective, hasty choices (including choosing not to choose); or choices derived from the limited, undesired, and undesirable options available in one's circumstances without satisfy-ing any authentic desires of the agent (except, perhaps, avoiding even less desirable options) is a thinner, or weaker, exercise of agency.

Agency actions can be self-regarding or other-regarding. One can exercise her agency in a manner that is morally positive (choosing to provide clothes for someone in need), morally negative (choosing to steal clothes from someone in need), or morally neutral (ceteris paribus, choosing to wear a blue shirt instead of a green one). Thus, simply act-ing as an agent is not necessarily a moral good. However, many ethical theories rightly hold that agency is a prerequisite of morally significant actions.[6] Moreover, both CST and the CA recognize that being an agent with a considerable degree of control over one's life is necessary for human flourishing. Thus, promoting agency, that is, one's ability to act as an agent, is—ceteris paribus—morally desirable.

The upshot is that, for our present purpose, agency exercises can be understood broadly as making choices about what one does and becomes. Or, to put it in terms of the CA, making choices about what functionings one achieves. Given that any capability x is the substantial freedom to achieve functioning *x*, our capability sets—that is, the set of real options we have—are important reflections of our agency. The capability sets of those with robust agency will not merely have more (merely trivial) capabilities but will have certain desirable capabilities. Capabilities not chosen in a person's capability set (the real freedom to avoid working a particular job or to refuse to align oneself with an unjust person of power) are also reflections of agency.

This rather broad understanding of agency can clearly be found in the overlapping conceptual space of CST and the CA. Moreover, CST and the CA both recognize that to be truly human is to be an agent and share the goal of expanding capability sets to allow individuals more robust agency and to live in accordance with their authentic and deeply held desires. Thus, from this conceptual space we can observe that when a person's capability set is systematically restricted, she is not simply diminished regarding achieving certain functionings but is also diminished as an agent and, in turn, as a human person.

FREEDOM

Freedom is at the very core of the CA. After all, capabilities are freedoms.[7] Freedom is also at the core of CST. Yet, within CST only a subset of our capabilities are considered to be true freedoms. Pope John Paul II (1995, 7) presents the CST view of freedom succinctly when he says that "freedom consists not in doing what we like, but in having the right to do what we ought." Thus, within CST freedom has a different, more focused, connotation than that typically used within the CA. Within a CST framework, not all capabilities are considered to be true freedoms. Specifically, capabilities to do what we desire when it is not what we ought to do are capabilities, but not freedoms. In this view, a person lacks freedom if she lacks the capability to do what she ought, even if she has many capabilities in her capability set, including capabilities to do as she likes.

Given my present goal of identifying and sketching aspects of the shared conceptual territory of the CA and CST, my focus on the conceptual space of freedom is restricted to the subset of capabilities that both the CA and CST recognize as freedoms. I use the phrase "authentic freedom" to represent the relevant concept of freedom at work in CST and within this subspace of the CA framework. A significant consequence of understanding agency and freedom as I find them in this shared CA-CST space is that it is possible to act simultaneously both as an agent in the sense of choosing what to do and in a way that is not in accordance with authentic freedom. An example is gratifying a self-indulgent desire that ultimately hinders rather than promotes one's flourishing. Concrete examples of such behaviors might include choosing to blow off steam by yelling at an innocent subordinate when frustrated by a work problem or choosing to eat too much junk food. This distinction allows us to think about agents choosing to act against freedom (discussed below).

Using this narrower space of authentic freedom as the space of freedom in our discussions is not only a legitimate use of CST; it is also a valuable and legitimate use of the CA. Restricting the conceptual scope of freedom to the more focused set of authentic freedom does not mean that those working within a CST framework are missing out on some worthwhile freedoms,[8] nor that we are no longer using a complete account of the CA. This narrower set is quantitatively narrow in that some capabilities will not be recognized as authentic freedoms, but in focusing on authentic freedoms, a qualitatively richer and more potent concept of freedom emerges.

Using this more focused concept of authentic freedom is a legitimate use of the CA because, as with agency, the concepts of capabilities and freedom can be appropriately fleshed out in various ways. Indeed, although I do not argue for the position here, I submit that the idea of identifying authentic freedoms is very similar to the much-discussed and debated task of identifying the set of capabilities that "we value and have reason to value" (Khader and Kosko 2019; Sen 1999) or are necessary for a life worthy of human dignity (Nussbaum 2000, 2011). For our present purpose, the capabilities that we have reason to value are exactly those capabilities that represent authentic freedoms, or the freedoms to do and be what we ought to do and be. Thus, the understanding of freedom as authentic freedom is clearly found in the overlapping conceptual space of CST and the CA; as such, it is an appropriate concept for our purposes. I now turn to the task of presenting and clarifying authentic freedom, or the freedom to do and be what we ought to do and be, and how it relates to our concept of agency.

AUTHENTIC FREEDOM

As explained above, both the CA and CST encompass the view that individuals are inherently morally valuable. Within CST the commitment to each and every individual follows from a recognition of universal and inalienable human dignity (PCJP 2006, 144). In this view, each and every human being has inalienable human dignity simply by virtue of the fact that he or she is human. This idea, which can be called the principle of universal human dignity, is not unique to CST. Many people who subscribe to various non-religious and religious outlooks can and do subscribe to some form of the principle of universal human dignity. Even more people subscribe to other accounts of human dignity in ways that justify recognizing the intrinsic and equal moral worth of individuals within theories of human rights (Carozza 2013) or capabilities (Nussbaum 2011). Thus, it is not only practically possible, but also theoretically coherent, to understand a commitment to human dignity and, in turn, to the inherent value of each person (ethical individualism) without embracing a Catholic anthropology.

Nevertheless, within CST, respect for human dignity is grounded in a Catholic anthropology that holds that human beings are made in the image and likeness of God (PCJP 2006, 36, 144). A certain moral perfectionism follows from this anthropology (PCJP 2006, 140).[9] A complete explanation of the moral perfectionism of CST is beyond the scope of this chapter. Therefore, I focus on the foundational principle of CST's perfectionism, which I suggest can be described as acting in accordance with human dignity.

Authentic freedom, or the freedom to be and act as we ought, is the freedom to be and act in accordance with dignity. According to CST's perfectionism, people achieve the proper development of human nature (or the fulfillment of our common human vocation) when they choose to "orient their lives toward God" (*Populorum Progressio* [Paul VI 1967], 15, 16)—in other words, when they act in accordance with their true selves, made in the image and likeness of God, that is, in accordance with human dignity.

Actions accord with dignity when they are grounded in a recognition of, or respect for, dignity. Careful consideration of the language used here may add some clarity to what is meant in this context. Recognition means to re-cognize, that is, to know again or to identify. Respect means to look back on, or to consider/see again. Dignity in a general context is worth or worthiness. In the context of CST, that which is worthy is that which is made in the image and likeness of God, or God-like, or divine (meaning proceeding from God). So, within CST when we act in accordance with human dignity, our actions are reflexive and grounded in awareness of the divine worthiness of ourselves and of others.

Actions, policies, and attitudes that mirror (or respect, or recognize) human dignity take many forms. We might show respect by making eye contact with a stranger or mirror dignity by nursing our own babies or bathing our elderly parents. Sometimes it is easier to notice when we feel that our own dignity or the dignity of others is not recognized. For example, we might feel slighted if an idle shopkeeper fails to acknowledge us or when vital health care or nutrition is denied to poor people. Efforts to care for the basic human needs of the poor are themselves dignified acts of human dignity recognition, or mirroring of dignity.

This mirroring of dignity—doing and being as the image and likeness of God—is the highest perfection for human beings. It is the telos of CST's moral perfectionism.[10] Mirroring dignity is an inherently social activity that is appropriate given CST's understanding of the human person as a social being (PCJP 2006, 34). Even actions that are not directed at others, but are instead simple acts of self-respect, are instances of mirroring the image and likeness of God and therefore affirm dignity because the agent is aware of and reflecting his or her own worth. Likewise, all dignified actions, including actions directed at others, are acts of self-respect.

In addition to the language of respect, CST also uses the relational language of love to convey this social nature of the human person acting in accordance with the common vocation of humanity. According to the *Compendium of the Social Doctrine of the Church*, "*The fundamental law of human perfection, and consequently of the transformation of the world, is … love*" (PCJP 2006, 54, italics original). This language of love makes clear that it is not only the act itself, but also the agent's internal state or attitude, with which the act is performed or activity sustained, that is essential to doing and being in accordance with dignity. This notion of love is rooted in an affectionate concern for well-being. The upshot is that authentic freedom is grounded in love in such a way that free actions actively recognize the dignity (divine worth) of the agent herself (PCJP 2006, 113), of other people, of non-human animals, and of other aspects of nature, or God's creation (*Laudato Si'* [Francis 2015], 33; PCJP 2006, 114).[11]

Moreover, within CST, we fail to achieve the perfectionist goal of acting in accordance with dignity when we lack an internal state or attitude of love. This is true even if our action improves our own or another's well-being.[12] (For example, a health care provider that administers medical treatment to the poor, but with contempt for their poverty or a detached attitude.) It is significant that authentic freedom requires that individuals actively stand in loving relationships with others. Moreover, some actions are the sorts of actions that always fail to recognize, but in fact violate, one's own dignity, the dignity of others, or that of creation. For example, substance abuse, hitting a child, and polluting a river all fail to recognize and respect dignity. Beings (including internal states devoid of love) and doings (including acts of exclusion and violence) that fail to recognize, or do violence to, dignity are contrary to the flourishing of human persons and undermine the authentic freedom of the agent. When agents choose such beings and doings over authentic freedoms, they act as agents against freedom.

It is important to understand that, in this view, dignity persists even when it is violated or not recognized. The alcoholic, the abused child, and the polluted river all have dignity even if others, or they themselves, fail to recognize and respect that dignity. Moreover, in this view, agents who choose to act in ways that fail to recognize, or do violence to, their own dignity or the dignity of others still have dignity. Human dignity, and the dignity of all, is inalienable. Thus, each person is called to treat all people with genuine love and respect (which should never be confused with gratifying or indulging a person's unworthy desires or morally negative behaviors). This is true even, or perhaps especially, if the person has historically, or is currently, not acting in a way that reflects dignity. After all, the reflexive nature of dignity entails that when one is treated with dignity (love and respect), she is often reminded of her dignity and is thereby better able to act in accordance with dignity. In other words, the mirroring of dignity enhances authentic freedom by facilitating action in accordance with dignity.

We have established that in this view acting in accordance with human dignity (that is, fulfilling our vocation) means being grounded in love and actively recognizing the dignity of ourselves and others. This means lovingly reflecting upon and striving to meet the truly human needs of the whole person and of every person (PCJP 2006, 38). Truly human needs, in this account, include physical needs (food, shelter, bodily safety, etc.), emotional needs (the ability to experience joy, to feel safe, to get angry, etc.), social needs (the ability to participate, to be heard, to appear in public without shame, etc.), intellectual needs (to imagine, to reason, to exchange ideas, etc.), and spiritual needs (freedom to reflect and form one's conscience, etc.), as well as many other needs.

Truly human needs do not include mere desires of the ego, for example, honorific titles (Professor, Monsignor, Vice President, Doctor, etc.) and other ornaments of status, including luxury goods (extravagant cars, designer clothing, the latest mobile phones, etc.). This is not to suggest that to seek, to have, or to use an honorific title or to wear a pair of designer shoes is in itself an act that fails to recognize dignity or is morally wrong. It is only that doing so does not meet any truly human need, nor does it enhance one's dignity or moral worth. So if we were to seek such artificial desires of the ego at the expense of meeting the truly human needs (respecting dignity) of ourselves or others, then we would be seeking something of no real value at the expense of something truly valuable, and that is wrong.

In this section I have argued that within CST being authentically free means being free to act as we ought. Catholic anthropology holds that all human beings are made in the image and likeness of God and that human dignity is grounded in this aspect of human nature. The moral perfectionism that follows from this anthropology holds that the highest achievement of human beings is to act in accordance with dignity. Such actions recognize, or mirror, the image and likeness of God, which can also be understood as acting with love. Therefore, being authentically free means being free to act in accordance with dignity, which in turn means recognizing and respecting dignity in ourselves, each other, non-human animals, and the environment. This concept of authentic freedom can be found in the shared conceptual space of CST and the CA because it is a CST position and because the CA is conceptually open to multiple realizations of freedom, including this application. Moreover, many who do not subscribe to the Catholic metaphysics of CST, but still subscribe to a universal principle of human dignity, might reasonably agree that the capabilities, or the freedoms that we have reason to value, are the capabilities to act in ways that accord with dignity and love.

AUTHENTIC FREEDOM AND RESPONSIBILITY

As discussed above, the perfectionist account of Catholic Social Teaching holds that the highest achievement of human persons is to act in accordance with human dignity. It follows from the moral dimension of this perfectionism that we have a responsibility to strive to act in accordance with dignity. Acting in accordance with dignity not only results in the perfection of the agent, but also benefits the common good and can result in the "transformation of the world" (PCJP 2006, 54). This is because we are relational beings situated in space and time whose very existence relies on and impacts the rest of the world. Thus, within CST there exists an ontological interdependence between freedom and responsibility. Where there is freedom, there is also responsibility, and where there is responsibility, there is also freedom. This account of the concept of authentic freedom is woven throughout Catholic documents and resources.

The *Compendium of the Social Doctrine of the Church* states: "Freedom is the highest sign [of a person's] being made in the divine image and, consequently, is a sign of the sublime dignity of every human person. . . . Every human person . . . has the natural right to be recognized as a free and responsible being" (PCJP 2006, 199). This passage captures how the Catholic understanding of the human person entails the freedom and responsibility of each individual person. Yet CST also recognizes that "freedom is exercised in relationships between human beings" (ibid.), such that the freedom of each person is linked to the freedom of every person:

> The meaning of freedom must not be restricted, considering it from a purely individualistic perspective and reducing it to the arbitrary and uncontrolled exercise of one's own personal autonomy: "Far from being achieved in total self-sufficiency and the absence of

relationships, freedom only truly exists where reciprocal bonds, governed by truth and justice, link people to one another."

. . .

The value of freedom, as an expression of the singularity of each human person, is respected when every member of society is permitted to fulfill his personal vocation; to seek the truth and profess his religious, cultural and political ideas; to express his opinions; to choose his state of life and, as far as possible, his line of work; to pursue initiatives of an economic, social or political nature. This must take place within a "strong juridical framework," within the limits imposed by the common good and public order, and, in every case, in a manner characterized by responsibility. (PCJP 2006, 199, 200)

The above passage makes clear (1) that each person should be free to pursue a lifestyle she values so long as her actions do not undermine the common good or public order; (2) that the structures of society, or the public order, should be arranged in such a way that promotes each person's authentic freedom; and (3) that each individual person's authentic freedom depends on relationships, bonds, and links between people. Thus, as argued above, ethical individualism entails concern for individuals as social beings and, in turn, for relationships and groups.

It is worth noting that CST explicitly advocates for the freedom of each person "to seek the truth and profess his religious, cultural and political ideas." Thus, once again, one need not be Catholic, nor seek to participate in or promote the Catholic faith, in order to operate within the conceptual space sketched in this chapter.[13] Instead, it is theoretically coherent to hold a different, nonreligious, perfectionist view of human nature that recognizes a similar notion of human flourishing, the social nature of people, and the significance of human dignity.

The *Compendium* also recognizes that authentic freedom requires both being able to choose to be and do things that make for a valuable lifestyle and the freedom to avoid being and doing things that are "morally negative," that is, to avoid being and doing things that obscure human dignity and impede human flourishing. Thus, CST is concerned not only with authentic freedom to be and do, but also authentic freedom from being and doing. Again, the freedom, *not* to exercise certain capabilities in our capability sets is important:

> Freedom must also be expressed as the capacity to refuse what is morally negative, in whatever guise it may be presented, as the capacity to distance oneself effectively from everything that could hinder personal, family or social growth. The fullness of freedom consists in the capacity to be in possession of oneself in view of the genuine good, within the context of the universal common good. (PCJP 2006, 200)

Unfortunately, our ability to act freely and refuse what is morally negative is often compromised by unjust structures. "The proper exercise of personal freedom requires specific conditions of an economic, social, juridic, political and cultural order that are too often disregarded or violated" (PCJP 2006, 137). In recognizing that individual freedom is inherently social, such that one is only authentically and fully free in the context of the universal common good, CST recognizes that complex interwoven economic, social, juridic, political, and cultural structures can determine whether or not it is possible for a person to fully experience authentic freedom, that is, the freedom to live in accordance with dignity.

In many cases when our authentic freedom is limited by entrenched inequalities and unjust structures, we continue to act as individual agents in the broad sense of making choices about what we do and become given our current set of options. However, in such cases our agency is weak, and we are diminished as agents (and therefore as humans), because we are not authentically free to avoid participation in social structures and systems that are morally negative. Because we are unable to act as agents in the robust sense, our responsibility for our actions is also relatively weak. Such cases are distinct from those in which an agent chooses to act against authentic freedom, which, as an offense to dignity, is a morally negative choice for which the agent bears significant responsibility. Yet even when our agency is diminished, we are each called to do what we can, to the extent that we are free to bring about economic, social, juridic, political, and cultural institutions that represent "truth and justice" in a "strong juridical framework" within the limits imposed by the common good and public order.

Concerns about the role of social and political institutions in protecting and promoting the common good are shared by those working with the CA. As Nussbaum (2011, 19) writes, "The [capabilities] approach is concerned with entrenched social injustice and inequality, especially capability failures that are the result of discrimination or marginalization. It ascribes an urgent task to government and public policy—namely to improve the quality of life for all people." Thus, both CST and the CA recognize that although individuals are the ultimate units of moral concern, no individual can flourish without social relationships or the support of just social, political, and corporate institutions that protect and promote the common good.

Furthermore, both CST and the CA recognize that entrenched social injustice and inequality undermine the common good and, in turn, authentic freedom for all people. It follows that if we want to promote the sort of authentic freedom found in this overlapping conceptual space, then we must work to eliminate economic, social, juridic, political, and cultural structures that hinder authentic freedom. We must expand capability sets, thereby eliminating capability failures in such a way that all people are allowed to act as agents who refuse what is morally negative and choose truly valuable capabilities.

FROM STRUCTURAL SIN TO STRUCTURAL INJUSTICE

Within CST the economic, social, juridic, political, and cultural structures that hinder authentic freedom are often identified as the sources of what is called structural sin, social sin, or sins of structure (Deneulin, Nebel, and Sagovsky 2006; Gutierrez, Inda, and Eagleson 1988; Nebel 2006; Romero 1980; see also John Paul II's encyclical *Sollicitudo Rei Socialis* [1987] 36 and *Catechism of the Catholic Church* [1992] 1869). Many people avoid the language of sin in public policy forums, and with good reason. To put forward a position that appeals to the language of structural sin would be to use language that not everyone can understand, much less accept, and would consequently undermine productive deliberation. Moreover, it would risk both provoking distracting debates about the nature of sin from believers with varied understandings of sin and raising the defenses of non-believers concerned that one might be judging them or trying to convert them, and would therefore be counter-productive.

In this section I risk a brief discussion of sin as I seek to provide an incomplete sketch of the concept of structural sin within CST with the hope of demystifying the concept for those less familiar with it. I attempt to demonstrate how this notion of sin relates to agency and authentic freedom as presented here. Finally, I suggest that one might discuss the challenges represented by structural sin using the language of structural injustice in a way that is not only productive but also faithful to the notion of structural sin within CST.

According to CST, there are "a great many kinds of sin," as the *Catechism of the Catholic Church* (*CCC*), published under John Paul II in 1992, puts it (*CCC* 1852). Yet it is important to distinguish between personal sin and social sin. Personal sin can be understood as "an offense against God" (*CCC* 1849). When individuals act as agents in opposition to authentic freedom, that is, in ways that fail to recognize dignity—the very image and likeness of God—it is an offense against God, or a personal sin. Structural sin occurs when there is a systematic failure to recognize and respect the dignity of others due to economic, social, juridic, political, and cultural structures.[14] Structural sin is distinct from the more familiar concept of personal sin, because structural sin is institutionalized. It affects all members of the relevant society (and often other creatures and the environment). Nevertheless, structural sin bears a complex relationship not only to personal sin but also to agency and authentic freedom.

Although no single individual alone can produce structural sin, it can be a result of personal sin. As Pope John Paul II (1987) said in *Sollicitudo Rei Socialis* (*SRS*): "It is a question of a moral evil, the fruit of many sins which lead to 'structures of sin'" (*SRS* 37). For example, when a policy-maker acts out of greed or fear and drafts a policy that fails to recognize the dignity of all people, the law-maker personally sins. When an individual makes sexist or racist comments, the individual personally sins. When there is a culture of support for and participation in such greedy policies and bigoted attitudes to the extent that some people are systematically disadvantaged and marginalized while others are privileged and empowered, there is structural sin. In this way, structural sin can be generated by the personal sins of creating, sustaining, or participating in unjust systems.

Structural sin also creates conditions that facilitate, or even encourage, personal sin and frustrate the agency and dignity of individuals. Marginalized, oppressed, and excluded people typically have diminished capability sets and suffer capability failures and corresponding agency deficits. Too often they are exploited by a system that fails to recognize the truly human material and social needs of every person. As a result of society's failure to recognize their human dignity, the marginalized, oppressed, and excluded experience alienation from their true nature (their divine image and likeness) (PCJP 2006, 374). Yet they are still agents who choose among the options they do have, even when they are not authentically free to meet all of their truly human needs. Given that within CST responsibility depends on freedom, all those without the freedom to live as we ought—that is, to live lives in full recognition of dignity—are damaged by structural sin. We can strive to avoid personal sin by continuing to recognize our own dignity and the dignity of others, despite any serious material and social deprivations.[15]

Unfortunately, such recognition of dignity is challenging—for all members of society—because systems of structural sin can distort one's perception of reality. From within our societies, the unjust structures of exploitation, disadvantage, and marginalization that make up social sin appear to be natural, appropriate, or necessary. Consequently, one's sense of what behaviors are acceptable, moral, and possible is susceptible to being distorted in a way that aligns with the biases of the system. Consider, for example, the following biases reflected in many cultures: Men make better (more appropriate) public leaders than women. Women are (naturally, and therefore necessarily,) more nurturing than men. Our biases include not only the general biases of the system, but also particular biases determined by our standpoint within the system. Both sets of bias shape our understanding and behavior as we navigate the system. For example, some may be led to think "people like me become primary school teachers, not prime ministers," others "I should not be kept waiting, even if others were here before me." Many of our biases are unconscious biases. Truth is obscured. Individuals act in ways that perpetuate the injustices of the system, thereby undermining the reciprocal bonds of freedom and the common good, often without the intention or even the realization that they are doing so. In this way, structural sin can be said to generate personal sin or offenses against dignity.

Structural sin is a detriment to all members of society. The privileged within the system are perhaps even more at risk of personal sin than the disadvantaged. This is because the system rewards attitudes and behaviors of the privileged, making it more difficult to recognize institutionalized wrongdoing. Working the system in a way that generates power and privilege might allow an individual to meet her material needs and an expansive set of capabilities, including many freedoms to do and be what she likes, even while the system prevents her from having the authentic freedom to do and be what she ought. For example, a privileged person may be unable to stand in genuine solidarity with the rest of the human family (because she cannot relate to the challenges they face) or to respect the dignity of the environment (because of the structure of consumption in society). Thus, the structure does not facilitate meeting the needs of the whole person.

Moreover, in a structure that celebrates gratifying desires of the ego, and glorifies the pursuit of accouterments of status, the privileged are at great risk of mistaking such hollow trophies for truly valuable human needs. Because their situation within the structure allows them to meet their material needs, the privileged are often at a loss for why they feel unfulfilled and alienated from their true nature (PCJP 2006, 47, 374). Thus, all members of society risk alienation in structures of sin.

Authentic freedom requires recognizing that each individual—privileged or marginalized—has an equal claim to meeting his or her genuine human needs. Reflecting on dignity can remind us of this truth. This incomplete description of structural sin is enough to show (1) that the authentic freedom of each person and of all people is affected by structural sin and (2) that no matter where we find ourselves within the economic, social, juridic, political, or cultural structure, we must strive to love and to recognize dignity to the extent that we are able. Individual human persons, with attitudes of love and actions in accordance with dignity, are the means for transforming the system and promoting the common good.

Thus far, I have described how structural sin facilitates personal sin and diminishes agency and freedom. I now sketch a description of the above damage to agency and freedom that avoids the language of personal and structural sin. I submit that the following description is consistent with (even faithful to) CST but can be adapted by those who subscribe to the sort of moral perfectionism grounded in universal human dignity as discussed above. While some may find the account disappointingly devoid of spiritual richness, others will find it refreshingly free of metaphysical baggage. In any case, the reader should find the account appealing as it enables us to build consensus across and beyond religious traditions.

In this non-religious view, structural injustice is a matter of collective dignity failures. Personal dignity failures occur when we fail to recognize dignity in ourselves and/or others. Structural injustice occurs when there is a systematic failure to recognize dignity. Individual dignity failures can both generate and be generated by structural injustice. For reasons discussed above, structural injustice harms all members of society to the extent that it distorts our view of reality and renders us alienated and confused about our true needs. Reflection on human dignity reveals a moral duty to work to promote the common good regardless of our position in society. This brief description is sufficient to show that we can capture the challenges CST describes in terms of personal and structural sin without using the language of sin. The account can be augmented in valuable ways, not only by drawing on the rich body of knowledge of CST but also through contemporary social political philosophy (see, for example, Young 2011).

CONCLUSION

I have argued that the conceptual space shared by Catholic Social Teaching and the capability approach yields (1) an understanding of agency as making choices about what one actually does and becomes and (2) an understanding of (authentic) freedom as the freedom to be and do in accordance with dignity. These notions allow us to draw the conclusion that although both CST and the CA value agency and hold that—ceteris paribus—promoting agency is morally good, not all agency expansion allows individuals the authentic freedom required for either their own perfection or the common good. Therefore, we ought to focus on promoting those capabilities that allow individuals to act in accordance with dignity. The promotion of such individual capabilities is an unavoidably social process that must recognize and strive to eliminate what CST calls sin, both personal and structural. However, the language of sin is problematic in deliberations within, across, and beyond faith traditions. For this reason, I have demonstrated how the relevant aspects of a nuanced account of personal and structural sin found in CST can be helpfully captured using the universal (non-religious) language of personal dignity failure and structural injustice.

NOTES

1. Nussbaum (2011, 34) describes affiliation as (1) being able to live with and toward others, to recognize and show concern for other humans, to engage in various forms of social interaction; being able to imagine the situation of another (protecting this capability means protecting institutions that constitute and nourish such forms of affiliation, and also protecting the freedoms of assembly and political speech); and (2) having the social bases of self-respect and non-humiliation as well as being able to be treated as a dignified being whose worth is equal to that of others. This entails provisions of non-discrimination on the basis of race, sex, sexual orientation, ethnicity, caste, religion, national origin, and species.

2. In focusing on individual human beings, I am leaving unexplored the rich literature on collective capabilities, collective agency, collective freedom, and non-human animals in both CST and the CA.

3. For a detailed discussion on Sen's and Nussbaum's agency concepts, see Keleher (2007; 2014).

4. Robeyns (2017) lists the "compulsory core" of the capability approach as follows: seeing A1: functionings and capabilities as core concepts; A2: functionings and capabilities as value-neutral categories; A3: conversion factors; A4: the distinction between means and ends; A5: functionings and/or capabilities as forming the evaluative space; A6: other dimensions of ultimate value; A7: value pluralism; and A8: the value of each person as an end.

5. By deeply held desires, I mean what philosophers often call *higher-order desires* or desires about desires. I hold that desires are especially deeply held desires when first-order desires and second-order desires (that is, our desires about our desires) are in alignment. For example, a desire to exercise is only deeply held when one both wants to exercise (a first-order desire) and one also wants to want to exercise (a second-order desire). A desire to exercise is not deeply held when one wants to hit snooze and sleep in, but is deeply held when one wants to want to get up and exercise.

6. Immanuel Kant (among others) is said to have subscribed to the idea that "ought implies can." Kant wrote: "For if the moral law commands that we ought to be better human beings now, it inescapably follows that we must be capable of being better human beings" (Kant 1998, 6:50)

7. As with so many other key concepts within the CA, there is considerable discussion about the sense in which capabilities can and should be understood as freedoms. See Robeyns (2017).

8. Scholars, including CST scholars, disagree about which freedoms are truly worthwhile and therefore disagree about which freedoms belong in the narrower set of capabilities that are compatible with authentic freedom. Thus, any particular account or list of authentic freedoms will invariably be a matter of some dispute among scholars.

9. Moral perfectionism is the idea that an objective account of the good, or at least the good for humans, can and should be understood in terms of the development of human nature. Within CST, human nature is revealed as a part of natural law. For more on the perfectionism of CST, see the CCC. For a general overview of moral perfectionism, see Wall (2017).

10. This idea of mirroring the likeness of God is not unique to Catholicism. It has roots in Aristotle's concept of God: "The divine mind, then, must think itself, and its thinking is a thinking of thinking" (Aristotle, *Metaphysics* 1074b). It can also be seen in the Hindu greeting namaste, which means "I bow to the divine in you" (Singh 2015) or "the sacred in me recognizes the sacred in you" (Oxhandler 2017, 168).

11. Given that the focus of this volume is human development, it is worth noting that within both CST and many applications of the CA, *human development*, or development that allows people to be "more human," is just development in accordance with human dignity.

12. The idea that even our seemingly impressive and heroic doings and beings lack worth, or dignity, if they are not informed by love is reflected in the following biblical passage from first letter of St. Paul to the Corinthians: "If I speak in human and angelic tongues but do not have love, I am a resounding gong or a clashing cymbal. And if I have the gift of prophecy and comprehend all mysteries and all knowledge; if I have all faith so as to move mountains but do not have love, I am nothing. If I give away everything I own, and if I hand my body over so that I may boast but do not have love, I gain nothing" (1 Cor. 13:1–3).

13. See also *Sollicitudo Rei Sociales* 32 (John Paul II 1987) and *Gaudium et Spes* (Vatican Council II 1965, 16).

14. CST documents grounding the concept of structural sin include Pope John Paul II's *Sollicitudo Rei Socialis* (published in 1987), Pope Benedict XVI's

Caritas in Veritate (published in 2009), Pope Francis's *Laudato Si'* (published in 2015), and the US Conference of Catholic Bishops (USCCB) document *Economic Justice for All* (published in 1986).

15. Scholars debate whether or not those living within structures of sin are authentically free *not* to commit personal sins and in which ways this may (or may not) be the case. For more analysis of structural sin and social justice, see Deneulin, Nebel, and Sagovsky (2006) and Nebel (2006).

WORKS CITED

Benedict XVI. 2009. *Caritas in Veritate: On Integral Human Development in Charity in Truth*. Encyclical. https://www.vatican.va/content/benedict-xvi /en/encyclicals/documents/hf_ben-xvi_enc_20090629_caritas-in-veritate .html.

Carozza, Paolo. 2013. "Human Rights, Human Dignity, and Human Experience," in *Understanding Human Dignity*, edited by Christopher McCrudden. Oxford: Oxford University Press, chap. 36.

Catechism of the Catholic Church. 1992. Vatican City: Libra Editrice Vaticana. https://www.vatican.va/archive/ENG0015/_INDEX.HTM.

Deneulin, Séverine, Mathias Nebel, and Nicholas Sagovsky. 2006. *Transforming Unjust Structures*. Dordrecht: Springer.

Francis. 2015. *Laudato Si': On Care for Our Common Home*. Encyclical. https:// www.vatican.va/content/dam/francesco/pdf/encyclicals/documents/papa -francesco_20150524_enciclica-laudato-si_en.pdf.

Gutierrez, Gustavo, Caridad Inda, and John Eagleson. 1988. *A Theology of Liberation: History, Politics, and Salvation*. Maryknoll, NY: Orbis.

John Paul II. 1987. *Sollicitudo Rei Socialis*. Encyclical. https://www.vatican.va /content/john-paul-ii/en/encyclicals/documents/hf_jp-ii_enc_30121987 _sollicitudo-rei-socialis.html.

———. 1995. Homily, Orioles Park at Camden Yards. https://w2.vatican .va/content/john-paul-ii/en/homilies/1995/documents/hf_jp-ii_hom _19951008_baltimore.html.

Kant, Immanuel. (1793) 1998. *Religion within the Bounds of Sheer Reason*. Translated by Philip McPherson Rudisill. https://kantwesley.com/Kant /RationalReligion.pdf.

Keleher, Lori [Loretta W. Kelecher]. 2007. "Empowerment and International Development." PhD diss., University of Maryland.

———. 2014. "Sen and Nussbaum: Agency and Capability-Expansion." *Ethics and Economics* 1, no. 2: 54–70.

Khader, Serene, and Stacy J. Kosko. 2019. "Reason to Value: Process, Opportunity, and Perfectionism in the Capability Approach." In *Agency and Democracy in Development Ethics*, edited by Lori Keleher and Stacy J. Kosko. Cambridge: Cambridge University Press.

Nebel, Mathias. 2006. *La Catégorie morale du péché structurel*. Paris: Cerf.

Nussbaum, Martha. 2000. *Women and Human Development*. Cambridge: Cambridge University Press.

———. 2011. *Creating Capabilities: The Human Development Approach*. Cambridge, MA: Harvard University Press.

Oxhandler, Holly. 2017. "Namaste Theory: A Quantitative Grounded Theory on Religion and Spirituality in Mental Health Treatment." *Religions* 8, no. 9. https://www.mdpi.com/2077-1444/8/9/168.

Paul VI. 1967. *Populorum Progressio: On the Development of Peoples*. Encyclical. https://www.vatican.va/content/paul-vi/en/encyclicals/documents/hf_p -vi_enc_26031967_populorum.html.

Pontifical Council for Justice and Peace (PCJP). 2006. *Compendium of the Social Doctrine of the Church*. https://www.vatican.va/roman_curia /pontifical_councils/justpeace/documents/rc_pc_justpeace_doc_20060526 _compendio-dott-soc_en.html.

Robeyns, Ingrid. 2017. *Wellbeing, Freedom and Social Justice: The Capability Approach Re-Examined*. Cambridge: Open Book Publishers.

Romero, Oscar. 1980. "La voz de la sin voz." In *La palabra viva de Monseñor Romero*, edited by Rodolfo Cardenal, Ignacio Martin-Baro, and Jon Sobrino. San Salvador: UCA Editorial.

Sen, Amartya. 1992. *Inequality Reexamined*. Oxford: Clarendon.

———. 1999. *Development as Freedom*. New York: Knopf.

Singh, V. K. 2015. *Hindu Rites and Rituals: Origins and Meanings*. India Penguin.

United States Conference of Catholic Bishops (USCCB). 1986. *Economic Justice for All*. https://www.usccb.org/upload/economic_justice_for_all.pdf.

Vatican Council II. 1965. *Gaudium et Spes*. Constitution. https://www.vatican .va/archive/hist_councils/ii_vatican_council/documents/vat-ii_const _19651207_gaudium-et-spes_en.html.

Wall, Steven. 2017. "Perfectionism in Moral and Political Philosophy." In *The Stanford Encyclopedia of Philosophy*. https://plato.stanford.edu/archives /win2017/entries/perfectionism-moral/.

Young, Iris Marion. 2011. "Structure as the Subject of Justice." In *Responsibility for Justice*, by Iris M. Young. New York: Oxford University Press.

FOUR

Dignity and Community in the Capability Approach and Catholic Social Teaching

Joshua Schulz

ABSTRACT

In this chapter I compare Martha Nussbaum's "intuitive" account of dignity with Catholic Social Teaching's "participative" account, highlighting their implications for thinking about the nature of practical reason, community, and the demands of social justice. Catholic Social Teaching articulates a metaphysical and theological account in which human dignity flows from our participation in three pre-political, "Leonine" societies. In this model, the family and civil society are natural developments of human sociality, implying pre-political norms for practical reason. In contrast, consistent with the anti-metaphysical methodological constraints of political liberalism, Nussbaum expresses a political account of dignity rooted in the vulnerabilities and needs of the human species. Using this model, she articulates a "liberal-egalitarian" model of community that regards families and states as political artifacts designed to lift individuals out of the dangers and injustices of a Rawlsian state of nature. Throughout the chapter, I explore convergences and divergences regarding who counts as a primary subject of justice and the role of communities in supporting several central human capabilities, especially practical reason and affiliation.

INTRODUCTION

Although the capability approach (CA) and Catholic Social Teaching (CST) represent convergent approaches to human development ethics, they understand dignity in very different ways, and this difference impacts their thinking about the nature and norms of community. Whereas CST believes that the family and civil society are natural developments of human sociality, implying pre-political norms for practical reason, the CA often defends a "liberal-egalitarian" model of community, one in which families and states are understood as political artifacts that should be designed to lift individuals out of the dangers and injustices of a Rawlsian state of nature (see Schulz 2016; Deneulin 2013). In this chapter I will explore these disagreements by comparing Martha Nussbaum's "intuitive" account of dignity with CST's "participative" account, highlighting their implications for thinking about the nature of community and the demands of social justice.

MARTHA NUSSBAUM'S CA

The way Martha Nussbaum justifies capability entitlements has changed over time. In the majority of this chapter I will focus on the version of the CA presented in *Creating Capabilities* (*CC*) (Nussbaum 2011a) and *Frontiers of Justice* (*FJ*) (Nussbaum 2006). For a listing of Nussbaum's central human capabilities, see Nussbaum 2011a, 33–34; they are also listed in the introduction to this book, p. 1–47. Nussbaum initially defended capability entitlements using quasi-Aristotelian "species-norms" but changed to a form of political liberalism in the mid-1990's.[1] Nevertheless, she has consistently invoked the concept of dignity as the basis for claiming that capabilities are rights.[2] This means the CA's claim that the central capabilities are political entitlements is based on a normative account of the relationship between dignity and the human community.

Following Jacques Maritain, John Rawls, and Amartya Sen, however, Nussbaum also accepts several theses from the liberal tradition that limit the ways capability entitlements can be justified. The most explicit of these are the Westphalian claim that ideological differences cannot be resolved by appeal to controversial metaphysical or religious arguments and the Cosmopolitan claim that political entitlements should be justified by premises that can be affirmed by citizens with a plurality of metaphysical and religious views.[3] One reason for favoring the capabilities approach (which holds a "partial, political conception of the good") over more comprehensive approaches is that framing political entitlements as capabilities (effective freedoms to do and to be) rather than functionings (actual beings and doings) avoids the intellectual quagmires of metaphysics, on the one hand, and the inevitable practices of social and ideological marginalization that accompany such views, on the other hand (cf. *CC*, 92).

To be persuasive, then, Nussbaum's CA must therefore satisfy two philosophical burdens. The substantive burden is to show that gaps between what others call status and achievement dignity create a moral duty of redress—specifically, in the state—and the methodological burden is to do so consistently with the anti-metaphysical commitments of political liberalism.[4] Nussbaum's strategy for meeting these burdens is to show that a life without access to the central capabilities is a life unworthy of dignity.

THE SUBSTANTIVE BURDEN

Nussbaum develops her conception of dignity in dialogue with several philosophical traditions. The first of these is the social contract tradition, which begins with the assumption that, on anything approaching the scale of the city, human beings will not spontaneously treat each other with justice, which can only be securely enjoyed after enforceable rules have been contracted by parties who are forced to cooperate with one another.[5] These parties, according to John Locke, must be "free, equal, and independent," for those who lack the power to compel cooperation or the productivity to attract it cannot be primary subjects of justice (Locke 1980, 95; cf. *FJ*, 28–33). As the Romans said, *non habentes personas*—such have no face in the civitas—and therefore no citizenship, no status, no dignitas with which to elicit the moral regard of citizens.[6]

Nussbaum offers two criticisms of this tradition in *Frontiers of Justice*. The first is that it is insensitive to the concrete realities of our animal life, particularly the normality of powerlessness and dependence. The second is that, by sidelining considerations of intrinsic human dignity, the social contract tradition both fails to explain our folk account of justice—which makes greater demands regarding a wider set of beings than the tradition allows (e.g., caring for infants)—and fails to justify these demands, since what ultimately motivates our acceptance of moral precepts is not (merely) self-interest, but an intuitive grasp of the fittingness of moral principles for dignified beings.[7]

However, Nussbaum argues the other major account of dignity, common to Kant and Stoicism, is likewise too narrow. For Kant, what distinguishes persons from non-persons is the possession of reason, which divides not only humans from animals but also the personal from the merely animal elements within human beings (*FJ*, 130). Insofar as Kantian accounts of dignity derive from reason's supposed transcendence over natural determined relations between things, nothing about animality per se has value (*FJ*, 131).[8] Nussbaum responds that this starkly dualistic picture ignores the evident fact that human dignity "just is the dignity of a certain sort of animal," that we find meaning and value in sex, emotion, artistic and athletic performances, and many other activities flowing from our embodiment.[9] Moreover, transcendental accounts of dignity treat "personhood" as an atemporal, self-sufficient, purely active quality of persons. This simply misdescribes our experience of dependence as we develop to maturity and decline toward death.

Nussbaum's own account is limned by these deficiencies: dignity must have a foundational role in an adequate theory of social justice, she argues, and it must be conceived as a feature of animality as such, one that supervenes on what she calls "striving" (cf. Nussbaum 2008, and see Formosa and Mackenzie 2014 for discussion). As she has written:

[The capability approach's] basic moral intuition concerns the dignity of a form of life that possesses both abilities and deep needs. Its basic goal is to address the need for a rich plurality of life activities. With Aristotle and Marx, the approach has insisted that there are waste and tragedy when a living creature with the innate or "basic" capability for some functions that are evaluated as important and good never gets the opportunity to perform those functions (Nussbaum 2006, 346–47). . . . [So] if we feel wonder looking at a complex organism, that wonder at least suggests the idea that it is good for that being to persist and flourish as the kind of thing it is. This idea is at least closely related to an ethical judgment that it is wrong when the flourishing of a creature is blocked by the harmful agency of another. That more complex idea is at the heart of the capabilities approach. (Nussbaum 2006, 349)

The abilities and needs characteristic of a form of life constitute its "species-norm," a concept necessary (a) for generating a list of individually necessary and incommensurable goods proper to a species, the lack of which define what counts as harm to its members, and (b) for identifying the natural, social, and (for human beings) political environments in which its members flourish.[10]

THE METHODOLOGICAL BURDEN

Importantly, however, liberalism's Westphalian and cosmopolitan commitments constrain how Nussbaum can justify and specify both (a) and (b) above. Insofar as the Westphalian account prohibits a metaphysical founding for a theory of justice, that account must overcome the is-ought gap: no "beings and doings" are held to be valuable in themselves but can only be interpreted as valuable from the point of view of a normative theory (*FJ*, 181ff.). The values chosen by the theory thus function as criteria for selecting which beings and doings are worth promoting. Nussbaum frequently notes that human beings have propensities to cruelty and patriarchy, for example, and suggests that without a normative theory with which to evaluate these propensities, we might be forced either (1) to conclude that such propensities are valuable entitlements or (2) to leave the interpretation of these propensities to the whims of cultural caprice.[11]

Nussbaum uses the concept of dignity to split the horns of this dilemma. She invokes dignity in order to specify which values will be used to interpret the various beings and doings of a species consistent with the cosmopolitan claim. "Dignity," she writes, is an "intuitive" notion referring to that quality of a living being that evokes an attitude of wonder and motivates us to treat something as an end in itself (CC, 29; FJ, 94, 347). Nussbaum primarily invokes dignity—described thus as a subjective impression motivating practical behavior, independently of any metaphysical foundation—as the reason people deserve equal respect in a pluralistic society, regardless of someone's level of functioning, thus avoiding horn 1 of the above dilemma (CC, 30–31; FJ, 183–86). Treating each person as an end requires sensitivity to ideological differences as we choose which beings and doings are valuable. This requires the list of political entitlements to be abstract, open-ended, and revisable. It also requires us to designate various liberties as basic—for example, immunities against coercion in speech, association, and religion—in order to avoid horn 2. Furthermore, we must understand the items on the list as capabilities rather than functionings, spaces of effective freedom one may choose to engage or forego (FJ, 171; CC, 25; see Nussbaum 2003, 42–43). In fact, this final freedom is central to Nussbaum's preferred justification of her capabilities list: it makes overlapping consensus possible even among persons whose comprehensive conceptions of the good would be violated were some functioning deemed basic (Nussbaum 2003, 43; cf. CC, 108–10).

More importantly, however—though contrary to Nussbaum's presentation of the argument—the concept of dignity must be invoked here to warrant the claim that these valued capabilities are political entitlements.[12] From the fact that I need x to flourish and will be harmed without it, it does not follow that I have a right to x. For that claim to follow, a "dignified life" must be something to which I am directed in such a way that my failure to achieve it is both tragic and possibly blameworthy, and in such a way that my being prevented or frustrated in achieving it is both tragic and an issue of social justice. It is precisely this teleological character that gives dignity the moral authority to make demands on people and social structures that merely aspirational claims lack.

To complete the argument, then: as Sen originally argued in works like *Development and Freedom* (Sen 1999) and *Capabilities and Commodities* (Sen 1985), someone's failure to convert resources into valuable functionings is often due to a variety of factors encompassing what Rawls called the natural and social lotteries: roughly, the unequally distributed sets of abilities and disabilities one possesses by brute luck.[13] Conversion failures thus constitute contingent gaps between someone's status as a dignified being and their real prospects for effectively choosing or achieving a life worthy of dignity. Dignity entails that insofar as these gaps can be rectified, they ought to be rectified: a minimally just society is one that overcomes morally arbitrary burdens and barriers to achieving a life worthy of dignity by protecting and provisioning the central capabilities.[14] To the extent that the CA specifies which capabilities need support, it creates a research imperative to discover how they are often blocked; to the extent it leaves open the particular manner in which the capabilities are to be satisfied in any given society, it constitutes a partial and political theory of social justice.

FROM DIGNITY TO ENTITLEMENTS: SOME CONFLICTS

None of the above arguments specify who should rectify gaps between status and achievement dignity. This lacuna is often regarded as a feature of a "partial" theory of justice, since various societies will presumably wish to assign these duties in unique ways. To anticipate a later disagreement, however, where the Catholic social tradition holds that the primary responsibility for securing social justice belongs to the diverse groups comprising civil society, Nussbaum clearly identifies the nation-state as the primary provider and enforcer of capability entitlements.[15] There seem to be two reasons for this. First, Nussbaum argues that the negative effects of forced care for dependent people constitutes an unjust burden on the capability right to self-determination, one that the state alone can rectify. Second, she argues that providing effective freedom of self-determination means providing "exit options" from people's inherited communities (such as families or religions) and that only the state can fulfill this role. Both arguments depend on a controversial understanding of the sixth item on Nussbaum's list of entitlements, practical reason.

Since CST and the CA will (perhaps irreconcilably) divide over these issues, we will articulate the controversies and their consequences by way of a transition to our discussion of CST.

According to the classical model used by CST, practical reason is a developed capacity to reason well about action and is fully exemplified in the virtue of prudence, understood as responsible deliberation about means within an order of ends specified by human nature. Call this weak self-determination. (See *Catechism of the Catholic Church* 2009 [*CCC*] 1806, which references St. Thomas Aquinas 1964, *Summa Theologica* [*ST*] II-II, 47.2–6.) In this model, practical and speculative/scientific reasoning are importantly analogous: both can issue true judgments, or fail to do so, because their operation depends on an accurate grasp of how the world is—of "being" in the case of speculative reason, and of the "human good" in the case of practical reason (*ST* I-II, 94.2).[16] As St. Thomas Aquinas says, reason is a measure of action only because it is itself first measured by nature, whose measure is eternal law (see *ST* I-II, 91.3 ad 3). Just as a metric ruler is a length used to measure other lengths, the prudent person likewise participates in the antecedent moral order established by Providence and is therefore the measure of good human action. In contrast, Nussbaum defines practical reasoning as the ability to "form a conception of the good and to engage in critical reflection about the planning of one's own life," what we will call strong self-determination (*FJ*, 77). Practical reasoning here means deliberation about ends rather than about means within an already-given order of ends. Possessing the capability of practical reasoning means having the opportunity to choose the meaning of one's life, what Nussbaum calls the "power of self-definition" (*CC*, 18). This is nominalism, whether metaphysical or methodological: there are no normative ends prior to the exercise of one's will.[17]

One consequence of the nominalist account of practical reason is that the demands of others, including one's dependents, can burden one's ability to direct one's life. Since practical reason, as an architectonic good, has a kind of priority over the other goods, it follows that if we are entitled to effectively choose the meaning of our lives, then individuals should have some freedom to divest themselves of burdensome dependents if these do not figure in their life-plans.

ABORTION AND CARE WORK

The tension between strong self determination and dependence is vividly illustrated in Nussbaum's discussions of abortion and "care work." Consider abortion (Nussbaum and Dixon 2012). "In a liberal society which prizes individual autonomy," Nussbaum and Dixon argue, "there will also be few circumstances in which it is legitimate" to force a woman to carry a child to term (ibid., 7). The harm caused by caring for (and perhaps the very existence of) an unwanted child could be catastrophic to a woman's sense of identity: she could lose her ability to exercise practical reason, and thus "all meaningful chance to determine the future course of her life" (ibid., 8). Thus, Nussbaum and Dixon argue, within the CA, "rights of access to abortion should be understood in terms that refer both to barriers against state interference and to affirmative duties on the part of the state to provide support. A life with human dignity requires protection of all the Central Capabilities up to a minimum threshold level: but all are conceived as opportunities for choice, and thus none has been secured unless the person has the opportunity to exercise choice in matters of actual functioning" (ibid., 10).

Nussbaum uses similar arguments regarding "care work." Consider a representative passage: "Good support for practical reason in this area [i.e., caregiving] would be public policies that make the choice to care for a dependent a real choice, not an imposition born of social indifference. Women would actually have the opportunity to make a plan of life for themselves and decide what role care for dependents would play in it" (*FJ*, 170–71). The central idea in both discussions is that an unwanted obligation to care for one's dependents constitutes an unjust burden on a woman's right to strong self-determination. The dignity of self-determining but vulnerable human beings is precisely what generates the need for the State as guarantor of capabilities here, for only an impersonal state is capable of protecting and providing for the central capabilities without itself suffering the crushing dignitary harms faced by those who must care for unwanted dependents. Whether by supporting abortion or paid care workers, Nussbaum argues, the state should relieve this burden.

Unfortunately, such arguments entirely undermine Nussbaum's previous account of dignity. Suppose, as she argued, that our account of dignity should be sensitive to the fact that animal striving is, in the normal case, undertaken in conditions of dependence. Such striving in dependence is found not only in children, the sick, the disabled, and animals, but, paradigmatically, also in the unborn. Either dependence excludes someone from being a primary subject of justice, or it does not; identifying one form of dependence (gestation) as lacking dignity is special pleading. Moreover, these arguments falsify the claim that the CA utilizes a non-metaphysical ("intuitive") concept of dignity. If dignity itself is subject to the democratic process of "ethical evaluation" that supposedly defines our species norm, then the intuition of dignity does no conceptual work in the theory, since it allows communities to bracket or ignore questions of intrinsic dignity for the sake of political expediency (e.g., as one way to secure women's political equality) or out of bias. (Recall that these were precisely the sorts of reasons Nussbaum invoked against Sen in defense of a list of capability entitlements.) These arguments also repudiate her criticism of the social contract tradition, since fetal persons are not counted as primary subjects of justice for the same reasons that the social contract tradition denied that women, children, and disabled people could be primary subjects of justice: because they are not presently either fully rational or sufficiently productive (i.e., independent) to count as political equals. In sum, to affirm that women bear no obligations of justice toward their children on the grounds that they are sometimes burdensome is thus to reaffirm the Kantian conception of the person, the Humean circumstances of justice, or the egoistic presumption that obligations of justice are conditioned on mutual advantage.[18] It is not to reject hierarchies between "normal" and dependent citizens; to base cooperation on dignity, love, and justice; or to affirm "that human beings are vulnerable temporal creatures, both capable and needy, disabled in many different stages and 'in need of a rich plurality of life-activities'" (FJ, 221).

THE RACINATION PROBLEM

A second consequence of Nussbaum's nominalist account of practical reason is the racination problem. The CA is fundamentally an account of states' positive obligations to ensure that their citizens meet minimum capability thresholds. The CA must therefore determine what level of practical reasoning is sufficient to constitute autonomous choice, what constitutes an impediment to the development of practical reasoning, and which means are appropriate to bring people below this threshold up to a minimum level of autonomy. Addressing these issues requires the CA to make problematic qualitative judgments about whether particular comprehensive doctrines and institutions racinate or deracinate us—facilitate or frustrate the development of practical reasoning—especially concerning dependent persons, such as children.

The problem runs thus. If the capability of practical reasoning is defined as the effective freedom for strong self-determination, then any worldview (such as CST) that advocates weak self-determination is morally suspect. Given their metaphysical and theological commitments to an antecedent reality that shapes our ends, rough-hew them how we will, weak self-determinists may well reject the claim that citizens must respect all alternative comprehensive doctrines, or people's freedom to move between them, on the grounds that following false doctrines is a misuse of reason (see *CCC* 1849). While the CA recognizes citizens' rights to hold doctrines of weak self-determination, it also regards this as an authentic choice only if one may believe otherwise, that is, if one has the effective freedom to be strongly self-determining. Thus, Nussbaum argues, citizens should possess "exit options" from their inherited worldviews and social practices, where this means access to the material, social, and conceptual resources—the effective freedom—necessary to move "from one comprehensive conception [of the good] to another" (*FJ*, 185).[19] Providing this access, however, requires all citizens to support and submit to legal and educational structures that may be contrary to their beliefs, such as permissive divorce laws, mandatory liberal sex education, and so on.[20] This is what we call the racination problem: weak self-determinists regard the attempt to provide these exit options as harmful to the proper development of practical reason in themselves, their dependents, and their society, while strong self-determinists regard the lack or obstruction of exit options as equally harmful. The point is that the nominalist definition of practical reason as strong self-determination is not philosophically or politically neutral. It entails that only someone with what Charles Taylor calls a "disengaged" conception of comprehensive doctrines as options one may adopt or alienate counts as possessing practical reason; someone with an immanent view of their own doctrine as an intellectually and morally binding condition for reasonable action does not qualify (Taylor 2007).[21] Since possession of a threshold capability for practical reasoning is part of a minimally just society, the nominalist definition has consequences for how the state should treat any community with an alternative account—including CST's.

Consider but one implication. While Nussbaum affirms the right of fully capacitated adults to choose hierarchical or authoritarian modes of affiliation, the CA requires her to reject the right of families, say, to raise children in this way—at least not in an immanent frame. She argues that the family is not a "natural" or "private" institution with unique rights and privileges against the state, but rather is a thoroughly artificial institution created by the state that ought to be regulated in light of the central capabilities, especially since "children are its captives in all matters of basic survival and well-being" and "it governs people's life chances pervasively" (Nussbaum 2001, 278; FJ, 105–6).[22] If capability failures follow from some aspect of family life, then "it is the job of the state to promote a more adequate structure" (FJ, 432, n. 19). The state must seemingly mandate "autonomy education" within a disengaged frame in order to correct the bad brute luck, say, of being born into a family that denies the relativity of comprehensive doctrines of the good or the intrinsic value of pluralism. Indeed, it is hard to avoid the conclusion that the CA must regard the practices of such families as deracinating children, that is, as impeding the development of their capacity for practical reasoning by depriving them of the conceptual and emotional resources for exercising "exit options," thus generating urgent moral concerns requiring correction as a matter of justice.

Elizabeth Anderson has argued that such luck-neutralizing actions would require the state to make impossible determinations about the extent of disability and compensation claims, and that state interventions would require quite illiberal policies of intrusiveness, insult, and painful revelation that contradict central capabilities, such as access to the social bases of respect and non-humiliation (Anderson 1999).[23] Even more substantially, borrowing again from Alasdair MacIntyre, the weak self-determinist would regard the compulsory public promotion of the view that all "alternative lives" are equally choice-worthy and deserving of public honor and support as deracinating children. If practical reason develops through creative participation in social practices defined by a shared conception of the common good, state action to minimize loyalty to these communities would frustrate rather than support the development of practical reasoning.

As we have seen, Nussbaum's theorization of justice based on the CA was intended to correct the social contract tradition in three areas: first, regarding the dignity of dependent, disabled, and non-human animal life; second, regarding the value of animality and the goods consequent upon it, including affiliation; and third, regarding the naturalness of benevolence and the desire for justice. Nevertheless, there are profound tensions between Nussbaum's conception of practical reason and the values of solidarity, affiliation, and community, tensions that challenge the CA's commitment to political liberalism and human dignity.

THE CATHOLIC ACCOUNT

In stark contrast to Nussbaum's CA, the Catholic account of dignity and community is inescapably metaphysical and theological. It is theological insofar as it claims that human beings have intrinsic value from the moment of their conception because they uniquely participate in ("image") the Trinitarian God. Specifically, says Pope Benedict XVI in *Caritas in Veritate*, just as the Trinitarian persons are defined by "pure relationality," so, too, "the human creature is *defined* through interpersonal relations" (Benedict XVI 2009, 53, my emphasis).[24] It is metaphysical because it claims that the meaning of human dignity is inseparable from our participation in several super-substantial totalities (see Clarke 1993, Schindler 1993, and especially Hittinger 2008). These part-whole relationships constitute the basis on which CST defines integral human development and the common good.

In particular, three non-contingent "Leonine societies" form the foundation of the Church's account of the person (see *CCC* 1882).[25] First, human beings are by nature ordered to family life. Insofar as every human being is descended from parents and sexually capacitated for reproduction, every person is essentially ordered to filial, nuptial, and familial relationships, or what Pope John Paul II called the "communio personarum" (see *Gratissimam Sane* [Letter to Families] [John Paul II 1994], 12). Second, insofar as everyone is traditioned by and into a culture, human beings are ordered to friendship and civic life, that is, to the common good of life in society. Finally, this same "from and for" model of relationality describes the supernatural origin and destiny of the human person. Because God creates and saves each person at every moment of her existence, human beings are the always-created site of God's redemptive activity. Every person is sacred because she is capacitated by and for grace (see *Evangelium Vitae* [John Paul II 1995], 38–39). Against the "unencumbered self" of liberal individualism, in which individuals possess dignity prior to having ends and all social relations are contingent and voluntary, the Church claims that the Leonine societies are natural and normative, specifying and shaping the meaning and value of human flourishing (*CCC* 1905–6; cf. Sandel 1984).

Consider an analogy.[26] A heart shares the end of health with the body of which it is a part. The heart contributes to the health of the body—part of being healthy is having a well-functioning heart—and is perfected by the health of the body since it is enabled to seek its own "internal" end of pumping blood by a body that is otherwise healthy. The excellence of the heart is thus both practically and conceptually inseparable from the good of its body. The relationship between heart and body is hierarchical but not exploitative since the transitive good of the whole body that the heart seeks also perfects the heart in an intransitive way. Thus the shared good of health defines the conceptual sphere in which the excellence of the heart qua heart is to be understood (as opposed to its color, its ability to produce noise in the chest, and so on). Similarly, we might say, human persons share ends with the Leonine societies in which they participate. As proper parts of these societies, our lives cannot but contribute to (or frustrate) the excellence of our families and other communities even as we ourselves are enabled to flourish by their flourishing or disabled by their failure.

The deep recognition of the social character of human flourishing is, I believe, the central insight shared by the CA and Catholic Social Teaching. The difference is that the former tends to understand the relation between the individual and society as a form of instrumental interdependence, while the latter views the relationship as constitutively complementary. To return to the analogy, just as the good of the heart cannot be conceptually or practically defined apart from its relationship to the body, so, too, do the Leonine societies constitute non-accidental spheres in which we seek our perfection. Familial, social, and spiritual relationships are not some goods among others—as if "affiliations" could be itemized and sought apart from health, practical reason, and so on, as on the CA's list. Just as "being rational" and "being virtuous" are not what we seek to do or be when we are not working or listening to music, neither is being familial, neighborly, and Christian something to do or be when we are not otherwise engaged. Whether I exercise at home with children underfoot before homeschooling prayerfully or split my time between gym and office while my children are socialized into a disengaged frame by salaried strangers in government institutions—these are all choices that are not only mine but are also familial, civic, and spiritual: they constitute how I am a husband, father, provider, educator, mentor, friend, citizen, and Christian. They are the irreducibly thick relational descriptions that constitute our lives.

Given the Catholic claim that because common goods are *boni honesti*, goods that flow back to persons and perfect them, there is, in principle, no conflict between the individual and social characters of human dignity. One does not possess dignity apart from family, community, and God; rather, one's dignity is realized with and in them as a daughter, neighbor, and Christian. That this does not happen automatically or inevitably does not make it contingent.[27] The claim is not that one is fully human only if one is raised by a good family but that, as dependent rational animals, every one of us is and cannot not be descended from and raised by some family or other, and this fact is a key part of any reasonable account of human dignity. In other words, CST agrees that the dignity of persons is just, as Nussbaum claims, "the dignity of a kind of animal," but it spells out in greater detail the consequences of this fact: that human dignity is inescapably sexual and therefore familial rather than voluntarily affiliational; that it is social, cultural, and political, and therefore inescapably ethnic, ideological, and traditioned rather than cosmopolitan; and that it is grounded in and seeks spiritual goods that transcend the *saeculum* and therefore grounds pre-political moral norms. All of this implies a wide, capability-based notion of human development, and, correspondingly, many kinds of poverty—material, intellectual, moral, social, legal, and spiritual—as well as structural forms of these poverties, some of which are recognized by the CA, while others, importantly, are not (see especially *Sollicitudo Rei Socialis* [John Paul II 1987], 9, 15, 29ff; *Populorum Progressio* [Paul VI 1967], 20–21).[28]

Much more should be said here, but let us return to our discussion of dignity. According to the participative account outlined thus far, human dignity has four dominant characteristics (*CCC* 1779). First, because it derives from the gifted participation of every person in God's loving act of creation, human dignity is universal, inherent, and inalienable. It is therefore more inclusive than threshold accounts of dignity, for it rejects the very idea that human beings need to pass performance thresholds—of sentience, independence, productivity, and so on—in order to count as primary subjects of justice. It is also more demanding than threshold accounts, for it requires respect for the dignity of those beyond Nussbaum's "frontiers of justice"—for example, the abandoned lab-grown embryo, the rapist's fetus, and the patient in a persistent vegetative state.[29]

Second, dignity is substantive rather than intuitive. The Leonine societies have intrinsic ends since, as real societies—like all real substances—they embody a natural law, an "ordering of reason," that provides the norms for the exercise of right reason (*CCC* 1881, 1910; see Hittinger 2008). That is, by providing the teleological framework that gives content to practical reason, these societies capacitate our moral agency by providing the ends necessary for the deliberation of prudence and the specification and pursuit of virtue.[30] This has two major consequences. First, it entails that the precepts of the natural law and the specification of (at least) the cardinal virtues are grounded in our unchosen participation in familial, social, and ecclesial totalities, and thus weak rather than strong self-determination. Second, it entails that natural rights are grounded in the pre-political protections every human being enjoys in pursuit of the goods proper to these societies, such as love, justice, and worship (see *Pacem in Terris* [John XXIII 1963], 8–37). Like the CA, the Church thus proclaims that we are made for positive liberty, but she also claims that this liberty is for the pursuit of our proper ends. Thus, the contemporary tendency to politicize and instrumentalize the Leonine societies—for example, to model the family on the contract, turn culture into propaganda, and privatize religious belief—does violence to the nature and moral authority of these societies, which is prior to and distinct from the contingent, fallible, positive authority of any state.[31] Moral rights are not primarily legal technologies for bringing about social change by liberating individuals from the accidents of family, culture, or religion, but are pre-political immunities against abuses of positive law by well-meaning bureaucrats and judges whose interventions would do violence to human nature rather than perfect the nature we have.

Third, although every being is directed to the God-given ends intrinsic to her essence, the human person participates in this providential order by freely and knowingly seeking her good within the societies of which she is a natural member. It follows that caritas and solidarity— the extent to which we identify with and deliberately contribute to the good of our neighbors—are in important respects the measures by which rational action is to be judged.[32] The account of human motivation in CST thus already transcends the egoist-altruist debates among the social contractarians because caritas sees our most important goods as common rather than competitive.

The fourth and final characteristic of the participative account of dignity is that it is self-regarding in ways Nussbaum's account is not. "Dignitary harm," for Nussbaum, seems to always have an external cause; it involves either the loss of some opportunity for autonomous action or an honorific loss of face. She offers no account of how an individual could commit an undignified act against herself. In contrast, the claim that dignity is participative and gifted entails that because we have responsibilities to steward our motherhood and fatherhood, our citizenship, and our status as divine image-bearers, we can therefore act in undignified ways that are not worthy of this status.

CONCLUSION: CHALLENGES FROM AND FOR CST

Taken together, these considerations bring CST into both fruitful and critical dialogue with the CA. Within CST, the norm of caritas implies that solidarity with the poor, marginalized, and disadvantaged is not supererogatory, that, as a matter of social justice, societies are to be judged by how they treat their poor (see *Centesimus Annus* [John Paul II 1991], 11; *Sollicitudo Rei Socialis* 42; *Caritas in Veritate* 6–7). These claims have clear echoes in the CA's claims that the poor and disabled are primary subjects of justice whose legitimate and urgent claims should direct the distribution of material and social goods within a society. Likewise,

CST's ancient defense of the social use of private property and the need to design economic life around supporting families' abilities to satisfy their vocation to raise and educate their children also echoes the CA's rejection of an absolutist approach to private property and desert-based defenses of material and social inequalities.

On the other hand, the participatory account of dignity is in deep conflict with the CA's account of society and the grounds of justice. For instance, CST does not regard all inequality as unjust, as arguments that derive our political obligations from inequalities generated by natural and social lottery tend to do. Rather, CST understands the diversity of human talents and disabilities, along with dependence and independence, as expressions of and calls to participate in the Providential order of the universe (see 1 Cor. 12; Aquinas on the diversity of creation, *ST* I, 47, II-II, 1847; and Dante Alighieri [1921] in the circle of Jupiter, XIX). Where the secularist sees inequality, CST sees complementarity: between male and female, yes, but also, recall, between workers and owners, the rich and the poor (*Rerum Novarum*), the Church and the laity (*Gaudium et Spes* [Vatican Council II 1965]), advanced societies and developing societies (*Sollicitudo Rei Socialis*), and even between those who suffer and those who care for them (*Salvici Doloris* [John Paul II 1984], 19–24). Complementarity is a structural and normative feature of a relational cosmos whose highest expression is gift.

CST therefore needs to draw careful distinctions between diversity and disability. While a complementarian approach to diversity implies respect for differences in capacity (such as the ability to gestate children) without implying diversity in dignity—men and women should equally enjoy the goods and dignity of family life—disabilities involve impediments to one's ability to contribute to or enjoy the common goods toward which one's complementary capacities are ordered. Disabilities generate just demands for rectification through the works of mercy and the reform of unjust social structures, especially those that marginalize the poor and vulnerable (see Robbins 2014; Belloc 2009; Médaille 2010). These reforms, however, must respect our participated dignity: rather than regarding women's unique child-bearing capacities as social disabilities that generate entitlements to motherhood-denying technologies, for instance, CST will demand that society organize itself in ways that support the full participation and dignity of parents and their children in the social order.

Finally, CST's affirmation of the normative priority of the Leonine societies over the state fundamentally shapes its approach to questions of religious and ideological pluralism. CST sometimes suggests that problems of political pluralism can be reduced to problems of scale, for example, that tolerance (as distinct from charity) is a virtue only in a world whose nations are too big for justice on a human scale. While liberalism claims to respect diversity but insists on massive states made of ideologically incompatible peoples, CST counsels turning to subsidiarity, the belief that investing smaller intermediate societies with creative authority is more likely to generate liberty-respecting solutions to pluralism than ever-widening structures of anonymous bureaucracy.

NOTES

1. The shift has arguably been incomplete and unstable. See Alison Jagger's analysis and evaluation of four distinct approaches employed by Nussbaum over the years in Jagger (2006).

2. This is despite the fact that she also claims that dignity cannot be defined "prior to and independently of the capabilities" because the two ideas are "intertwined" (*FJ*, 162; *CC*, 29–30). Scholars note that the list of basic capabilities has not changed despite the changing foundations of the theory, raising questions about the actual work dignity does in Nussbaum's theory. See Claassen and Düwell (2013).

3. Nussbaum offers pragmatic reasons for the Westphalian claim, and argues that the Cosmopolitan claim best satisfies the norm of respect for persons (cf. *FJ*, 163, 183–86); see also Nussbaum (2011b). The Catholic tradition disagrees with both claims. First, it accepts the possibility of well-justified metaphysical and religious views, and second, it holds that truth is a condition of love (and therefore respect). See, e.g., Benedict XVI, *Caritas in Veritate* (2009).

4. For discussion of the role of the two kinds of dignity in Nussbaum, see Formosa and Mackenzie (2014).

5. It is often argued that the benevolent sentiments required for other-regarding behavior are limited in scope, unreliable, or altogether absent in some (or all) members of the population.

6. Traditionally, this meant that women, children, slaves, the disabled, the elderly, the uneducated and unskilled, zealots, and the poor were considered *secondary* subjects of justice—*at best* tolerated objects of charity. See *FJ*, 48.

7. Together, these objections motivate the problematic character of the three "frontiers of justice" to which Nussbaum calls our attention, namely, the systematic inability of the social contract tradition to conceive as primary subjects of justice anyone disabled from fully participating in society by uncontrollable circumstances. These include not only physically and cognitively disabled human beings but also underdeveloped countries that lack the power or productivity to engage with more developed countries on equal terms and non-human animals whose welfare is increasingly affected by human activity.

8. See Kant (1998).

9. For discussion, see Nussbaum (2008).

10. See Nussbaum's influential defense of the need for a specific list of capability entitlements in Nussbaum (2003).

11. To understand the importance of the Westphalian claim, consider that, as a political liberal, Nussbaum must accept the Enlightenment's understanding of *nature* as "whatever happens frequently" rather than the Aristotelian sense of "what belongs to something's essence." Yet, for an Aristotelian, it is entirely possible for something to happen frequently that is contrary to something's nature in the Aristotelian sense, such as disease or cruelty. Thus, for an Aristotelian (and CST), the first horn of this dilemma is not persuasive, the Westphalian claim is unmotivated, and there is no need to worry about the second horn. Given her commitments, Nussbaum must take both horns seriously. She discusses the second horn of the dilemma at some length in her defense of the need for a list of central capabilities against Amartya Sen's reticence to affirm such a list (Nussbaum 2003, 47).

12. Nussbaum denies this by claiming that dignity and entitlements are "intertwined," a notion I can make no sense of (*FJ*, 162; *CC*, 29–30); see n. 4.

13. The Rawlsian lotteries form the basis of *Frontiers of Justice*, roughly defining the three groups treated as secondary subjects—those marginalized by physical and mental impairments, national origin, or species (*FJ*, 14–22). For Rawls, social justice is measured by a society's willingness to rectify these morally arbitrary barriers or burdens to achieving a life worthy of dignity. This claim spawned an entire field investigating the relation between luck and justice. For discussion, see Knight and Stemplowska (2011).

14. The requirement to meet such thresholds is a "minimum account of social justice," says Nussbaum: "A society that does not guarantee these to all its citizens, at some appropriate threshold level, falls short of being a fully just society" (*CC*, 40).

15. *CC*, 64: "In my view [contrary to Sen], there is a conceptual connection between Central Capabilities and government."

16. For discussion, see MacIntyre (2007, chap. 4).

17. Nussbaum's CA thus presupposes liberalism's "unencumbered self," which Michael Sandel famously discusses in Sandel (1984).

18. These were the motivations for developing a politically liberal CA in the first place: "My argument has suggested that liberal theory needs to question some of its most traditional starting points—including the Kantian notion of the person, the Humean account of the Circumstances of Justice, and the contractarian idea of mutual advantage as the purpose of social cooperation" (*FJ*, 220).

19. For discussion, see Claassen (2018).

20. For reasons such as these, Deneulin (2006) argues that "Nussbaum's politically liberal capabilities approach is a perfectionist approach in disguise" (42). Nussbaum denies this in Nussbaum (2011b).

21. This theme is an important one in recent conservative thought. See MacIntyre (2007), who argues that the essential characteristic of modern selfhood is "the capacity to detach oneself from any particular standpoint or point of view . . . and view and judge that standpoint or point of view from the outside" (126). Nussbaum's review of MacIntyre's *Whose Justice, Which Rationality* is telling here: she explicitly accuses MacIntyre of misogyny (Nussbaum 1989).

22. Nussbaum argues that "there is no reason for the state to take traditional groupings as given: in light of the human capabilities, the state should consider what groupings it wishes to protect, and on what basis. And I have argued further that there is no way in which the state can really avoid constructing the family unit in accordance with some norms or other; so it had better do so self-consciously, with full awareness of the goals in view" (Nussbaum, 2001, 278).

23. Although Anderson does not address Nussbaum's CA itself, see Moschella's critique of autonomy education on grounds similar to those I suggest here in Schulz (2016).

24. Benedict continues: "The Christian revelation of the unity of the human race presupposes a metaphysical interpretation of the '*humanum*' in which relationality is an essential element." See his earlier article, written as Cardinal Ratzinger (1990), for similar claims. See Pontifical Council for Justice and Peace (PCJP, 2004), esp. secs. 108–10 and 149–51, and *Gaudium et Spes* (Vatican Council II 1965), 24–25.

25. These societies appear prominently in Aquinas's exposition of natural law in *ST* I-II.94. Human beings are teleologically ordered to the creation and

preservation of life, to friendship and society, and to knowing the truth about God and the world. They play an explicit role in Catholic teaching on many issues, including private property, just wages, education, and integral human development.

26. For extended analogical and normative discussions of the part-whole relationships found in organisms, artifacts, and societies, see Pope Pius XII (1952). See also Schulz (2015).

27. PCJP (2004, 150): "The social nature of human beings does not automatically lead to communion among persons, to the gift of self. Because of pride and selfishness, man discovers in himself the seeds of asocial behavior, impulses leading him to close himself within his own individuality and to dominate his neighbor."

28. With the CA, CST recognizes the injustice of marginalization from the sources of wealth and respect embodied in scientific knowledge and know-how, but adds further forms of marginalization: marginalization from communities of moral virtue; the objectification of women and disrespect for the feminine vocation within the family; a culture of death that treats the poor, sick, weak, and vulnerable as non-valuable; the liberal expectation of public atheism; and so on.

29. For an impassioned extension of the Catholic critique of what Pope John Paul II (1995) called the "culture of death" in *Evangelium Vitae* 19–23, see Pope Francis's 2020 critique of the "throwaway world" that treats the unborn, elderly, and poor as disposable waste in *Fratelli Tutti*, 18–21.

30. For discussion, see Barrera (2001, 291ff).

31. Consider that in *Rerum Novarum* 14, Leo XIII (1891) calls it a "great and pernicious error" to believe that "the civil government should at its option intrude into and exercise intimate control over the family and the household," as Nussbaum advocates.

32. See Benedict XVI (2009, 3): Truth needs to be sought, found, and expressed within the "economy" of charity, but charity, in turn, needs to be understood, confirmed, and practiced "in the light of truth."

WORKS CITED

Alighieri, Dante. 1921 (1320). *The Paradisio of Dante Alighieri*. London: J. M. Dent.

Anderson, Carl, and José Granados. 2009. "The Nuptial Mystery: From the Original Gift to the Gift of Self." In *Called to Love: Approaching John Paul II's Theology of the Body*. New York: Doubleday.

Anderson, Elizabeth. 1999. "What Is the Point of Equality?" *Ethics* 109 (2): 287–337.

Aquinas, Thomas. 1964 (1485). *Summa Theologiae*, II-II, 47.2–6. Translated by Edmund Hill, OP. London: Blackfriars with Eyre & Spottiswoode.

Barrera, Albino. 2001. "The Common Good as Due Order and Due Proportion." In *Modern Catholic Social Documents and Political Economy*. Washington, DC: Georgetown University Press.

Belloc, Hilaire. 2009 (1936). *An Essay on the Restoration of Property*. 2nd ed. Norfolk, VA: IHS Press.

Benedict XVI. 2009. *Caritas in Veritate*. Encyclical. https://www.vatican .va/content/benedict-xvi/en/encyclicals/documents/hf_ben-xvi_enc _20090629_caritas-in-veritate.html.

Catechism of the Catholic Church. 1992. Vatican City: Libra Editrice Vaticana.

Claassen, Rutger. 2018. *Capabilities in a Just Society: A Theory of Navigational Agency*. Cambridge: Cambridge University Press.

Claassen, Rutger, and Marcus Düwell. 2013. "The Foundations of Capability Theory: Comparing Nussbaum and Gewirth." *Ethical Theory and Moral Practice* 16, no. 3: 493–510.

Clarke, W. Norris. 1993. *Person and Being*. Milwaukee, WI: Marquette University Press.

Deneulin, Séverine. 2006. *The Capability Approach and the Praxis of Development*. New York: Palgrave Macmillan.

———. 2013. "Recovering Nussbaum's Aristotelian Roots." *International Journal of Social Economics* 40, no. 7: 624–32.

Formosa, Paul, and Catriona Mackenzie. 2014. "Nussbaum, Kant, and the Capabilities Approach to Dignity." *Ethical Theory and Moral Practice* 17: 875–92.

Francis. 2020. *Fratelli Tutti*. Encyclical. https://www.vatican.va/content /francesco/en/encyclicals/documents/papa-francesco_20201003_enciclica -fratelli-tutti.html.

Hittinger, Russell. 2008. "The Coherence of the Four Basic Principles of Catholic Social Doctrine: An Interpretation." In *Pursuing the Common Good: How Solidarity and Subsidiarity Can Work Together*. Vatican City: Pontifical Academy of Social Sciences, Acta 14.

Jagger, Alison. 2006. "Reasoning about Well-Being: Nussbaum's Methods of Justifying the Capabilities." *Journal of Political Philosophy* 14, no. 3: 301–22.

John XXIII. 1963. *Pacem in Terris*. Encyclical. https://www.vatican.va/content /john-xxiii/en/encyclicals/documents/hf_j-xxiii_enc_11041963_pacem .html.

John Paul II. 1984. *Salvici Doloris*. Apostolic letter. https://www.vatican.va
/content/john-paul-ii/en/apost_letters/1984/documents/hf_jp-ii_apl
_11021984_salvifici-doloris.html.

———. 1987. *Sollicitudo Rei Socialis*. Encyclical. https://www.vatican.va
/content/john-paul-ii/en/encyclicals/documents/hf_jp-ii_enc_30121987
_sollicitudo-rei-socialis.html.

———. 1991. *Centesimus Annus*. Encyclical. https://www.vatican.va
/content/john-paul-ii/en/encyclicals/documents/hf_jp-ii_enc_01051991
_centesimus-annus.html.

———. 1994. *Gratissimam Sane* (Letter to Families). Apostolic letter. https://
www.vatican.va/content/john-paul-ii/en/letters/1994/documents/hf_jp
-ii_let_02021994_families.html.

———. 1995. *Evangelium Vitae*. Encyclical. https://www.vatican.va
/content/john-paul-ii/en/encyclicals/documents/hf_jp-ii_enc_25031995
_evangelium-vitae.html.

Kant, Immanuel. 1998 (1785). *Groundwork for the Metaphysics of Morals*.
Edited and translated by Mary Gregor. 1998. Cambridge: Cambridge
University Press.

Knight, Carl, and Zofia Stemplowska. 2011. *Responsibility and Distributive
Justice*. Oxford: Oxford University Press.

Leo XIII. 1891. *Rerum Novarum*. Encyclical. https://www.vatican.va/content
/leo-xiii/en/encyclicals/documents/hf_l-xiii_enc_15051891_rerum
-novarum.html.

Locke, John. 1980 (1689). "Second Treatise of Government." In *John Locke
Second Treatise of Government*, edited by C. B. McPherson. Indianapolis,
IN: Hackett.

MacIntyre, Alasdair. 2007. *After Virtue*. 3rd ed. Notre Dame, IN: University of
Notre Dame Press.

Médaille, John. 2010. *Toward a Truly Free Market*. Wilmington, DE: ISI Books.

Moschella, Melissa. 2016. "Is Mandatory Autonomy Education in the Best
Interests of Children?" *Proceedings of the American Catholic Philosophical
Association*. doi: 10.5840/acpaproc201713159.

Nussbaum, Martha. 1989. "Recoiling from Reason." In *New York Review of
Books*, December 7.

———. 2001. *Women and Human Development*. Cambridge: Cambridge University Press.

———. 2003. "Capabilities as Fundamental Entitlements: Sen and Social Justice." *Feminist Economics* 9, nos. 2–3: 33–59.

———. 2006. *Frontiers of Justice: Disability, Nationality, Species Membership*.
Cambridge, MA: Belknap Press.

————. 2008. "Human Dignity and Political Entitlements." In *Human Dignity and Bioethics: Essays Commissioned by the President's Council on Bioethics*. US Independent Agencies and Commissions.

————. 2011a. *Creating Capabilities: The Human Development Approach*. Cambridge, MA: Belknap Press.

————. 2011b. "Perfectionist Liberalism and Political Liberalism." *Philosophy & Public Affairs* 39, no. 1: 3–45.

Nussbaum, Martha, and Rosalind Dixon. 2012. "Abortion, Dignity, and a Capabilities Approach." In *Feminist Constitutionalism: Global Perspectives*, edited by Beverly Baines, Daphne Barak-Erez, and Tsvi Kahana. Cambridge: Cambridge University Press. https://papers.ssrn.com/sol3/papers .cfm?abstract_id=1799190.

Paul VI. 1967. *Populorum Progressio*. Encyclical. https://www.vatican.va /content/paul-vi/en/encyclicals/documents/hf_p-vi_enc_26031967 _populorum.html.

Pius XII. 1952. "Address to the First International Congress on the Histopathology of the Nervous System." *AAS* 44: 779–89.

Pontifical Council for Justice and Peace (PCJP). 2004. *Compendium of the Social Doctrine of the Church*. Vatican City: Libreria Editrice Vaticana.

Ratzinger, Joseph. 1990. "Concerning the Notion of Person in Theology." *Communio* 17, no. 3: 439–54.

Robbins, Harold. 2014 (1938). *The Sun of Justice*. United Kingdom: Agnus Dei Publishing.

Sandel, Michael. 1984. "The Procedural Republic and the Unencumbered Self." *Political Theory* 12, no. 1: 81–96.

Schindler, David. 1993. "Norris Clarke on Person, Being, and St. Thomas." *Communio* 20, no. 3: 580–92.

Schulz, Joshua. 2015. "The Principle of Totality and the Limits of Enhancement." *Ethics and Medicine* 31, no. 3: 143–57.

————. 2016. "The Capabilities Approach and Catholic Social Teaching: An Engagement." *Journal of Global Ethics* 12, no. 1: 29–47.

Sen, Amartya. 1985. *Capabilities and Commodities*. Oxford: Oxford University Press.

————. 1999. *Development as Freedom*. Oxford: Oxford University Press.

Taylor, Charles. 2007. *A Secular Age*. Cambridge, MA: Belknap Press.

Vatican Council II. 1965. *Gaudium et Spes*. Pastoral constitution. https://www .vatican.va/archive/hist_councils/ii_vatican_council/documents/vat-ii _const_19651207_gaudium-et-spes_en.html.

FIVE

Persistent Gender Inequality

Why Catholic Social Teaching Needs
the Capability Approach

Katie Dunne

ABSTRACT

*Catholic Social Teaching (CST) is a valuable resource for confront-
ing global justice issues. Many magisterial documents and pastoral
constitutions have commented on trends of inequality and lamented
social and economic disparity. Moreover, CST consistently professes
the human dignity of all people. Undeniably, however, the conception
of the human person in CST does not find its full potentiality in providing a resource for confronting injustice against women. Indeed, it
can reasonably be argued that it fails to engage, in a meaningful way,
with the social and cultural realities of women's experiences. The subsequent theological landscape is inevitably androcentric and results in
accounts of human development that tend to eclipse the social realities*

that affect women. In contrast to CST, writings based on the capability approach (CA) have dealt with questions of achieving full justice for women by creating the appropriate space in which to analyze inequality and deprivation by focusing on human capabilities. In this chapter I propose that Martha Nussbaum's writings on the CA are particularly well placed to confront the androcentric nature of CST. Therefore, the CA not only offers more substance to CST, but it also provides a site for serious moral and political debate in terms of human development and social justice.

INTRODUCTION

Catholic Social Teaching (CST) is a valuable resource for confronting global justice issues. As many contributors to this volume have argued, it provides a distinctive interpretation of human persons, their intrinsic dignity, and their worth. Importantly, CST consistently professes the human dignity of all people. Undeniably, however, the conception of the human person in CST does not find its full potentiality in providing a resource for confronting injustice against women. Indeed, it can reasonably be argued that it fails to engage, in a meaningful way, with the social and cultural realities of women's experiences. Remarkably, for example, CST predominantly focuses on women's relationship to motherhood and the family and does not engage in a sustained analysis of the issue of justice for women, nor does it draw conclusions, or offer solutions, to combat the injustices that women face. At the same time, many contemporary magisterial documents explicitly and unequivocally endorse the dignity of all people. Consequently, there is a certain amount of ambivalence surrounding how gender is considered in CST. The subsequent theological landscape is inevitably androcentric, and this results in accounts of human development that tend to eclipse the social realities that affect women (Hicks 2002).[1]

It has been well established that, as a theoretical and practical framework, the capability approach (CA) can enhance a theological analysis of human development.[2] With its predominant focus on agency and well-being, the CA is also a significant resource for analyzing gender discrimination. In contrast to CST, writings based on the CA have dealt with questions of achieving full justice for women by creating the appropriate space in which to analyze inequality and deprivation by focusing on human capabilities. As such, the CA not only offers more substance to CST but also provides a site for serious moral and political debate in terms of human development and social justice. In this chapter I propose that Martha Nussbaum's writings on the CA are particularly well placed to confront the androcentric nature of CST.[3] In her attempt to build a partial theory of justice on the basis of the CA, Nussbaum directly asks which capabilities are the most valuable for a woman's life that is worthy of human dignity. As a set of inter-related opportunities, she proposes her ten central capabilities (which are listed toward the end of the chapter) as ones that any just society ought to protect, promote, and nurture so that human development can be authentic for all, especially women (Nussbaum 2011, 2001). In her list of capabilities for a dignified life, she seeks to address impoverishment and deprivation in comprehensive ways. She works to discern the necessary conditions for a just society and provides compelling reasons to engage the moral claims of human flourishing. Asking what people are actually able to do and to be in life ensures that her theory foregrounds the inequalities experienced by women. In this chapter, therefore, I aim to explore the value of the CA for CST, particularly in terms of the demands of gender justice, and to illuminate what Karl Rahner refers to as "the practical theological questions of what is and what ought to be" (Rahner 1972, 102). In order to fulfil this aim, I proceed by explicitly considering the nature of CST and its discourse on gender. I then explore the value of Nussbaum's politically liberal (partial) theory of justice based on the CA. I conclude by proposing a responsible theological anthropology, in dialogue with the CA, that fully affirms women's equality and personhood in CST.

CST: THE LACUNA

As part of a responsive tradition, social encyclicals, which form part of CST, are usually prefaced with the economic conditions at the particular time of promulgation. These encyclicals document the trajectory of human progress, including worsening inequalities, the disparity between the rich and the poor, technological advances, and power dynamics. They also emphasize that authentic human development, a concept introduced in the 1967 encyclical *Populorum Progressio* (Paul VI 1967) and developed by encyclicals written since, is constituted by much more than socio-economics. They outline that inequality is also framed by social, cultural, and political issues. Fundamental to CST is the understanding that the concept of development cannot be defined solely in terms of material accumulation. To depict development in these terms alone impoverishes the entire process and annuls the many other facets that give meaning to it (Lawler and Salzman 2001). For progress to be achieved, people must exercise, and have the opportunity to exercise, their agency. The principles of the social teachings of the Catholic tradition add unique value to this process by advocating that people exercise their agency collectively and responsibly for the common good. It can reasonably be suggested, therefore, that the value of CST to development theory and policy is found in the key concepts that it proposes. Moreover, CST is versatile and lends itself easily to interdisciplinarity. It is this dynamic nature of CST that allows it to address many diverse issues, including the economy, religious freedom, nuclear warfare, ecology, human rights, and human development.

One of the most valuable contributions made by CST to human development discourse is the notion of integral, or authentic, human development. As presented in CST, integral development rejects policies that focus primarily on economic growth as an indicator of a person's well-being. In place of such notions of development, CST calls for a holistic conception of development in which the dignity of all is affirmed. Consequently, participation, a preferential option for the poor, the just distribution of goods and services, solidarity, a sense of community, ecological concern, the common good, and respect for diverse cultures all figure as prominent concerns in CST's current presentation of authentic development. However, a significant criticism can be levelled at CST's conception of integral human development: it fails, in both process and content, to adequately address the demands of gender justice and the realities of women's experiences (Marshall et al. 2011).[4] Indeed, its appropriation of human development fails to engage in a meaningful way with the economic and empirical realities that affect development and equality, particularly for women. This methodology serves to diminish the concrete circumstances of life that have a very real impact on human development and gender justice. There is an undeniable tension: on the one hand, CST provides beneficial guiding principles for the process of development on both a micro and a macro level; on the other hand, it is permeated by an imbalanced focus on gender. In essence, CST relegates women, and also the social realities that they face, to the margins, thereby ensuring an unbalanced discourse on human development. To show this, it may be helpful to turn to specific teachings in this regard.[5]

CST: THE SPECIFIC NATURE OF WOMEN

Gender inequalities persist in all corners of the globe, and they are often insidious and deeply entrenched. With its ground in the principle of human dignity as the fundamental basis for its discourse on integral human development, CST affirms women's full humanity. Yet it paradoxically endorses a reductive theological anthropology that defines women according to their "nature," and it does not adequately identify, or engage with, the complex, multifaceted nature of gender issues, whose adequate understanding is critical for the promotion of the dignity of all human lives, especially female ones. Indeed, issues around gender and embodiment have critically shaped CST's discussion of women, and reinforced their inferiority. CST's implicit suspicion of the body, in particular the female and non-heteronormative body, ensures that we find ourselves entangled in ambiguities concerning the rhetoric of egalitarianism on the one hand and the legacy of patriarchy on the other. Also characteristic of magisterial documents on women is the absence of women's experiences. Natalia Imperatori-Lee (2015) captures the problematic:

> The gendered struggle for authority and truth has a long history in the Catholic Church. From Catherine of Siena's rebukes of Pope Gregory XI to Teresa of Avila's theological ruminations, Catholic theology is shot through with women's words and work. The tendency of the Roman Catholic hierarchy to obfuscate, silence, and otherwise undermine women's theological production represents an unfortunate companion piece to women's long theological trajectory.

One need only look at the absence of women's voices in the theological canon of saints to know that in the Roman Catholic Church, women have not been considered reliable witnesses to their own lives, or faith, or the faith of the Church that they love. Feminist theology has grown in response to women's desire to claim theological truth as their property (90).

Crucially, there was a notable change in Church teaching on gender and equality in the late twentieth century. The results of this change, however, are not easily negotiated. Undoubtedly, the Church moved to endorse the full equality of women in society and in the domestic sphere.[6] At the same time, it also endorsed a form of gender essentialism that endowed women with a "special nature" that was complementary to, but different from, that of men. This "special nature" is intimately connected with the family for women in CST. The emphasis of CST on women's primary vocation in the family disenfranchises men from fatherhood while simultaneously disenfranchising women from their full personhood. Representative examples may help to illustrate the changing patterns in CST and the increasing recognition of women's rights. In *Pacem in Terris* John XXIII (1963) wrote:

> The part that women are now playing in political life is everywhere evident ... women are gaining an increasing awareness of their natural dignity. Far from being content with a purely passive role or allowing themselves to be regarded as a kind of instrument, they are demanding both in domestic and in public life the rights and duties which belong to them as human persons (41).

In *Laborem Exercens* (1981a) Pope John Paul II observed:

> It is a fact that in many societies women work in nearly every sector of life. But it is fitting that they should be able to fulfil their tasks in accordance with their own nature, without being discriminated against and without being excluded from jobs for which they are capable, but also without lack of respect for their family aspirations and for their specific role in contributing, together with men, to the good of society (19).

In *Mulieris Dignitatem* John Paul II (1981b) further maintained:

> A woman's dignity is closely connected with the love which she re-
> ceives by the very reason of her femininity. . . . The moral and spiri-
> tual strength of a woman is joined to her awareness that God
> entrusts the human being to her in a special way. Of course, God
> entrusts every human being to each and every other human being.
> But this entrusting concerns women in a special way—precisely by
> reason of their femininity—and this in a particular way determines
> their vocation. . . . In our own time, the successes of science and
> technology make it possible to attain material well-being to a de-
> gree hitherto unknown. While this favours some, it pushes others to
> the edges of society. In this way, unilateral progress can also lead to
> a gradual loss of sensitivity for man, that is, for what is essentially
> human. In this sense, our time in particular awaits the manifestation
> of that "genius" which belongs to women, and which can ensure
> sensitivity for human beings in every circumstance: because they are
> human (30).

Ecclesiastical commentaries on women concentrate on women's
equality, with discrimination against women being strongly condemned.
Gaudium et Spes (Vatican Council II 1965), for example, clearly affirms
that women possess fundamental human rights:

> With respect to the fundamental rights of the person, every type of
> discrimination, whether social or cultural, whether based on sex,
> race, colour, social condition, language, or religion, is to be overcome
> and eradicated as contrary to God's intent. For in truth it must still
> be regretted that fundamental personal rights are not yet being uni-
> versally honoured. Such is the case of a woman who is denied the
> right and freedom to choose a husband, to embrace a state of life, or
> to acquire an education or cultural benefits equal to those recog-
> nized for men (29).

When dealing with the issue of women's work outside domestic roles, the
pastoral constitution later explains that "at present women are involved
in nearly all spheres of life: they ought to be permitted to play their part

fully in ways suited to their nature" (Vatican Council II 1965, 60). Here we see a limited articulation of social justice permeated with a decidedly androcentric bias: CST contends that the fundamental rights of women are interpreted in accord with women's "own nature." In *Laborem Exercens* Pope John Paul II (1981a) reinforced this point by claiming that "the true advancement of women requires that labour be structured in a way that women do not have to pay for their advancement by abandoning what is specific to them and at the expense of the family, in which women as mothers have an irreplaceable role." (19). This example again highlights that CST reduces women's embodiment to her biological structure, that is, her "nature," as it is dictated by men. As a result, the concrete circumstances in which women live—their oppression, their deprivation, their specific struggles, and the discriminative practices against them—are neither described, condemned, nor even lamented.

A letter by the Congregation for the Doctrine of the Faith (CDF, 2004) titled *On the Collaboration of Men and Women in the Church and in the World* also reflects the Church's position on gender binarity and what is at stake in terms of the demands of gender justice. Although long, it is worth quoting at length to frame the task at hand:

> Recent years have seen new approaches to women's issues. A first tendency is to emphasize strongly conditions of subordination in order to give rise to antagonism: women, in order to be themselves, must make themselves the adversaries of men. Faced with the abuse of power, the answer for women is to seek power. This process leads to opposition between men and women, in which the identity and role of one are emphasized to the disadvantage of the other, leading to harmful confusion regarding the human person, which has its most immediate and lethal effects in the structure of the family. A second tendency emerges in the wake of the first. In order to avoid the domination of one sex or the other, their differences tend to be denied, viewed as mere effects of historical and cultural conditioning. In this perspective, physical difference, termed sex, is minimized, while the purely cultural element, termed gender, is emphasized to the maximum and held to be primary. The obscuring of the difference or duality of the sexes has enormous consequences on a variety of levels. This theory of the human person, intended to promote

prospects for equality of women through liberation from biological determinism, has in reality inspired ideologies which, for example, call into question the family, in its natural two-parent structure of mother and father, and make homosexuality and heterosexuality virtually equivalent, in a new model of polymorphous sexuality.... According to this perspective, human nature in itself does not possess characteristics in an absolute manner: all persons can and ought to constitute themselves as they like, since they are free from every predetermination linked to their essential constitution. This perspective ...strengthens the idea that the liberation of women entails criticism of Sacred Scripture, which would be seen as handing on a patriarchal conception of God nourished by an essentially male-dominated culture. Second, this tendency would consider as lacking in importance and relevance the fact that the Son of God assumed human nature in its male form (2–3).

In this letter gender is appropriated almost entirely negatively: it is associated with competition and struggle, resulting in the destruction of the family structure, and is irremediably linked to biological sex (Schaab 2001, 342). This prevailing emphasis again depreciates the complexity of norms relative to women's experiences (Schaab 2001). Moreover, the normative assumption that sex and gender are binary has led to a hierarchical endorsement of gender complementarity. In short, CST holds that men and women are equal but different.[7] This understanding of the human person as ontologically and theologically either male or female has profound consequences for theological anthropology, sexual ethics, and human development, particularly from a justice perspective. And, this interpretation of sexual difference has consistently reinforced the inferiority of women and afforded predominantly heterosexual white men a place of uninterrogated privilege. It is, in fact, hard to escape androcentric bias in CST.

More recent pronouncements have continued to retain a strong emphasis on gender binarity, but there has also been a move to explicitly acknowledge the equal dignity of women. In *Evangelli Gaudium* (2013), his apostolic exhortation on the proclamation of the Gospel in today's world, Pope Francis says that he has always been

distressed at the lot of those who are victims of human trafficking. . . . Doubly poor are those women who endure situations of exclusion, mistreatment, and violence, since they are frequently less
able to defend their rights. Even so, we constantly witness among
them impressive examples of daily heroism in defending and protecting their vulnerable families. . . . It is not "progressive" to try to
resolve problems by eliminating a human life. On the other hand, it
is also true that we have done little to adequately accompany women
in very difficult situations, where abortion appears as a quick solution to their profound anguish (211–14).

It is certainly positive that Pope Francis mentions human trafficking and
the plight of women, albeit briefly. However, it may be argued that gender
expectations also permeate this extract, with women being immediately
associated with the family and, shortly after, with abortion. This analysis
appears to be in line with previous exhortations and proclamations on
women whereby CST reverts to gender expectations in its social analysis,
thereby relegating women to the family and, ultimately, sees their lives in
terms of their biology. In this instance, Pope Francis moves from briefly
mentioning human trafficking to women and the family and to abortion.
He also fails to note that these are complex realities in the lives of *both*
women and men. In the more recent *Amoris Laetitia* (Francis 2016) we
read: "If certain forms of feminism have arisen which we must consider inadequate, we must nonetheless see in the women's movement the
working of the Spirit for a clearer recognition of the dignity and rights
of women" (54). *Fratelli Tutti* (Francis 2020), more helpfully, explicitly
comments on the insufficiently universal human rights of women: "The
organisation of societies worldwide is still far from reflecting clearly that
women possess the same dignity and identical rights as men. We say one
thing with words, but our decisions and reality tell another story" (23).

In his analysis of women in CST, Donal Dorr explains that a significant result of such a one-dimensional understanding of women "is that
CST does not give as much prominence as it should to certain key areas
of exploitation of women, such as the extraordinary increase in pornog-
raphy, especially through the internet, and the trafficking of women for
sexual exploitation" (Dorr 2012, 461). To extend this point: except for

procreation and the family, CST is bereft of any sustained analysis of the historical, social, and cultural realities that face women in society today. For example, issues around bodily autonomy, health justice, domestic violence, human trafficking, maternal mortality rates, educational deprivation, female genital mutilation, HIV/AIDS, and the systemic causes of women's inequality, oppression, and subordination remain either absent from CST or feature as ancillary themes (Beattie 2015). Furthermore, it seems reasonable to suggest that women ought to appropriate the discourse about their own lives and bodies, and yet the Catholic tradition and its social teachings seem to continue to insist upon according women roles that are suitable to their "nature." What must be negotiated now is the ambivalent inheritance the Catholic tradition leaves in its wake: it professes the human dignity of all people, but the social encyclicals, pastoral constitutions, and apostolic exhortations essentially render issues of justice for women invisible. There is an opportunity for the Catholic tradition, and its social teachings in particular, to compensate for this radical inequality by engaging with the CA.

THE CA AND GENDER JUSTICE: THE CENTRAL CAPABILITIES

A significant advantage of the CA is its focus on what people are able to do and to be. By focusing on this, the approach foregrounds and addresses inequalities that women suffer: "inequalities in resources and opportunities, educational deprivations, the failure of work to be recognised as work, and insults to bodily integrity" (Nussbaum 2001, 39). In short, the CA provides distinctive insight for ethical analyses of gender discrimination because it recognizes that all persons should have an equality of basic opportunity. This fundamental aspect of the approach works to conceptualize, confront, and respond to discrimination and persistent inequality (Nussbaum 2011). Moreover, there is a strong ethical component of the CA that mandates confrontation of discrimination in all aspects of life. As Nussbaum explains of her account of the CA:

> The capabilities approach is a powerful tool in crafting an adequate account of social justice. But the bare idea of capabilities as a space within which comparisons are made and inequalities assessed is

insufficient. To get a vision of social justice that will have the requisite critical force and definiteness to direct social policy, we need to have an account, for political purposes, of what the central human capabilities are, even if we know that this account will always be contested and remade. Women all over the world are making critical proposals in public discussion, proposals that embody their radical demand for lives with full human dignity. While we await the day when the world as a whole accepts such ideas, the capabilities list is one way of giving theoretical shape to women's definite, and justified, demands. (Nussbaum 2001, 56)

Nussbaum's methodology is explicitly committed to involving women, especially those who are marginalized, in the process of defining capabilities essential to their own lives (Nussbaum 2011). She constructs her list of capabilities as a "normative conception of social justice, with critical potential for gender issues" (Nussbaum 2001, 35). This is only the case, she points out, if a set of definite capabilities is specified (Nussbaum 2001). In other words, she develops her theory with women's capabilities and equality prominently in view.

TEN CENTRAL CAPABILITIES

"All over the world, people struggle to live lives that are worthy of human dignity, with women, in particular, lacking the essential support and opportunities to lead fully human lives" (Nussbaum 2000a, 222). Therefore, women's full empowerment, economic and otherwise, remains a distant goal. And, as Nussbaum (2000a) puts it, "This lack of support is frequently caused by them being women" (222). Fundamental capabilities, such as being well nourished, well educated, and healthy, evade women. Women have fewer opportunities than men. They are less well nourished, less healthy, and more vulnerable, particularly to sexual abuse and physical violence, and less likely to receive education or have political opportunities:

In many nations, women are not full equals under the law, they do not have the same property rights as men, the same rights to make a contract, the same rights of association, mobility, and religious liberty . . . women have fewer opportunities than men to live free from fear and to enjoy rewarding types of love—especially when, as often, they are married without choice in childhood and have no recourse from a bad marriage. In all these ways, unequal social and political circumstances give women unequal human capabilities. (Nussbaum 2000a, 220)

According to Nussbaum, a life with or without dignity is easily identifiable. She therefore generates her list of central capabilities by asking, "Which things are so important that we will not count a life as a human life without them?" (Nussbaum 2000a, 74). Her central capabilities signify both the freedoms and the opportunities to lead a life that one has reason to value. In her view, each capability is required for one to be capable of a truly human life. In other words, a life without any one of the capabilities on her list would not be recognizably dignified. It is worth relaying the list in her own words:

1. **Life.** Being able to live to the end of a human life of normal length; not dying prematurely, or before one's life is so reduced as to be not worth living.
2. **Bodily Health.** Being able to have good health, including reproductive health; to be adequately nourished; to have adequate shelter.
3. **Bodily Integrity.** Being able to move freely from place to place; having one's bodily boundaries treated as sovereign, that is, being able to secure against assault, child sexual abuse, and domestic violence; having opportunities for sexual satisfaction and for choice in matters of reproduction.
4. **Senses, Imagination, and Thought.** Being able to use the senses, to imagine, think and reason—and to do these things in a "truly human" way, a way informed and cultivated by an adequate education, including, but by no means limited to, literacy and basic mathematical and scientific training. Being able to use imagination and thought in connection with experiencing and producing self-expressive works and events of one's own choice, religious, literary, musical, and so forth. Being able to use one's

mind in ways protected by guarantees of freedom of expression with respect to both political and artistic speech, and freedom of religious exercise. Being able to search for the ultimate meaning of life in one's own way. Being able to have pleasurable experiences, and to avoid non-necessary pain.

5. **Emotions.** Being able to have attachments to things and people outside ourselves; to love those who love and care for us, to grieve at their absence; in general, to love, to grieve, to experience longing, gratitude, and justified anger. Not having one's emotional development blighted by overwhelming fear and anxiety, or by traumatic events of abuse or neglect. (Supporting this capability means supporting forms of human association that can be shown to be crucial in their development.)

6. **Practical Reason.** Being able to form a conception of the good and to engage in critical reflection about the planning of one's life. (This entails protection for the liberty of conscience.)

7. **Affiliation. A.** Being able to live with and toward others, to recognize and show concern for other human beings, to engage in various forms of social interaction; to be able to imagine the situation of another and to have compassion for that situation; to have the capability for both justice and friendship. (Protecting this capability means protecting institutions that constitute and nourish such forms of affiliation, and also protecting the freedom of assembly and political speech.) **B.** Having the social bases of self-respect and non-humiliation; being able to be treated as a dignified being whose worth is equal to that of others. This entails, at a minimum, protections against discrimination on the basis of race, sex, sexual orientation, religion, caste, ethnicity, or national origin. In work, being able to work as a human being, exercising practical reason and entering into meaningful relationships of mutual recognition with other workers.

8. **Other Species.** Being able to live with concern for and in relation to animals, plants, and the world of nature.

9. **Play.** Being able to laugh, to play, to enjoy recreational activities.

10. **Control over One's Environment. A. Political**. Being able to participate effectively in political choices that govern one's life; having the right of political participation, protections of

free speech and association. **B. Material**. Being able to hold property (both land and movable goods), not just formally but in terms of real opportunity; and having property rights on an equal basis with others; having the freedom from unwarranted search and seizure. (Nussbaum 2011, 33–34)

This list, Nussbaum tells us, functions as a focus for comparative quality-of-life assessment and for the formulation of political principles (Nussbaum 2001, 40). All ten capabilities constitute dimensions of life that are recognized in all cultures across the world. Of course, how people experience these realities of embodiment, in their concrete circumstances of life, will inevitably differ from culture to culture or even within one particular society (Nussbaum 2000). It is, however, reasonable to suggest that people share commonality in certain human experiences.

Of note, the capabilities of affiliation and practical reason are of special importance in Nussbaum's list (Nussbaum 2000a, 2000b). Nussbaum is therefore concerned with the realities of how the capability of affiliation, in particular, is manifested for women. Commenting on how issues of gender present themselves, Nussbaum explains that women have long been associated with traditional roles involving their families, especially the rearing of their children and the care for their homes and husbands (Nussbaum 2000, 242). She further explains that these roles have been associated with some important moral virtues, such as "altruistic concern, responsiveness to the needs of others, and a willingness to sacrifice one's own interests for those of others" (Nussbaum 2000, 242). Given her special endorsement of a variety of forms of affiliation, Nussbaum is keen to "confront the questions posed by the presence of the family, and the roles that it constructs for women" (Nussbaum 2000, 244). Her central concerns in this endeavor are the human capabilities that are at stake in the family structure. As Nussbaum puts it: "It would be difficult to deny that the family has been a, if not the, major site of the oppression of women. Love and care do exist in families. So too do domestic violence, marital rape, child sexual abuse, undernutrition of girls, unequal health care, unequal educational opportunities, and countless more intangible violations of dignity and equal personhood" (Nussbaum 2000, 242). A brief example may help to illustrate how Nussbaum's CA engages gender issues.

Gender-based violence against women and girls is a global pandemic that affects one in three women in their lifetimes. According to the World Bank, 35 percent of women worldwide have experienced physical and/or sexual violence from an intimate partner or non-partner. Globally, 7 percent of women have been sexually assaulted by someone other than a partner, 200 million women have experienced female genital mutilation/cutting, and 38 percent of murders of women have been committed by intimate partners. By September 2020, 52 countries had integrated prevention of and response to violence against women and girls into COVID-19 response plans, and 121 countries had adopted measures to strengthen services for women survivors of violence during the global crisis (UNDP 2020).

These sobering statistics confirm that the configuration of embodiment, gender, and power cannot be abstracted from the reality of violence, often familial. What this means experientially for those who suffer it is difficult to fully comprehend and is further compounded by significant social and economic costs. Domestic violence is especially pernicious given that "it occurs in a space that is also central to the development of human capabilities—the family" (Agarwal and Panda 2007, 362). Nussbaum, therefore, "reads the signs of the times," to borrow the language of *Gaudium et Spes* (Vatican Council II 1965), and draws attention to this reality of women's experience. Violence demonstrates how comprehensively a person's capabilities can be diminished and denied. In fact, it interferes with every capability on Nussbaum's list (Nussbaum 2011, 2005, 2000a). Throughout the world, Nussbaum says:

> Women's bodies are vulnerable to a range of violent assaults that include domestic violence, rape within marriage, rape by acquaintances or dates, rape by strangers, rape in wars and communal conflicts, honour killing, trafficking and forced prostitution, child sexual abuse, female infanticide, female genital mutilation, and sex-selective abortion. Other practices that are not as obviously violent also contribute to the atmosphere of threat in which all women live the entirety of their lives: sexual harassment, stalking, threats of violence, deprivation of bodily liberty, the under nutrition of girls. (Nussbaum 2005, 167)

These forms of violence have an extensive impact on women's capabilities. Furthermore, it is generally agreed that there is a clear link between violence and violation of rights. Taking each capability in turn, Nussbaum illustrates the toll that various forms of violence—and the threat of violence—take on a woman's life (Nussbaum 2005).[8] Women often lose their lives through violence, particularly sexual violence. Bodily health and bodily integrity are also profoundly impacted by violence. When the capability of bodily health is diminished, the capability of bodily integrity is also automatically annulled. Violence has cumulative devastating effects on the agency of women. The fear of violence inevitably and radically impacts the senses, imagination, and thought by curtailing women's experiences of the pleasurable things in life. Indeed, Nussbaum (2005) effectively highlights the fact that the impact that violence has on the emotions is devastating: fear can cripple a life. Violence and the threat of it affects independence, limits the capability of affiliation, and inevitably affects the ability to have meaningful relationships and to enjoy leisure time, laughter, and play. Finally, the last capability, control over one's environment, is radically affected by violence or the threat of it. In certain nations, for example, a woman's ability to participate in politics, to seek employment, and to enjoy a successful work life is prohibited by law if she has no male guardian (Nussbaum 2005). The threat of violence maintains this state of affairs. And, as Nussbaum points out, "Even where women enjoy legal equality, threats of violence, sexual harassment, and actual violence often impede them from effective participation" (Nussbaum 2005, 173).

Looking at the example of violence through the lens of Nussbaum's list demonstrates how a person's capabilities can be radically diminished. It seems obvious that freedom from violence should be central to any discussion of a person's well-being, development, and quality of life (Agarwal and Panda 2007). Indeed, given that violence is an undeniable reality of the human condition, it demands investigation in any discourse that aims to discern and improve human well-being. It may also be suggested that a discussion of women's embodiment would invariably recognize the multifaceted nature of embodiment. Often, however, as Bina Agarwal and Pradeep Panda note, "It is the obvious that is most neglected" (Agarwal and Panda 2007, 383).

A sense of inherent worth and dignity grounds Nussbaum's CA. Key to the central capabilities, then, is the notion of combined capabilities. In other words, people ought to actually be able to function in society; its structures and institutional environment must be conducive to genuine choice. Nussbaum's CA, as an evaluative framework and a partial theory of justice, provides an important basis for thinking about the goals of development. Agency, freedom, and well-being are particularly important goals for women, who have long been marginalized and characterized as passive dependents. Consequently, Nussbaum's commitment to substance is hugely beneficial for CST. It provides fresh insight into, and respect for, the dignity of the person. Nussbaum's partial account of social justice causes her to name the capabilities that every person needs to live a full and dignified life. She highlights that any conception of authentic human development must correspond to the true realities facing women. Conceptually, therefore, the CA is well placed to diagnose, analyze, and engage with the reality of oppression and deprivation, especially for women.

AN INTEGRATED APPROACH

Similarities abound between CST and the CA in terms of human development and social justice. Both take a universalist standpoint on values, and both take embodiment as the basis for defining human values and obligations. Shared foundations, such as the inviolable dignity of the human person and emphatic concern for those living impoverished lives, illustrate that these quite different perspectives share a similar starting point. Of fundamental importance, too, is the creation of conditions for people to live fully human lives. In this regard, contemporary CST has consistently highlighted the complexities of human development, most notably from John XXIII's pontificate onward. In *Pacem in Terris*, for example, John XXIII emphasizes the importance of choice in life: "Man has the right to live. He has the right to bodily integrity and to the means necessary for the proper development of life, particularly food, clothing, shelter, medical care, rest, and, finally, the necessary social services. . . . Human beings have also the right to choose for themselves the kind of life which appeals to them" (John XXIII 1963, 11).

Anticipating a key element of the capabilities discourse, opportunity of choice, *Gaudium et Spes* also highlights the complexities that permeate human development discourse: "While an immense number of people still lack the absolute necessities of life, some, even in less advanced areas, live in luxury or squander wealth. Extravagance and wretchedness exist side by side. While a few enjoy very great power of choice, the majority are deprived of almost all possibility of acting on their own initiative and responsibility, and often subsist in living and working conditions unworthy of the human person" (Vatican Council II 1965, 63).

More recently, in his exhortation *Evangelii Gaudium* Pope Francis again echoes the language of the CA when he says that "the culture of prosperity deadens us; we are thrilled if the market offers us something new to purchase; and in the meantime, all those lives stunted for lack of opportunity seem a mere spectacle" (Francis 2013, 54). Again, the importance of opportunities for choice in life is evident. In his discussion of the social dimensions of global change in *Laudato Si'* (2015) Francis also provides a commentary on the nature of development: "The human environment and the natural environment deteriorate together; we cannot adequately combat environmental degradation unless we attend to causes related to human and social degradation. In fact, the deterioration of the environment and of society affects the most vulnerable on the planet" (48). And yet Francis fails to offer any gender analysis of how climate change disproportionately affects women.

Despite its many notable insights in terms of human development, it is unfortunate that CST is woefully deficient in its lack of gender awareness and inclusivity. Even at a semantic level, CST fails to be inclusive. The repeated use of "man's integral development" in official documents from the Catholic Church cannot be dismissed as a product of its time, though in *Laudato Si'* and *Fratelli Tutti* Francis has adopted more inclusive language. Androcentric language inevitably renders women invisible and ensures an incomplete discourse on human development. Consequently, to have theological legitimacy, and to contribute to wider public debate, there is an urgent need for CST to embrace an inclusive theological anthropology. The CA affords CST this opportunity.

The CA highlights that discrimination on the basis of gender reinforces the notion that some people are not fully equal (Nussbaum 2011, 149). Conceptually, therefore, the CA is well placed to diagnose deprivation and to analyze and engage in public debate: it reframes moral imperatives and asks what is fundamentally at stake if a person's freedom is radically limited. The CA offers a more detailed picture of the constraining conditions that impact what people view as possible in their lives. Thus, supplementing CST with the substantive language of capabilities allows CST an opportunity to address deprivation, impoverishment, and gender discrimination in comprehensive ways. The CA demonstrates clearly that issues of justice affecting women must be understood in the concrete circumstances in which women live and in light of the overarching issues within patriarchal society. Crucially, the CA's focus on agency and well-being, and its principle of "each person as an end," holds particular value for assessing gender discrimination. An integrated approach to authentic development, infused with capability-based social analysis, the preferential option for the poor, solidarity, and distributive justice, would offer a more inclusive and comprehensive methodology for confronting justice issues. In sum, the CA can give more specification to the complexities that constitute human life and well-being in theological discourse.

CONCLUSION

The prevailing emphasis of CST remains characterized by power and androcentrism. While this is not surprising, given that the teachings of the Catholic tradition predominantly reflect a centralized "top-down" ecclesial practice, it is harmful for its human development discourse. Indeed, there is a need to overcome the tension in CST and how it envisions development. This is particularly problematic when it is formulated almost exclusively by men and remains rather general in its proposals. As an evaluative framework that has practical value, the CA can animate CST's mandate to act justly. It can also ensure that CST's depiction of integral human development can extend beyond a disproportionate emphasis on the family for women. In a time of radical deprivation, when 1.3 billion people are living in multi-dimensional poverty and are unable to live lives worthy of their human dignity, it is imperative that CST respond in an inclusive, credible, and pragmatic way (OPHI 2021). Incorporating the CA into theological discourse on development sheds much-needed light on the struggles women and girls face in their quest for equality in all aspects of life.

NOTES

1. This is not surprising given that CST's official discourse on women has been written predominantly, if not exclusively, by men.

2. See, for example, Tenai 2016, Schulz 2016, Deneulin 2021, Deneulin and Zampini-Davies 2020, 2016.

3. Some capabilities scholars argue that the CA is subject to much misunderstanding. By way of clarification, Ingrid Robeyns suggests that "there is one capability approach and there are many capabilities theories, and keeping that distinction sharply in mind should clear-up many misunderstandings in the literature" (Robeyns 2017, 300). It follows, for some capabilitarians, that Nussbaum's capabilities theory is best understood as a development of Amartya Sen's CA, not as an independent approach in its own right. This work acknowledges that such disagreement exists around the classification of Nussbaum's CA. However, it understands her CA as a partial theory of social justice. This is not to depreciate the importance of Sen's work; it is simply to highlight the importance of Nussbaum's method, particularly in terms of a fuller theory of justice for women: "My own version of this approach (which began independently of Sen's work through thinking about Aristotle's ideas of human functioning and Marx's use of them) is in several ways different from Sen's, both in its emphasis on the philosophical underpinnings of the approach and its readiness to take a stand on what the central capabilities are. Sen has focused on the role of capabilities in demarcating the space within which quality of life assessments are made; I use the idea in a more exigent way, as a foundation for basic political principles that should underwrite constitutional guarantees" (Nussbaum 2000a, 71).

4. It is important to note that this is not unique to the Catholic tradition. Kathryn Marshall and colleagues remind us that many religions and religious communities are inherently patriarchal and discriminate against women. Many traditions, they tell us, deny women leadership positions in their organizations, and women are often prevented from gaining access to clerical roles or pursuing education that allows them to interpret their religious traditions with authority (Marshall et al., 2011, 12–13).

5. It is inevitable that the parameters of this chapter do not allow for a systematic exposition of CST and its implications for women, so we must limit our analysis to representative examples.

6. *Pacem in Terris* (John XXIII 1963), for example, was the first encyclical to mention the issue of women's rights and the role that women play in economic and political life.

7. Of note, this approach embodies the failed "separate but equal" logic that led to racial segregation in the United States.

8. The following is a brief summary of Nussbaum's argument. For a more detailed discussion, see Nussbaum 2000a, 171–73, 2000b).

WORKS CITED

Agarwal, Bina, and Pradeep Panda. 2007. "Toward Freedom from Domestic Violence: The Neglected Obvious." *Journal of Human Development* 8: 359–88.

Beattie, Tina. 2015. "Dignity Beyond Rights: Human Development in the Context of the Capabilities Approach and Catholic Social Teaching." *Australian eJournal of Theology* 22: 273–95.

Congregation for the Doctrine of the Faith (CDF). 2004. *Letter to the Bishops of the Catholic Church on the Collaboration of Men and Women in the Church and in the World.* https://www.vatican.va/roman_curia/congregations /cfaith/documents/rc_con_cfaith_doc_20040731_collaboration_en.html.

Deneulin, Séverine. 2021. *Human Development and the Catholic Social Tradition: Towards an Integral Ecology.* Abingdon, UK: Routledge.

Deneulin, Séverine, Mathias Nebel, and Nicholas Sagovsky, eds. 2006. *Transforming Unjust Structures: The Capability Approach.* Dordrecht: Springer.

Deneulin, Séverine, and Augusto Zampini-Davies. 2016. "Theology and Development as Capability Expansion." *Theological Studies* 72, no. 4: 1–9.

———. 2020. "Religion and the Capability Approach." In *The Cambridge Handbook of the Capability Approach*, edited by Siddiq Osmani, Mozaffar Qizilbash, and Enrica Chiappero-Martinetti. Cambridge: Cambridge University Press, 686–705.

Dorr, Donal. 2012. Option for the Poor and for the Earth: Catholic Social Teaching. Mayknoll, NY: Orbis.

Francis. 2013. *Evangelii Gaudium (EG): The Joy of the Gospel.* Papal exhortation. https://www.vatican.va/content/francesco/en/apost_exhortations /documents/papa-francesco_esortazione-ap_20131124_evangelii-gaudium .html.

———. 2015. *Laudato Si' (LS): On the Care for Our Common Home.* Encyclical. https://www.vatican.va/content/francesco/en/encyclicals/documents /papa-francesco_20150524_enciclica-laudato-si.html.

———. 2016. *Amoris Laetitia (AL): On Love in the Family.* Papal exhortation. https://www.vatican.va/content/dam/francesco/pdf/apost_exhortations

/documents/papa-francesco_esortazione-ap_20160319_amoris-laetitia
_en.pdf.

———. 2020. *Fratelli Tutti (FT)*: *On Fraternity and Social Friendship*. Encyclical. https://www.vatican.va/content/francesco/en/encyclicals/documents
/papa-francesco_20201003_enciclica-fratelli-tutti.html.

Hicks, Douglas A. 2002. "Gender, Discrimination, and Capability: Insights
from Amartya Sen." *Journal of Religious Ethics* 30: 137–54.

Imperatori-Lee, Natalia. 2015. "Father Knows Best: Theological 'Mansplaining' and the Ecclesial War on Women." *Journal of Feminist Studies in Religion* 31: 89–107.

John XXIII. 1963. *Pacem in Terris (PT)*: *On Establishing Universal Peace in Truth,
Justice, Charity, and Liberty*. Encyclical. https://www.vatican.va/content/john
-xxiii/en/encyclicals/documents/hf_j-xxiii_enc_11041963_pacem.html.

John Paul II. 1981a. *Laborem Exercens: On Human Work*. Encyclical. https://
www.vatican.va/content/john-paul-ii/en/encyclicals/documents/hf_jp-ii
_enc_14091981_laborem-exercens.html.

———. 1981b. *Mulieris Dignitatem: On the Dignity and Vocation of Women*.
https://www.vatican.va/content/john-paul-ii/en/apost_letters/1988
/documents/hf_jp-ii_apl_19880815_mulieris-dignitatem.html.

Lawler, Michael G., and Todd Salzman. 2001. "Human Experience and
Catholic Moral Theology." *Irish Theological Quarterly* 76: 35–56.

Marshall, Katherine, Susan Hayward, Claudia Zambra, and Esther Breger.
2011. *Women in Religious Peacebuilding*. Berkeley, CA: Georgetown.

Nussbaum, Martha. 2000a. *Women and Human Development: The Capabilities
Approach*. Cambridge: Cambridge University Press.

———. 2000b. "Women's Capabilities and Social Justice." *Journal of Human
Development and Capabilities* 1: 219–47.

———. 2001. "Capabilities as Fundamental Entitlements: Sen and Social Justice." *Feminist Economics* 9: 33–59.

———. 2005. "Women's Bodies: Violence, Security, Capabilities." *Journal of
Human Development* 6: 167–83.

———. 2011. *Creating Capabilities: The Human Development Approach*. Cambridge, MA: Belknap.

Oxford Poverty and Human Development Initiative (OPHI). 2021. *Global
MPI 2021*. https://ophi.org.uk/multidimensional-poverty-index/global
-mpi-2021/.

Paul VI. 1967. *Populorum Progressio*. Encyclical. https://www.vatican.va
/content/paul-vi/en/encyclicals/documents/hf_p-vi_enc_26031967
_populorum.html.

Rahner, Karl. 1972. *Theological Investigations IX*. London: Darton, Longman, and Todd.

Robeyns, Ingrid. 2017. *Wellbeing, Freedom and Social Justice: The Capability Approach Re–Examined*. Cambridge: Open Book.

Schaab, Gloria L. 2001. "Feminist Theological Methodology: Toward a Kaleidoscopic Model." *Theological Studies* 62: 34–65.

Schulz, Joshua. 2016. "The Capabilities Approach and Catholic Social Teaching: An Engagement." *Journal of Global Ethics* 12.1: 29–47.

Tenai, Noah K. 2016. "Is Poverty a Matter of Perspective? Significance of Amartya Sen for the Church's Response to Poverty: A Public Practical Theological Reflection." *Theological Studies* 72, no. 2: 1–10.

United Nations Development Programme (UNDP). 2020. COVID-19 Global Gender Response Tracker. https://undp.org/publications/covid-19-global-gender-response-tracker.

Vatican Council II. 1965. *Gaudium et Spes: Pastoral Constitution on the Church in the Modern World*. https://www.vatican.va/archive/hist_councils/ii_vatican_council/documents/vat-ii_const_19651207_gaudium-et-spes_en.html.

SIX

Integral Ecology

Autonomy, the Common Inheritance of the Earth, and Creation Theology

Cathriona Russell

ABSTRACT

Autonomy implies that morality is not conformity with the norms of society or found in the teleological structure of nature but is rooted in a first-person perspective that acknowledges our likeness to one another as the very condition of our being moral agents. In this chapter I begin from that perspective and examine themes from two domains—political philosophy and creation theology—that provide potential interpretative categories for "integral ecology" at the intersection of teachings of the Catholic social tradition (CST) and the capability approach (CA) associated with Amartya Sen. First I revisit the concept of the common inheritance of the earth as it has been defined and applied in relation to co-operation on common

*resources since the eighteenth century, and in its ongoing applica-
tion in the CST and its related influence on the CA. Second I argue
for an approach to creation theology in environmental theology and
ethics that does not overplay "order" in creation or "holism" in ethics
and acknowledges the reflexive capacities in human societies to build
upon and revise the terms on which they coexist and interact with
one another in a finite world.*

INTRODUCTION

I write this chapter from the perspective of the autonomy approach
in Christian ethics (cf. Mieth 1982; Junker-Kenny 2019). Eberhard
Schockenhoff has described this approach as a "legitimate continuation
of the natural law approach in the circumstances created by the modern consciousness of freedom," or indeed as a "late representative of the
classical Catholic natural law ethics" (Schockenhoff 2003, 2). However,
the emphasis on freedom, from which this position takes its starting
point, offers related but distinct interpretative categories for expressing
the theological message of salvation in Christian ethics. What are considered to be specifically Christian in this position are the intensifying, motivational, heuristic, integrating, and relativizing dimensions of a
Christian faith background rather than the "content" of ethical obligations (Mieth 1982).

After first introducing the autonomy perspective in Christian ethics,
I will investigate two themes from very different domains, one from political philosophy and the other from creation theology. My intention
is to explore what might belong to this emerging concept of "integral
ecology" in the Catholic tradition (CST). From political ethics I will
characterize the question of the common possession of the earth—
understood in the CST in terms of the concept of "the universal destination of goods"—first from the perspective of classical natural law and
then from an autonomy perspective.[1] The idea of the common possession
of the earth has been foundational for international co-operation on
common resources since the eighteenth century. It has also played a role
in the debates about not-yet-appropriated common areas in our world:
the ocean floor, the moon, outer space, and more recently, the proximal

sky (Russell 2021). This analysis also operates as an example of the difference that an emphasis on autonomy rather than classical natural law can make for theorizing distributive justice internationally and for the dialogue between the CST and Amartya Sen's capability approach (CA) to development.

Second I will examine how coherently creation theology has been interpreted in the many emerging theologies of nature and deployed in environmental ethics as justification for action. The thought, for example, that creation is good and destined for salvation, and that "creatureliness" is an abiding aspect of human anthropology, should convey more than that we should engage in environmental conservation and preservation for utilitarian reasons. Theological categories—stewardship, the autonomy of creation, contemplative approaches—all carry semantic and moral potential that cannot be simply reduced to questions of systems integrity. Finally, I will point to some implications of these background analyses for "integral ecology," a concept extensively incorporated into the encyclical *Laudato Si'* (*LS*; 2015), which is itself a text "now added to the body of the Church's social teaching" (*LS* 15).

AUTONOMY IN A CHRISTIAN CONTEXT

The autonomy position in Christian ethics differs from classical natural law in that the good is not based on a given nature but is a reflection of historical experience, a shift that it shares with revised natural law (Junker-Kenny 2019, 154ff). Also in common with revised natural law, the autonomy approach gives a greater role to human self-determination and thematizes a plurality in forms of the good life.[2] There is an assumption in the autonomy approach that a teleological ethics needs a deontological framework to prevent it from being co-opted by instrumentalist readings. Kant's categorical imperative, for this position in ethics, secures the individual from the violation of others and from violation in the name of the collective.

Too often autonomy in theological ethics circles is understood reductively as "atomistic individualism" or "unfettered choice," liberal in the polemical sense and subversive of community and shared commitment. It is perhaps no coincidence that a certain anti-individualism is loudly articulated in North American moral philosophy and theology where the cultural history of that society has led it to identify atomistic individualism as *the* danger to social coherence. In Europe, cultural history resists a different danger, that of totalitarianism. Lisa Sowle Cahill, an American moral theologian and advocate for the Catholic social doctrine of the common good (and in dialogue with the German theologian Dietmar Mieth) remarked on this difference and on "the importance of presenting a theory of the common good in a manner attractive to those whose cultural history posed totalitarianism as a greater social danger than the individualism that I as a North American theologian had been trained to battle" (Sowle Cahill 2001, 378).

The corrosive impact of atomism—the emphasis on personal choice and not responsibility, for example—is not inherent in Kant's account of autonomy, although many critics of Kant suggest that it is. As Heiner Bielefeldt argues, it is, ironically, quite the contrary in Kant. It "is our awareness of duty which opens the way to a profound understanding of human freedom and to a genuinely normative concept of rights" (Bielefeldt 1997, 527). Kant's *Kingdom of Ends* is a world in which "we first acknowledge our likeness to one another as the very condition of our being moral agents" (Mieth 1999, 7). It is inherently intersubjective and thereby social, identifying a constraint or limit on our actions in relation to others that we may not over-ride or control (Junker-Kenny 2005, 48).

In its Christian reconfiguration, this position shares much with revised natural law approaches, including the respect for self-legislation in morality, understood as conscience. As Bielefeldt notes, citing *Summa Theologiae* (II/I, qu. 19, art. 5, resp.), Thomas Aquinas also acknowledged that in a conflict between an external norm and an inner command of conscience, "the latter should prevail even in the case that the norm were right and the conscience erring" (Bielefeldt 1997, 528). Kant, Bielefeldt says, acknowledged that the categorical imperative—the criterion of moral self-legislation—is not new but only a new formula (ibid., 530). Nevertheless, Kant rejects the idea of "erring conscience" in natural law thinking since it "only half-heartedly acknowledges the significance of the inner will," will is more than the faculty of choice, it is "the faculty of binding oneself to self-given principles" (ibid., 529).

Kant also recognizes that "the moral will belongs to a finite human being who often fails to live up to her own self-legislated moral principles"

(Bielefeldt 1997, 529). And, famously, in the *Critique of Practical Reason* he argues that the moral law—exactly by "revealing both the unalienable moral vocation and the unavoidable frailty of the human being— . . . implicitly points to the idea of an absolute divine justice that on earth can never be achieved" (ibid.). Although his approach remains within the boundaries of the context of the late eighteenth century, Kant's moral philosophy lies behind many current discourses in political theory (ibid., 526). He developed a demanding and sophisticated concept of human freedom and a liberalism whose core is the dignity of every human person. At the same time, as Junker-Kenny points out, understanding ourselves as being made in the image of God may have parallels with the concept of human dignity established on purely philosophical grounds, but it is not exhausted by it. She adds that the "thought that we are made in the image of God should be both more disconcerting and more uplifting than being a religious parallel to insights which can be gained on secular grounds" (Junker-Kenny 2001, 81).

Finally, rather than being a past paradigm (now also long replaced in theological ethics by positions with more overtly Christian credentials), these distinctions between natural law approaches and Kant's understanding of autonomy still lie at the root of recent interpretations of and approaches to development and are significant for theorizing from an international standpoint in environmental ethics. In the next section I distinguish between a classical natural law approach on the idea of the common inheritance of the earth and that of Kant. This is directly relevant to the discussion of integral human development in the CST. The intention is not primarily to revisit the early modern debates but, as Jacob Huber puts it, to redevelop promising perspectives from which to theorize shared international problems.

THE COMMON INHERITANCE OF THE EARTH

The idea of the common possession of the earth[3] has its origins in the Christian natural law idea of God's common gift of the earth to humanity, given to satisfy human needs (or fundamental desires) (Pinheiro Walla 2016, 163). Huber argues that it received its most systematic development in the seventeenth century in the work of early modern thinkers, where it helped to explain why private property was to be understood as a social construct devised by human reason and not by divine plan, but nonetheless compatible with natural law (Huber 2016, 232). In the *Catechism of the Catholic Church* (1992) we find this idea presented in relation to the right to private property and the universal destination of the goods of the earth: "The right to private property, acquired or received in a just way, does not do away with the original gift of the earth to the whole of mankind. The universal destination of goods remains primordial, even if the promotion of the common good requires respect for the right to private property and its exercise" (2403). This approach to private property is understood as flexible enough to allow a "right of necessity" and the revival of the original-use right in cases of extreme need (Pinheiro Walla 2016, 164).

Hugo Grotius, the Dutch natural law jurist, employed this idea in his discussion of the property rights and state boundaries of his own time. He argued that these were "the result of an (idealized) historical process that saw the division of an initially common stock" (Huber 2016, 232). Nothing belongs to anyone in this original community, although "this initial, universal use-right is gradually transformed into a scheme of property rights and territorial boundaries" (ibid.). And, as Alice Pinheiro Walla writes, The "introduction of use-rights and ... property rights is a means of avoiding conflict and creating security" (Pinheiro Walla 2016, 164). Grotius appeals to God and His divine gift to secure this as part of the wider account of the evolution of society, arguing, according to Huber, that what happened is what ought to have happened. Meanwhile, "rights in property and territory retain a close connection to the original purpose of basic needs satisfaction" (Huber 2016, 233).

This original idea of common possession was not focused on how individuals relate to each other but on questions of "legitimate particularization" or the "conditions under which parts of the global common can be privatized and rights to rule ... allocated" (Huber 2016, 235). As Huber puts it, by prioritizing our "relationship to the planet as a whole," not how we relate to each other, Grotius—and, by implication, natural law approaches—reduce questions of global justice to those of legitimate distribution (ibid., 236).

Immanuel Kant, in *Perpetual Peace: A Philosophical Sketch*, takes a different approach, although it may not seem so at first glance (Huber

2016, 231–49). In *Perpetual Peace*, first published in 1795, Kant (2009) begins with the observation that since "the earth is a globe they [people] cannot disperse of an infinite area, but must necessarily tolerate one another's company. And no one originally has any greater right than anyone else to occupy any particular portion of the earth" (ibid., 29). Yet it is clear that he is focused elsewhere, on the interdependence in "relations that persist between agents" that act and coexist in finite space (Huber 2016, 237). The original common possession of the earth is not Kant's starting point but his conclusion, and it is used metaphorically "to illustrate the way in which embodied agents that jointly inhabit a bounded territory are united in an original community" (ibid., 238). He is less interested, therefore, in rightful entitlement and more interested in how people live together in a finite place, "constrained to occupy a portion of space on the earth." The common possession of the earth is understood by Kant as an "idea of reason" and not a "fictitious historical fact" (Pinheiro Walla 2016, 162).

Indeed, for Kant, "empirical facts about human nature are insufficient to generate obligations . . . in a way compatible with the freedom of all" (Pinheiro Walla 2016, 163). Consequently, he focuses on human freedom, where legal relations pertain between persons as being capable of obligation and as subjects of rights. He makes the exercise of freedom in a finite space the basis for rights, not the needs of individuals. And, in contrast to Grotius, Kant argues that it is the relationship between individuals that constitutes the human community (not God's gift to humanity) (ibid., 178). The community is an idea of reason, not a community that was instituted. The "peoples of the earth have thus entered in varying degrees into a universal community, and it has developed to the point where a violation of rights in one part is felt everywhere" (Kant 2009, 30). Only under this condition, he argues in that text, can we advance toward perpetual peace. Pope Francis, in *Fratelli Tutti* (*FT*, 2020), reflects this in his interpretation of the human family; to "be part of a people is to be part of a shared identity arising from social and cultural bonds. And that is not something automatic, but rather a slow and difficult process . . . advancing towards a common project" (*FT* 158).

Kant continues to inspire because of this early recognition of the interdependent nature of international politics and for providing an interdependent standpoint (Milstein 2010). The urgent demand for just transformative change that humanizes the transition to low-carbon and circular economies requires such theorizing. It is the reflexivity of agents that recognize this interdependence—not a carving up of resources to meet indeterminate needs—that will be the driver of change.[4] There are several parallels here with Amartya Sen's capability goals-rights approach, where freedom is both the goal (end) of development but also the means of development (Sen 1999). This focus on freedom is in contrast to a model of development that begins with need. It is reflected in Sen's reinterpretation of the Brundtland definition of sustainability, groundbreaking as that achievement had been (Sen 2004).[5]

Sen identified potentially self-defeating problems with a focus on needs. First, it is assumed that there is a self-evident universal understanding of human needs, as opposed to opulence, and this is simply not the case. Second, a needs approach operates with a reductive anthropology: the human person is reduced to a list of needs rather than being understood as a capable agent. Sen refuses to develop a canonical list of capabilities, as Martha Nussbaum has done, not because it might not be useful but because such a list, he argues, could subvert democratic public processes of "open impartiality." As he writes: "My own reluctance to join the search for such a canonical list arises partly from my difficulty in seeing how the exact lists and weights would be chosen without appropriate specification of the context of their use (which could vary), but also from a disinclination to accept any substantive diminution of the domain of public reasoning" (Sen 2006, 155). David Hollenbach, in his *Common Good and Christian Ethics*, is clear that deliberative approaches can also fall far short. The possibility for what he calls "intellectual solidarity" requires citizens' commitment to co-operate in a spirit of genuine reciprocity and respect, which is not always in evidence (Hollenbach 2002, 145). Nevertheless, the emphasis on freedom and environmental citizenship, rather than demands, in Sen's CA resonates with Hollenbach's model of the common good in the CST. This would suggest that the constitutive elements of integral human development in the CST are better understood as developing in a "historically incremental way through deep encounter and intellectual exchange across traditions" (ibid., 159).

Laudato Si' reiterates the longstanding interpretation in the CST that the earth is a shared inheritance and that this is the more fundamental principle; the right to private property is legitimately subordinated to it. It borrows here from *Laborem Exercens* (*LE*; 1981), which claims it as "the first principle of the whole social and ethical order" (*LE* 93). *Fratelli Tutti* (2020) also recognizes the "social purpose of all forms of private property" (*FT*, 120). Its remarkable subtitle, *On Social Fraternity and Friendship*, does not allow us to hesitate in interpreting distant strangers as our neighbor (*FT*, 80ff), and the encyclical calls for a "new network of international relations ... to resolve the serious problems of our world" (*FT*, 126). *Fratelli Tutti* also elaborates on the positive implications of the right to property and what this means: "I care for and cultivate something that I possess, in such a way that it can contribute to the common good of all" (*FT*, 143).

Having investigated above an interdependence based not on need but on agency and intersubjectivity in political ethics, in the next section I draw from a different but inter-related domain: the interpretations and deployment of creation theology in environmental ethics. My intention is to investigate how aspects of creation theology are applied in ecological theology and ethics.

CREATION AND OTHER COSMOLOGIES: INTERPRETING NATURE AS CREATION

Creation theology is central to classical accounts of divine action, free will, grace, finitude, theodicy, time, and eternity (Russell 2018). It carries within itself a double meaning: creation as an unprecedented origin and God's continuing relationship with creation in history. It is a term often used synonymously with "nature," "universe," or "cosmos" in dialogue with the physical sciences—or with the "earth" and earth systems in ecology. It should come as no surprise that, from a theological perspective, creation is understood to be more than an analogue of cosmos or earth. It implies many things, not least a Creator who is classically, in Christianity, the "transcendent" God of Scripture. Such a Creator is redundant in modern accounts of order in the world, and physical cosmology is methodologically, if not always metaphysically, atheistic. In this section I will present a brief account of models of creation in the theological tradition, some relevant parallels and differences with cosmologies in the natural sciences, and the implications for theologies of nature (or ecotheologies) and for an "integral ecology."

Although in the popular imagination the biblical accounts of beginnings are always associated with the first chapters of Genesis, as Paul Ricoeur points out, the drama of creation is not simply captured in any one literary form; there are many accounts in the text. And there is more than one model of creation: there is creation by generation from God's-self (not thought to be found in the biblical text); from combat (Ps. 89 and Job); by fabrication (Gen. 2–3); and, radically, by divine fiat, by the Word of God alone (Gen. 1 and Ps. 33) (Ricoeur 1998, 37). Each one of these presents different possibilities for addressing the Creator-creation relationship.

Creation texts are concerned with much more than the physical order of the universe, fascinating and revealing as that is. They present, in plural literary forms, aspects of the Creator-creation relationship that include (but are not confined to) the idea that God is not dependent on creation yet is deeply involved, that the creation is not "necessary" but willed by God and is thereby loved, and that matter is neither divine nor demonic but good. This last affirmation of the goodness (not perfection) of creation emerges from enduring disputes with forms of world-rejecting dualisms that interpret the God of the Hebrew Bible as the demiurge who created radically fallen matter and the God of the New Testament as a hidden God known only to those with special knowledge, or gnosis. Finally, but not insignificantly, there is a degree of promise in creation: the promise "of an orderly world, or of a responsible humanity, of many descendants, of a common identity, of a land in which to dwell" (Ricoeur 1998, 50). These are theological and not empirical claims about primal mystery that leave "world causality" in place.

Just as, for the narrator of Genesis, seeking the principle of order in the universe is part of what it means to seek God, the creation texts testify to the same wonder, the same will to understand found in any modern scientific thinker who hopes to start "from experiences belonging to their own sphere of observation" (Ricoeur 1998, 51). There is a kinship that relates the mythic with the scientific point of view that is "not negligible." In that light, creation theology does seek a coherent metaphysics that can account for an immanent and personal God. The application of historical consciousness in the disciplines of geology, biology, and physics—respectively, in the recalibration of the age of the earth, the evolution of life, and the models of an emergent universe—has brought new, previously incredible, insights to human understanding of the physical world.

Creation theologies are not immune to or ignorant of developments in the natural sciences, nor to the implications for rethinking divine action in a world described by those disciplines. The quiet turn to panentheistic (literally all-is-in-God) theologies of creation, influenced by process theologies, has allowed modern theology to retrieve the fundamental intimacy of God in his creation (Clayton and Peacocke 2004). These paradigm shifts in modeling Creator-creation do have great heuristic potential, not least in that they are also profound reminders of the limits of all language in mediating realities. They help us to seek out "slightly less inadequate ways," as John Feehan puts it, to interpret creation (Feehan 2016). Expressed in the form of a question, panentheism is a thought experiment in reimagining the Creator-creation relationship. As Paul Clayton and Arthur Peacocke ask: "Is it better to state with qualifications that the cosmos is in God or with qualifications that the cosmos is not in God?" (Clayton and Peacocke 2004). These alternatives, like the grammar of all analogies, represent the ongoing interplay between the apophatic tradition, according to which we cannot affirm anything about God, and the cataphatic or affirmative tradition, which nonetheless perseveres in attempting to speak about God in the service of understanding (Ricoeur 1998, 347). We can therefore affirm that God creates and creates order—from nothing or something—but that does not mean we know exactly what that order is.

The implication of this analysis is that creation and cosmos are not equivalents without remainder. Creation theology does not forge a totalizing concept of order; creation, justice, and redemption are different modes of thought not captured in the concept of "order" (Ricoeur 1998, 60). To "think in terms of the idea of creation is not the same thing as thinking in terms of the idea of order" (ibid., 57). To paraphrase Ricoeur, creation theology proclaims that despite his hiddenness, God is not entirely unknown; despite suffering, humankind is not delivered over to evil and death; and despite order this is not a self-explanatory world (ibid., 66).

There is also in creation an aspect of order that is related to fragility, vulnerability intrinsic to that order itself, what can be called the "contingency of order." This fragility is there in diverse representations: such as the struggle against chaos; the quasi-artisanal fabrication; the word that calls forth, that brings into existence (Ricoeur 1998, 57). It is constitutive of creation. The implications of this are significant; first, fragility is not the origin of evil, and it is there even after the victory over chaos, and second, the vulnerability of this order has an ethical form, as we see in the theodicy question. It demands justice in the face of injustice, not by a systematic, unassailable defense of the justice of the Creator but by pointing to the danger of turning "order" into an idol (ibid.). "Resistance to order," including oppressive and coercive order, is also "inherent to a creation that is in essence vulnerable and fragile" (ibid., 59). Physical cosmologies, by definition, are silent on such evaluations.

IMPLICATIONS FOR THEOLOGIES OF NATURE AND ENVIRONMENTAL ETHICS

There are, I suggest, some significant implications of this analysis of order, fragility, and vulnerability in creation for "integral ecology." A theology of nature seeks to understand that reality, named "nature"—which is also the subject of the natural and social sciences—through the lens of creation theology. Eco-theologies have drawn on systems approaches to develop arguments in environmental ethics. And there are profound interpretations of creation that make much of concepts like the "prior order in nature," understood more and more as the "deep relationality" in nature and the "interdependence" in the cosmos, particularly in contemplative theologies (Feehan 2016).

These creation themes, however, often emerge truncated into environmental ethics as a totalizing interdependent system, presented uncritically as some version of "holism" (Thompson 1995). Yet "holism," like order in cosmology, requires some interpretation. It carries several meanings at once, often confusing things that differ. In terms of behavior, holism is sometimes understood as the intuitive absorption of ecology's lessons, a grasping of strategies for change and reform, the belief that if we change our philosophical or narrative views we will change our behavior. One such example, and there are many, can be found in Ryszard Sadowski's review of "integral ecology" in *Laudato Si'*. He writes that, in "turn, the relationship to nature, in which a person has a deep sense of unity with all that exists, results in adopting a spontaneous attitude of moderation and concern for others" (Sadowski 2016, 71). However, behavioral change is complex, and there is much yet to investigate about the value-action gap: what engenders pro-environmental behavior (Van den Noortgaete and de Tavernier 2014) and in what way commitment is important for rationality (Sen 2005). Human freedom is in danger of being reduced to a re-alignment with a prior order in creation, poorly understood, rather than the response of a capable agent to a complex of possibilities.

Paul B. Thompson also argues convincingly that appeals to holism can be philosophically and ethically paralyzing because methodologically they can require neutrality toward other values that are equally pressing (Thompson 1995, 142). For example, the transition to low-carbon-emission economies entails burden sharing, both as an efficient *means* to transition and as the effective *realization* of intergenerational justice in the present. All societies and economies have common responsibilities, but to different degrees. Justice cannot be delayed to some unattainable future when targets have been met and carbon budgets balance. As Paul Sober writes, holisms can be as "monolithic as the most single-minded individualism"; the only difference being that the unit of value is assumed to be at a higher level of organization (Sober 1995, 241).

However, more problematically, holisms can, Thompson writes, "invest a particular representation of nature with scientifically or metaphysically grounded authority, and . . . conclude that human action must conform to norms that support and reproduce that order" (Thompson 1995, 142). James Lovelock's *Gaia*, he suggests, is a case in point; in it determinism returns in ecological guise. Holism, Thompson adds, can be a source of insight and personal commitment, but we also need accountability, documented evidence, and good governance (ibid.).

The biblical text and tradition attest to both a given order in the cosmos but also the contingency of that order. Contingency is likewise thematized in physical cosmology, referring to events that could be otherwise, are dependent on starting conditions, or for which we cannot give sufficient cause (Evers 2017). These considerations of contingency pivot on the contrasts between determinism and indeterminism in philosophy and physics. In theology there is an additional layer of interpretation to be added; contingency recaptures the idea that God continually creates and is active in creation, and, however we envisage salvation, it is neither simply a return to the garden nor the naturalistic outworking of physical forces.

CONCLUSION: INTERPRETING "INTEGRAL ECOLOGY" IN THE CST

There are two implications, from this analysis, for interpreting "integral ecology" in the CST. The first comes from political ethics. If for Kant the purpose of moral philosophy is to accomplish the self-clarification of moral consciousness (Bielefeldt 1997, 531), then this, according to Bielefeldt, helps us first to clarify what moral philosophy is not. "Morality is not simply a part of our natural inclinations; it is not identical with a good behavior that is in conformity with the norms of society; it cannot be found in the teleological structure of nature" (ibid.). Sen is avowedly influenced by Kant's philosophy. Sen could also be said to move us away from the model of what Huber describes as the "Archimedean observer that distributes global shares" and begins instead with a "first-person standpoint through which agents recognize their unavoidable interdependence" (Huber 2016, 246). This approach does not come with ready-made solutions but commit us to a process that assumes that human societies can "retain the reflexive capacities to build upon, critique, or revise the terms on which they coexist and interact with one another" (ibid., 231).

The second implication is that creation is not reducible to a physical cosmology or systems theory in ecology, whether static or emergent; nor is creation a "totalizing order" or "holism" the highest goal. What remains significant, theologically, is that reality—in all its particularities—is an open system, opening up an unforeseeable history. Creation, justice, and salvation, remain different modes of thought not captured in the concept of "order." From a faith perspective, the fact that creation is not of human making but nonetheless demands our response is not alienating or, indeed, all-consuming. The world is affirmed as home for the human person, the graced creature of a benevolent Creator.

NOTES

1. For an introduction to the complex history of natural law argumentation in CST, see Pope (2004).

2. Autonomy and revised natural law share what Junker-Kenny calls "an inductive route to establishing norms through the reflection of reason (both philosophical and in its social scientific applications) on experience; highlighting the role of freedom; understanding identity as a gift that becomes the basis of the capability of acting morally; and spelling out the heuristic and motivational power of the Christian vision, as well as questioning the status and the way of dealing with morality" (Junker-Kenny 2019, 201).

3. The original phrase, in the work of the Dutch Jurist Hugo Grotius and in Kant's philosophy, is "the common possession of the earth." It is modified here to "inheritance" since in the tradition ownership is understood not as an absolute right of possession but as a "use right" (Huber 2016, 231–49).

4. For example, according to Billé, Lapeyre, and Pirard (2012), biodiversity loss in all economies is more directly related to inequality than it is to poverty; inequality may be the missing piece in the biodiversity-poverty puzzle (cf. Russell 2017).

5. The Brundtland Report defined sustainable development as meeting "the needs of the present without compromising the ability of future generations to meet their own needs" (Sen 2004, 10).

WORKS CITED

Bielefeldt, Heiner. 1997. "Autonomy and Republicanism." *Political Theory* 25, no. 4: 524–58.

Billé, Raphaël, Renaud Lapeyre, and Romain Pirard. 2012. "Biodiversity Conservation and Poverty Alleviation: A Way Out of the Deadlock?" Edited by Gaëll Mainguy. *SAPIENS* 5, no. 1.

Catechism of the Catholic Church. 1992. Vatican City: Libreria Editrice Vaticana.

Clayton, Paul, and Arthur Peacocke. 2004. *In Whom We Live and Move and Have Our Being.* Grand Rapids, MI: Eerdmans.

Evers, Dirk. 2017. "Creation and Contingency." In *Oxford Research Encyclopedia of Religion.* doi: 10.1093/acrefore/9780199340378.013.35.

Feehan, John. 2016. *The Dipper's Acclaim and Other Essays.* Dalgan Park, Ireland: Columban.

Francis. 2015. *Laudato Si'*. Encyclical. https://www.vatican.va/content/francesco
/en/encyclicals/documents/papa-francesco_20150524_enciclica-laudato
-si.html.

———. 2020. *Fratelli Tutti*. Encyclical. https://www.vatican.va/content
/francesco/en/encyclicals/documents/papa-francesco_20201003_enciclica
-fratelli-tutti.html.

Hollenbach, David. 2002. *The Common Good and Christian Ethics*. Cambridge:
Cambridge University Press.

Huber, Jacob. 2016. "Theorising from the Global Standpoint: Kant and Grotius on Original Common Possession of the Earth." *European Journal of
Philosophy* 25, no. 2: 231–49.

Junker-Kenny, Maureen. 2001. "The Image of God—Condition of the Image
of the Human." In *The Human Image of God*, edited by H. G. Ziebertz,
F. Schweitzer, and H. Häring. London: Brill.

———. 2005. "Valuing the Priceless: Christian Convictions in Public Debate
as a Critical Resource and as a 'Delaying Veto' (J. Habermas)." *Studies in
Christian Ethics* 12, no. 1: 43–56.

———. 2019. *Approaches to Theological Ethics: Sources, Traditions, Visions*. London: Bloomsbury/T&T Clark.

Kant, Immanuel. 1795. *Perpetual Peace: A Philosophical Sketch*. Reproduced in
Penguin Great Ideas, "In Answer to the Question: What Is Enlightenment?" London: Penguin, 2009.

Mieth, Dietmar. 1982. "Autonomy of Ethics—Neutrality of the Gospel?"
Concilium: Is Being Human a Criterion of Being Christian? 5, no. 18:
32–39.

———. 1999. "Bioethics, Biopolitics, Theology." In *Designing Life? Genetics,
Procreation and Ethics*, edited by Maureen Junker-Kenny. Aldershot: Ash-
gate, 6–22.

Milstein, Brian. 2010. "Kantian Cosmopolitanism beyond 'Perpetual Peace':
Commercium, Critique, and the Cosmopolitan Problematic." *European
Journal of Philosophy* 21: 118–43.

Paul VI. *Laborem Exercens*. 1981. Encyclical. https://www.vatican.va/content
/john-paul-ii/en/encyclicals/documents/hf_jp-ii_enc_14091981_laborem
-exercens.html.

Pinheiro Walla, Alice. 2016. "Common Possession of the Earth and Cosmopolitan Right." *Kant-Studien* 106, no. 1: 160–78.

Pope, Stephen. 2004. "Natural Law in Catholic Social Teaching." In *Modern Catholic Social Teaching: Commentaries and Interpretations*, edited by
K. Himes. Washington, DC: Georgetown University Press, 41–71.

Ricoeur, Paul. 1998. "Thinking Creation." In *Thinking Biblically: Exegetical and Hermeneutical Studies*, edited by A. LaCocque and P. Ricoeur. Chicago: University of Chicago Press, 31–67.

Russell, Cathriona. 2009. *Autonomy and Food Biotechnology in Theological Ethics*. Oxford: Peter Lang.

———. 2017. "Demography, Poverty and Planetary Boundaries in *Laudato Si'*." In *Laudato Si': An Irish Response*, edited by S. McDonagh. Dublin: Veritas, 173–96.

———. 2018. "Creation: An Invitation to Share God's Love." *Search: A Church of Ireland Journal* (Summer): 91–99.

———. 2021. "Creation, the Biosphere as Common Inheritance and the Commodification of the Proximal Sky." Paper presented at the International Congress of the European Catholic Theological Society, Osnabrück, Germany, August 2021.

Sadowski, Ryszard F. 2016. "Inspirations of Pope Francis's Concept of Integral Ecology." *Seminare* 37, no. 4: 69–82. doi: http://doi.org/10.21852/sem.2016.4.06.

Schockenhoff, Eberhard. 2003. *Natural Law & Human Dignity: Universal Ethics in an Historical World*, translated by Brian McNeil. Washington, DC: Catholic University of America Press.

Sen, Amartya. 1999. *Development as Freedom*. Oxford: Oxford University Press.

———. 2004. "Why We Should Preserve the Spotted Owl." *London Review of Books* 26, no. 3: 10–11.

———. 2005. "Why Exactly Is Commitment Important for Rationality?" *Economics and Philosophy* 21, no. 1: 5–14.

———. 2006. "Human Rights and Capabilities." *Journal of Human Development* 6, no. 2: 151–66. doi: 10.1080/14649880500120491.

Sober, Elliot. 1995. "Philosophical Problems for Environmentalism." In *Environmental Ethics*, edited by R. Elliot. Oxford: Oxford University Press, 226–47.

Sowle Cahill, Lisa. 2001. "Genetics, Individualism, and the Common Good." In *Interdisziplinäre ethik: Grundlagen, methoden, bereiche; Festgabe für Dietmar Mieth zum sechzigsten geburtstag*, edited by A. Holderreg and J. P. Wils. Freiberg: Herder, 378–92.

Thompson, Paul. 1995. *The Spirit of the Soil*. London: Routledge.

Van den Noortgaete, Francis, and Johan de Tavernier. 2014. "Affected by Nature: A Hermeneutical Transformation of Environmental Ethics." *Zygon* 49, no. 3: 572–92.

SEVEN

Caring for the Earth

Challenges for Catholic Social Teaching and the Capability Approach

Clemens Sedmak

ABSTRACT

In this chapter I intend to offer a comparison of Catholic Social Teaching (CST) to the capability approach (CA) through the perspective of "sustainable development." This endeavor is a challenging one given the fact that CST is part of a wide tradition (the "Catholic social tradition") and that this tradition may be more appropriately understood as referring to "Catholic social traditions," plural. This endeavor is also challenging since "the capability approach" with a unified doctrine and an established Magisterium to control and create standards of "orthodoxy" does not exist, as it does for the Catholic social tradition. Following an illustration of the situation in which we find ourselves, I offer a reconstruction of the relationship between CST and the sustainability discourse (with a special focus on the encyclical Laudato Si'*) together with a discussion of the CA and its relation to sustainability. In a third and final step, I will compare CST to the CA with respect to common ground and differences, making use of the term "(intellectual) comfort zones."*

INTRODUCTION: WHERE WE ARE AND WHO WE WANT TO BE

How are we to understand our present situation? Reference points may be derived from three modern "topoi." Fukushima as the site of a nuclear catastrophe, Lampedusa as a reality and symbol of the recurrent refugee struggle, and New Moore Island, the small rocky islet in the Bay of Bengal that disappeared due to climate change, are three places that convey the drama of our present situation. These three places represent "*loci theologici,*" signatures of our time, struggling with risks, exclusion, and imponderables; they can also be considered "non-places," or places where it is not good to be. The discourse on and the experience of challenges to sustainability are marked by these topoi and by what they represent.

Fukushima, Lampedusa, and New Moore Island reflect four notable characteristics: irreversibility, urgency, inescapability, and inequality. (1) Irreversibility: Certain events trigger causal chains that are no longer reversible; the events flow like a river in one direction and may be modified, slowed, or stopped, but the initial state can no longer be created. The realities of nuclear energy, the dynamics of migration, and the seeming inexorability of climate change have resulted in irreversible circumstances that have become starting points for further events. It is not without reason that, following the disaster in Fukushima, the famous saying "I cannot get away from the ghosts I called" was frequently quoted. (2) Urgency: Fukushima, Lampedusa, and New Moore Island, in the language of catastrophe and disaster, address processes of imminence that necessitate swift and far-reaching action and a transformation of agency. The three topoi demand decision, resolution, and appropriate action. We do not pass the test of these disasters by plunging our heads into the sand and waiting for disaster to pass. Rather, time presses on with the risk that worse things will come to pass unless action is taken quickly and energetically. It is a distressing fact that we have already lost important years since the Rio de Janeiro Earth Summit in 1992. (3) Inescapability: Urgency arises precisely because the risks mentioned cannot be contained locally. Questions of nuclear energy are global issues, as are refugee flows and climate change. These challenges speak a language of inescapability: we cannot arrange our future lives so as to be unaffected by these topoi. As signatures of our time, they are constituent of the structure of destiny that we must confront. They do not allow for neutrality or non-involvement. (4) Inequality: Even if urgency and inescapability create a certain equality, and thus egalitarianism, in the face of the global catastrophic scenarios brought about by climate change, people are affected differently. In other words, inequality among people manifests itself, among other things, in the differential ways people are affected by these signs of the times. Some people can protect themselves more effectively given their privileges of wealth or education or birth lottery. Fukushima obviously bears different implications for Japan than for Austria; New Moore Island may be far from a European's daily concerns, but not from a Bengali's. In a remarkable book on the 2001 El Salvador earthquake, Jon Sobrino (2004) remarked that the earthquake was a "natural disaster" whose tremors reached people irrespective of their social status. However, it could not be denied that poor populations—given their lower levels of protection and support and higher levels of vulnerability—experienced the quake's greatest impact. These three signpost locations reflect new entry points for inequality. And yet the sense of uncontrollability has escalated, calling for a new culture of cooperation—synchronic cooperation among persons and diachronic cooperation among generations.

Fukushima, Lampedusa, and New Moore Island point to a new *moral* reality: we cannot live our lives in a spirit of innocence. "Never such innocence again" was Jonathan Glover's characterization of the driving attitude of the First World War, examining the multitudes of "sleepwalkers" (the title of a book by Christopher Clark) who entered into war (Glover 2001). In the wake of Fukushima, Lampedusa, and New Moore Island, the luxury of innocence has been discredited as irresponsible naïveté—making for an uncomfortable and inconvenient awakening. In a different context, Robin DiAngelo (2018) coined the term "white fragility" to bring to light inconvenient truths: the tendency to create comfort zones without race-based stress allowing for a positive self-image and the tendency to operate within polite contexts without looking into matters of complicity and the reality of a system that privileges white people. By analogy, there is the bitter insight that we benefit from Fukushima (we need the energy!), Lampedusa (we dismiss increased taxes to support those less privileged in the birth lottery!), and New Moore Island (we desire exciting lives of travel and consumption!).

There is a nuclear, residential, and green fragility in each of us who would prefer to see ourselves as "basically decent people." Who would like to admit that he or she benefits from environmental disasters and large-scale displacement? We are beholden to toothless good will, that is, good will without the willingness to make sacrifices.

How are we, therefore, to respond to our present situation? How are we to live after Fukushima, Lampedusa, and New Moore Island? This chapter highlights differences and common ground between Catholic Social Teaching (CST) and the capability approach (CA) through the lens of "responding to the ecological crisis."

CATHOLIC SOCIAL TEACHING

Faced with Fukushima, Lampedusa, and New Moore Island, CST provides a language that surpasses technological or ethical paradigms. It expresses the social dimension of the Christian faith and, as result, has the potential to draw upon a tradition and community of concrete examples ("the communion of saints"). It is distinct from a social theory, although it makes use of socially relevant categories like "structures," "market," "governance," "working conditions," and "wages." Yet these categories are set against a horizon of not only "the transcendent" in the abstract but of a personal God who became human. CST considers "peace" and "peace building," but it does so from a position that recognizes the power of the words "Peace I leave with you; my peace I give to you. Not as the world gives do I give it to you" (John 14:27). CST is not another ethical approach situated within the philosophical tradition; it is constituent of moral theology with its commitment to revelation, including biblical revelation. Thus, one of its central aspects is its biblical foundations, which are not "arguments" or "systematic treatises" but expressions of an encounter between the human and the divine. CST is an expression of discipleship, an expression of the social dimension of following Christ. Hence, it regards sustainable development as both a responsibility (in the sense of stewardship for creation) and a transitory reality (there will be a new heaven and a new earth). "Development" cannot be separated from "growth" toward God. The relationship between God and the human person is most vividly described and revealed in the biblical texts.

Biblical Foundations of *Populorum Progressio*

Let us explore the use of biblical sources in the groundbreaking encyclical *Populorum Progressio* (*PP*; Paul VI 1967), which opened CST to the global discourse and perspective. With this document, Paul VI ushered in a new era for the social teachings of the Catholic tradition.

The text quotes the Gospel of Matthew as well as the Gospel of Luke four times. The Gospel of Matthew appears in the form of the Sermon on the Mount (Matt. 5:3 according to footnote 18) and in eschatological speech on the final judgment (Matt. 25:35–36 according to footnote 61). Interestingly, the Sermon on the Mount is embedded in the discussion of decent living conditions and is consonant with the thesis that, after covering the necessities of life, a taste for the spirit of poverty may be developed pursuant to Matt. 5:3. The eschatology represents, in the context of committed young people in humanitarian service, an appeal to all people of good will who may have the capacity to embrace Matt. 25:35–36 and meet Christ in the poor. This motivation is specific to the Christian tradition. In the same context, the encyclical includes a quotation from the Gospel of Mark in which Jesus expresses his compassion for the crowd, thus preparing to feed the four thousand (Mark 8:2: "My heart is moved with pity for the crowd"); this is a powerful image for the mission and vocation of those working in international development. Whereas "indifference" has sometimes been identified as the key challenge for moral philosophy (Margalit 2002), the encyclical, with its reference to Mark's Gospel passage, offers a particular path for overcoming indifference: "No one is permitted to disregard the plight of his brothers living in dire poverty, enmeshed in ignorance and tormented by insecurity. The Christian, moved by this sad state of affairs, should echo the words of Christ: 'I have compassion on the crowd'" (*PP* 74).

Matthew 19:66, on marriage, is drawn upon to understand and educate readers about the position of the family—a passage also cited in *Rerum Novarum* (Leo XIII 1891) and in *Quadragesimo Anno* (Pius XI 1931). Matthew 16:26 ("What good does it do to a man if he gains the whole world, but at the same time loses his life? At what price can a person buy back his life?") is echoed by Pope Paul VI in the context of defending the preservation of local culture insofar as it embodies true values. Pope Paul VI also references the Gospel of Luke's famous passage, Luke 7:22 (the Gospel is proclaimed to the poor), to underline the mission of the Church to support progress: "True to the teaching and example of her divine Founder, who cited the preaching of the Gospel to the poor as a sign of His mission . . . the Church has never failed to foster the human progress of the nations to which she brings faith in Christ" (*PP* 12). There follows a reference to the building work of the Church, which, in addition to churches, had constructed hospices, hospitals, schools, and universities—concretizing and anchoring the verse of Luke in contemporary realities.

The Gospel of Luke is made normatively fruitful in *Populorum Progressio* 47 in the form of a union of the Lazarus passage (Luke 16:19–31) with the mandate to build one world for all. In *Populorum Progressio* 49, a passage on the micro level of individuals (Luke 12:20) is raised to the level of states and intergovernmental relations:

> We must repeat that the superfluous goods of wealthier nations ought to be placed at the disposal of poorer nations. The rule, by virtue of which in times past those nearest us were to be helped in time of need, applies today to all the needy throughout the world. And the prospering peoples will be the first to benefit from this. Continuing avarice on their part will arouse the judgment of God and the wrath of the poor, with consequences no one can foresee. If prosperous nations continue to be jealous of their own advantage alone, they will jeopardize their highest values, sacrificing the pursuit of excellence to the acquisition of possessions. We might well apply to them the parable of the rich man. His fields yielded an abundant harvest and he did not know where to store it. "But God said to him, 'Fool, this very night your soul will be demanded from you.'" (Luke 12:20)

Ultimately, it is reconnection with God that provides the basis for the proper commitment to international development, a recapitulation, conveyed in the sincerity of the spiritual search expressed in Luke 11:9:

> It must be admitted that men very often find themselves in a sad state because they do not give enough thought and consideration to these things. So We call upon men of deep thought and wisdom—Catholics and Christians, believers in God and devotees of truth and justice, all men of good will—to take as their own Christ's injunction, "Seek and you shall find" (Luke 11:9). Blaze the trails to mutual cooperation among men, to deeper knowledge and more widespread charity, to a way of life marked by true brotherhood, to a human society based on mutual harmony. (*PP* 85)

The encyclical's approach of linking the micro level with the macro level and translating personal ethical claims into normative structural challenges conveys an important means of making the Gospels fruitful for social doctrine, namely, by transferring a personal ethic into a macro ethic such that the moral concepts expressed in the Gospels become structurally relevant. Rather than mere illustrations or authority arguments, the biblical references in *Populorum Progressio* point to the deeper layers of fundamental motivations; they demonstrate that a commitment to the transformation of structures, in a Christian reading, is based on discipleship.

Laudato Si': A Plea for Conversion

Another important aspect of CST is the theological language of "conversion" and "creation" in regard to sustainable development. The key document here is Pope Francis's encyclical *Laudato Si'* (*LS*; Francis 2015).

In *Laudato Si'* Pope Francis defends "the light of faith" (*LS* 63), acknowledging that many discard a faith-informed perspective (*LS* 62). Similar to *Populorum Progressio*, the text provides a faith-based motivation for action (*LS* 64). An emphasis on theological categories like sinfulness and sin (*LS* 2, 8, 66) demonstrates that CST is not "another ethical approach"; rather, the encyclical uses the language of "repentance" (*LS* 8) and "conversion" (*LS* 5), recognizing God's authority (*LS* 6) and the implications of the truth: "We are not God" (*LS* 67). The text also reminds readers of the implications of this truth as regards the ownership of created things: they "are not free of ownership"; they belong to God (*LS* 89, making use of a Hebrew Bible quotation from the Book of Wisdom 11:26). Consequently, the text criticizes practical relativism, which gives centrality to human beings (*LS* 122–23), and a technocratic paradigm that reflects misled anthropocentrism. For believers, relationship with the earth is a question of fidelity to the Creator (*LS* 93). In the encyclical Pope Francis conveys these truths through thick descriptions of exemplary figures like St. Francis of Assisi (*LS* 10–12).

Again we find biblical sources at work: Pope Francis engages the Gospel of Matthew in order to indicate the specific power of Christianity (Matt. 20:25–26; *LS* 82), the equality of dignity of both rich and poor (Matt. 5:45; *LS* 94), the paternal concern of God for His creation (Matt. 11:25 and 6:26; *LS* 96), the small beginnings of the kingdom of God (Matt. 13:31–32; *LS* 97), Jesus's harmony with nature (*LS* 98; Matt. 8:27), and the meaning of conversion (*LS* 220; Matt. 6:3–4). *Laudato Si'* 99 recalls the mystery of creation by reference to the prologue to the Gospel of St. John without diminishing the clear significance of the Gospel of Matthew within the encyclical. Twice, mentioning it as a marginal curiosity, Pope Francis cites Luke 12:6 ("Are five sparrows sold for a few pennies? Yet God does not forget any of them," *LS* 96, 221), which also expresses a certain spiritual orientation (namely, confidence in the providence of God and an attitude of "hope against hope," even in the face of Fukushima, Lampedusa, and New Moore Island).

The perspective of *Laudato Si'* also considers future generations. Nature is recognized as "creation" and "gift" (*LS* 71, 76, 146, 155, 159, 220) with language that is based on relationship with God. This understanding of the human-divine relationship generates an understanding of the world as a gift intended for all—for all people now and for all people to come: "We realize that the world is a gift which we have freely received and must share with others. Since the world has been given to us, we can no longer view reality in a purely utilitarian way, in which efficiency and productivity are entirely geared to our individual benefit. Intergenerational solidarity is not optional, but rather a basic question of justice, since the world we have received also belongs to those who will follow us" (*LS* 159), and "the notion of the common good also extends to future generations. The global economic crises have made painfully obvious the detrimental effects of disregarding our common destiny, which cannot exclude those who come after us. We can no longer speak of sustainable development apart from intergenerational solidarity" (*LS* 159). The theological language provides a context for generating a perspective that recognizes limits. *Laudato Si'* 191 calls for "a decrease in the pace of production and consumption" while *Laudato Si'* 193 addresses "irresponsible growth."[1]

In the encyclical Pope Francis makes an appeal for "a change in lifestyle" (*LS* 206). This change requires "an awareness of the gravity of today's cultural and ecological crisis [which] must be translated into new habits" (*LS* 209). This appeal represents an invitation to realize the messages of *Laudato Si'* in everyday common practice. It calls upon each of us to inspect our ways of life—our "pace of life and work" (*LS* 18), "to become painfully aware, [of] what is happening to the world" (*LS* 19, 66). It exhorts us to open our eyes to "pollution, waste and the throwaway culture" (*LS* 21, 123) and to "the depletion of natural resources" (*LS* 27, 55, 211); to pause and contemplate the world's beauty (*LS* 34, 53, 97, 103, 112, 150, 215, 235) and to approach nature with openness to awe and wonder (*LS* 11). It is a summons to conversion in the domains of "interpersonal relations" (*LS* 47), "harmful habits of consumption," human beings'"dominant lifestyle" (*LS* 55, 145, 203, 204), transportation (LS 153), and "environmental responsibility," specifically the "use of plastic and paper" (*LS* 211). It exhorts people to become aware of ecological change, "the harm done to nature and the environmental impact" (*LS* 59, 117), and the ecology of daily life (*LS* 147, 152) and to cultivate practices of "simplicity of life" (*LS* 214, 222), abstinence (*LS* 9), and promoting the common good (*LS* 232). The encyclical is notoriously critical of the technocratic paradigm that, paradoxically, enhanced human capabilities (*LS* 106–14): "Never has humanity had such power over itself" (*LS* 104).

This change of lifestyle, however, is embedded in language of personal conversion (*LS* 5) and community conversion (*LS* 219); the heart has to overcome indifference (*LS* 91). "The ecological crisis is also a summons to profound interior conversion" (*LS* 217); this conversion is described in language of prayer and encounter with Christ: "What they all need is an 'ecological conversion,' whereby the effects of their encounter with Jesus Christ become evident in their relationship with the world around them. Living our vocation to be protectors of God's handiwork is essential to a life of virtue; it is not an optional or a secondary aspect of our Christian experience" (*LS* 217). Pope Francis grounds the encyclical's central message not on a set of abstract principles but rather on a concrete person, St. Francis of Assisi (*LS* 218), who witnesses to the kind of conversion that is called for, a conversion that "calls for a number of attitudes which together foster a spirit of generous care, full of tenderness" (*LS* 220).

Here again, we see that CST is the result and expression of discipleship. *Laudato Si'* invites all to develop a sense of limits and restrictions, even a sense of sacrifice: "An ecological conversion can inspire us to greater creativity and enthusiasm in resolving the world's problems and in offering ourselves to God 'as a living sacrifice, holy and acceptable' (Rom. 12:1)" (*LS* 220).

THE CA AND SUSTAINABILITY

The CA does not use the language of discipleship or creation; it does not work with concrete role models (like the one Pope Francis finds in Francis of Assisi); as such, the approach may be less exclusive and employ language less "esoteric" than that of CST. Committed to the idea of freedom, the CA envisions the human person primarily as an agent, with an emphasis on capabilities and choices (rather than resources, commodities, possessions). Within the CA, the development of the person and the whole person (what CST calls integral human development) is understood as the expansion of real freedoms—an expansion that is understood in holistic terms, applying to all areas of life that people inhabit and shape and by which they are affected. Development is the intentional effort to increase and expand capability sets, that is, choices for the realization values and opportunities for valuable achievements. The concept and value of sustainability comes into play not only with regard to the sustainability of people's livelihoods but also with regard to natural resources and the future of the planet. Hence, there is a tension between "present" and "future," between "expanding capabilities" and "accepting limits, even degrowth." One could argue that it takes a new set of capabilities to deal with the challenges of climate change. In order to illustrate the connection between the sustainability discourse and the CA, I will explore some aspects of the Human Development Reports; thereafter, I will discuss certain challenges at the theoretical level of the CA.

The Human Development Reports and Sustainable Human Development

The connection between the sustainability discourse and the CA can be and has been translated into concrete political action, as the Human Development Reports of the United Nations Development Programme (UNDP) illustrate. The series of Human Development Reports reflect a highly impactful global policy application of the CA. These reports have dealt explicitly with the challenge of sustainability since the 1990s. Let us take a look at some selected reports. The 1994 Human Development Report developed the concept of "sustainable human development," making it a central issue of policy discourse. Arguing that there is no tension between human development and sustainability, the report puts forth the concept of the "universalism of life claims." It underlines the importance of enhancing capabilities: "Development must enable all individuals to enlarge their human capabilities to the fullest and to put these capabilities to the best use in all fields—economic, social, cultural and political" (UNDP 1994, 13); it seems that "all" (individuals) include future generations. Moreover, the report explicitly states that "the strongest argument for protecting the environment is the ethical need to guarantee to future generations opportunities similar to the ones previous generations have enjoyed" (ibid.), echoing the Brundtland Report's definition of sustainability. In recognizing that universal life claims bind "the demands of human development today with the exigencies of development tomorrow" (ibid.), the report begs the question of whether present lifestyles are acceptable; to that end, it suggests: "A major restructuring of the world's income distribution, production and consumption patterns may therefore be a necessary precondition for any viable strategy for sustainable human development" (UNDP 1994, 4). The challenge of "expanding the right kinds of capabilities" undeniably arises: the expansion of capabilities is compatible with a sustainable future for the planet under the condition that certain capabilities are expanded, while others are not. The former could be called "sustainability-promoting capabilities" such as the capability to change mobility patterns; the latter would be "sustainability-adverse capabilities" such as particular patterns of consumption. Negotiating the distinction between these two types of capabilities would require democratic discourse and a commitment to rationality.

The 2003 Human Development Report addresses the United Nations' Millennium Development Goals, including a chapter on public policies to ensure environmental sustainability. It reiterates the necessity of change: "Many environmental problems arise from the production and consumption patterns of non-poor people, particularly in rich countries. . . . To ensure the sustainability of Earth and its resources, including the development prospects of poor countries, these harmful production and consumption patterns must change" (UNDP 2003, 123). The report bespeaks an optimism that rational debates will generate the motivation to accept limits and bring about this change. This optimism that optimal outcomes are attainable is also expressed in the commitment to an integral policy response: "Environmental management cannot be treated separately from other development concerns. To achieve significant, lasting results, it must be integrated with efforts to reduce poverty and achieve sustainable development" (UNDP 2003, 126). The rather vague language, however, does not help to address the challenge of opportunity costs that emerge when attempting, at once, to address both present and future generations, both poverty reduction and environmental protection.

The 2007/08 Human Development Report ("Fighting Climate Change") anticipates a motif of *Laudato Si'*, arguing that climate change affects all people in all countries while identifying the poorest as the most vulnerable to the harmful effects of climate change. The report suggests an inverse relationship between climate change vulnerability and responsibility, and it appeals to solidarity as well as to agreements: "Climate change is a global problem that demands an international solution. The starting point must be an international agreement on the limitation of greenhouse gas emissions" (UNDP 2007/08, 44). Here again, the questions remain: Can transnational solidarity be motivated by rationality (and, if so, by which kind of rationality)? And is the motivational structure of transnational solidarity comparable to the motivational structure of solidarity on the micro level of interpersonal relationships?

The 2010 Human Development Report reconfirms the centrality of ethical universalism and suggests an equivalence between "human development" and "sustainable human development": "Human development is about enabling people to lead long, healthy, educated, and fulfilling lives. Sustainable human development is about making sure that future generations can do the same" (UNDP 2010, 19). And, even more explicitly: "Human development, if not sustainable, is not true human development" (ibid.). Hence, an understanding of "authentic" or "true" human development needs to reflect the centrality of sustainability; the report connects the concept, however, more closely with an anthropocentric approach—"Sustainability implies that improvements in human development can be sustained" (UNDP 2010, 79)—and does not allow much space for ideas of degrowth and reduction. There is the potential for conflicts, which the report recognizes in acknowledging the need for "a frank and open discussion of links, conflicts and complementarities" (UNDP 2010, 118).

The 2011 Human Development Report on sustainability and equity highlights the links between (environmental and ecological) sustainability and (social) equity. It stresses "empowerment, equity and sustainability in expanding people's choices" (UNDP 2011, 13); it characterizes "human development" in the well-known manner of the CA as "the expansion of the freedoms and capabilities people have to lead lives they value and have reason to value" (UNDP 2011, 17). The report defines "sustainable human development" as "the expansion of the substantive freedoms of people today while making reasonable efforts to avoid seriously compromising those of future generations" (UNDP 2011, 18).[2] Attending to the question of limits, the report states that the answer "is clear: our development model is bumping up against concrete limits" (UNDP 2011, 15). Here again, the document does not provide guidance about the negotiation between "limits" and "expansion"; however, it clearly favors efficiency measures of production (rather than reduction of consumption, including energy consumption, with the corollary restriction of individual freedoms).

The 2013 Human Development Report discusses the temporality of justice: "Sustainable human development is about understanding the links between temporal choices of different generations and about assigning rights to both present and future generations" (UNDP 2013, 34). It glosses over real conflict potentials when discussing "the need for technological innovations and shifts in consumption that can facilitate movement towards sustainable human development" (ibid.). Once again, democratic debate is suggested as the key means to negotiating different interests: "Equitable and sustainable human development requires systems of public discourse that encourage citizens to participate in the political process by expressing their views and voicing their concerns" (UNDP 2013, 91).

The 2020 Human Development Report discusses "human development and the Anthropocene." It describes the dynamic of our destabilizing the planetary systems we rely on for survival. The pressures put on the planet mirror the strains on societies. There is a need for new social norms and new incentive structures. The report proposes a "planetary pressures–adjusted Human Development Index." Given the flashing warning lights that cannot be overlooked, we need to respond to the planetary and social imbalances that reinforce each other. We are entering a new era: "Whether we wish it or not, a new normal is coming. COVID-19 is just the tip of the spear. Scientists generally believe that we are exiting the Holocene, which spanned some 12,000 years, during which human civilization as we know it came to be" (UNDP 2020, 4). The message is very clear: We cannot continue with our established patterns. The situation we are in has been created through human agency and human choices and has to be addressed through human choices and human agency.

Challenges

The brief discussion of sustainable human development in the Human Development Reports illustrates that the CA has much to offer to the discourse and policy planning (Burger and Christen 2011). It provides a view of the person not primarily as a consumer or a being with needs, but as an agent of change who, according to Amartya Sen, "can—given the opportunity—think, assess, evaluate, resolve, inspire, agitate, and, through the same means, reshape the world" (Sen 2013, 7).[3] (This is also, one might say, the strongest message of the 2020 Human Development Report.)

The human person is an agent who is capable of rational discourse, which is the key instrument in planning and implementing sustainability-strengthening policies. Generating change may also generate the need for new (types of) capabilities, for example, moving from material to immaterial values.[4] This could even result in different sets of freedom beyond consumer stress. For example, Breena Holland (2008) has proposed "sustainable ecological capacity" as a meta-capability that involves the ability to live in the context of ecological conditions that can provide environmental assets that enable people's capabilities, now and in the future. On this basis, she develops a concept of environmental justice.

However, there are also significant challenges for the CA when facing the question of sustainability. The literature lists a number of challenges to which it needs to respond. Martin Binder and Ulrich Witt argue that the CA is essentially a static normative framework, whereas, sustainability economics demands a systematic, long-term view with a focus on wide-ranging societal change (Binder and Witt 2012). In a similar vein, Ortrud Lessmann and Felix Rauschmayer (2013) suggest that the CA struggles to negotiate between the individual and system levels and the issue of dynamics and dynamic modeling. The more serious challenges, however, concern the limits and limitations of freedoms: there is the challenge of "sustainability-promoting," "sustainability-compatible," and "sustainability-adverse" capabilities; relatedly, there is the challenge of the motivational basis for accepting limits, the need for degrowth and reduction, and the restriction of freedoms. The CA has not developed within a context of understanding "limits" but rather with an emphasis on "expansion" (of freedoms); this constitutes the challenge of an ethos of restraint (how to justify "reduced consumption"). The CA is (not unlike CST) traditionally anthropocentric and tends to value the natural world insofar as it contributes to people's freedoms. Additionally, the approach tends to focus on the evaluation of choices of present stakeholders. As Kin Hubbard has remarked, "The hardest thing is to take less when you can get more" (quoted in Oral and Thurner 2019, 277). The hardest thing is not to make use of capabilities.

One could argue, as the Human Development Reports suggest, that future generations should not be constrained in their possibility to live worthwhile lives because of the adverse effects of exacerbated anthropogenic climate change. This idea would introduce a new dimension to the CA, namely a dimension of "ceilings." People would have to exercise their freedoms and manage their capability sets while negotiating a limited environmental budget. As Peeters, Dirx, and Sterckx (2013) have argued, capabilities need to be defined as forming a triadic relation among an agent, constraints, and possible functionings. The goal of enhancing people's capabilities and well-being is situated within (the biophysical)

constraints (of the ecosphere). One implication of this attempt to reconcile the CA with limits could be that the goals of sustainable human development include the expansion of people's freedoms and capabilities up
to a threshold level such that capabilities become "bounded capabilities"
(Jackson 2017). Determining thresholds would be a matter for democratic
debate in each nation and, thus, open to the risk of paternalism; this begs
the additional question of whether we need to accept the concept of "basic
capabilities" in order to better understand the thresholds.[5] But what are
our options if the resources for the "threshold level" are not available?

Tough questions persist. Sen (2013, 13) articulates one such question as follows: "If sustainability requires a behavioural change that makes
people less inclined towards massive—and massively resource-depleting—
consumption (and more towards seeking fulfilment in activities that take
a less improvident form), can this valuational change happen voluntarily?
Or is coercion or compulsion the only feasible route (if any)?" Whereas
Sen is optimistic concerning the reasoning skills of persons and the power
of public debate (and he makes the point that behavioral change for fer-
tility decline worked best with more freedom, not less), it is telling that a
significant number of dystopic scenarios describe eco-dictatorships (such
as that in the classical book *Go! Die Ökodiktatur*, by Dirk Fleck, set in
2040). Must we "sacrifice freedoms" (in the spirit of "laws of fear") (Sunstein 2005)?

To add another tough question (the point here is not a discussion of
past or present politics, but a more fundamental question for the CA):
On June 1, 2017, U.S. President Donald Trump announced the United
States' withdrawal from the Paris Climate Accord. In his official statement the president mentioned "the onerous energy restrictions" that the
Paris Climate Accord had placed on the United States, with the loss
of 2.7 million jobs and significant production reductions in the paper,
cement, iron and steel, coal, and natural gas industries. His statement
included the following:

We have among the most abundant energy reserves on the planet,
sufficient to lift millions of America's poorest workers out of poverty.
Yet, under this agreement, we are effectively putting these reserves
under lock and key, taking away the great wealth of our nation—its
great wealth, its phenomenal wealth; not so long ago, we had no idea

we had such wealth—and leaving millions and millions of families trapped in poverty and joblessness. . . . My job as President is to do everything within my power to give America a level playing field and to create the economic, regulatory and tax structures that make America the most prosperous and productive country on Earth. . . . Beyond the severe energy restrictions inflicted by the Paris Accord, it includes yet another scheme to redistribute wealth out of the United States through the so-called Green Climate Fund—nice name— which calls for developed countries to send $100 billion to developing countries all on top of America's existing and massive foreign aid payments. . . . There are serious legal and constitutional issues as well. Foreign leaders in Europe, Asia, and across the world should not have more to say with respect to the U.S. economy than our own citizens and their elected representatives. Thus, our withdrawal from the agreement represents a reassertion of America's sovereignty. (Trump 2017)

Here is the question: Can this decision to withdraw from the Paris Climate Accord (given Trump's emphasis on freedoms, agency, and quality of life) be justified on the basis of a certain understanding of the CA? I would assume that this is not a trivial question; it points to a challenge of the CA and fundamental challenges to approaches focused on the agency and choices of individuals.

CST AND THE CA IN DIALOGUE

On the basis of the two sketches of CST and the CA insofar as they relate to sustainability, I will enter a dialogue between these two traditions. One route toward conceptualizing the relationship between CST and the CA is through the concept of "comfort zones." Human beings have comfort zones, that is, contexts of familiarity within which they operate best, with minimal effort and minimal cognitive adaptions. Comfort zones are contexts in which a person's abilities are not challenged or tested. The concept of comfort zones seems to be relevant for frameworks, models, and approaches. There are contexts within which a particular conceptual framework, a particular model, or a sufficiently sophisticated approach works best; these would be the areas of "best examples," primary concerns, or original intentions. We could call these "operational" or "discursive" comfort zones. Approaches and frameworks have operational or discursive comfort zones. The term "comfort zone" indicates that people committed to a certain framework or approach would be willing to stretch the approach beyond its comfort zone to defend its plausibility; they would be open to testing its cognitive capacity and would be optimistic about the possibilities for expanding its range beyond the area of primary concerns or best examples. This may lead, however, to the phenomena associated with leaving comfort zones, namely, a sense of uneasiness and a suspicion that others might excel in these areas, which remain comfort zones for some but are already learning zones or panic zones for others.

CST, to offer a relevant example, works best in a context in which a concept of the family with two married, heterosexual, primary caregivers is understandable without much instruction or persuasive labor; CST is less comfortable providing language for a scenario of diverse family situations: it may be challenged to leave its discursive comfort zone when trying to dialogue with certain persons, such as homosexuals. As an Austrian archbishop once put it: how can we credibly tell homosexual persons that they are fully respected and really welcome in the Catholic Church? But again, a defender of CST will say that it is possible for the framework provided by CST to move beyond established discursive comfort zones, though so doing may reflect a more forced and less effortless posture than in other domains.

The CA, on the other hand, functions most naturally in contexts that are primarily concerned with "agency," "achievement," and "striving." It seems most at home in areas in which these terms can be appropriately engaged; the operational or discursive comfort zone of the CA exists in areas in which we might consider "control," "choices," "rights," and "entitlements." Martha Nussbaum undertakes a prioritization of those capabilities on her renowned list (see the chapters by Katie Dunne and by Joshua Schulz in this volume). Perhaps especially, she has prioritized the capability for (personal and political) control over one's environment, thus reflecting a commitment to a particular understanding of "autonomy." The CA seems to be moving into a discursive learning zone when talking about "duties."

Again, a defender of the CA may argue that the approach can accommodate challenges of non-agency-based discourses, but this could imply, as I would perceive it, an invitation to leave an operational or discursive comfort zone.

Common Ground: Beyond the Material Dimension

One important insight of the CA is the primacy of "good-related agency" over "goods." The primary question regards not the goods and commodities at a person's disposal but rather the agency made possible through and related to these available and accessible goods and commodities. Similarly, CST stresses the importance of values and education. Both traditions concur that there is no value-free space in development. Development necessarily involves evaluation.[6] Both traditions insist on the role of dialogue and process as explained in Sen's *The Idea of Justice* (Sen 2009) and stressed in *Laudato Si'* (the need for an honest debate: *LS* 14, 61, 189).

Both traditions are committed to intangible infrastructure and immaterial resources, stressing "values," "freedoms," and "reason." This kind of "transcendence" is appropriate after Fukushima, Lampedusa, and New Moore Island; these topoi remind us that we have reached the limits of money, the limits of what money can buy. There was a time when German sociologist Niklas Luhmann (2001) had good reason to regard money as a symbolically generalized communication medium and universal symbol that enables the exchange and settlement of goods of all kinds. Money enables translatability from one language to another, from one context to another. There seem to be two basic questions, articulated in the twentieth century for challenges of all kinds, namely: How much does it cost? And who pays? The cost issue and the payment question were established as central to contingency design. When the questions of costs and payments are clarified, a catastrophe loses its ghostly veneer, takes shape, and becomes a dimension of action planning. If, following an accident, there is identification of who assumes the costs, the situation is regarded as clarified and completed—because answering these questions clears up the causal aspects and etiology and establishes the possibility for reversibility. Even questions of "the value of human life" have adopted this approach through two basic questions of cost and payment (Feinberg 2005).

Now these two questions of cost and payment find their legitimacy and their value above all in a suitably equipped legal system that may be regarded as a machine for their clarification. At once, it is clear that these two issues are reaching their limits by reason of the limits of reversibility, on one hand, and the limits of the monetary sphere, on the other hand. The catastrophes of Fukushima, Lampedusa, and New Moore Island reveal the limits of answering principally questions of costs and payments. In other words: if the world becomes uninhabitable due to nuclear contamination (a scenario that Michael Frayn described in his 1968 dystopia *A Very Private Life*), the question "Who should pay for it?" becomes obsolete.

Both CST and the CA seem well equipped to address the limits of the material and monetary and to enter into a discourse that stresses the immaterial—values, freedoms, and reasons (without denying the need for an appropriate material and ecological base). Both traditions stress the primacy of relationship with a good over the good itself; both traditions recognize the human person as equipped with reason and the human condition as having a political aspect that allows for public debates and cooperative decision-making. However, some differences remain.

Distinct and Defining (and Lasting) Differences

CST—see the *Compendium for the Social Doctrine of the Church* (PCJP 2006), chapter 3, part 2—regards the human person primarily as a creature, as a being created by God in the image and likeness of God (para. 108) (see chapters by Amy Daughton and Meghan Clark in this volume). This facilitates a vocabulary that includes terms like "life as gift," "imago Dei," "dependency," "recipient," "child of God," "need for salvation," and "eternal destination." In this area, the theological foundations of Catholic Social Teaching are most obvious, and there is a primacy of creation language. As Rowan Williams (2000) put it in his powerful essay "On Being Creatures": "From this perspective, identity is not constructed or negotiated, it is not based on achievements or agency, it is primarily given as a gift." Consequently, the concept of freedom is closely related to "surrender" rather than described primarily in terms of "agency." *Laudato Si'* 6 stresses the limits of human freedom in light of the doctrine of creation. One prominent example of this semantic shift is Alfred Delp, a Jesuit who was involved in the resistance movement against Hitler. He was imprisoned in July 1944, sentenced to death in January 1945, and executed on February 2, 1945. During Advent of 1944, with his hands chained, he wrote on freedom from his prison cell in Berlin Tegel, reflecting that there can be no real freedom without surrendering to God's will. The human person has to take "the essential first step of relinquishing his personal self of his own free will. Only thus can he come to the necessary state of receptivity. It is an attitude conditioned by the relationship of the creature to the Creator" (Delp 1963, 49). These words reflect the conviction of a man who was arrested and killed because of his strong commitment to the social and political dimension of faith, his commitment to CST, especially to *Quadragesimo Anno*, which provided him with a vision of order that he saw destroyed by the Nazi regime. Freedom in the Christian understanding, which is the basis of CST, cannot be separated from a kind of relationality that involves God. In his essay *Theology of Freedom*, Karl Rahner (1969, 179–80) remarked:

> It would be a complete misconception of the nature of freedom to try to understand it as the mere capacity of choice between objects given a posteriori, among which, besides many others, there is also God; so that God would only play a special role in the choice made by this freedom of choice from among these many objects on account of his own objective characteristics but not on account of the nature of freedom itself. Freedom only exists ... because there is spirit understood as transcendence ... God is present unthematically in every act of freedom as its supporting ground and ultimate orientation.

The theological concept of freedom cannot be separated from the concepts of "transcendence" and "redemption." This takes us beyond a language of agency and rights. In other words, there are rooms in the house of human dignity that cannot be unlocked by the key proffered through the language of rights and entitlements; these rooms are inaccessible by terms such as "fairness" or "agency"—and it is in these rooms that CST, with its reading of the person in a theological light, may feel at home. I would like to suggest that CST as a framework is moving at once in two discursive comfort zones that cannot be separated. Gustavo Gutierrez (1987), in his interpretation of the Book of Job, has offered language for these two discursive comfort zones: the prophetic and the mystical; the prophetic is the context appropriated by social justice language, a hunger and thirst for justice, a wrestling with injustice; and the mystical is the space of silence and surrender, contemplation and letting go, trusting and handing over. The Book of Job, as Gutierrez interprets it, is a learning journey wherein Job must leave the discursive comfort zone of the prophetic and enter the discursive comfort zone of the mystical. This may approximate Simone Weil's reflection on "waiting" and "attention" in her approach to the philosophy of religion, or in her atheist belief in God (Weil 2010). Neither the human person nor even God is primarily described as an "agent." Religion, thus, is not to be grasped in a language of capabilities (discipleship as a "resource"). If we cease to see faith as a resource and source of good life, we will leave "the prophetic" and enter "the mystical." CST is to be understood in discursive comfort zones in which the prophetic is ultimately anchored in the mystical.

CONCLUSION

Fukushima, Lampedusa, and New Moore Island have at least four notable characteristics: irreversibility, urgency, inescapability, and inequality. In other words, we are faced with limits and the need to deal with these limits. CST and the CA address these limits by emphasizing the primacy of the immaterial over the material, the primacy of the intangible over the tangible. But they do so by operating within different discursive comfort zones. Why does this matter?

First, the suggestion of "discursive comfort zones" does not imply a language of "right" or "wrong" but rather one of "accommodation" (can A accommodate x?). And by "accommodate" we could understand this: to integrate, to give meaning without betraying the foundations of the framework. CST will find it challenging to accommodate certain types of pluralism; the CA will find it difficult to accommodate the language of the cross. Second, a plea for the recognition of the mystical as an important dimension of the human condition is not irrelevant to development work with its traps of compassion fatigue, burnout, cynicism, or—to use a more ancient term—"acedia." The foundation for the character of commitment shown by Gandhi, the Dalai Lama, Leymah Gbowee, Mother Teresa, and Sophie Scholl can be found in the mystical, not only the prophetic. In the face of our present ecological challenges, we might feel tired and frustrated. We need motivation for the long run and "the deep run." We need to draw upon the mystical. Third, the distinction between the prophetic and the mystical may give us an insight into the negotiation of operational or discursive comfort zones between the CA and CST: a philosophical reading of CST, emphasizing its appeal to common-sense roots and its approach to the human condition from an Aristotelian-Thomist tradition, is most convincingly suited to finding common ground with the CA. As Vivencio Ballano (2019) has argued, despite methodological and theoretical differences, sociology and the moral theology of CST can share a common ground in their treatment of the social order.

A more theological reading of CST, that is, a recognition that CST is closer to moral theology than to social philosophy, that it is part of the Catholic Magisterium, and that it is grounded in the theologies of creation, salvation, and eschatology would make it more difficult to find the common ground. But this, again, could be fruitful and helpful. There is a political dimension to the mystical that the CA may be able to unpack, and there is a mystical dimension to politics that may be expressed in the simple statement "My Kingdom is not of this world" (John 18:36).

NOTES

1. In *Laudato Si'* 193 Pope Francis poses an interesting variety of translations. The official English version states: "The time has come to accept decreased growth in some parts of the world, in order to provide resources for other places to experience healthy growth." The Spanish version (the version that Pope Francis approved) states: "Ha llegado la hora de aceptar cierto decrecimiento en algunas partes del mundo aportando recursos para que se pueda crecer sanamente en otras partes." Obviously, there is a difference between "decreased growth" and "degrowth!" But the point is an acceptance of limits, which is, within a capitalist and technocratic paradigm, a real challenge. Why do less if you could do more? Why take less if you could take more?

2. This definition is quoted again in UNDP (2016, 93).

3. Amartya Sen makes the point of seeing human persons as agents as an explicit critique of the Brundtland Report's well-known definition of sustainable development as one "that meets the needs of the present without compromising the ability of future generations to meet their own needs (Sen 2013, 8). Persons are not to be seen primarily as "needy beings." Lessmann and Rauschmayer (2013) argue, however, that a simple replacement of "needs" with "capabilities" when working with the Brundland definition is challenging and actually demands individuals to make heroic choices when faced with sustainability challenges. This brings us to this question: Does the situation we are in require moral saints and moral overachievers?

4. Similar to Lars Tornstam's concept of "gerotranscendence" (the possibility for aging well is connected to a new commitment to immaterial values), one could think of a concept of "eco-transcendence" (accepting a commitment to immaterial needs on the basis of concern for the environment and the long-term future of the planet). See Tornstam (1994).

5. Nuno Martins argues that this concept can accommodate the concerns with freedoms and limits: "We need a conception where we can define a certain *limited* standard of human well-being, which enables the reproduction of economy, society and nature, in a circular process. The capability approach provides a framework within which we can engage in discussions about the standard of living, defined in terms of basic capabilities" (Martins 2013, 229, emphasis original).

6. See *LS* 5 ("authentic human development has a moral character") and Sen (1988, 20): "One of the difficulties in adequately characterizing the concept of development arises from the essential role of evaluation in that concept. What is or is not regarded as a case of 'development' depends inescapably on the notion of what things are valuable to promote"; Sen mentions explicitly "the dependence of the concept of development on evaluation" (ibid.).

WORKS CITED

Ballano, Vivencio. 2019. "Catholic Social Teaching, Theology, and Sociology: Exploring the Common Ground." *Religions* 10, no. 10: 557. doi:10.3390/rel10100557.

Binder, Martin, and Ulrich Witt. 2012. "A Critical Note on the Role of the Capability Approach for Sustainability Economics." *Journal of Socio-Economics* 41: 721–25.

Burger, Paul, and Marius Christen. 2011. "Towards a Capability Approach to Sustainability." *Journal of Cleaner Production* 19: 787–95.

Delp, Alfred. 1963. *The Prison Meditations of Father Delp: With an Introduction by Thomas Merton*. New York: Herder and Herder.

DiAngelo, Robin. 2018. *White Fragility: Why It's So Hard for White People to Talk about Racism*. Boston: Beacon.

Feinberg, Kenneth R. 2005. *What Is Life Worth?: The Inside Story of the 9/11 Fund and Its Effort to Compensate the Victims of September 11th*. New York: Public Affairs.

Francis. 2015. *Laudato Si'* (*LS*). Encyclical. https://www.vatican.va/content /francesco/en/encyclicals/documents/papa-francesco_20150524_enciclica -laudato-si.html.

Glover, Jonathan. 2001. *Humanity: A Moral History of the Twentieth Century*. New Haven: Yale University Press.

Gutierrez, Gustavo. 1987. *On Job: God-Talk and the Suffering of the Innocent*. Maryknoll, NY: Orbis.

Holland, Breena. 2008. "Justice and the Environment in Nussbaum's 'Capabilities Approach': Why Sustainable Ecological Capacity Is a Meta-Capability." *Political Research Quarterly* 61, no. 2: 319–32.

Jackson, Tim. 2017. *Prosperity without Growth*. London: Routledge.

Leo XIII. 1891. *Rerum Novarum*. Encyclical. https://www.vatican.va/content /leo-xiii/en/encyclicals/documents/hf_l-xiii_enc_15051891_rerum -novarum.html.

Lessmann, Ortrud, and Felix Rauschmayer. 2013. "Re-conceptualizing Sustainable Development on the Basis of the Capability Approach: A Model and Its Difficulties." *Journal of Human Development and Capabilities* 14, no. 1: 95–114.

Luhmann, Niklas. 2001. "Einführende Bemerkungen zu einer Theorie symbolisch generalisierter Kommunikationsmedien." In *Aufsätze und Reden*. Stuttgart: Reclam, 2001, 31–75.

Margalit, Avishai. 2002. *The Ethics of Memory*. Cambridge, MA: Harvard University Press.

Martins, Nuno O. 2013. "The Place of the Capability Approach within Sustainability Economics." *Ecological Economics* 95: 226–30.

Oral, Cansu, and Joy-Yana Thurner. 2019. "The Impact of Anti-consumption on Consumer Well-being." *International Journal of Consumer Studies* 43: 277–88.

Paul VI. 1967. *Populorum Progressio* (*PP*). Encyclical. https://www.vatican .va/content/paul-vi/en/encyclicals/documents/hf_p-vi_enc_26031967 _populorum.html.

Peeters, Wouter, Jo Dirx, and Sigrid Sterckx. 2013. "Putting Sustainability into Sustainable Human Development." *Journal of Human Development and Capabilities* 14, no. 1: 58–76.

Pius XI. 1931. *Quadragesimo Anno.* Encyclical. https://www.vatican.va /content/pius-xi/en/encyclicals/documents/hf_p-xi_enc_19310515 _quadragesimo-anno.html.

Pontifical Council for Justice and Peace (PCJP). 2006. *Compendium of the Social Doctrine of the Church.* https://www.vatican.va/roman_curia/pontifical _councils/justpeace/documents/rc_pc_justpeace_doc_20060526 _compendio-dott-soc_en.html.

Rahner, Karl. 1969. *Theology of Freedom: Theological Investigations* 6 (essay 13). Translated by K.-H. and B. Kruger. London: Darton, Longman, and Todd.

Sen, Amartya. 1988. "The Concept of Development." In *Handbook of Development Economics*, edited by H. Chenery and T. N. Srinivasan. Vol. 1. Elsevier Science Publishers B.V. 9–26.

———. 2009. *The Idea of Justice.* Cambridge, MA: Belknap Press of Harvard University Press.

———. 2013. "The End and Means of Sustainability." *Journal of Human Development and Capabilities* 14, no. 1: 6–20.

Sobrino, Jon. 2004. *Where Is God? Earthquake, Terrorism, Barbarity and Hope.* Maryknoll, NY: Orbis.

Sunstein, Cass. 2005. *Laws of Fear: Beyond the Precautionary Principle.* Cambridge: Cambridge University Press.

Tornstam, Lars. 1994. "Gerotranscendence—A Theoretical and Empirical Exploration." In *Aging and Religious Dimension*, edited by L. E. Thomas and S. A. Eisenhandler. Westport, CT: Greenwood Publishing. 203–25.

Trump, Donald. 2017. "Statement by President Trump on the Paris Climate Accord," Rose Garden. Washington, DC: Trump White House Archives. https://trumpwhitehouse.archives.gov/briefings-statements/statement -president-trump-paris-climate-accord/.

United Nations Development Programme (UNDP). 1994. *Human Development Report: New Dimensions of Human Security.* New York: UNDP. https://hdr.undp.org/content/human-development-report-1994.

———. 2003. *Human Development Report: Millennium Development Goals: A Compact among Nations to End Human Poverty.* New York: UNDP. https://hdr.undp.org/content/human-development-report-2003.

———. 2007/8. *Human Development Report: Fighting Climate Change; Human Solidarity in a Divided World.* New York: UNDP. https://hdr.undp.org /content/human-development-report-20078.

———. 2010. *Human Development Report: The Real Wealth of Nations; Pathways to Human Development*. New York: UNDP. https://hdr.undp.org/content/human-development-report-2010.

———. 2011. *Human Development Report: Sustainability and Equity; A Better Future for All*. New York: UNDP. https://hdr.undp.org/content/human-development-report-2011.

———. 2013. *Human Development Report: The Rise of the South; Human Progress in a Diverse World*. New York: UNDP. https://hdr.undp.org/content/human-development-report-2013.

———. 2016. *Human Development Report: Human Development for Everyone*. New York: UNDP. https://hdr.undp.org/content/human-development-report-2020.

———. 2020. *Human Development Report: The Next Frontier; Human Development and the Anthropocene*. New York: UNDP. https://hdr.undp.org/content/human-development-report-2020.

Weil, Simone. 2010. *Waiting for God*. New York: Routledge.

Williams, Rowan. 2000. "On Being Creatures." In *On Christian Theology*. Oxford: Blackwell, 63–78.

PART 2

Common Ground for Action

EIGHT

Development as Freedom Together

Human Dignity and Human Rights in Catholic Social Teaching and the Capability Approach

Meghan J. Clark

ABSTRACT

What is the relationship between human dignity and human rights? Appeals to human dignity are emotionally persuasive, but there is much disagreement on the role of human dignity in the human rights project; however, the deep connection between them remains central to the international development agenda. The intersection between development, human rights, and human dignity is a fertile nexus for conversation between Catholic Social Teaching (CST) and the work of Amartya Sen focusing on the capability approach (CA). In this chapter I focus on the relationship between human rights and human dignity in three parts. First, I identify the use of human dignity by the United Nations human rights documents alongside similar developments in CST. Second, I examine Amartya Sen's understanding of human rights as both ethical claims (ideas) and a discipline (practice) linked to freedom and capabilities. Finally, turning back to CST, I argue that there is a dynamic relationship between human dignity and human rights that is deepened through attention to solidarity and the common good. I also argue that CST contributes a vision of an inherent and aspirational sense of human dignity and human rights within communities that typifies integral human development and offers a vision of development as freedom together.

INTRODUCTION

The *Universal Declaration of Human Rights* (UN 1948) begins with the affirmation of "the inherent dignity of and the equal and inalienable rights of all members of the human family." This "universal vocation to protect the dignity of every human being," notes Mary Robinson (1998), "captured the imagination of humanity." Political scientist Tom Banchoff (2014, 257) notes that "to claim that something violates human dignity is to assert it contradicts basic moral precepts and must be remedied"; and, beyond that, the idea of human dignity "has informed an ambitious development agenda around poverty, healthcare, and education." Over the past seventy years, despite significant debates and a seemingly insurmountable gap between said universal vision and lived realities around the world, human rights has emerged and continues to be the primary mode of moral discourse at the United Nations. For almost twenty years, the stated goal of both human rights and development agendas has been lives of dignity for all human persons. "Human rights and human development share common vision and a common purpose—to secure the freedom, well-being and dignity of all people everywhere," began the 2000 United Nations Development Programme's *Human Development Report*, which argued for the centrality of human rights to human development (UNDP 2000, xv). Secretary General Ban Ki-moon (2013) echoed this by titling his 2013 report to the General Assembly *A Life of Dignity for All*, setting the priorities for the sustainable development agenda, then still being negotiated. "Ultimately," he argued, "the aspiration of the development agenda beyond 2015 is to create a just and prosperous world where all people realize their rights and live with dignity and hope" (Ban 2013). Human dignity and human rights, then, continue to be central to sustainable development, as the international community envisions it.

Framing the human rights agenda through the lens of dignity is emotionally persuasive, but it is complicated. As Amartya Sen (2004, 315) notes, "There is something deeply attractive to the idea that every person anywhere in the world, irrespective of citizenship or territorial legislation, has some basic rights, which others should respect." However, one does not have to look far for examples of the failure to respect the rights of others. The relationship between human dignity and human rights is a point of serious contention within human rights discourse. Human rights scholars cannot agree on the role of human dignity in the human rights project. As Charles Beitz (2013, 259) noted, "Many friends of human rights believe we cannot understand their special importance without a grasp of the value of human dignity. On the other hand, it is easy to remain suspicious of the idea that human dignity can do useful work in our thinking about the nature and basis of human rights." Beitz and others prefer to focus on the practice of human rights. However, human dignity continues to be invoked in international discussions of human rights. Similarly, despite debates questioning the value and universal force of human rights both politically and intellectually, the language of human rights retains moral force within international debates. Despite the ambivalence or hesitance of scholars and activists, human rights, human dignity, and the deep connection between them remain central to the international development agenda.

The intersection of development, human rights, and human dignity is one place for productive conversation between the capability approach (CA) and Catholic Social Teaching (CST). In this chapter I will focus on the relationship between human dignity and human rights for the shared goal of a world where men and women "become dignified agents of their own destiny" (Francis 2015a). First, I will examine the concept of human dignity as it is invoked within the United Nations founding documents and as it developed in CST, as simultaneously inherent yet aspirational.[1] Second, I will examine Amartya Sen's understanding of human rights as both ethical claims (ideas) and a discipline (practice) tied to freedom and to capabilities in which human rights present themselves as inherent, yet aspirational. Finally, I will argue that this dynamic aspect of human dignity and human rights is connected to solidarity and the central role of the community in integral human development.[2] Ultimately, the contribution of CST to larger debates concerning development and human rights is this acceptance of the "already, but not yet" quality of integral human development.[3] It is the recognition, by Pope Paul VI (1963) in *Populorum Progressio* (*PP*), that "there can be no progress toward the complete development of the person without the simultaneous development of all humanity in the spirit of solidarity" (*PP* 43). Twenty years later, in *Sollicitudo Rei Socialis* (*SRS*), Pope John Paul II (1987b) expanded this vision of "a different world, ruled by concern for the common good of all humanity," or by concern for the "spiritual and human development of all" instead of by the quest for individual profit. He wrote that peace would be possible as the result of a "more perfect justice among people" (*SRS* 10), tying together even more explicitly human rights, the common good, and solidarity. In his encyclical *Fratelli Tutti* (*FT*), Pope Francis (2020b) reiterated that it is an ongoing communal task in which "justice and solidarity are not achieved once and for all; they have to be realized each day" (*FT* 11).

INHERENT AND ASPIRATIONAL: HUMAN DIGNITY AND HUMAN RIGHTS IN CATHOLIC SOCIAL TEACHING

The *Universal Declaration of Human Rights* (*UDHR*; UN 1948) and the *Charter of the United Nations* (UN 1945) both invoked human dignity as a primary value but intentionally avoided explaining further.[4] Even clarifying how human dignity functions within United Nations practice is complicated. "Some utterances seem to refer to human dignity as an inherent property of human beings, a status they constantly have rather than one they can achieve," notes philosopher Pablo Gilabert (2015, 197). A paradigmatic example is the preamble to the *UDHR* (UN 1948), which begins thus: "Whereas recognition of the inherent dignity and of the equal and inalienable rights of all members of the human family is the foundation of freedom, justice and peace in the world . . . ." At the same time, writes Pablo Gilabert, "some statements appear to refer to dignity as a more contingent state that human beings may come to enjoy (and this includes certain treatment of them by others)" (Gilabert 2015, 197), including the fact that dignity can be attacked or violated (as described in *UDHR* article 23 or *Vienna Declaration* [World Congress on Human Rights 1993] article 23) (Gilabert 2015, 197). Surveying the United Nations' key documents and practices, Gilabert (2015, 208, emphasis in original) argues for two categories of dignity: "status-dignity" and "condition-dignity." Status-dignity refers to *"circumstances of human dignity* ... these clearly include the capabilities concerning reason, conscience, and solidaristic action." Human dignity is intimately tied to freedom and self-determination. It is something that everyone has. At the same time, elaborate social conditions are required in order for human persons to substantively develop and exercise these capabilities, and this provides the context for condition-dignity. Gilabert (2015, 209) argues, "Human beings are agents with capabilities of prudential and moral reasoning, imagination, knowledge, productive labor and social cooperation. ... We can identify various kinds of social conditions in which human dignity is fostered." Human dignity here is difficult to fully separate from human rights, echoing the basic thrust of a capability approach to human rights: "if there is a human right to *x*, then every human person ought to have the capability to get *x*" (Gilabert 2015, 209). While this dynamic tension between what Gilabert labels status-dignity and conditions-dignity can make human dignity seem elusive and fuzzy, for CST it is this complex dynamic that makes it an effective reference point for human rights. It is this appreciation of human dignity that is both inherent and conditional or, as I will argue, aspirational.

Human dignity, in Catholic theology, begins with the theological principle of the human person as created *imago Dei*, in the image and likeness of God (Gen. 1:26–27). While this has been understood differently throughout history, the universality and uniqueness of the *imago Dei*, that is, of the human person as equally created by God, in God's image, has been consistently, albeit at times only nominally, asserted. In *Human Rights and the Image of God*, Roger Ruston (2004, 55) posits, "All created beings are like God in their own way—they bear 'traces' of God (in the sense, perhaps that a work of art bears traces of its maker). But whereas everything is like God insofar as it exists, and every living creature insofar as it lives, only human beings are like God in any significant sense, in that they too are capable of knowledge and understanding."

"Human dignity," then, aims to capture the unique connection between humanity and God. In CST the theological starting point for human rights, human development, and social ethics more broadly is this theological anthropology of dignity. As a matter of creation, Pope John XXIII (1963, 9) holds up this vision of the person as foundational for human rights in *Pacem in Terris*, stating, "Any human society, if it is to be well-ordered and productive, must lay down as a foundation this principle, namely, that every human being is a person; that in his [or her] nature is endowed with intelligence and free will. Indeed, precisely because he [or she] is a person he [or she] has rights and obligations. . . . And as these rights and obligations are universal and inviolable, so they cannot in any way be surrendered."[5] As such, notes Ruston (2004, 56), human persons are "moral beings, capable of self-direction, and of responsibilities towards ourselves, towards God, towards one another." Built upon this understanding of dignity, Pope Benedict XVI (2009, 17) notes in *Caritas in Veritate* (*CV*): "*Integral human development presupposes the responsible freedom* of the individual and of peoples" (emphasis in original).

Firmly rooted in creation by God, human dignity is inherent. By virtue of being a human person, one has a dignity or value that others are obliged to respect. Examining lived reality, however, history provides far more examples of the violation of human dignity than of its celebration. Recognizing the reality of sin, also going back to the beginning of the Bible, CST approaches dignity as both a matter of creation and a part of salvation through Christ. Anna Rowlands (2021, 55) notes, "Believing that we live within an unfolding economy of salvation means that dignity is something seen as something we *possess* and something we *become*. Dignity is something we can seriously debase in ourselves or for others but it is not something we can fundamentally lose or completely alienate" (emphasis in original).[6] This sense of human dignity as something that is *already, but not yet* grounds CST's radical commitment to dignity as inviolable while also recognizing that profound exploitation and degradation exist (grappling with the same dynamic Gilabert (2015) identifies in UN documents as "status-dignity" and "condition-dignity"). More fundamentally, this dynamic of *already, but not yet* applies to all people, such that everyone is called to become more fully human, to embrace more fully the human community and recognize the dignity within themselves and others. At the same time, the fullness of justice eludes us within a world of injustice and brokenness. In this way, human dignity is both gift and responsibility. Or, to quote Protestant theologian Jürgen Moltmann (1984, 10), "The dignity of the human being consists in this, that they are human and should be human. Their existence is gift and task simultaneously." Theologically, the task of dignity is tied to justice and the responsibility to bring about greater justice within the community.

Accepting this dynamic, wherein human dignity is simultaneously inherent and still aspirational, is crucial if it is to have credibility as a concept. Despite the deep attraction of ascribing value to every person regardless of citizenship, race, gender, and so on, as one looks around the world, lived reality is often marked more by inequality and violations of human dignity than by its embrace. For Pope Francis, a major source of violations of human dignity is linked to a culture of indifference or a throwaway culture in which "some parts of our human family, it appears, can be readily sacrificed for the sake of others considered worthy of a carefree existence (*FT* 11). In his diagnosis of society, Francis identifies an indifference to the equal humanity of others as foundational to myriad ways in which the dignity of persons is violated individually and as members of groups. Thus, "it frequently becomes clear that in practice human rights are not equal for all" and that many of these human rights violations are a matter of exclusion (*FT* 22). Part of the gift and task of human dignity is that everyone must be included as a full member of the community. Poverty as exclusion is an important element of CST's approach. Therefore, participation in the economic, social, cultural, and political life of the community is integral to justice, as well as development.[7] Practically, dignity is lived or denied in complex and contingent social realities—the questions of condition-dignity for the United Nations. Seeking a life of dignity for all is a collective goal or responsibility because "others are not yet able to live in a way worthy of their human dignity," explains Pope Francis in his 2015 encyclical *Laudato Si'* (*LS* 93). *Gaudium et Spes* (Vatican Council II 1965) and Catholic social encyclicals since the Second Vatican Council have noted that in addition to "a growing awareness of the exalted dignity proper to the human person" there is an associated responsibility to make "available to all people everything necessary for leading a life truly human, such as food, clothing, shelter; the right to choose a state of life freely"; and so on (Vatican Council II 1965, 26).

Two aspects of CST here help clarify dignity and its relationship to human rights and help set the boundaries for establishing bonds of global solidarity. First, dignity incorporates the developmental aspect of human life—the centrality of becoming. Working for peace and justice is predicated on the idea that we can become more—more fully human, more just, more free—and can create a more peaceful community. Tina Beattie (2015, 159) notes, "The idea of human dignity roots the language of human rights in a bodily and ethical quest for the good life, which constitutes more than simply providing the basic needs of human existence." Second, dignity is not merely individual but also communal. Each of us has equal human dignity, and, at the same time, communities have dignity as well. In his encyclical *Lumen Fidei* (*LF* 38), Pope Francis (2013b) explains human relationality, stating, "Persons always live in relationship. We come from others, we belong to others, and our lives are enlarged by our encounter with others. Even our own knowledge and self-awareness are relational; they are linked to others who have gone before us. . . . Self-knowledge is only possible when we share in a greater memory." For CST, this is linked to theology's understanding of salvation. As Pope Francis noted, "No one is saved alone, as an isolated individual, but God attracts us looking at the complex web of relationships that take place in the human community. God enters into this dynamic, this participation in the web of human relationships" (Francis, quoted in Spadaro 2013). Thus an overarching and inclusive vision emerges that truly seeks a life of dignity for all. Protestant theologian Martin Luther King Jr. (2001, 45–46) expressed the connection between dignity and interdependence, stating, "I can never be what I ought to be until you are what you ought to be. This is the way our world is made. No individual or nation can stand out boasting of being independent. We are interdependent." When your dignity is being violated, my ability to live more fully in dignity is diminished. Similar to Dr. King's view, the vision of CST is that we have dignity.[8]

Achieving a life of dignity for all requires embracing that we are one human family. In his 1987 World Day of Peace message, "Development and Solidarity," Pope John Paul II (1987a) insisted, "We are one human family. Simply by being born into this world, we are of one inheritance and one stock with every other human being. This oneness expresses itself in the richness and diversity of the human family." The universality of human rights depends upon the dignity of the human person inviolably present in all human persons, but its universality is not uniformity. In this focus on equality and reciprocity, Pope Francis (2014) argues, "There are no disposable lives. All men and women enjoy as equal and inviolable dignity . . . this is the reason why no one can remain indifferent before the lot of our brothers and sisters." Thus, interdependence and community are integral to our understanding of the persons who are the subject of human rights.

IDEAS AND PRACTICES: HUMAN RIGHTS, FREEDOM, AND CAPABILITIES IN AMARTYA SEN

Despite the dominance of human rights rhetoric in international development, the agreement and commitment to the human rights project has always been a fragile one. In "Elements of a Theory of Human Rights," Amartya Sen (2004, 317) raises an urgent concern for the future of the human rights agenda, pleading that "the conceptual doubts must also be satisfactorily addressed, if the idea of human rights is to command reasoned loyalty and to establish a secure intellectual standing. It is critically important to see the relationship between the force and appeal of human rights, on the one hand, and their reasoned justification and scrutinized use, on the other." In the absence of said reasoned justification, human rights risk being limited only to those codified in particular laws and the important connection between human rights, substantive freedom, and capabilities risks being lost. According to Sen (2009, 357), human rights are first and foremost ethical assertions: "Proclamations of human rights, even though stated in the form of recognizing the *existence* of things that are called human rights, are really strong ethical pronouncements as to what *should* be done" (emphasis in original). In this section I will examine Sen's discussion of human rights and its dialectic of freedom, capabilities, and public scrutiny. In parallel to his philosophy of global justice, human rights as ethical assertions emerge with a similar inherent yet aspirational quality to human dignity.

Freedom and capabilities provide the foundation for Sen's philosophical approach to human rights. Rejecting utilitarianism, he prioritizes substantive freedoms or the actual, realizable opportunities people have.

By focusing on substantive freedoms, he is concerned with a human person's agency "as someone who acts and brings about change, and whose achievements can be judged in terms of her own values and objectives ... as a participant in economic, social, and political actions" (Sen 1999, 19). A central component of his book *Development as Freedom* (1999) is the argument for participation as a primary criterion for evaluating freedom. Participation provides the foundation for his focus on both the opportunity and process aspects of freedom, as well as undergirding development as freedom. The idea of capability, he argues, addresses the opportunity aspect of freedom. "A capability reflects the alternative combinations of functionings from which the person can choose one combination," he writes (Sen 2005, 154), and this opportunity aspect of freedom is crucial for evaluating freedom. Sen is careful to distinguish between opportunity (combinations of functionings) and what a person is actually doing (the person's chosen path). If we focus on participation as central for agency, writes Séverine Deneulin, we view each and every person "as subject and actor of her own life rather than as an object of actions that are being made for her" (Deneulin 2006, 356). Participation and agency, as they are understood within the CA as well as CST, include self-determination. It is not enough to nominally "take part in" society in a passive sense if one does not have the ability to discern and decide about values and the direction of one's own life and that of the community.[9]

Linking human rights to capabilities, according to Sen, is ultimately more akin to a philosophy of justice that "has to be alive both to the fairness of the processes involved and to the equity and efficiency of the substantive opportunities involved that people can enjoy" (Sen 2005, 156). The denial of due process or the freedom to choose for oneself is central for substantive freedom and human rights regardless of outcome. For example, even if a young woman wishes to cook dinner or to become a lawyer, her freedom is violated if she is forced to do either. Sen (2009, 370–71) acknowledges that the violation of freedom would be greater if she was being forced to do something she "would not otherwise choose," as in that case both the process and opportunity aspects of her freedom would be violated. The process and opportunity aspects of freedom are both centered on the human person as agent. Capabilities are mainly a matter of the opportunity aspect of freedom, and the centrality of process illustrates why Sen is careful not to reduce human rights to capabilities. Both aspects of freedom, however, demonstrate, for Sen, why human rights are predominantly ethical claims and should not be seen primarily as legal ones.

In declaring a human right, Sen (2009, 358) argues, "the ethical assertion is about the critical importance of certain freedoms (like the freedom from torture or the freedom to escape starvation) and correspondingly about the need to accept some social obligations to promote or safeguard these freedoms." Why is it critical that we understand human rights as ethical assertions rather than legal rights? First, a primary claim of human rights is that they are universal in application; they apply to all human persons merely by virtue of their being human and not as a function of their citizenship or membership in a particular group. Additionally, as ethical rather than legal assertions, human rights declarations are not merely statements of "what is already legally guaranteed" (Sen 2009, 359). Human rights declarations may involve new legislation, but not all human rights are most effectively thought of in terms of laws. In thinking beyond the confines of law, Sen seeks to make room for actions on behalf of human rights by activist and non-governmental organizations as well as for specific human rights that may not be best codified in law. Sen (ibid.) argues that "recognizing and defending a wife's right to have an effective voice in family decisions, often denied in traditionally sexist societies, may well be extremely important," but at the same time this kind of participation cannot be substantiated effectively merely through the law. Seeing human rights as primarily ethical statements can broaden and deepen their reach. Here Sen (2012, 91) himself seems to be concerned not only with human rights as concepts but also with their effectiveness in practice, revealing his concern with both interpreting and changing the world.[10]

Human rights as ethical claims also prioritize the need for reasoned public debate. In *The Idea of Justice* Sen (2009, 387) argues, "The force of a claim for a human right would be seriously undermined if it were possible to show [it is] unlikely to survive open public scrutiny." Additionally, Sen (2004, 349) expressly denies that human rights claims can be rejected because in "politically and socially repressive regimes, which do not allow open public discussion, many of these human rights are not taken seriously at all." His basic argument is that human rights claims can and would hold up to scrutiny were open public debate to occur, and that if, in fact, such public reasoning took place and human rights did not hold up—then the force and justification of said rights would in fact be questionable, as "uncurbed critical scrutiny is essential for dismissal as well as for justification" (Sen 2009, 387). The process aspect of freedom, as it pertains to democracy, is to be upheld whether or not said freedom is currently exercisable. Expanding the real or substantive freedoms that people enjoy is the driver of *development as freedom*, and thus the absence of one or more freedoms currently does not suffice as an argument against the valuing of said freedom.

Drawing on both John Rawls and Adam Smith, in his book *The Idea of Justice* Sen understands public reasoning more broadly and expands it to include both human rights claims as well as systems of domestic justice. Previously Sen had dismissed ideologies that set up "uncrossable barriers" between civilizations (e.g., Samuel Huntington's famous clash of civilizations) and those who would dismiss public reasoning and human rights as inescapably Western realities (invoking Nelson Mandela's example of learning democracy in watching Xhosa village proceedings) (Sen 2004, 352–53). Furthermore, he rejects any vision of public reasoning that seeks a monolithic or homogenous reasoning, arguing that engaging a plurality of reasons is necessary (and should not be automatically treated as a threat to universal human rights) (Sen 2009). While an in-depth analysis of Sen's discussion of public reasoning is outside the scope of this chapter, it is his emphasis on public reasoning that reveals that human rights as ethical claims share an inherent yet aspirational quality with human dignity.

Sen's appreciation of development in the realization of human rights, expanding the substantive freedoms people enjoy, and public reasoning, all reveal a vision of the human person and human agency that appreciates *becoming more*. This *already, but not yet* quality is clearest when we examine second-generation rights or the international development focus on poverty eradication as a human rights priority. For Sen (2009, 381), "The inclusion of second-generation rights makes it possible to integrate ethical issues underlying general ideas of global development with the demands of deliberative democracy, both of which connect with human rights and quite often with an understanding of the importance of advancing human capabilities." The economic and social rights most directly relate to what Gilabert (2015) called condition-dignity, focusing on the conditions necessary for a human person to live a life of dignity, expand substantive freedoms, and exercise the agency of self-determination central to the CA. Most frequently, these rights are rejected based upon their feasibility in practice. Rejecting the feasibility critique, Sen (2009, 385) argues, "non-realization does not, in itself, make a claimed right a non-right. Rather, it motivates further social action."

Sen's understanding of freedom recognizes the intimate connection between the social and economic life of a community and the substantive freedoms of individual persons. This drives his argument that human rights as ethical assertions include but are not limited to questions of legal statutes. At the same time, however, Sen is himself rather apprehensive about any further statements about the role of the community in general. What emerges throughout his idea of justice is a deep commitment to the idea that communities matter in protecting the process and opportunity aspects of substantive freedom, but said communities remain instrumental realities.[11] Despite this, the way in which he integrates his approach to development and human rights avoids a static list of capabilities and builds a broader understanding of justice. It emphasizes public reasoning and creates a dynamic and evolving relationship to the community, which reveals an aspirational quality to freedom that is not limited merely to achieving a particular basic list of human capabilities, as does Martha Nussbaum.[12]

SOLIDARITY: A REQUIREMENT FOR INTEGRAL HUMAN DEVELOPMENT

Throughout this chapter I have attempted to examine the way that Catholic Social Teaching understands human dignity and the way Sen approaches human rights reveal an *inherent and aspirational* quality to both. In both cases, this reveals an *already, but not yet* quality to how we can understand respect for human dignity or human rights in practice. This is part of the broader dialogue between the CA and CST, which this volume contributes to. Both traditions emphasize that human persons are the ultimate end of development. Most recently, the growing focus on multi-dimensional poverty has demonstrated the ever-growing recognition of the interdependence of substantive freedoms of persons.

Addressing poverty within and across communities is not merely an economic reality, as recognized by both the CA and CST.[13] Yet in these efforts to put the human person and her dignity at the core of development the community largely remains instrumental, with recognition of the reality of interdependence but not much further reflection on the community as such. Within this context, CST is distinct from the CA because it is teleological by nature—the human flourishing it aspires to is not only one of expanding substantive freedoms but also seeks the common good marked by solidarity. While there is a sense of solidarity implicit in Sen's emphasis on participation, justice, and responsibility for others, my claim is that CST goes further, defining solidarity as a virtue by which, in the words of Pope John Paul II, "it is a firm and persevering determination to commit oneself to the common good; that is to say to the good of all and of each individual, because we are all really responsible for all" (*SRS* 38). In this final section I will briefly point to CST's understanding of the common good as providing a vision of *development as freedom together*.

The relationship between the individual and the community has tended to be seen in the literature as a point of divergence between CST and the CA (Clark 2007). In particular, the most common criticism is that the CA "does not accommodate very well the idea that such a common good has an existence in its own right" (Deneulin 2006, 367). In *The Idea of Justice* Sen (2009, 245) himself addresses the challenge of "methodological individualism," arguing that "the entire approach of the 'impartial spectator' . . . focuses on the relevance of the society—and people far and near—in the valuation exercise of individuals." According to Johan Verstraeten (2017, 218), despite an inherent tension, placing capabilities within the broader context of "the universality of justice, or more precisely, the idea of an open impartiality: every human being is 'neighbor' and his or her interests and perspectives need to be taken into account in reasoning about realizing a more just state of affairs in the world," provides new points of convergence between CST and the CA. On this point, Deneulin and Clausen (2018) agree that what previously seemed like a divergence now appears more as a difference of emphasis with CST.

A hallmark of both CST and Amartya Sen's vision of justice is that they value participation greatly, with both arguing that process, or the

way that ends are achieved, matters greatly. Within the CA, public reasoning and participation are integral to substantive freedoms. For CST
as well, "participatory discourse [holds up] as an explicit goal the creation
of connective practices among interlocutors in order that shared social
practices may be transformed," as Lisa Cahill (2005, 38) writes. Participation is an essential component of integral human development. In his
address to the United Nations General Assembly, Pope Francis (2015a)
stated, "Integral human development and the full exercise of human dignity cannot be imposed. They must be built up and allowed to unfold for
each individual, for every family, in communion with others, and in a
right relationship with all those areas in which human social life develops—friends, communities, towns and cities, schools, businesses and
unions, provinces, nations, etc." This resonates deeply with an understanding of development as expanding substantive freedoms.

For CST, the common good is something dynamic and aspirational.
As *Gaudium et Spes* (*GS*) explains: "The common good embraces the
sum total of all those conditions of social life which enable individuals,
families, and organizations to achieve complete and effective fulfillment"
(*GS* 74). Persons and communities are linked in profound ways, such
that the whole is greater than the part or the mere sum of the parts; as
Pope Francis (2013a) notes in *Evangelii Gaudium* (*EG*), "It is the convergence of peoples who, within the universal order, maintain their own
individuality; it is the sum total of persons within a society which pur-
sues the common good, which truly has a place for everyone" (*EG* 236).
CST argues for simultaneously upholding the dignity of each individual
person and that of the one human family (without exception). Integral
human development, interdependence, and this vision of the one human
family are intergenerational, transcending space and time. Pope Benedict
XVI (2009) argued, "Projects for integral human development cannot
ignore coming generations, but need to be *marked by solidarity and intergenerational justice*, while taking into account a variety of contexts: ecological, juridical, economic, political and cultural" (*CV* 48, emphasis in
original).[14] With *Laudato Si'*, Francis extends the common good even
further to include future generations and "the expansion of the 'universal common good' beyond human societies to include other species,
ecosystems and the planet" (Cahill 2018, 887). This longitudinal gaze on
future generations is one aspect of CST's understanding of the dignity

of the one human family that goes beyond simply upholding the dignity of each individual person.

With the incorporation of integral ecology into the vision of the common good, Pope Francis broadens integral human development to include the rest of creation within CST's approach to the common good and solidarity. In doing so in *Laudato Si'*, he does not weaken but doubles down on the importance of the common good, solidarity, and addressing poverty as exclusion for integral human development within CST. It is one unified vision. As Francis (2015b) explains:

> Underlying the principle of the common good is respect for the human person as such, endowed with basic and inalienable rights ordered to his or her integral development. . . . Finally, the common good calls for social peace, the stability and security provided by a certain order, which cannot be achieved without particular concern for distributive justice; whenever this is violated, violence always ensues. . . . In the present condition of global society, where injustices abound and growing numbers of people are deprived of basic human rights and considered expendable, the principle of the common good immediately becomes, logically and inevitably, a summons to solidarity and a preferential option for the poorest of our brothers and sisters. (*LS* 157–58)

Practically, David Hollenbach (2002, 195) identifies three strategic moral priorities of the common good, which simultaneously should also serve as priorities of integral human development:

1. The needs of the poor take priority over the wants of the rich.
2. The freedom of the dominated takes priority over the liberty of the powerful.
3. The participation of the marginalized takes priority over the perseveration of an order that excludes them.

These strategic priorities coalesce with attention to the real freedoms people enjoy. In light of *Laudato Si'*, a fourth priority could be added: 4. Sustaining creation and biodiversity takes priority over preserving established patterns of economic development. These priorities also reveal the common focus on persons living on the margins of society, those whose basic needs and rights are denied. However, for CST these strategic priorities are not only normative claims, but also methodological ones. They identify the location from which CST evaluates questions of development or human rights.

In practice, these strategic priorities for the common good help to concretely build up solidarity. They provide a practical path for greater realization of the aspirational. Pope Francis (2020b) notes, "Solidarity means much more than engaging in sporadic acts of generosity. It means thinking and acting in terms of community" (*FT* 116). The common good is present "in a community of solidarity among active equal agents," explains Hollenbach (2002, 189), and "when these relationships form reciprocal ties among equals, the solidarity achieved [is] itself a good that cannot otherwise exist." Thus, as I noted at the beginning, Pope Paul VI (1963) frames integral human development, stating: "There can be no progress toward the complete development of the person without the simultaneous development of all humanity in the spirit of solidarity" (*PP* 43). For CST, we seek *development as freedom together*.

NOTES

1. During the COVID-19 pandemic, Pope Francis himself noted, "In modern culture, the closest reference to the principle of the inalienable dignity of the person is the Universal Declaration of Human Rights" (Francis 2020a).

2. Within CST, "community" as it is used here is a multifaceted and complex word; it is meant to capture all of the communities within which human persons exist. These include but are not limited to local communities and political communities such as the state. While examining this is outside the scope of this chapter, this holistic approach to "community" is meant to attend to the centrality of social bonds. Together with the principle of subsidiarity, which affirms that decision making and action should be attended closest to the situation possible and at the highest ordering necessary, CST recognizes that all of the levels of community, from the family and local groups to the state to the international community and one human family, are valued and have their own proper functions.

3. Theologically, to speak of the "already, but not yet" character of human dignity and human development frames this within the greater responsibility

to cooperate with God and work for greater justice "on earth as it is in heaven." It is rooted in the virtues of faith and hope but also intimately tied to the virtue of justice. As such, this already but not yet is a matter not only of eschatology but also of human rights and the common good. As Pope Benedict XVI notes in *Caritas in Veritate*, "In an increasingly globalized society, the common good and the effort to obtain it cannot fail to assume the dimensions of the whole human family, that is to say, the community of peoples and nations, in such a way as to shape the *earthly city* in unity and peace, rendering it to some degree an anticipation and a prefiguration of the undivided *city of God*" (Benedict XVI 2009, 7).

4. For more on this particular debate, see Glendon (2001), Hollenbach (1979), Maritain (1944).

5. Gender-inclusive language added, not in original text but true to original intent. This is the preferred translation of the encyclical and the one that is often cited by Vatican documents themselves (such as John Paul II's 2003 World Day of Peace Message). Translation from O'Brien and Shannon (1992), not from the Vatican website.

6. See also Hanvey (2013).

7. For more on this, see USCCB (1986).

8. For more information on this theological point, see Clark (2014), where I develop the connection among human dignity, the community, and the Trinity. Central to the theology of human dignity is creation *imago Dei*, examining what it means to be created *imago Trinitatis*.

9. For Karol Wojtyla (who became Pope John Paul II), authentic solidarity includes opposition: "Experience with diverse forms of opposition . . . teaches that people who oppose do not wish to leave the community because of their opposition. They are searching for their own place in the community— they are searching for participation and such a definition of the common good that would permit them to participate more fully and effectively in the community" (Wojtyla 1981, 49).

10. It is worth noting that many of Sen's articles and *The Idea of Justice*, which examine the philosophy of human rights, take note of Marx's distinction between interpreting and changing the world as important for examining human rights theory and practice.

11. For more on this see Clark (2007) and Deneulin (2006).

12. For more on Martha Nussbaum's approach to capabilities and human rights, see Nussbaum (1988, 2000, 2011). For an examination of Nussbaum in conversation with CST, see O'Connell (2009).

13. Reducing multi-dimensional poverty is the first of the seventeen Sustainable Development Goals (SDGs) adopted by the United Nations in 2015.

For more information on multidimensional poverty, see OPHI (2022). For more information on the United Nation's SDGs, see https://sdgs.un.org/goals.

14. See also Francis's (2013a) *Evangelii Gaudium*, paragraphs 217–22.

WORKS CITED

Ban, Ki-Moon. 2013. *A Life of Dignity for All: Accelerating Progress towards the Millenium Development Goals and Advancing the United Nations Development Agenda Beyoned 2015. Report of the Secretary General.* https://www.un.org/millenniumgoals/pdf/A%20Life%20of%20Dignity%20for%20All.pdf.

Banchoff, Thomas. 2014. "Religion and the Global Politics of Human Dignity." In *Human Dignity and the Future of Global Institutions*, edited by Mark P. Lagon and Anthony Clark Arend. Washington, DC: Georgetown University Press, 257–74.

Beattie, Tina. 2015. "Dignity beyond Rights: Human Development in the Context of the Capabilities Approach and Catholic Social Teaching." *Australian eJournal of Theology* 22, no. 3: 150–65.

Beitz, Charles. 2013. "Human Dignity in the Theory of Human Rights." *Philosophy & Public Affairs* 41, no. 3: 259–90.

Benedict XVI. 2009. *Caritas in Veritate: On Integral Human Development in Charity in Truth.* Encyclical. https://www.vatican.va/content/benedict-xvi/en/encyclicals/documents/hf_ben-xvi_enc_20090629_caritas-in-veritate.html.

Cahill, Lisa Sowle. 2005. *Theological Bioethics: Participation, Justice, Change.* Washington, DC: Georgetown University Press.

———. 2018. "Laudato Si': Reframing Catholic Social Ethics." *Heythrop Journal* 59: 887–900.

Clark, Meghan J. 2007. "Integrating Human Rights: Participation in John Paul II, Catholic Social Thought and Amartya Sen." *Political Theology* 8, no. 3: 299–331.

———. 2014. *The Vision of Catholic Social Thought: The Virtue of Solidarity and the Praxis of Human Rights.* Minneapolis: Fortress.

Deneulin, Séverine. 2006. "Amartya Sen's Capability Approach to Development and *Gaudium et Spes*." *Journal of Catholic Social Thought* 3, no. 2: 355–72.

Deneulin, Séverine, and Jhonatan Clausen. 2018. "*Collective Choice and Social Welfare* by Amartya Sen: A Review Essay with Reference to Development in Peru." OPHI Working Paper 113, University of Oxford, Oxford.

Francis. 2013a. *Evangelii Gaudium*. Apostolic exhortation. https://www
.vatican.va/content/francesco/en/apost_exhortations/documents/papa
-francesco_esortazione-ap_20131124_evangelii-gaudium.html.

———. 2013b. *Lumen Fidei*. Encyclical. https://www.vatican.va/content
/francesco/en/encyclicals/documents/papa-francesco_20130629_enciclica
-lumen-fidei.html.

———. 2014. "Fraternity, the Foundation and Pathway to Peace." World Day
of Peace Message. https://www.vatican.va/content/francesco/en/messages
/peace/documents/papa-francesco_20131208_messaggio-xlvii-giornata
-mondiale-pace-2014.html.

———. 2015a. Address to the United Nations General Assembly, New York,
September 25. http://w2.vatican.va/content/francesco/en/speeches/2015
/september/documents/papa-francesco_20150925_onu-visita.html.

———. 2015b. *Laudato Si': On Care for Our Common Home*. Encyclical. https:
//www.vatican.va/content/dam/francesco/pdf/encyclicals/documents
/papa-francesco_20150524_enciclica-laudato-si_en.pdf.

———. 2020a. "Heal the World: 2. Faith and Human Dignity." Audience
on Wednesday, August 12. https://www.vatican.va/content/francesco
/en/audiences/2020/documents/papa-francesco_20200812_udienza
-generale.html.

———. 2020b. *Fratelli Tutti: On Fraternity and Social Friendship*. Encyclical.
https://www.vatican.va/content/francesco/en/encyclicals/documents
/papa-francesco_20201003_enciclica-fratelli-tutti.html.

Gilabert, Pablo. 2015. "Human Rights, Human Dignity, and Power." In *Philosophical Foundations of Human Rights*, edited by Rowan Cruft, Matthew
Liao, and Massimo Renzo. Oxford: Oxford University Press, 196–213.

Glendon, Mary Ann. 2001. *A World Made New: Eleanor Roosevelt and the Universal Destination of Human Rights*. New York: Random House.

Hanvey, James. 2013. "Dignity, Person, Imago Trinitatis." In *Understanding
Human Dignity*, edited by Christopher McCrudden. Oxford: Oxford
University Press, 209–28.

Hollenbach, David. 1979. *Claims in Conflict: Retrieving and Renewing the
Catholic Human Rights Tradition*. Mahwah, NJ: Paulist Press.

———. 2002. *Common Good and Christian Ethics*. Cambridge: Cambridge
University Press.

John XXIII. 1963. *Pacem in Terris*. Encyclical. https://www.vatican.va/content
/john-xxiii/en/encyclicals/documents/hf_j-xxiii_enc_11041963_pacem
.html

John Paul II. 1987a. "Development and Solidarity: Two Keys to Peace." World
Day of Peace Message. http://w2.vatican.va/content/john-paul-ii/en

/messages/peace/documents/hf_jp-ii_mes_19861208_xx-world-day-for
-peace.html.

———. 1987h. *Sollicitudo Rei Socialis* (*SRS*). Encyclical. https://www.vatican.va
/content/john-paul-ii/en/encyclicals/documents/hf_jp-ii_enc_30121987
_sollicitudo-rei-socialis.html.

King, Martin Luther Jr. 2001. *Measure of a Man.* Minneapolis: Fortress.

Maritain, Jacques. 1944. "Introduction." In United Nations Educational, Scientific, and Cultural Organization (UNESCO): *Human Rights: Comments
and Interpretations; A Symposium Edited by UNESCO.* Paris, 9–17.

Moltmann, Jürgen. 1984. *On Human Dignity: Political Theology and Ethics.*
Translated by M. Douglas Meeks. Minneapolis: Fortress.

Nussbaum, Martha. 1988. "Nature, Function, and Capability: Aristotle on Political Distribution." In *Oxford Studies in Ancient Philosophy, Supplementary
Volume* (vol. 6). Oxford: Oxford University Press, 145–84.

———. 2000. *Women and Human Development: The Capabilities Approach.*
Cambridge: Cambridge University Press.

———. 2011. *Creating Capabilities: The Human Development Approach.* Cambridge, MA: Harvard University Press.

O'Brien, David J., and Thomas A. Shannon. 1992. *Catholic Social Thought: The
Documentary Heritage.* Maryknoll, NY: Orbis.

O'Connell, Maureen. 2009. *Compassion: Loving Our Neighbor in an Age of
Globalization.* Maryknoll, NY: Orbis.

Oxford Poverty and Human Development Initiative (OPHI). 2022. *Policy:
A Multidimensional Approach to Poverty.* https://ophi.org.uk/policy
/multidimensional-poverty-index/.

Paul VI. 1963. *Populorum Progressio: On the Development of Peoples.* Encyclical.
https://www.vatican.va/content/paul-vi/en/encyclicals/documents/hf_p
-vi_enc_26031967_populorum.html.

Robinson, Mary. 1998. "The Declaration of Human Rights: A Living Document." Symposium for Human Rights in the Asia Pacific Region. United
Nations University, Tokyo. https://archive.unu.edu/unupress/Mrobinson
.html.

Rowlands, Anna. 2021. *Towards a Politics of Communion: Catholic Social Teaching in Dark Times.* London: T&T Clark.

Ruston, Roger. 2004. *Human Rights and the Image of God.* London: SCM Press.

Sen, Amartya. 1999. *Development as Freedom.* Oxford: Oxford University Press.

———. 2004. "Elements of a Human Rights Theory." *Philosophy and Public
Affairs* 32, no. 4: 315–56.

———. 2005. "Human Rights and Capabilities." *Journal of Human Development* 6, no. 2: 151–66.

———. 2009. *The Idea of Justice*. London: Allen Lane.

———. 2012. "The Global Reach of Human Rights." *Journal of Applied Philosophy* 29, no. 2: 91–100.

Spadaro, Antonio, SJ. 2013. "A Big Heart Open to God: An Interview with Pope Francis." *America Magazine*, September 30. https://www.americamagazine.org/faith/2013/09/30/big-heart-open-god-interview-pope-francis.

United Nations (UN). 1945. *Charter of the United Nations*. San Francisco: United Nations.

———. 1948. *Universal Declaration of Human Rights (UDHR)*. New York: United Nations.

United Nations Development Programme (UNDP). 2000. *Human Development Report*. New York: UNDP. https://hdr.undp.org/sites/default/files/reports/261/hdr_2000_en.pdf.

United States Conference of Catholic Bishops (USCCB). 1986. *Economic Justice for All*. https://www.usccb.org/upload/economic_justice_for_all.pdf.

Vatican Council II. 1965. *Gaudium et Spes*. Constitution. https://www.vatican.va/archive/hist_councils/ii_vatican_council/documents/vat-ii_const_19651207_gaudium-et-spes_en.html.

Verstraeten, Johan. 2017. "Catholic Social Thought and Amartya Sen on Justice." In *Economics as a Moral Science*, edited by Peter Rona and Laszlo Zsolnai. Dordrecht: Springer, 215–23.

Wojtyla, Karol. 1981. *Toward a Philosophy of Praxis*. New York: Crossroad.

World Congress on Human Rights. 1993. *Vienna Declaration and Programme for Action*. https://www.ohchr.org/en/instruments-mechanisms/instruments/vienna-declaration-and-programme-action.

NINE

Encounter and Agency

An Account of a Grassroots Organization in Uganda

Ilaria Schnyder von Wartensee and Elizabeth Hlabse

ABSTRACT

In this chapter we bring into dialogue Catholic Social Teaching (CST), the capability approach (CA), and the results of a qualitative study in Kampala, Uganda, to consider the crucial role of interpersonal encounter in catalyzing local actors' agency. We suggest that encounter catalyzes an expression of development that is deeply personal, emerging from the person as agent, and thus becoming the basis for a constructive and lasting process of integral human development. Through the study of Meeting Point International (MPI), a grassroots development organization in Kampala, we present the central features of encounter that have emerged in MPI's efforts to promote the health and well-being of vulnerable people. After considering each dimension of encounter in relation to CST, we propose that encounter brings to light a crucial yet unexplored aspect of the CA, for it is through encounter that agency is fostered and expressed. We conclude by highlighting distinct points of emphasis between CST and the CA as regards the experience of encounter in development interventions.

INTRODUCTION

In the early 1990s, a Ugandan nurse named Rose Busingye began working with HIV/AIDS patients in Kireka, a slum in Kampala, Uganda. Home to approximately 68,000 people, Kireka is known for its significant population of internally displaced persons from Northern Uganda. Many of the displaced women residents had suffered intense trauma before arriving at Kireka: some had been kidnapped and forced to commit violence; others had been victims of rape, contracted HIV, and been rejected by their families. Rose began her work with the women by providing anti-retrovirals and medical treatment. After several years, however, the standard interventions were proving ineffective. Many patients were rejecting the medicines or refusing the treatment. Rose began to consider what was lacking in her approach. She recalls questioning: "Who are these people to me? ... And who am I to them?" (Busingye 2001). She asked what the women needed beyond medicine and began listening to their aspirations, needs, and longings. She started to discern a common cry, a cry for love and affirmation, for something or someone to give meaning to their existence. She came to recognize the reality described by a patient of hers: "If you are sick, though they have given you everything, [if] there is no love ... you will never respond to the treatment, but when someone who is attending to you ... shows you all that love, you respond very fast."

Through sharing daily life with her patients, Rose Busingye founded Meeting Point International (MPI), an organization that provides not only medical and psychological services but also social support. Today MPI serves over 1,000 persons, primarily women, and provides indirect services for more than 13,800. Women who had refused the medication from Rose now participate fully in the activities of MPI. The organization has initiated new socioeconomic enterprises, built two schools, and sponsored fundraising efforts for vulnerable populations abroad. The central vision of MPI is to facilitate a space of encounter wherein each person served can rediscover her value and dignity.

The experience of MPI highlights that development is not just a matter of economic growth or improvement across material dimensions, whether health and housing or education and employment. Rather, as articulated both within the capability approach (CA) and Catholic Social Teaching (CST), the human person is the subject and ultimate end of the development process. The example of MPI suggests, however, that something is needed to animate and awaken the capacity of people to act as subjects of their own development and to promote their flourishing, a capacity that is described in the development studies literature as "agency" (Sen 1999; Gammage et al. 2018). There is, in other words, a precondition to agency. Rose's relationship with the women suggests that a key element whereby a person is awakened to her dignity and value, one that catalyzes her agency, is what we call encounter. In this chapter we bring our qualitative research on MPI into dialogue with CST and the CA.[1] We proceed by discussing the central features of encounter that emerged in our research, and we consider each feature in terms of how it is treated within CST. We suggest that encounter brings to light a crucial yet unexplored aspect of the CA, for it is through encounter that agency is fostered and expressed. Encounter catalyzes an expression of development that is deeply personal, emerging from the person as agent. We conclude by discussing the distinct points of emphasis between CST and the CA as regards the experience of encounter in development interventions.

AGENCY THROUGH THE LENS OF CST

As this edited volume highlights, the CA and CST are both person-centered approaches, and they share a central focus on the human person as the primary development actor. Following Sen, well-being and agency are seen as "the two central ideas that give cogency to the focus on human development. That focus relates, on one side, to a clearer comprehension of how—and in what ways—human lives can be lived much better and, on the other, to a fuller understanding of how this betterment can be brought about through a strengthening of human agency" (Sen 2003, vii). CST takes this vision a step further, understanding the person in her integrality. As we read in *Populorum Progressio* (*PP*; Paul VI 1967, 14) and *Sollicitudo Rei Socialis* (*SRS*; John Paul II 1987, 1, 29), development involves the person's interior dimension, including her religious sense. As elaborated in *SRS* 29, "Development which is not only economic must be measured and oriented according to the reality and vocation of man seen in his totality, namely, according to his interior dimension." This case study examines the centrality of the human person, and her agency, to human development.

The literature on the CA highlights that the subjective dimension of agency exercises an important role in the process of empowerment and the expansion of human capabilities (Davis 2004; Teschl and Derobert 2008). This subjective dimension—while pertaining to the person and involving psychological agency, internal motivation, and self-belief—is found to have also an essentially relational character that is expressed in and through one's relationships (Klein 2014). Nonetheless, there is little in the existing literature that treats the interplay among subjective agency, human relationship, and capability expansion. In a previous article we consider how quality of relationship awakens a person's identity, catalyzing agency (Schnyder von Wartensee et al. 2018). Considering the CA in light of CST, we discuss how it is in the experience of encounter that agency is awakened and development fostered. We describe in the following paragraphs some key stages of this awakening.

The Longing of the Human Heart

When Rose began her work in Kireka, she recognized that many of the women were not only materially but also emotionally vulnerable. They had internalized past experiences of violence, rejection, and abuse. In qualitative interviews, many women discussed their lives prior to Kampala when they were "in the bush" and detained by rebels from the Lord's Resistance Army (LRA) in Northern Uganda. As one woman described her earlier life: "In 1997 I was abducted; then I stayed in the bush for three years. In 2000, when I came back, life was not easy; whenever I passed, people talked about me." Upon escaping from the LRA, many women returned to their villages but were rejected by their families and communities.

As result of the violence and trauma they had endured, the women reflected feelings of fear, shame, and isolation. One woman described her situation upon arriving at MPI: "I was looking like I was the tiny lady. . . . I saw my friends [and] I said, . . . They do not have [problems] like me. Sometimes I feared being near to them. I would stay in the corner there, just quiet." Another woman remarked: "I felt I was not fitting anywhere, I had that fear, in fact I was traumatized." The women's woundedness was not only physical but also internal, where medicines could not reach. As one woman said: "You know . . . me telling people my problem is not easy: I laugh with you, I play with you, I share with you, but inside my heart it is not easy to get. That is my problem. . . . I felt like I did not want to give someone my burden and [I wanted to] fight alone."

Through spending time with the women, Rose realized the depth of their psychological and spiritual suffering. She recognized that anti-retrovirals and medical treatment were insufficient to promote the women's healing and that, more fundamentally, they needed to re-discover a reason for living. In CST the human person's profound desire for meaning is described in terms of "heart." St. Augustine (1960) wrote of the restless heart of the human person who longs for God (Lib. 1, 1–2, 2.5, 5: CSEL 33, 1–5). In a general audience Pope Benedict XVI (2012) explained that nothing finite can satisfy the human heart and its infinite desire, which is realized in God alone. The heart is the place of the human person wherein we locate the aspirations for love, truth, and justice (Giussani 2015). Hence, the treatment of "heart" is related to the experience of love described by CA scholar Flavio Comim (2018): "Love is about how we look at ourselves and how we perceive ourselves as objects of value. Love is also about how we look at other people. Thus, love is about self-recognition and about mutual-recognition." In their experience of shame and isolation, the women of MPI struggle to recognize their value and express a longing for love and for meaning.

The Heart's Awakening: An Encounter

It is the encounter that stirs the heart of a person and awakens her to an awareness of her value and a newfound sense of hope. In repeated interviews and as confirmed through field observation, the women of

MPI described their relationship with Rose as an encounter. As one woman explains: "The first time I met her, at first I didn't understand her properly. The way she could talk with me, she really saw that love." The woman describes Rose as *seeing the love* to communicate how Rose recognized the woman's goodness and invited her to share in an awareness of her dignity. Another woman reflected: "[Rose] told me, 'Agnes, do you know that you still have the value?'... She talked to me, she really counseled me." Another recalled:

> Rose looked at me . . . and told me: "Vicky, . . . you can do it, you just need to find hope, you have a value and this value is great." I was silent while Rose kept looking at me. Only these words she pronounced, but the eyes, the eyes that looked at me, the eyes spoke much more than her mouth. She looked at me with eyes that invited me to believe them, as if she were telling me: there is something above you in which you must place your hope. (Aryenyo 2008)

The women's experience has brought to light several key characteristics of encounter. First, encounter is a personal invitation. Rose calls the women by name. Second, the encounter invites each woman to rediscover her value and inherent dignity. Third, with the rediscovery of one's value, a person can re-envision her future with hope, not limited by the confines of suffering. In this way, the encounter is a gaze of mercy. Encounter *happens*. It is an unforeseen and unforeseeable transformative event in a person's life.

Within CST, encounter is discussed primarily in terms of a person's encounter with Christ. The Christian faith understands that Christ—in becoming man, an embodied, incarnate God—invites human persons to an encounter with Himself. Recalling the encyclical *Populorum Progressio* (Paul VI 1967), Pope Benedict XVI explains in *Caritas in Veritate* (2009, 8), "Pope Paul VI illuminated the great theme of the development of peoples with the splendour of truth and the gentle light of Christ's charity. He taught that life in Christ is the first and principal factor of development." In the introduction to *Deus Caritas Est* (2005, 1) he highlighted that "being Christian is not the result of an ethical choice or a lofty idea, but the encounter with an event, a person, which gives life a new horizon and a decisive direction." Similarly, in the opening line of

Evangelii Gaudium (2013, 1), Pope Francis expressed this idea: "The joy of the gospel fills the hearts and lives of all who encounter Jesus."

Hence, the essential qualities of encounter with Christ become the defining characteristics of one's encounter with neighbors. The encounter with Christ can be understood in light of the three aforementioned characteristics, which we find in the experience of the dialogue between Rose and the women of MPI. First, Christ calls each by name. In describing Mary Magdalene's encounter with the resurrected Christ in a general audience, Pope Francis (2017) recalls that Christ called her by her name, "Mary" (John 20:1–2, v. 16):

> How nice it is to think that the first apparition of the Risen One—according to the Gospels—took place in such a personal way! To think that there is someone who knows us, who sees our suffering and disappointment, who is moved with us and calls us by name. . . . He calls each of us by our name: he knows us by name; he looks at us; he waits for us; he forgives us; he is patient with us. . . . Jesus calls her: "Mary!": the revolution of her life. Being called by name is a personal invitation, requiring a personal response.

Second, the encounter with Christ awakens the human person to the mystery of her dignity as being made in the image and likeness of God and belonging to God in love.[2] Resuming his catechetical addresses on mercy, in 2016 Pope Francis devoted a general audience to the Gospel account of the healing of the woman suffering from a hemorrhage (Matt. 9:20–22). He explains that Jesus, by looking upon her with tenderness and mercy, acknowledges her dignity: "He knows what has happened and he seeks a personal encounter with her, which is essentially what the woman desired. This means that Jesus not only welcomes, but considers her worthy of this encounter, to the point of giving her his word and his attention." Pope Francis adds, "We do not know her name, but the few lines in the Gospels describing her encounter with Jesus outline a journey of faith that is capable of restoring the truth and greatness of the dignity of every person." In such an encounter, Christ affirms the person at the depth and foundation of her being; he affirms her as made in his image.

In *Redemptor Hominis* Pope John Paul II (1979) describes that to encounter love is to encounter Christ who "fully reveals man to himself"

(10). The encounter with Christ changes the way a person understands herself. It awakens the person to her identity through the awareness of her fundamental value and dignity. As Pope Francis said in a 2014 address to UN representatives at the Vatican, the rebel Zaccheus rediscovered himself and his dignity in his encounter with Christ: "It is the encounter between Jesus Christ and the rich tax collector Zacchaeus, as a result of which Zacchaeus made a radical decision of sharing and justice, because his conscience had been awakened by the gaze of Jesus." It was through the love of Jesus that Zacchaeus began to look at himself and to act in a transformed way.

In *Fratelli Tutti* Pope Francis (2020, 87) describes how the encounter with another mirrors the encounter with Christ, for in and through encounter the person experiences self-discovery and fulfillment:

> Human beings are so made that they cannot live, develop and find fulfilment except "in the sincere gift of self to others." Nor can they fully know themselves apart from an encounter with other persons: "I communicate effectively with myself only insofar as I communicate with others." No one can experience the true beauty of life without relating to others, without having real faces to love. This is part of the mystery of authentic human existence.

This brings us to the third characteristic of encounter, that it moves one to a response of hope. Becoming aware of one's identity and dignity involves the recognition of one's vulnerability and sinfulness. In reflecting on the conversion of St. Matthew, also known as Levi (Luke 5:25–28, Mk 2:13–14), in a general audience, Pope Francis (2016) explained that in the encounter with Christ, Christ's gaze carried such love and mercy that St. Matthew could not resist. The Pope reflected on the encounter with Christ's mercy in relation to his own experience of the call to priesthood at age 17 on the feast of St. Matthew (Enright 2018). "That finger of Jesus, pointing at Matthew. That's me. I feel like him. Like Matthew" (Francis, quoted in Spadaro 2013). Pope Francis explained how the recognition of one's own sinfulness opens the door to Christ's mercy. The encounter of love and mercy evokes agency just as it moved St. Matthew to act, to follow Christ.

Finally, by affirming the person's dignity, encounter catalyzes the inner state of the person, awakening agency such that the person becomes the protagonist of her development. In this sense, encounter is a transformative event in the person's life. Prades (2014) uses the metaphor of a spark to describe the encounter through which a person becomes conscious of her value and her aspirations. Encounter acts as a catalyst to agency. Hence, human flourishing and development become possible through relationships of encounter that transform the way a person understands and approaches her life in light of her dignity.

Rose attributes her capacity to encounter and to share life with the women of MPI to faith. She recognizes faith as the foundation for self-consciousness, identity, and aspirations; this is a central reason for which she invites the women to reflect on the meaning of their lives. Following Rose, some of the women of MPI find that faith becomes the source of meaning for their personal growth and belonging to the community. In interviews, several women described how in community meetings, when asked to reflect on the meaning of their lives, they came to recognize faith as an animating factor. Some women asked to be baptized, and some chose to take part in additional weekly discussions about faith.

THE INNER DIMENSION OF DEVELOPMENT

Focusing on the experience of encounter—the awakening of one's heart—brings to light the role of the inner life, or the soul, in development. As one woman of MPI explains, "One day, Rose invited me to her office. She looked me in the eyes and said, 'You are valuable and this value is greater than the sickness! . . . you just need to find hope again'" (Aryenyo 2008). Development is not only a matter of physical capacity or material dimensions; Rose points to the starting point of development as the inner life of the human person. She recognizes that in realizing their dignity, the women find the strength to endure physical difficulties because they rediscover a reason for living and a newfound sense of purposefulness. Hence, Rose's insight that healing and recovery are not solely matters of anti-retroviral treatment applies to development more broadly. As Rose explains, "It's very easy to confuse or substitute the human person with what we are doing for him or her. You reduce the person to a project; even you can reduce her to a sickness" (Busingye 2012, 2). Development interventions are secondary to the person's will to live, based on a recognition of one's value and life's meaning.

Clemens Sedmak discusses the person's inner life in relationship to development when describing the soul as home to one's deepest desire. He explains: "The soul as inner space can be depicted as 'active agent' as well as backdrop where the events of life are 'staged' and come to pass." It is in the soul that one's "intellect, will, memory, attitudes, and emotions" exist together and facilitate the expression of agency (Sedmak 2017, 28). Pope Benedict XVI (2009, 76) describes this inner dimension of development in *Caritas in Veritate*: "The question of development is closely bound up with our understanding of the human soul." He builds on Pope John Paul II's (1987, 41) writings in *Sollicitudo Rei Socialis*: "Whatever affects the dignity of individuals and peoples, such as authentic development, cannot be reduced to a 'technical' problem. If reduced in this way, development would be emptied of its true content, and this would be an act of betrayal of the individuals and peoples whom development is meant to serve." In *Laudato Si'* (2015, 112), Pope Francis reflects that the present ecological crisis is a moral crisis. He remarks, "An authentic humanity, calling for a new synthesis, seems to dwell in the midst of our technological culture." CST understands that technocratic approaches, which conceive of development in terms of material dimensions, are insufficient; rather, the challenges of development can be addressed adequately through the transformation of each person.

Encounter presents an invitation to share in the journey of development and flourishing, and this invitation is open always to the freedom of each person. Taking into account the inner dimension of development also entails a recognition of the freedom of the person to accept or reject the encounter. Rose recognizes that the women of MPI are free to accept or to reject the invitation, the opportunity, to share in community life. Initially, the women declined to take the anti-retroviral medication. The decision, however, was not made freely because their earlier trauma and their negative social context had occluded the women's vision of their dignity and their reason for living. Rose persisted in her efforts to engage the women. As Pope Benedict XVI reflected in a 2006 homily, this persistence of encounter reflects the persistence of

God's beckoning the person to awaken to her dignity and to the fullness of life to which she is called. Those who accept the invitation, wondering "What does this mean for me?" choose to enter into a relationship of belonging. As we describe in the next section, through belonging and accompaniment the MPI women are sustained in their reflection on life's meaning, and they continue to integrate this understanding into their daily lives.

BELONGING AND ACCOMPANIMENT

Through encounter, the women of MPI enter into relationship with Rose and with one another, relationship of mutuality and shared responsibility, which can be described as belonging. When they describe their experience of freedom, they reference specifically this relationship of belonging. They regularly perform a song, re-enacting their lives prior to meeting Rose: "When I was a widow, . . . When I was a mad one, . . . a street kid, . . . a witch doctor, . . . in the bush, . . . in the quarry." They conclude each verse by singing, "Since I met Rose, she brought my heart and saved me. Rose set me free. I'm now free." By coming to recognize their dignity through their encounters with Rose and one another, the women deepen in awareness of their freedom, which is experienced and expressed in relationship. Freedom, within CST and as exhibited at MPI, implies the responsibility to look after and care for one another, realizing that the other's flourishing is intimately united with one's own. Within CST, Pope Benedict XVI said in a 2012 general audience, the journey of freedom is expressed in self-gift, and the ultimate fulfillment of one's freedom is in communion with God. In becoming aware of their dignity, belonging, and need to be in relationship with Christ and fellow members of humanity, the women of MPI are moved to encounter others and to invite them into an awareness of their dignity.

In other words, belonging both generates accompaniment and is generated by it. It is "the vehicle by which the consciousness of local actors grows by being invited to share what is most important to them in a process of constructive dialogue" (Schnyder von Wartensee 2018, 638). Reifenberg and Hlabse (2020, 248) describe accompaniment as "an approach of deep listening and of walking with." At MPI, the accompaniment process can be understood in light of several key characteristics.

First, accompaniment involves a deepening reflection on the meaning of one's life, which fosters further expressions of agency. Rose encourages a reflection of life's meaning in one-to-one interactions with the women as well as in community meetings, which take place twice a week. During these meetings Rose guides the women in dialogue around a central theme, such as love or life's meaning. She prompts the women to reflect on central questions such as these: Who am I? How am I living? By giving testimony and engaging in dialogue, the women deepen in the realization of their value and the meaning they ascribe to their experience. Rose accompanies the women in their discernment. One woman recounts, "In Meeting Point, actually in meetings, we have learnt many things. Rose has taught us how to share, how to love each other and [forgive] each other." Through accompaniment, the women reflect on their aspirations in a manner that is supported and sustained within the community.

A second defining feature of accompaniment is mutuality. Rose exhibits an openness and willingness to grow with, and learn from, the women that makes the experience of belonging possible. Rose's own self-awareness and agency are expressed and developed in and through relationship with the women. One woman describes her experience: "Rose is not in front or behind. She moves in the middle. She is not the leader. She stays within and we learn together." Rose's relationships with the women can be interpreted in the light of Paterson and Zderad's (1976, 132) description of humanistic nursing as "a mode of being available or open in a situation with the wholeness of one's unique individual being; a gift of self which can only be given freely." Moreover, Rose's relationships reflect the dynamic of development described by Quarles van Ufford and Giri (2003, 255): "Development is not only meant for the other, it is also meant for the self . . . both the development of the other and development of self should go hand in hand." The encounter is deepened over time in a relationship of accompaniment.

Third, accompaniment situates development in a time frame that is dependent on the person and her unique needs and aspirations; as such, the process cannot be confined to a time-specific, metrics-based evaluation. MPI's approach varies by length and circumstances, responsive to the freedom, needs, and aspirations of those involved. For some women of MPI, the positive impact of the relationship occurs when they first meet Rose and other members of the MPI community; others live at MPI for years before coming to an awareness of their value. One woman explained that she had lived at MPI nearly ten years before she believed the mantra she'd long been repeating, "I have a value." Another woman explained: "She [Rose] is somehow different; she keeps on ... she keeps on coming to me and counsel me." This quality of relationship, reflected in the encounter, implies a vision of development with a longer and more flexible timeline for fostering the deepening awareness of people's value. This vision stands in contrast to the predominant mode of conceptualizing development through short-term impact evaluations.

Awakened to their dignity and supporting one another in community life, the women of MPI are moved to acts of charity and generosity. One woman explains: "If you don't love yourself you cannot love the others." The women reflect that because of their experience of joy and gratitude, which arises from belonging and accompaniment and which encounter has generated, they are able to embrace others. They have initiated various efforts including the fundraising and construction of a primary and secondary school for their children and fundraising for relief efforts abroad.[3] More basically, the women of MPI recognize that they transmit the richness of encounter through their witness. Recognizing their own dignity, they can perceive the dignity of each person and bear responsibility for the lives of other human persons.

As Pope Benedict XVI (2009, 11) puts it in *Caritas in Veritate*, "In the encounter with God we are able to see in the other something more than just another creature, to recognize the divine image in the other, thus truly coming to discover him or her and to mature in a love that 'becomes concern and care for the other.'" Pope John Paul II, in *Sollicitudo Rei Socialis* (1987, 26), describes the phenomenon of being "linked together in a common destiny." Awakened to one's own dignity, a person becomes aware of the dignity of her neighbor—and aware that their dignity is shared, bound up in relationship. In *Laudato Si'* Pope Francis (2015, 240) likens encounter to nurturing the bounds of solidarity: "Everything is interconnected, and this invites us to develop a spirituality of that global solidarity which flows from the mystery of the Trinity." Hence, encounter gives birth to development through relationships of solidarity.

FREEDOM, ENCOUNTER, AND DEVELOPMENT IN THE CA AND CST

The centrality of the person is a common foundation of human development, both for the CA and for CST. Human development is something that happens to a person and through a person. As Alkire (2010, 40, emphasis in original) expresses it, "Human development is development *by* the people *of* the people and *for* the people." The alternative to this approach is to measure development directly through the outcomes, forgetting the personal inner dimensions and the process through which a person comprehends, desires, and acts on her values and aspirations. This reduction is present, for example, in the literature that identifies the measurement of human development principally in terms of multidimensionality. Ponzio and Gosh (2016) describe the tendency of human development to approach multidimensionality as an end in itself rather than the measure for evaluating how people pursue ways of life they deem valuable.

Sen explains that the CA necessarily implies a multidimensional approach because human development requires a change in life conditions (Shaikh 2004). The primacy Sen assigns to human freedom, hence agency, prevents human development from being reduced to a list of material conditions. CST takes this vision a step further, providing a substantive vision of human flourishing. Because the human person is the subject, not only the "object," of development, Pope Francis writes (*LS* 81), the various dimensions emerge from one's needs and aspirations. He further cautions against the "technocratic paradigm," or the tendency to evaluate human progress in terms of technological and material advances without considering the full measure of human flourishing and without accounting for the interdependency of members of the human community (2015, 101). In other words, personal growth cannot be separated from inner growth; integral development involves the whole of the person, including the moral and spiritual dimensions (Sedmak 2017).

The focus of both the CA and CST on the person as the subject of her own and others' development is the strongest point of relation between the two approaches, and it underlines the importance of freedom. The whole of CST regards the path of human freedom (PCJP 2004, 63), and freedom, following Sen (1992, 36), is "the primary end . . . and principal means of development." In the CA, freedom involves two related dimensions: freedom as opportunity and freedom as a process. The first dimension relates to the space of capabilities and to the ability of a person to achieve those things that she has reason to value. The second dimension relates to the concept of agency; freedom is the process through which a person acts to achieve desired capabilities (see Sen 2002, 10, quoted in Alkire and Deneulin 2009, 10).

How might we, then, understand how freedom, as both opportunity and process, happens—how it is fostered and expressed? CST articulates a vision of human freedom that is essentially relational. The example of MPI brings forth a further insight: that freedom as opportunity and process cannot be expressed without the encounter. Prior to meeting Rose, the women of MPI could not identify a reason for living. The encounter with her was necessary to awaken their sense of meaning (opportunity freedom) and to catalyze their agency (process freedom). In fact, the MPI women identify the encounter as the decisive experience by which they come to recognize their value and the value of living. In their experience of being loved, and of belonging, the women recognize their responsibilities to care for themselves and for one another. Their pursuit of aspirations is bound by choosing to live and act in a manner that stewards the common goods of community life.

Development, thus, cannot be understood as an individual pursuit; rather, through encounter, a person enters into a relationship of belonging and responsibility whereby agency is expressed. This brings to light a point of distinction between the CA's and CST's respective understandings of freedom as opportunity. Paolo Carozza (2017, 38) argues that opportunity freedom, following the CA, can lend itself to reductionism, suggesting "that human self-realization is fundamentally about the maximization of individual choice without regard to the substance of ends chosen." CST goes a step further than the CA in elaborating its understanding of human freedom, which is experienced properly in one's belonging to one's relationships, one's community, and to God, which awakens one to her humanity.

CONCLUDING REMARKS ON ENCOUNTER AND THE INTERSECTION OF THE CA AND CST

Through qualitative research on the experience of MPI, in this chapter we have explored the role of encounter in catalyzing agency by awakening in a person an awareness of her dignity and value. Beginning with the centrality of freedom and agency, as identified in the CA and CST, we have discussed how agency was fostered in the women of MPI. The importance of encounter has been dealt with at length within CST, including in Pope Francis's recent encyclical *Fratelli Tutti* (2020), in which he elaborates on the CST's treatment of one's encounter with Christ to inform an understanding of one's encounter with neighbors. Bringing this discussion of encounter into dialogue with the experience of MPI, we have analyzed some of the central features of encounter and how an appreciation for encounter, drawing upon both CST and the CA, can advance our understanding of human development.

NOTES

1. Field research and subsequent analysis of MPI's experience were conducted between February 2014 and May 2015. The specific tools included participant observations, in-depth interviews, and focus group discussions.

2. The understanding of human dignity as deriving from being created in the image and likeness of God is attributable to Genesis 1:26. It is expounded on in John XXIII, *Pacem in Terris* 10 and Vatican Council II, *Gaudium et Spes* 22.

3. In response to Hurricane Katrina and the earthquake in L'Aquila, Italy, the women of MPI garnered funds through their labor of breaking rocks into gravel to send donations to the victims.

WORKS CITED

Alkire, Sabina. 2010. "Human Development: Definition, Critiques and Related Concepts." OPHI Working Paper 36, University of Oxford, Oxford.

Alkire, Sabina, and Séverine Deneulin. 2009. "Introducing the Human Development and Capability Approach." In *An Introduction to the Human*

Development and Capability Approach, edited by Séverine Deneulin and Lila Shahani. London: Earthscan.

Aryenyo, Vicky. 2008. "Is Saying 'Yes' to the Mystery." Presentation at the Meeting for Friendship among People, Rimini, Italy. http://archivio .traces-cl.com/2008E/09/issayingyes.html.

Augustine. 1960 (400). *The Confessions of St. Augustine*. Translated by John K. Ryan. New York: Doubleday.

Benedict XVI. 2005. *Deus Caritas Est*. Encyclical, December 25. http://w2 .vatican.va/content/benedict-xvi/en/encyclicals/documents/hf_ben-xvi _enc_20 051225_deus-caritas-est.html.

———. 2006. "Holy Mass with the Members of the Bishops' Conference of Switzerland: Homily of His Holiness Benedict XVI." Homily, November 7. https://w2.vatican.va/content/benedict-xvi/en/homilies/2006 /documents/hf_ben-xvi_hom_20061107_swiss-bishops.html.

———. 2009. *Caritas in Veritate*. Encyclical, August 28. http://w2.vatican .va/content/benedict-xvi/en/encyclicals/documents/hf_ben-xvi_enc _20090629_caritas-in-veritate.html.

———. 2012. "General Audience," Saint Peter's Square, Wednesday, November 7. http://w2.vatican.va/content/benedict-xvi/en/audiences/2012 /documents/hf_ben-xvi_aud_20121107.html.

Busingye, Rose. 2001. "Presentation of the Lenten Message of the Holy Father for Lent 2001 on the Theme 'Love Is Not Resentful' (1 Cor. 13:5)," Vatican City. http://www.vatican.va/roman_curia/pontifical_councils /corunum/documents/rc_pc_corunum_doc_20010219_Attivita_Iniziative _PresentazioneMQ01_en.html.

———. 2012. "Communion in Suffering and Healing." Personal Testimony at the 50th International Eucharistic Congress, Dublin, Ireland, June. http:// meetingpoint-int.org/wp-content/uploads/2014/12/Rosew-testimony -Intyernational-Eucaristich-Congress.pdf.

Carozza, Paolo G. 2017. "The Structures of Development and the Structure of the Human Person." In *Questione sociale, questione mondiale: La permanente attualità del magistero di Paolo VI*, edited by Ferdinando Citterio, 63–76. Milan: Vita e Pensiero.

Comim, Flavio. 2018. "The Common Good and the Rejection of the Poor." Lecture at the Kellogg Institute for Development Studies, University of Notre Dame, Notre Dame, IN, October.

Davis, John. 2004. "Identity and Commitment: Sen's Conception of the Individual." Tinbergen Institute Discussion Paper 055, no. 2. http://papers .tinbergen.nl/04055.pdf.

Enright, Nancy. 2018. "Pope Francis and Caravaggio's 'The Calling of St. Matthew' Share a Gaze of Mercy." *National Catholic Reporter*. https://www .ncronline.org/news/opinion/pope-francis-and-caravaggios-calling-st -matthew-share-gaze-mercy-0.

Francis. 2013. *Evangelii Gaudium*. Encyclical, November 24. https://www .vatican.va/content/francesco/en/apost_exhortations/documents/papa -francesco_esortazione-ap_20131124_evangelii-gaudium.html.

———. 2014. "Address to the UN System Chief Executives Board for Coordination." Consistory Hall, Vatican City, May 9.

———. 2015. *Laudato Si'*. Encyclical, May 24. http://w2.vatican.va/content /francesco/en/encyclicals/documents/papa-francesco_20150524_enciclica -laudato-si.html.

———. 2016. "General Audience." Saint Peter's Square, Wednesday, April 13. http://w2.vatican.va/content/francesco/en/audiences/2016/documents /papa-francesco_20160413_udienza-generale.html.

———. 2017. "General Audience." Saint Peter's Square, Wednesday, May 17, 2017. http://w2.vatican.va/content/francesco/en/audiences/2017 /documents/papa-francesco_20170517_udienza-generale.html.

———. 2020. *Fratelli Tutti*. Encyclical. Vatican Website. October 3, 2020. https://www.vatican.va/content/francesco/en/encyclicals.index.html #encyclicals.

Gammage, Sarah, Naila Kabeer, and Yana van der Meulen Rodgers. 2018. "Voice and Agency: Where Are We Now?" *Feminist Economics* 22, no. 1 (2018): 1–29. doi: 10.1080/13545701.2015.1101308.

Giussani, Luigi. 2015. *Christ, God's Companionship with Man*. Montreal: McGill-Queen's University Press.

John Paul II. 1979. *Redemptor Hominis*. Encyclical, March 4. http://w2 .vatican.va/content/john-paul-ii/en/encyclicals/documents/hf_jp-ii_enc _04031979_redemptor-hominis.html.

———. 1987. *Sollicitudo Rei Socialis*. Encyclical, December 30. http://w2 .vatican.va/content/john-paul-ii/en/encyclicals/documents/hf_jp-ii_enc _30121987_sollicitudo-rei-socialis.html.

Klein, Elise. 2014. "Psychological Agency: Evidence from the Urban Fringe of Bamako." OPHI Working Paper 69. https://www.ophi.org.uk/wp -content/uploads/OPHIWP69.pdf.

Paterson, Josephine, and Loretta Zderad. 1976. *Humanistic Nursing*. New York: John Wiley and Sons.

Paul VI. 1967. *Populorum Progressio*. Encyclical, March 26. http://w2.vatican .va/content/paul-vi/en/encyclicals/documents/hf_p-vi_enc_26031967 _populorum.html.

Pontifical Council for Justice and Peace (PCJP). 2004. *Compendium of the Social Doctrine of the Church*. Vatican City: Libreria Editrice Vaticana.

Ponzio, Richard, and Arunabha Ghosh. 2016. *Human Development and Global Institutions: Evolution, Impact, Reform*. New York: Routledge.

Prades, Javier. 2014. "Knowing the Truth through Witness: The Christian Faith in the Context of Interreligious Dialogue." In *Retrieving Origins and the Claim of Multiculturalism*, edited by Antonio Lopez and Javier Prades. Translated by Mariangela Sullivan, 176–90. Grand Rapids, MI: William B. Eerdmans.

Quarles van Ufford, Philip, and Ananta Giri. 2003. Reconstituting Development as a Shared Responsibility. In *A Moral Critique of Development: In Search of Global Responsibilities*, edited by Philip Quarles van Ufford and Ananta Giri, 253–78. London: Routledge.

Reifenberg, Stephen, and Elizabeth Hlabse. 2020. "Dignity in Accompaniment: Integrated Health Care in the Sierra Madres." In *Human Dignity in the Practice of Human Development*, edited by Paolo G. Carozza and Clemens Sedmak. Notre Dame, IN: University of Notre Dame Press.

Schnyder von Wartensee, Ilaria. 2018. "At the Root of Participatory Approaches: Uncovering the Role of Accompaniment." *Development in Practice* 28, no. 5: 636–46. doi: 10.1080/09614524.2018.1467880.

Schnyder von Wartensee, Ilaria, Elizabeth Hlabse, Giuseppi Folloni, and Gabriella Berloffa. 2018. "The Role of Personal Identity in Human Development." *European Journal of Development Research*: 1–19. https://doi.org/10.1057/s41287-018-0163-2.

Sedmak, Clemens. 2017. "The Soul of Development." *Journal of Moral Theology* 6, no. 1: 21–38.

Sen, Amartya Kumar. 1992. *Inequality Reexamined*. Oxford: Clarendon.

———. 1999. *Development as Freedom*. New York: Anchor.

———. 2002. Rationality and Freedom. Cambridge, MA: Harvard University Press.

———. 2003. "Foreword." In *Readings in Human Development: Concepts, Measures and Policies for a Development Paradigm*, edited by Sakiko Fukuda-Parr and A. K. Shiva Kumar. Oxford: Oxford University Press.

Shaikh, Nermeen. 2004. "Interview with Amartya Sen." Asia Source Q&A Interview, December 6, 2004. https://asiasociety.org/amartya-sen-more-human-theory-development.

Spadaro, Antonio. 2013. "A Big Heart Open to God: An Interview with Pope Francis." *America Magazine*, September 30. https://www.americamagazine.org/faith/2013/09/30/big-heart-open-god-interview-pope-francis.

Teschl, Miriam, and Laurent Derobert. 2008. "Does Identity Matter? On the Relevance of Identity and Interaction for Capabilities." In *The Capability Approach: Concepts, Measures and Applications*, edited by Flavio Comim, Mozaffar Qizilbash, and Sabina Alkire, 125–56. Cambridge: Cambridge University Press.

TEN

Agency, Power, and Ecological Conversion

The Case of the Conflict-Free Technology Campaign

Guillermo Otano Jiménez

ABSTRACT

In this chapter I show how the conceptual framework of the capability approach (CA)—especially regarding the understanding of agency and power analysis—can be applied to the promotion of ecological conversion. It focuses on the Conflict-Free Technology campaign launched in 2014 by the Alboan Foundation, an international Jesuit non-governmental organization (NGO) from Spain. The chapter is divided in three sections. I start with briefly explaining the context of Alboan and the reasons behind its turn toward the field of integral ecology and socio-environmental justice. In the second section I discuss the advantages of framing the "conflict minerals" issue, which is at the core of the campaign, through the lens of the encyclical Laudato Si' *(Francis 2015). Finally, it analyzes the objectives, strategies, and lines of work carried out since 2014 using the 3C-Model approach to social innovation (conscientization, conciliation, and collaboration) proposed by Ibrahim (2017). I argue that these three elements are related to different understandings of power and, therefore, are central for encouraging ecological conversion at the personal, societal, and institutional levels.*

INTRODUCTION

As Amartya Sen has pointed out on many occasions, public reasoning and social participation—in other words, democracy—play a key role in the collective achievement of human development (Sen 1999a and b, 2009). However, in a book co-authored with Jean Drèze Sen has stressed that "democracy stands not just for electoral politics and civil liberties but also for an equitable distribution of power" (Drèze and Sen 2013, xi). The question of power and its implications for human agency is something that went unnoticed by most of the pioneers of the capability approach (CA) during the 1980s and the 1990s (Fukuda-Parr 2003). This is most likely because the theorization of the CA was dominated from the beginning by economists and philosophers, and other disciplines, such as sociology and anthropology, took longer to join the debate (Otano Jiménez 2015). Be that as it may, the fact remains that the first priority back then was improving the methodological applications of Sen's ideas to assess well-being in terms of human capabilities in order to demonstrate that they offered a better alternative to conventional welfare measures (such as income, resources, or primary goods) in policy planning.

Nevertheless, the perspective of freedom proposed by Sen is not limited to the "evaluative aspect" of human development; it also includes the "process aspect" of freedom (Sen 2002; 2009, 228–30 and 370–71). While the former focuses on evaluating improvements in people's capability to live the life they have reason to value as an explicit development goal, the latter analyzes the interactions between individual and collective agency in the pursuit of such progress. Since the early 2000s, there has been a growing interest in the concept of "agency" and its link with the question of power, as both elements are key to understanding the "process aspect" of freedom (see also Keleher in this volume).[1] In a glo-balized world, where individuals feel increasingly powerless in the face of world-wide socio-economic dynamics and climate threats, there is an urgent need to rethink solidarity and the links among agency, power, and social change.

In this chapter I will argue that the literature on agency and the CA offers interesting insights to promote the idea of "ecological conver-sion," which arises from the teachings of the Catholic social tradition, in practice. This notion was first introduced in January 2001 by Pope John Paul II during a general audience, and more recently, in 2015, it has been developed in depth in Pope Francis's encyclical *Laudato Si'* (*LS*). In both cases it refers to the need to restore the harmony of men and women with God, with their fellow human beings, and with creation. According to the book of Genesis, men and women were created in the "image of God," and they were conceived by God as stewards of His creation. Unfortunately, as Pope John Paul II pointed out in his general audience of 2001, "If we scan the regions of our planet, we immediately see that humanity has disappointed God's expectations" (John Paul II 2001). The advance of deforestation in the Amazonian rainforest or the melting of the West Antarctic ice sheet are only the most visible examples of man-made devastation on earth, but there are many others. As Braden (2021) puts it, "ecological conversion" is "a process of acknowledging our contri-bution to the social and ecological crisis and acting in ways that nurture communion: healing and renewing our common home."

My aim is to show how the conceptual framework of the CA—especially regarding the understanding of agency and power analysis—can be applied to the promotion of social change inspired by the values of ecological conversion. I will do so by focusing on the Conflict-Free Technology campaign launched in 2014 by the Alboan Foundation, an international Jesuit non-governmental organization (NGO) from Spain. The chapter is divided in three sections. I start with briefly explaining the context of Alboan and the reasons behind its turn toward the field of integral ecology and socio-environmental justice. In the second section I discuss the advantages of framing the "conflict minerals" issue, which is at the core of the campaign, through the lens of the encyclical *Laudato Si'*. Finally, I analyze the objectives, strategies, and lines of work car-ried out since 2014 using the 3C-Model approach to social innovation (conscientization, conciliation, and collaboration) proposed by Ibrahim (2017). I argue that these three elements are related to different understandings of power, and therefore, are central for encouraging ecological conversion at the personal, societal, and institutional levels.

ALBOAN'S TURN TOWARD ECOLOGY AND SOCIO-ENVIRONMENTAL JUSTICE

Alboan is a Jesuit international NGO founded in 1996 with headquarters in the Basque Country and Navarre, northern Spain. Its name is taken from the Basque language and means "alongside" or "together with," and it works side by side with many excluded communities and other local organizations from Latin America, Africa, and India. As a Jesuit NGO, Alboan is a "faith-based organisation" inspired by "Ignatian spirituality"—a kind of spirituality "geared towards contemplation in action and which finds fulfilment in mission" (Segura 2013, 8). It is about a way of being in the world with others, and engaging with the social realities of those who suffer structural injustices. The mission of the Society of Jesus (the Jesuits) is characterized by individual, communal, and institutional discernment in search of an apostolic response to people in need (Álvarez de los Mozos 2013). It is a process that is open to dialogue with other religious traditions and cultures. Accordingly, Alboan understands integral human development as "a process of shared construction, in which the style, methods of interacting and ways of doing things are important, as well as the activities and the results themselves" (Alboan 2014).

During the past decade, this commitment to integral human development has led the Society of Jesus as a whole—and most of the Jesuit institutions and organizations, such as Alboan—to pay increasing attention to ecology and socio-environmental justice. The call for "reconciliation with God, with one another, and with Creation" was clearly identified as one of the most important challenges for the Jesuit Mission in the 35th General Congregation of the Society of Jesus, convened in 2008 (Society of Jesus 2008, 3–9). Since then, the theme of "reconciliation with Creation" has been developed in depth in other doctrinal texts, such as the document "Healing a Broken World" written by the Ecology Task Force of the Social Justice and Ecology Secretariat (SJES 2011) and, of course, Pope Francis's encyclical *Laudato Si'* (2015).

This process of collective discernment around the idea of socio environmental justice and ecological conversion has major implications. In the case of the Society of Jesus, this has led to an increasing networking among Jesuit institutions worldwide. In 2008 the Society created the Global Ignatian Advocacy Networks (GIAN), which are centered around four thematic networks: Right to Education (GIAN-Education), Migration and Forced Displacement (GIAN-Migration), Integral Ecology (EcoJesuit), and Governance of Natural Mineral Resources (GIAN-GNMR). Ten years later, the General Superior, Fr. Arturo Sosa, renewed the Universal Apostolic Preferences (UAPs) of the Society around four purposes: "showing the way to God," "walking with the excluded," "journeying with the youth," and "caring for our Common Home" (Sosa 2019). These four points set the Jesuit framework for collaboration in the years to come (2019–29).

Alboan has been deeply involved in the creation of the GIAN, especially in the GNMR. A first research project conducted during 2009–11 showed that the organization's allies in Guatemala, India, and the Democratic Republic of Congo (DRC) were affected by serious human rights abuses caused by environmental conflicts (Aleman Arrastio 2012). Two of the most controversial issues in this regard were the social and environmental impacts of extractive activities such as mining. This finding echoed informal consultations led by the core group of GIAN-GNMR with the Jesuit social centers and organizations from the Jesuit Conferences of Canada and the United States, Africa and Madagascar, South Asia, the Asia Pacific, Europe, and Latin America (SJES 2015). So in 2015, GNMR decided to rename itself "Justice in Mining—A Jesuit Network." The new name emphasizes the focus on mining conflicts and the network's commitment to join forces in the fight for justice in these contexts.

The idea of "global advocacy" is always embedded in the reality of struggles that are experienced "locally" and, therefore, are usually subject to particular power dynamics. However, as we will see in the next section, the holistic framing provided by the encyclical *Laudato Si'* is a powerful tool with which to link both the local and the global dimensions inasmuch as it offers a values-driven approach to the social and environmental challenges of today's world.

READING THE CONFLICT MINERALS ISSUE THROUGH
THE LENS OF LAUDATO SI'

After the Second Congo War, initiated in 1998 and officially ended in 2003, the "resource course" (Ross 1999) took on a dramatic dimension in the eastern DRC—which may still qualify as a conflict zone or high-risk area. The mineral reserves of tin, tantalum, tungsten, and gold found in that region are some of the largest in the world. They are worth millions of dollars, but the DRC remains one the countries in the world that ranks lowest on the Human Development Index (UNDP 2020). Even if the struggles to take control over natural resources are not the main drivers of the political instability in the region (as there are other economic, social, and ethnic factors), they play a key role in fueling the violence, according to the United Nations (UN) group of experts for the DRC.

Despite the local character of the conflict, the smuggling of minerals is a regional problem, since most of these precious metals and ores enter illegally into neighboring countries such as Rwanda and Burundi. Moreover, it has a global dimension, as the minerals then go to smelters and refiners in Southeast Asia to supply the international electronics industry, for these minerals have unique properties that make them useful in the manufacturing of electronic devices such as mobile phones, laptops, and other electronic devices.

The deadly consequences of this trade have also been addressed by the Organization for Economic Co-operation and Development (OECD), which launched the first edition of the *OECD Due Diligence Guidelines for Responsible Supply Chains of Minerals from Conflict-Affected and High-Risk Areas* in 2011 (OECD 2016). The Guide, as it is known, establishes a five-step framework of due diligence as a basis for the responsible supply-chain management of minerals, including tin, tantalum, tungsten, and gold, as well as all other minerals. On the international stage, the OECD Guidelines can be considered the main benchmark against which to assess business practices in the responsible sourcing of minerals. However, the OECD's recommendations are, by definition, not mandatory, so there are very good reasons to be skeptical about the implementation of the guidelines by corporations and businesses alike.

This is why many international NGOs, grassroots organizations, and global social movements have been demanding the translation of these voluntary principles into legally binding regulations. This demand was met first in the United States in the wake of the 2008 financial crisis, when in 2010 President Obama approved the Wall Street Reform Act (also known as the Dodd-Frank Act), whose purpose was to provide tighter regulation of the financial industry and promote corporate transparency. The legislators included a clause, Section 1502, that requires US companies that use tin, tungsten, tantalum, and gold to implement due-diligence systems if these resources come from conflict zones in the DRC and nine adjoining countries.

Following this trend, in October 2010 the European Parliament passed a resolution calling for the regulation of commodity markets and supply chains. Four years later, in 2014, the European Commission announced its proposal to introduce due-diligence obligations for supply chains of minerals from conflict zones or high-risk areas (European Commission 2014). Many international NGOs interpreted this as a window of opportunity to push toward an effective European regulation on the responsible sourcing of minerals coming from conflict areas. Such a law would increase the accountability of companies involved in the mining trade, forcing them to implement due-diligence systems that can identify and prevent risks related to human rights abuses in their supply chains. Accordingly, it would help cut the funds obtained illicitly by organized crime and armed groups operating in the eastern DRC, who are the ones that have been benefiting from the smuggling of minerals for decades.

Alboan joined the informal coalition of NGOs (henceforth, "the Coalition") formed to coordinate lobbying strategies in Brussels and in other EU Member States. By that time, Alboan's campaigns team was clear about the necessity to launch a specific campaign on conflict minerals. It was an opportunity to link accompaniment and service to partner organizations affected by mining with the defense of their rights. As mentioned above, since 2008 at least, Alboan has also been involved in the process of collective discernment around the meanings of "integral ecology" and "Ignatian advocacy." In the terms proposed by the "see-judge-act" hermeneutic cycle characteristic of Catholic Social Teaching (CST; see the Deneulin and Zampini-Davies chapter in this volume), it could be said that Alboan was ready to take action in 2014. A first version of the Conflict-Free Technology Campaign was launched that year alongside the first stage of the negotiations on an EU regulation on conflict minerals at the European Parliament (EP). However, from conversations with members of the EP, policy-makers, and other activists with expertise in this matter, it was clear that the negotiation process could take several years. Many conflicting interests were at stake. From the point of view of the NGOs, the European Commission's initial proposal was too weak.[2] It conceived the due-diligence obligations implicit in the future EU regulation as voluntary, whereas corporate lobbies were pushing against the conflict minerals legislation per se, and some policy-makers and political representatives would rather not have had any regulation at all. The Coalition needed to make much more noise in order to be heard. Alboan—and other NGOs from the core group—had to work out how to gain the utmost support by the European citizens in every EU Member State.

Listening to the voices of those affected by the conflict in the DRC was not enough to convince policy-makers and political representatives of the need for legislation. They were more concerned about the potential impacts of the law on European companies, as well as the unintended consequences for European consumers and Congolese artisanal and small-scale mining communities.[3] So the Coalition needed to ensure, on the one hand, that its demands reflected the views of Congolese civil society and had social support among European citizens, and, on the other, that its solutions were fact-based and "technically feasible," addressing the potential side effects of such a regulation. The initial challenge was how to awaken a sense of solidarity between those remote communities, which suffer on a daily basis from the conflict minerals trade, and European citizens, who are themselves benefiting indirectly from that trade. Without a powerful narrative that linked both realities it would very difficult to persuade individual citizens from Member States to engage in collective actions to reach the EU legislative bodies and push for a binding regulation.

By the time Alboan's campaign team was figuring out how to put together the pieces of this jigsaw, *Laudato Si'* was published, and it greatly facilitated the framing of Alboan's narrative on conflict minerals. If one reads the issue of "conflict minerals" in the DRC (or anywhere else) through the lens of *Laudato Si'*, one easily realizes that it is not just a problem of "underdevelopment" understood in terms of poverty, insecurity, and lack of access to basic education and health care services. It is also a problem of the global dynamics of consumption and production.

As Pope Francis argues in *Laudato Si'*, "We are faced not with two separated crises but one complex crisis which is both social and environmental" (*LS* 139), one with moral and cultural roots. He points out the unsustainability of our consumption patterns and lifestyles. So the search for social justice in the case of conflict minerals should address not only human rights violations, the lack of transparency of global supply chains, and the environmental impacts of mining, but also the drivers behind the demand for tin, tungsten, tantalum, and gold, among other minerals. In other words, it must say something about the "throwaway culture" promoted by the electronics industry and about our individual and collective responsibilities as consumers of electronic devices in a global world.

This integral framing calls for an all-encompassing ecological conversion that goes from the social to the institutional, from individual to collective action. For Alboan's campaigns team, it was clear that the message of the Conflict-Free Technology Campaign should not encourage technophobia. On the contrary, it should aim to start a public conversation about the social and environmental impacts of our patterns of consumption of electronic goods. Global supply chains of minerals are complex systems that bring together many different actors and corporations. They connect our reality as consumers with other people's reality as producers. Even if we do not experience how it feels to be on the other side of the value chain, we cannot skip our responsibility to the rights of the people who occupy that space. As Pope Benedict XVI stated in his 2009 encyclical *Caritas in Veritate* (*CV*), "purchasing is always a moral—and not simply economic—act. Hence the consumer has a specific social responsibility, which goes hand-in-hand with the social responsibility of the enterprise" (*CV* 66). Therefore, consumers have the moral duty to search for as much information as possible about the ethical and environmental aspects of each product purchased. In the next section I analyze the strategies set in motion by Alboan to promote individual and collective agency at the institutional, social, and individual levels using Ibrahim's model for processes of social change (Ibrahim 2017).

PROMOTING ECOLOGICAL CONVERSION AT THREE LEVELS TO TACKLE THE CONFLICT MINERALS ISSUE

In an article published in 2017 in the *Journal of Human Development and Capabilities*, Solava Ibrahim presents what she calls a "3C-Model for Grassroots-Led Development." It is a conceptual framework designed to analyze three social processes (conscientization, conciliation, and collaboration), which, she argues, are key for fostering social innovations at the grassroots. These three processes, she writes, "promote social change at three highly interdependent levels: the individual, collective, and institutional levels. By exploring the dynamics of each of these processes and examining the factors that affect them, the model demonstrates the importance of *individual* behavioural changes, *collective* agency, and local *institutional* reforms for social innovations at the grassroots" (Ibrahim 2017, 199, emphasis in original). Her proposed framework focuses on human capabilities, power dynamics, and the processes that lead to social change. On the one hand, the model explores how each of the 3C processes can be initiated and supported. On the other, it examines their impact "in terms of (1) success (i.e., achievement of objectives), (2) sustainability (i.e., focus on long-term impact), and (3) scalability (i.e., broader institutionalization rather than one-off solutions)" (ibid.).

Even if initially proposed in the context of "Grassroots-Led Development," Ibrahim's 3C-Model can be used to analyze a wide range of social change processes driven by individual and collective actors who decide to act—through conscientization, conciliation, and collaboration—as agents of change. Ibrahim links her 3C-Model to Oxfam's categorization of power (Rowlands 1997): "Conscientization addresses the *power within*, conciliation enhances *power with*, and collaboration emphasizes the importance of *power over* and *power to* challenge unequal power relations" (Ibrahim 2017, 204). I apply her model to the Conflict-Free Technology campaign to examine the repertoire of individual and collective actions displayed to promote conversion at the individual, social, and institutional levels.

Conscientization: Conversion at the Individual Level

As I mentioned in the previous section, back in 2014, international NGOs and policy officers from several countries and the private sector had already discussed how to regulate the "conflict minerals" trade, but the issue was not discussed in the wider citizenry of EU Member States (at least in Spain). As consumers of electronic devices, citizens have agency that is reduced to the act of choosing among those devices that they would like to buy. Therefore, the scope of their freedom is as large as their purchasing power. In addition, their choice is also biased by the limited product information they get from technological companies and retailers, which usually refers only to technical characteristics, aesthetics, or prices. It is very complicated for a consumer to find reliable information about the origins of electronic components, the supply chain, or the company's track record in protecting human rights.[4]

Moreover, most cutting-edge electronic devices are designed in such a way that they cannot be repaired by users. The concept of "planned obsolescence" sums up this tendency to shorten the lifespan of electronic products by design, making them easier, and often cheaper, to replace than repair; for instance, the average smartphone lasts just two to three years. This is the case of almost any electronic device and creates new problems, such as the overexploitation of natural resources and increasing e-waste. Despite how irrational it may seem from an ethical or ecological point of view, public opinion accepts planned obsolescence as normal.

Following Pope Francis's call in *Laudato Si'*, Alboan's campaigns team included in the Conflict-Free Technology campaign a line of work to counteract the "throwaway culture" with regard to electronic devices. At the individual level, the campaign adopted a bottom-up approach to incentivize Alboan's different stakeholders (volunteers, educators, partners, and the general public) to stop behaving as passive consumers and to become active citizens. As Ibrahim highlights, conscientization processes (in the sense understood by Paolo Freire) integrate three stages, "reflection-perception-action" (Freire 1972, 51, quoted in Ibrahim 2017, 206). For an individual to become an agent, Ibrahim argues, "she or he needs to *reflect* critically about his/her life" (ibid., emphasis in original). In this case, what the campaign seeks to address critically is the narrowness of consumers' preferences of electronic devices. It does so by *challenging perceptions* of what a "good electronic device" is. Is "good" a synonym for "cheap" or "fancy"? Is a smartphone really "smart" considering its social and environmental impacts? Which kind of information should one use to make value judgments regarding technology?

Alboan invested a lot of effort in posing these questions to its different audiences. The campaign's narrative focused on smartphones. Under the slogan "What Your Mobile Hides," in 2015 the organization launched a promotional video and a photo exhibition that tell the story of the artisanal mining communities of Rubaya, in the eastern DRC. Alongside these resources, Alboan edited a set of pedagogical materials covering different aspects of the "conflict minerals" problematic (such as life in the mines, sexual violence against women, the mineral supply chain, consumer preferences, e-waste, and so on). These materials were specifically designed for schools and groups of volunteers and educators from Alboan's Youth Network. They were aimed at, on the one hand, improving young people's knowledge of the "conflict minerals" problem, questioning their beliefs and values about the market and their preferences, and, on the other hand, giving them the opportunities to act as active citizens in the search for solutions. Since 2014, Alboan has delivered hundreds of training sessions about different issues related to conflict minerals and electronic devices to groups of volunteers, students, and teachers. The process of self-scrutinizing and developing a critical consciousness has been reflected many times in these sessions' evaluation forms:

> We barely pay attention to the things that are present in our daily lives, such as the case of electronic devices that we use all the time. They have a history of exploitation behind them and we just ignore it because we prefer so ... what I liked most about the training is that I have learned a lot and it has made me think. (19- year-old girl)

> [I've learned] that citizen participation is indispensable in the face of the internal crisis that the DRC is experiencing, in one way or another we are all responsible regardless of nationality, because everyone is using electronic devices that end up generating social, political, and illiteracy inequalities, corruption, economic, and social crisis. (20-year-old girl)

Awakening this critical consciousness is important. But if a process of conscientization does not create opportunities to make a difference, it can lead to frustration—or, what is worse, a sense of powerlessness. Conscientization is about discovering the *power within us* to take control over our lives and our circumstances. First individuals have to believe in their ability to change something; then they have to take advantage of their opportunities to make the changes they have reason to value. Civil society organizations (CSOs) can play a crucial role, providing the means for action and creating channels for social participation.

Conciliation: Conversion at the Social Level

Following Ibrahim's 3C-Model, "conscientization" paves the way for "conciliation," understood as a process that aims "to reconcile individuals own self-interests with communal goals" (Ibrahim 2017, 208). That is not an easy goal to achieve because it requires a sense of shared purpose and a certain degree of consensus about the meaning of "the common good." Even if such a thing is highly unlikely in pluralistic societies, Ibrahim, following Sen's emphasis on public reasoning in his *Idea of Justice* and other works (Sen 2009, chaps. 15 and 16), has stressed the importance of *public reasoning* and *inclusive decision-making* for the emergence of shared values and commitments. Open dialogue requires social interaction and, by definition, leaves space for the confrontation of ideas. When it is genuine, it can also contest our own views, "changing the quality of conversation and the thinking that lies behind it" (Alemanno 2017, 128). This is the purpose behind the Conflict-Free Technology campaign, inasmuch as it raises ethical concerns—based on facts related to human rights violations and other environmental damages—that call into question our ever faster-growing consumption and demand for electronic devices.

The campaign's target population at the grassroots included volunteers and educators from Alboan's Youth Network and schools from the Basque Country and Navarre. It is hard to predict how many participants in the campaign's awareness-raising activities will be motivated to change their behaviors as a consequence. But, to be effective, public campaigns must offer alternative solutions to the problems they address. "Dealing with conflict minerals, consumer electronics, and human rights violations," one educator told me in an informal encounter, "one of the questions that people ask more often is 'Which mobile phone should I buy?' And this is not an easy question to solve." He was right, as there is just one manufacturer of mobile phones that has an outstanding record on human rights and environmental protection: the Dutch company

Fairphone. However, its price is still a little higher than those of other makers of mobiles with similar features, and if there is no stock availability, buyers have to join a waiting list they can be on for months. In this sense, even if the Fairphone is aligned with the campaign's goals, Alboan does not encourage buying any particular brand of mobile phones or any other electronic devices. It endorses responsible consumption by making consumers aware of how their phones are produced and letting them make consumption choices accordingly.

An important part of the campaign's narrative is about reducing the environmental impact of technology. Conciliation in that regard is easier to foster, as ecological issues affect us all and taking care of our "Common Home" is something that "all men and women of good will" can have good reasons to do (*LS* 3). Nonetheless, recycling and reusing are practices that people usually do not engage in until they are given the opportunity to do so. Hence, the campaigns team launched an initiative called Mobiles for the Earth to foster recycling and reusing among Alboan's stakeholders. Working in partnership with RECUINTEC, a company specializing in the treatment of e-waste, the campaigns team designed a cardboard box where people could dispose of their old mobile phones. For each phone collected, RECUINTEC donates a small amount of money for development and humanitarian projects implemented by Alboan's partners in the eastern DRC and Colombia, where some regions are also affected by the conflict minerals problem.

The main purpose of this initiative was not fundraising but networking with different schools, institutions, and other organizations to promote responsible consumption. Many other initiatives have grown from this one, such as setting up collection points at schools,[5] collecting signatures during the legislative process to support civil society demands, and sending letters to politicians and policy-makers. As noted above, conciliation is about enhancing the *power* we have *with* others to change things. It requires alignment between self-interest and communal goals, and it can lead to a process of "collaboration" with different actors.

Collaboration: Conversion at the Institutional Level

Transforming unjust structures requires changes that are sustainable and therefore durable. Laws and public policies are powerful tools to bring about changes. Not surprisingly, the process of passing them often becomes a battlefield among different corporate and citizen lobbies. However, such struggles open up the possibility of collaboration among actors who share similar interests and concerns. Shortly after the European Commission published its proposal to regulate conflict minerals, numerous international NGOs and CSOs from different EU Member States decided to create a broad advocacy coalition to push for strong regulation and counter the arguments of those opposed to such a law. The Coalition's main goal was to achieve a law that would include human rights due-diligence obligations for all companies involved in the supply chain—both downstream and upstream companies, including smelters and refineries.

Under the leadership of a few international NGOs (such us Global Witness, Amnesty International, and Action Aid), the Coalition developed an advocacy strategy that mixed public campaigning and traditional inside lobbying activities with representatives from different EU Member States and EU institutions. Reaching out to the different stakeholders (both in Brussels and in the main capital cities) and targeting the general public of the European Union with a single voice was possible thanks to collaboration among diverse agents with different organizational skills and resources. International NGOs provided the core group with firsthand information about the negotiations in Brussels and put out policy drafts and fact sheets that could be used to lobby national governments; this made it possible for the fifteen or twenty NGOs participating in the core group to mobilize other organizations in their respective countries, at some points numbering more than 150 organizations (Global Witness 2015b).

The participation of other networks in the Coalition was also crucial. The European Network for Central Africa (EurAc) played a key role, bringing to the table views from Congolese CSOs (EurAc 2017) and attracting influential personalities to the cause, such as the Congolese gynecologist Dr. Denis Mukwege, a Nobel laureate and winner of the EU's Sakharov Prize (EurAc 2015). Coopération Internationale pour le Développement et la Solidarité (CIDSE), the international network of Catholic social justice organizations, based in Brussels, also succeeded in getting more than 145 bishops and religious leaders from more than thirty-eight countries and five continents to sign a joint statement asking for a stronger regulation (CIDSE 2015). The successful mobilization of diverse actors and the ability to reach wider audiences helped to swing the European Parliament's vote during May 2015 in favor of the Coalition's demands. These collaborations were a good example of collective agency developed by the Coalition, in the sense that influencing the vote was something that could not have been achieved by any organization acting on its own. Following the types of power suggested by Rowlands (1997), collaboration is about *power over* and *power to* challenge unequal power relations, and that is precisely the aim of broad-based citizen coalitions.

Despite this success, votes in the Council of the European Union in December 2015 went in the opposite direction, watering down the most ambitious proposals and delaying the possibility of reaching an agreement until the following year. The EU legislators reached a political agreement in November 2016, and finally the EU conflict minerals regulation was approved in May 2017 by the Council and the European Parliament (OJEU 2017). Even if the final agreement did not satisfy the demands expressed by the civil society during the negotiations (see Global Witness 2016; CIDSE 2017), the collaboration was valuable for most of the organizations involved—not just because the law was finally passed but because of the lessons learned in the process. In the case of Alboan, it provided the organization with firsthand knowledge about the OECD due-diligence principles (which is essential to understand corporate responsibility in mineral supply chains but also in other business activities) and the EU legislative process (which is key for CSOs to involve European citizens in the functioning of the EU institutions). This collective learning process with other organizations also opened up new windows of opportunity to keep on pushing to strengthen legal frameworks on business and human rights. The existing loopholes in the EU regulation on conflict minerals encouraged Alboan's team to launch new lines of work in order to promote due-diligence practices among the manufacturers of electronic devices (e.g., through the ethical public procurement of electronic goods); in a broader context, it also encouraged them to engage with other organizations to follow up by offering input to the current negotiations of the United Nations Binding Treaty on Business and Human Rights,[6] as well as the forthcoming EU directive on corporate governance, human rights, and environmental due diligence.[7]

CONCLUSION: BRIDGING THE GAP BETWEEN SPIRITUAL CONTEMPLATION AND SOCIAL ANALYSIS

The dialogue between CST and the CA offers a common ground for reflection and discernment that can be very useful for development practice. There are two main reasons to welcome this dialogue. On the one hand, the world's current problems are so immense that there is an urgent need for hope and inspiration. In this sense, the diagnosis of the climate crisis and the call for ecological conversion, alongside the values-driven nature of spiritual reflection, can be more inspiring than conventional development narratives and social analysis, which usually are framed with a much more technocratic view. On the other hand, the CA offers a set of concepts, philosophical assumptions, and methodological tools—in other words, a language (Deneulin 2014)—with which to describe the situation of less advantaged people in a given context. It can be applied to the assessment of their well-being and also their individual and collective agency, as this chapter has illustrated.

The case study of the Conflict-Free Technology campaign shows how both CST and the CA can not only help to frame unjust situations—the conflict minerals issue—but also to explore possible solutions in an inspiring and more systematic way. What CST teaches us is that there cannot be reflection and discernment without commitment, solidarity, and action. As the encyclical *Laudato Si'* reminds us, "Everything is interconnected" (*LS* 138), and we have the moral duty to deepen this interconnectedness. When Alboan decided to launch a campaign on conflict minerals, it knew that local violence was the visible part of a much more complex situation that needed to be assessed carefully. Identifying the many actors involved and addressing the structural root causes is not easy without identifying responsibilities at local, regional, and global levels.

But for each party involved to assume its responsibility, it is necessary to promote, through individual and collective action, a change of mentality that can be translated into concrete actions—the so-called "conversion" at the individual, social, and institutional levels. The CA, especially the literature on individual and collective agency, can be of great help in that regard. As has been argued, the insights provided by Ibrahim's 3C-Model for grassroots innovations can help us better understand the link between processes of conscientization, conciliation, and collaboration.

Over the years, the way to embrace change at these three levels has been evolving, and it will continue to evolve given new emerging realities. When *Laudato Si'* came out, Alboan had already started a process of collective reflection, which is the first stage in the journey toward its own "ecological conversion." It is a long and very challenging journey that will go beyond this campaign and affect the whole organization (e.g., implementing an environmental policy, reducing the organization's ecological footprint, stimulating sustainable lifestyles, and so on). But in *Laudato Si'* we find good reasons to carry on down the path undertaken by Pope Francis and not let ourselves be carried away by discouragement. As the encyclical concludes: "Let us sing as we go. May our struggles and our concern for this planet never take away the joy of our hope" (*LS* 244).

NOTES

1. This is reflected in discussions on the individualism implicit in the CA (see Robeyns 2005, 107–10); the role of collectivity and collective action in the CA (Stewart 2005; Ibrahim 2006; Leßman and Roche 2013; Fernandez-Baldor, Hueso, and Boni 2012; Pelenc, Bazile, and Ceruti 2015; Boni, G. Millán Franco, and M. Millán Franco, 2018; Leßman 2020; and the interdependence between individual agency and social structures (Cleaver 2007; Crocker 2008; Deneulin 2008). Some of these contributions use the concept of "collective capabilities"—understood broadly as those capabilities that can be achieved only by working alongside others, together, with a common purpose—to emphasize that there are capabilities that the individual alone would never have or be able to achieve (Ibrahim 2006). This definition has been criticized for theoretical and practical reasons (Ibrahim 2018). Some authors, such as Robeyns (2017), discourage its use to avoid conceptual confusion. For reasons of clarity and concision, I will use instead the concepts of individual agency and collective agency.

2. See the policy briefing published in February 2015 by Global Witness and thirteen NGOs, titled "A Conflict Minerals Regulation That Works" (Global Witness 2015a).

3. Discussions on the European conflict minerals regulation were marked by previous debates on the US law and its consequences for the DRC. Opponents of the EU regulation argued that Section 1502 of Dodd-Frank had resulted in a *de facto embargo* on trade in minerals coming from the DRC,

further worsening the situation for local communities. The exaggeration of these effects gave rise to competing narratives about the unintended effects of these regulations and forced European policy-makers to adopt a different approach to the US law (Koch and Kinsbergen 2018). For more on the arguments for and against regulation, see Koch and Burlyuk (2020).

4. In the United States, consumers can compare the information provided by the US companies subject to Section 1502 of the Dodd-Frank Act via the analysis provided by third parties, such as the Responsible Sourcing Network (2019). Despite their obligation, "a majority of the largest electronics, jewelry, and automotive companies are still not requiring suppliers to source from conflict-free refiners and smelters" (Lezhnev 2021). In Europe, even though the conflict-minerals law came into force on January 1, 2021, the competent authorities responsible for implementing the regulation in each Member State diverge in their transparency policies; see EurAc & Pax for Peace (2021).

5. This initiative was inspired by the "Conflict-Free Campus Initiative" launched by the US NGO Enough Project as part of its campaign on conflict minerals.

6. The seventh session of the open-ended intergovernmental working group on transnational corporations and other business enterprises with respect to human rights took place on October 2021, when the third draft of the UN Binding Treaty was discussed. The final text is still waiting for approval.

7. On April 29, 2020, Didier Reynders, the European commissioner for justice, announced that the European Commission (EC) will pass new rules for mandatory corporate environmental and human rights due diligence. Almost a year later, the European Parliament passed a resolution with recommendations to the Commission on corporate due diligence and corporate accountability (European Parliament 2021). After several delays due to the objections expressed by the EC's internal Regulatory Scrutiny Board (an independent body charged with quality control and impact assessment of legislation), on February 23, 2022, the European Commission adopted a proposal for a Directive on corporate sustainability due diligence (European Commission, 2022). The aim of this Directive is to foster sustainable and responsible corporate behavior and to anchor human rights and environmental considerations in companies' operations and corporate governance. The new rules will ensure that businesses address adverse impacts of their actions, including in their value chains inside and outside Europe. It is expected that during 2022 the proposal will go to the European Parliament and the European Council for approval.

WORKS CITED

Alboan. 2014. *Strategic Plan 2014–2018*. https://www.alboan.org/sites/default /files/publicaciones/pdf/2017/04/plan_2014-2018_alboan.pdf.

Aleman Arrastio, Alicia. 2012. *¿Tiene dueño la naturaleza? Tres Experiencias de acción social y recursos naturales*. Bilbao: ALBOAN.

Alemanno, Alberto. 2017. *Lobbying for Change. Find Your Voice to Create a Better Society*. London: Icon.

Álvarez de los Mozos, Patxi, SJ. 2013. "The Cycle of the Mission in the Society of Jesus." *Promotio Iustitiae* 110, no. 1: 13–20.

Benedict XVI. 2009. *Caritas in Veritate: On Integral Human Development in Charity in Truth*. https://www.vatican.va/content/benedict-xvi/en/encycli cals/documents/hf_ben-xvi_enc_20090629_caritas-in-veritate.html.

Boni, Alejandra, Gynna F. Millán Franco, and María Alejandra Millán Franco. 2018. "'When Collectivity Makes a Difference: Theoretical and Empirical Insights from Urban and Rural Communities in Colombia." *Journal of Human Development and Capabilities* 19, no. 2: 216–31.

Braden, Jonathon. 2021. "What Is Ecological Conversion?" *Laudato Si' Movement*. https://laudatosimovement.org/news/what-is-an-ecological -conversion-en-news.

Cleaver, Frances. 2007. "Understanding Agency in Collective Action." *Journal of Human Development and Capabilities* 8, no. 2: 223–44.

Coopération Internationale pour le Développement et la Solidarité (CIDSE). 2015. "'We Need Supply Chain Due Diligence to Stop Complicity in Funding Conflicts'—Catholic Leaders' Statement." https://www.cidse .org/2015/04/30/catholic-leaders-statement-on-conflict-minerals.

———. 2017. "New Legislation on Conflict Minerals, a Missed Opportu- nity for the European Union." https://www.cidse.org/2017/03/16/new -legislation-on-conflict-minerals-a-missed-opportunity-for-the-european -union.

Crocker, David A. 2008. *Ethics of Global Development: Agency, Capability, and Deliberative Democracy*. Cambridge: Cambridge University Press.

Deneulin, Séverine. 2008. "Beyond Individual Freedom and Agency: Struc- tures of Living Together in Sen's Capability Approach to Development." In *The Capability Approach: Concepts, Measures and Application*, edited by S. Alkire, F. Comim, and M. Qizilbash. Cambridge: Cambridge Univer- sity Press, 105–24.

———. 2014. *Wellbeing, Justice and Development Ethics*. New York: Routledge.

Drèze, Jean, and Amartya Sen. 2013. *An Uncertain Glory: India and Its Contra- dictions*. Princeton, NJ: Princeton University Press.

European Commission. 2014. *Joint Communication to the European Parliament and the Council: Responsible Sourcing of Minerals Originating in Conflict-Affected and High-Risk Areas*. Brussels: European Commission. https:// eur-lex.europa.eu/LexUriServ/LexUriServ.do?uri=JOIN:2014:0008: FIN:En:PDF.

———. 2022. *Proposal for a Directive of the European Parliament and of the Council on Corporate Sustainability Due Diligence and Amending Directive (EU) 2019/1937*. https://ec.europa.eu/info/publications/proposal-directive -corporate-sustainable-due-diligence-and-annex_en.

European Network for Central Africa (EurAc). 2015. "Conflict Minerals in the DRC: Dr. Mukwege and a Group of 34 NGOs Call on the European Parliament to Make a Difference!" https://www.eurac-network.org/sites /default/files/conflict_minerals_in_the_drc._dr._mukwege_ngos_call_on _the_ep_to_make_a_difference_-_may_2015.pdf.

———. 2017. *Accompanying Measures to the EU Regulation on the Responsible Sourcing of Minerals; Towards a Strengthening of the Governance of the Artisanal Mining Sector in the DRC*. https://www.eurac-network.org/en/press -releases/new-report-accompanying-measures-eu-regulation-responsible -mineral-sourcing-towards.

European Network for Central Africa (EurAc) and Pax for Peace. 2021. *The EU Conflict Minerals Regulation: Implementation at the EU Member State Level*. https://www.eurac-network.org/en/review-paper-eu-conflict -minerals-regulation-implementation-eu-member-states-level.

European Parliament. 2021. *European Parliament Resolution of 10 March 2021 with Recommendations to the Commission on Corporate Due Diligence and Corporate Accountability (2020/2129 (INL)*. https://www.europarl.europa .eu/doceo/document/TA-9-2021-0073_EN.html#title1.

Fernandez-Baldor, A., A. Hueso, and A. Boni. 2012. "From Individuality to Collectivity: The Challenges for Technology-Oriented Development Projects." In *The Capability Approach, Technology and Design*, edited by Ilse Oosterlaken and Jeroen Hoven. London: Springer.

Francis. 2015. *Laudato Si': On Care for Our Common Home*. http://www .vatican.va/content/francesco/en/encyclicals/documents/papa-francesco _20150524_enciclica-laudato-si.html.

Freire, Paolo. 1972. *Education of Critical Consciousness*. New York: Continuum.

Fukuda-Parr, Sakiko. 2003. "The Human Development Paradigm: Operationalizing Sen's Ideas on Capabilities." *Feminist Economics* 9, nos. 2–3: 301–17.

Global Witness. 2015a. "A Conflict Minerals Regulation That Works." https:// www.globalwitness.org/en/campaigns/conflict-minerals/conflict-minerals -shaping-eu-policy.

————. 2015b. "More than 150 Civil Rights Groups Call on MEPs to Strengthen the EU Conflict Minerals Regulation." https://www.global witness.org/en/campaigns/conflict-minerals/conflict-minerals-europe -brief/more-150-civil-rights-groups-call-meps-strengthen-eu-conflict -minerals-regulation.

————. 2016. "EU: Conflict Minerals Agreement Reached as Exemptions Added." https://www.globalwitness.org/en/campaigns/conflict-minerals /eu-conflict-minerals-agreement-reached-exemptions-added.

Ibrahim, Solava. 2006. "From Individual to Collective Capabilities: The Capability Approach as a Conceptual Framework for Self-help." *Journal of Human Development and Capabilities* 7, no. 3: 398–416.

————. 2017. "How to Build Collective Capabilities: The 3C-Model for Grassroots-Led Development." *Journal of Human Development and Capabilities* 18, no. 2: 197–222.

————. 2018. "Colectividades y capacidades." In *Introducción al Enfoque de las Capacidades: Aportes para el desarrollo humano en América Latina*, edited by Séverine Deneulin, Jhonatan Clausen, and Areli Valencia. Buenos Aires: Ed. Manantial, FLACSO, Fondo Ed. PUCP.

John Paul II. 2001. "God Made Man the Steward of Creation." General Audience, January 17. https://www.vatican.va/content/john-paul-ii/en /audiences/2001/documents/hf_jp-ii_aud_20010117.html.

Koch, Dirk-Jan, and Sara Kinsbergen. 2018. "Exaggerating Unintended Effects? Competing Narratives on the Impact of Conflict Minerals Regulation." *Resources Policy* 57: 255–63.

Koch, Dirk-Jan, and Olga Burlyuk. 2020. "Bounded Policy Learning? EU Efforts to Anticipate Unintended Consequences in Conflict Minerals Legislation." *Journal of European Public Policy* 27, no. 10: 1441–62.

Leßmann, Ortrud. 2020. "Collectivity and the Capability Approach: Survey and Discussion." *Review of Social Economy*. doi: 10.1080/00346764 .2020.1774636.

Leßmann, Ortrud, and José Manuel Roche. 2013. "Collectivity in the Capability Approach." *Maytreyee: E-Bulletin of the Human Development & Capability Association* 22.

Lezhnev, Sasha. 2021. "Conflict Minerals: Are Companies Sourcing From Conflict-Free Refiners & Smelters?" Op-ed. https://thesentry.org/2021 /05/25/6004/op-ed-conflict-minerals-companies-sourcing-conflict-free -refiners-smelters.

Official Journal of the European Union (OJEU). 2017. *Regulation 2017/821 of the European Parliament and of the Council of 17 May 2017: Laying Down Supply Chain Due Diligence Obligations for Union Importers of Tin,*

Tantalum and Tungsten, Their Ores, and Gold Originating from Conflict-Affected and High-Risk Areas. http://eur-lex.europa.eu/legal-content/EN /TXT/HTML/?uri=OJ:L:2017:130:FULL&from=EN.

Organization for Economic Cooperation and Development (OECD). 2016. *OECD Due Diligence Guidance for Responsible Supply Chains of Minerals from Conflict-Affected and High-Risk Areas.* 3rd ed. Paris: OECD.

Otano Jiménez, Guillermo. 2015. "La libertad como relación social: Una aproximación sociológica del enfoque de las capacidades de Amartya K. Sen." *Revista Iberoamericana de Estudios sobre Desarrollo* 4, no. 1: 98–127.

Pelenc, Jérôme, Didier Bazile, and Cristian Ceruti. 2015. "Collective Capability and Collective Agency for Sustainability: A Case Study." *Ecological Economics* 118: 226–39.

Responsible Sourcing Network. 2019. *Mining the Disclosures, Year 2019.* https://www.sourcingnetwork.org/mining-the-disclosures.

Robeyns, Ingrid. 2005. "The Capability Approach: A Theoretical Survey." *Journal of Human Development* 6, no. 1: 93–114.

———. 2017. *Wellbeing, Freedom and Social Justice: The Capability Approach Re-Examined.* Cambridge: Open Book. https://www.openbookpublishers .com/books/10.11647/obp.0130.

Ross, Michael L. 1999. "The Political Economy of the Resource Curse." *World Politics* 51, no. 2: 297–322.

Rowlands, Jo. 1997. *Questioning Empowerment.* Oxford: Oxfam.

Segura, José María, SJ. 2013. "A Theological Foundation for Ignatian Advocacy." *Promotio Iustitiae* 110, no. 1: 6–12

Sen, Amartya. 1999a. "Democracy as Universal Value." *Journal of Democracy* 10, no. 3: 3–17.

———. 1999b. *Development as Freedom.* New York: Knopf.

———. 2002. *Rationality and Freedom.* Cambridge, MA: Belknap Press of Harvard University Press.

———. 2009. *The Idea of Justice.* Cambridge, MA: Harvard University Press.

Social Justice and Ecology Secretariat (SJES). 2011. *Promotio Iustitiae* 106, no. 2. Special Issue, *Ecology: Healing a Broken World—Task Force on Ecology.* https://www.sjesjesuits.global/media/2021/04/PJ_106_ENG.pdf.

———. 2015. *Promotio Iustitiae* 118, no. 2. Special Issue, *Governance of Mineral Resources: Challenges and Responses.* https://www.sjesjesuits.global /media/2021/02/PJ_118_ENG.pdf.

Society of Jesus. 2008. *General Congregation 35, Decree 3*: 3–9. http://www .sjweb.info/35/documents/Decrees.pdf.

Sosa, Arturo, SJ. 2019. "Universal Apostolic Preferences of the Society of Jesus, 2019–2029: Letter to the Whole Society." https://www.jesuits .global/sj_files/2020/05/2019-06_19feb19_eng.pdf.

Stewart, Frances. 2005. "Groups and Capabilities." *Journal of Human Development* 6, no. 2: 185–204.

United Nations Development Program (UNDP). 2020. *Human Development Report 2020: The Next Frontier: Human Development and the Antrophocene.* New York: UNDP. http://hdr.undp.org.

ELEVEN

Integral Human Development

A Role for Children's Savings Accounts?

James P. Bailey

ABSTRACT

Catholic Social Teaching (CST) has long argued that ownership of private property can contribute to human flourishing and, partly because of this, it has supported policies that enable savings and widespread ownership of property for all persons, including the poor. This chapter looks at one vehicle for facilitating savings in lower-income families, namely, children's savings accounts (CSAs). CSAs are a policy response to the growing body of literature that suggests that even small amounts of savings and other assets can have a dramatic impact on the material and psychological well-being of children in ways that have a direct bearing on human flourishing. For example, CSAs have been shown to increase future-oriented thinking in parents and children, stimulating more hope about the future and leading children and parents to take concrete steps to realize this imagined future. For this and other reasons, in this chapter I suggest that CSAs are consistent with many of the goals of CST, including the aim of integral human development.

INTRODUCTION

Catholic Social Teaching (CST) articulates an understanding of development that includes, but goes beyond, mere economic well-being. Because each person is embodied, more or less rational, relational, social, political, and spiritual, authentic human development must address all of these qualities. For development to be truly integral it must take account of these complex and interrelated aspects of human personhood and do so in a way that facilitates human flourishing. Put another way, the promotion and facilitation of human flourishing must address the whole person (including the social and political context in which she lives).

One could delineate how this commitment to integral human development is embodied across a range of principles, values, and commitments found in the body of the CST literature. But in this chapter I want to focus first on one programmatic recommendation within CST and briefly indicate how this recommendation can be understood in light of a commitment to integral human development and the formation of important human capabilities. I will then turn my attention to a particular proposal to develop children's savings accounts, arguing that such accounts are one means of beginning to actualize an aspect of human flourishing.

The programmatic recommendation I am going to focus on is the Church's persistent support for, and defense of, the institution of private property. The Church's affirmation of a regime that respects the right to private property is often and perhaps primarily understood as a critique and repudiation of certain kinds of socialism, particularly those forms in which the state has complete control over the means of production. And this is true as far as it goes. But there is something much more important and interesting in the Church's emphasis on private ownership than simply a critique of particular economic and/or political systems.

Consider (among other things) that, more often than not, talk of private ownership in social encyclicals is almost always accompanied by the suggestion that ownership ought to be widespread, significantly more widespread than what has been the norm up to now.

Why would that be? What sort of value does this tradition see in private ownership? Sometimes a commitment to private property is seen as a compromise, a concession to the reality that property held in common is just not well taken care of. And sometimes private ownership is linked to justice—one ought to be able to keep what is one's own (up to certain limits).[1] But more frequently, CST sees private property—especially the expansion of private property ownership to those who do not yet own property—as helping not only to alleviate poverty but also as fostering important aspects of human development that go beyond the merely economic. Pope Leo XIII noticed, for example, in his encyclical *Rerum Novarum* (*RN*), published in 1891, that a person who has a certain amount of savings or owns some amount of property is better able to plan for the future than one who does not—not merely in a financial sense but in the sense of identifying and executing a plan for one's life. In this way, ownership enables the possibility for people to exercise prudential judgment about their lives rather than simply reacting and surviving from one day to the next (*RN* 6–7). This ability to think about and plan for one's future can also be read as enabling a capacity for hope about the future, and human beings do find it very difficult to flourish without some aspect of hope.

Many other examples of the non-economic benefits of property ownership abound within CST. Here are a few: *Gaudium et Spes* (*GS*; Vatican Council II 1965) argues that "ownership and other forms of private control over material goods contribute to the expression of personality," going so far as to speak of the holding of private property or some form of ownership of goods as "an extension of human freedom" (*GS* 71). The US Catholic Bishops suggest that expanding ownership to those who do not yet own property is an effective way not only to support family life but also to increase participation in society as a whole (USCCB 1986, 91).[2] Nearly all the papal encyclicals that address the issue of property ownership insist that gross inequalities in levels of wealth are harmful, both to individual members of society and to society as a whole. That is to say, wide disparities in degrees of asset ownership have significant negative effects on the common good.

Martin Luther King Jr., who retrieved insights from the Christian tradition to critique racial discrimination and economic inequalities in the United States, gestures toward many of these same ideas in a talk he gave to the AFL-CIO in 1961. There will come a time, King argued, that

> we shall bring into full realization the American dream—a dream yet unfulfilled. A dream of equality of opportunity, of privilege *and property widely distributed*; a dream of a land where men will not take necessities from the many to give luxuries to the few, a dream of a land where men will not argue that the color of a man's skin determined the content of his character; a dream of a nation where all our gifts and resources are held not for ourselves alone but as instruments of service for the rest of humanity; the dream of a country where every man will respect the dignity and worth of human personality—that is the dream.[3]

King understood that equality of opportunity (an important aspect of human freedom) depends upon privilege and property that are widely distributed and that human dignity and the common good are served when societies are not characterized by extreme levels of economic inequality. In this chapter I will focus on recent efforts to expand the distribution of property (and the privileges that follow from this) in the form of children's savings accounts (CSAs). I will begin, however, with a brief look at the connection between material well-being and human flourishing, as understood by two important historical figures, Aristotle and Thomas Aquinas. I will then turn our attention to economic inequality in the United States, with a particular focus on wealth inequality and how the latter affects children. This will lead to a discussion of the differential impact of income and assets and why both are important for human well-being. Finally, we will look more closely at the rationale for CSAs and why they may be one important mechanism for reducing wealth inequality and for promoting integral human development and enhancing the capabilities of people.

PHILOSOPHICAL AND THEOLOGICAL UNDERPINNINGS
OF CST AND THE CA

While there are important differences between Catholic Social Teaching (CST) and its vision of integral human development and the capability approach (CA), they share several features that are relevant to the subject of this chapter. First, both approaches recognize that people are social and political beings; we are not self-sustaining individuals, capable of flourishing separate and apart from others. Rather, our well-being is linked to other persons and institutions, including but not limited to families, schools, and a range of civic organizations (including churches); well-functioning local, state, national, and global political institutions; businesses large and small; and well-functioning economies. We are also increasingly aware that our own well-being and the well-being of non-human animals and other living entities depends upon the protection and promotion of healthy and thriving environments. Additionally, both CST and the CA recognize that some in society have greater needs than others and, consequently, have claims to greater levels and/or different kinds of resources in order to achieve an adequate level of what is called, in CA jargon, "functioning."[4] Both approaches to development also acknowledge, for a variety of reasons, that human flourishing is facilitated at least in part by material well-being, including some degree of income and wealth.[5] Income and wealth are not ends in themselves, of course, but means to a flourishing life.

Both the CA and CST articulate and endorse a robust and comprehensive conception of development. Their proponents are often critical of the narrow and limited understandings of development that have tended to dominate public policy in much of the twentieth and early twenty-first centuries. These approaches are ones that tend to equate increases in quantifiable indicators of aggregate economic activity with social progress more generally. Thus the "developed" nations are those with relatively high levels of gross domestic products (GDPs), relatively high average incomes, and so forth. The weakness of this approach to development can be seen readily enough if one scratches the surface of the aggregate indicators of development. Within so-called developed nations (those with high GDPs, relatively high average incomes, and so on) one finds not just widespread economic inequality but also unequal educational systems, unequal access to institutions that support and facilitate wealth accumulation, unequal access to their health care systems, and so on. So, the CA and CST direct our attention beyond aggregate measures of economic activity to the importance of inclusive education, widespread political participation, robust and vibrant associations within civil society, reasonable work hours, humane vacation and sick leave policies, access to health care, widespread access to quality education, and care for those who are most in need.

It is worth pointing out that there is nothing new to the assertion that economic activity does not exhaust the meaning and purpose of development. The basic insights behind CST and the CA have been part of moral and political discourse for quite some time, even if they have been neglected in recent years in policy implementation. Aristotle, for example, understood all human activity to be motivated by the desire to achieve human happiness (*eudaimonia*), where happiness is understood as a state of flourishing. He was quite clear that material well-being alone would not secure the happiness we seek. For example, as he put it near the beginning of his *Nicomachean Ethics* (*NE*; 1980), "Wealth is evidently not the good we are seeking; for it is merely useful and for the sake of something else" (*NE* Book I, chap. 5, 1096a5). For Aristotle, human flourishing (*eudaimonia*) in its fullest and richest sense involves the development and perfection of a wide range of human capacities that he associated with certain virtues. The proper exercise of these virtues presumes adequate material resources (including some degree of wealth) and sufficient levels of education, without which human beings could not flourish. Given that the development of virtues is mediated by social and political communities within which people find themselves, it is important that these communities be of a certain type, namely, ones that promote human flourishing in a full and complete sense. This is why Aristotle suggests that the aim of every legislator is (or ought to be) the formation of certain kinds of habits (virtues) and that one can evaluate political arrangements based on how effective they are at doing this. As he put it: "Legislators make the citizens good by forming habits in them, and this is the wish of every legislator, and those who do not effect it miss their mark, and it is in this that a good constitution differs from a bad one" (*NE* Book II, chap. 1, 1103b). The achievement of *eudaimonia*, in other words, depends upon well-functioning social and political institutions.

Likewise, Thomas Aquinas, in his *Summa Theoligica* (*ST*; 1981), also stressed that human activity aimed at a telos whose realization required the acquisition of certain human capacities that he, too, named virtues. And, just as Aristotle did, Aquinas stressed the social and political nature of human beings. Consequently, he saw the acquisition of virtues as not a solitary achievement but one requiring the presence of social and political institutions that would facilitate and enable humans' development.[6] Aquinas, of course, sought to situate the good human life within a larger Christian eschatological framework, and this led him to expand Aristotle's conception of human flourishing to entail that its full achievement could be obtained only through the acquisition of the grace-bestowed supernatural virtues of faith, hope, and love and to see the telos of all human activity in terms not only of terrestrial fulfillment (*eudaimonia*) but of heavenly fulfillment (*beatitudo*; Aquinas, *ST* I-II q. 3, art. 8).

Yet it is also true that those who focus too narrowly on economic aspects of development are not wrong to insist that economic well-being is an important human good. This is especially true, as Aristotle and Aquinas both believed, when income and wealth (whether viewed individually or in the aggregate) are not viewed as ends in themselves. A certain level of economic well-being is very important to human flourishing, since human flourishing in the fullest sense depends upon not only meeting the material needs of the body but also the development of a range of important human capacities. In many societies, this depends upon an adequate level of not only subsistence income but the ability to save and accumulate wealth. Crucially, the ability to do this is almost always tied to access to institutions that enable and incentivize savings so that wealth can accumulate over time. And, just as importantly, those with limited incomes are often most likely to have limited access to these wealth-building institutions.[7]

READING THE SIGNS OF THE TIMES: ECONOMIC INEQUALITY IN THE UNITED STATES

Because proposals to develop children's savings accounts (CSAs) and other similar savings instruments for children, are made in the United States against a backdrop of historic levels of income and wealth inequality, it is important to be clear about the nature and extent of this inequality. Both income and wealth inequality in the United States are significant and growing. However, wealth inequality far exceeds income inequality. Indeed, in the United States today, according to Ganesh Sitaraman (2017, 227), the "twenty wealthiest individuals in America alone are wealthier than the bottom half of the American population—152 million people." A more complete assessment of income and wealth inequality paints just as bleak a picture: the top 20 percent of households earn about 64 percent of the nation's income—but command nearly 90 percent of its wealth. The bottom 60 percent, the majority of US households, earn about 19 percent of the nation's income—but own less than 3 percent of the wealth. And the bottom 40 percent earn 9 percent of national income but own less than 1 percent of the wealth (Wolff 2017). Moreover, wealth inequality in the United States varies dramatically by race and ethnicity. For example, in 2016 the median white, Latino, and black household assets were valued at $140,600, $6,300, and $4,160 respectively (Nieves and Asante-Muhammad 2018).

This data on wealth inequality helps underscore the precarious financial state of many US households. The Federal Reserve Bank reported that in 2013 some 48 percent of a nationally representative sample had so little savings that they did not believe they could cover a $400 emergency expense without having to borrow money or sell something they owned (Board of Governors of the Federal Reserve Bank 2014, 3). Unsurprisingly, the precarious state of US household wealth does not leave children untouched. In fact, in a recent study researchers found that nearly two-thirds of children in the United States live in households that are asset-poor (Rothwell, Ottusch, and Finders 2019, 412).[8]

The impact of great disparities in wealth and income has not gone unnoticed by those working within the frameworks of the CA and CST. Amartya Sen, for example, argues that "being poor in a rich society itself is a capability handicap" (Sen 1992, 115). And CST contains frequent references to, and worries about, extreme levels of inequality. To take two examples, Pope Benedict XVI writes in *Caritas in Veritate* (*CV*), published in 2009, that the "dignity of the individual and the demands of justice require, particularly today, that economic choices do not cause disparities in wealth to increase in an excessive and morally unacceptable manner" (*CV* 32). Taking note of the growing levels of inequality across the globe, Pope Francis insists in *Evangelii Gaudium* (*EG*), published in 2013, that "inequality is the root of social ills" (*EG* 202). In *Fratelli Tutti* (*FT*), published in 2020, Pope Francis observes that some "economic rules have proved effective for growth, but not for integral human development. Wealth has increased, but together with inequality, with the result that 'new forms of poverty are emerging'" (*FT* 21, Pope Francis is quoting Pope Benedict XVI from *CV* 22).

Pope Francis, like his predecessors, understands that extreme levels of inequality do not simply happen, nor are they inevitable. Extreme levels of inequality, like all forms of social injustice, are products of unjust structures. As he puts it in *Evangelii Gaudium*:

> We can no longer trust in the unseen forces and the invisible hand of the market. Growth in justice requires more than economic growth, while presupposing such growth: it requires decisions, programmes, mechanisms, and processes specifically geared to a better distribution of income, the creation of sources of employment and an integral promotion of the poor which goes beyond a simple welfare mentality. I am far from proposing an irresponsible populism, but the economy can no longer turn to remedies that are a new poison, such as attempting to increase profits by reducing the work force and thereby adding to the ranks of the excluded. (*EG* 204)

Other commentators from a variety of perspectives have joined in critiquing extreme levels of economic inequality. For example, Richard Reeves (2017, 58) of the Brookings Institution has noted that the United States is no longer "the land of opportunity" but is instead characterized by a class structure that is now "more rigid ... than many European nations, including the United Kingdom."[9] Likewise, sociologist Robert Putnam (2015) worries that increased income and wealth inequality is contributing to a coarsening of our public life, in part because extreme income and wealth are leading to significant numbers of wealthy persons separating themselves geographically and socially from those who come from lower economic classes, a phenomenon he suggests is relatively recent. While it would be naïve to think the United States was ever, at any point in its history, an egalitarian state, it is nevertheless true that income and wealth inequality have both grown dramatically over the past several decades

(Kent, Rickets, and Boshara 2019).[10] Today, US political institutions cater to an ever-smaller number of members of the body politic, the nation's wealthiest citizens. There are, of course, structural reasons for this—but the structures themselves are there largely at the behest of the nation's wealthy. Given this degree of wealth inequality—and the paltry share of the nation's wealth that is owned by those with lower incomes—we ought not be surprised that so many children find themselves in families on precarious economic footing, even in families that could be said, based upon their income, to be part of the middle class.

WHY ASSETS?

But why concern ourselves with disparate levels of asset ownership at all? Why not, instead, focus our attention on income alone? After all, most official definitions of poverty do, in fact, focus entirely on income levels. In the United States, for example, the so-called "poverty line" denotes a specific income threshold beneath which a household is said to be in poverty and above which it is said not to be. That threshold is defined by a dollar amount equal to "three times the [inflation-adjusted] cost of a minimum food diet in 1963 and adjusted for family size" (Institute for Research on Poverty 2021). When poverty is defined in this way, it makes sense that the remedies proposed to alleviate poverty almost always aim at raising the incomes of the poor by various means: direct cash payments, supplying income substitutes (food stamps, housing subsidies, and others), establishing or raising minimum wage standards, and so on.

Over the past several decades, however, social scientists and policy analysts have carefully delineated the differences that income and wealth make for the well-being of individuals and households. The differences that CSAs can make for children, parents, and households will be explored in greater depth below. Here it is enough to notice that deficiencies in income and deficiencies in savings or assets impact different dimensions of human flourishing. This is because income and wealth have different functions in the lives of individuals and families. A shorthand way to think about the distinctive impacts of income and wealth is that while income helps people to get by, wealth helps them to get ahead. Or, alternatively, income helps people to survive, wealth helps them to thrive. This is because income and wealth secure different kinds of goods that serve very different kinds of purposes. Generally speaking, income helps to secure the necessary goods of daily living, and it is these goods that the majority of current US poverty policies are aimed at securing. As Melvin Oliver and Thomas Shapiro (1995, 2) put it, income helps us to "purchase milk and shoes, and other necessities." While securing these goods is important and necessary, policies that focus only on helping lower-income people secure the goods of daily living can fairly be described as "subsistence" or "survival" policies (Elliott and Lewis 2018, xix).[11] But, as has been noted throughout this book, the vision of human flourishing described by CST and the CA is not one of mere survival but rather facilitates human thriving. And, increasingly, thriving depends at least in part upon having some degree of household wealth.

To understand why this is so, we need to have a better understanding of the complex and varied ways that savings and wealth contribute to human flourishing. A partial list would include the following:

- Wealth helps act as a buffer against temporary interruptions in income flows, helping individuals and families to better manage economic shocks (the loss of a job, an unexpected expense or illness, and so on).
- Wealth also helps people "to create opportunities, secure desired stature and standard of living, or pass class status on to one's children" (Oliver and Shapiro 1995, 2).
- Just as importantly, wealth helps to shape expectations about the future and encourages people to meet goals leading to that future (Shobe and Page-Adams 2001). In the context of educational attainment, for example, the presence of wealth has been shown to shape parental expectations of their children in school and, in turn, to motivate children to do well in school (Kim et al. 2017; Zhan 2006). Data from the first randomized control study of the effects of CSAs has shown that parents in the "experimental group" (parents who participated in the CSA program) "have higher expectations for their children's future education and that their expectations are more likely to remain constant or increase, compared to parents whose children did not receive the CSA" (Elliott and Lewis 2018, 109).

- Wealth has also been shown to encourage greater civic and political participation and in this way strengthens democratic institutions. In the United States there is concern bordering on alarm about the way in which extreme levels of wealth inequality are eroding the institutions and processes necessary for a functioning democracy while also barring large numbers from full participation in society (Putnam 2015; Sitaraman 2017). It is worth noting that participation in the civic and political life of one's own society is, in CST, a basic human right and is fundamental to the duty to contribute to the common good (USCCB 1986).[12]
- And, finally, the presence of wealth is associated with greater marital and family stability (Lerman and McKernan 2008; Scanlon and Page-Adams 2001).

Because of these and other effects of wealth, Oliver and Shapiro write that "the command over resources that wealth entails is more encompassing than is income or education and closer in meaning and theoretical significance to our traditional notions of economic well-being and access to life's chances" (Oliver and Shapiro 1995, 2).

Another reason for broad public concern about wealth inequality has to do with the way in which federal and state policies are exacerbating wealth inequality. These policies incentivize and reward the savings and asset accumulation behaviors of those at the higher end of income distribution while neglecting to do the same for lower-income households. In effect, public policy in the United States has developed in such a way that the wealthy are, in the words of William Elliott and Melinda Lewis (2018, 44), "given access to 'growth policies' through subsidization of investments while the poor are given access to 'survival' policies that help subsidize consumption." For example, in 2013 the federal government invested over $540 billion dollars in household saving and asset building. The largest of these investments went to savings and investments accounts, retirement accounts, homeownership, and postsecondary education. However, according to Ezra Levin, Jeremie Greer, and Ida Rademacher (2014, 6), because these expenditures were largely delivered through the tax code, "most individuals and families—those in the bottom 60%—received less than 12% of the benefits" of these expenditures. By contrast, those in the top 1% of the income distribution received greater subsidies for asset building and savings than the combined total of the bottom 80% of income earners (ibid.). The very unequal distribution of these benefits can fairly be described as a preferential option for the non-poor, exacerbating the vulnerability of those who most need such assistance. Among the population of those left behind are significant numbers of children.

We will now turn our attention to a policy proposal for CSAs, with a particular focus on how such measures might help alleviate extreme inequalities while promoting human capabilities and flourishing.

WHY CHILDREN'S SAVINGS ACCOUNTS?

Why is there interest in facilitating savings accounts or baby bonds for children? The reasons are many, but five seem especially important. First, as Ray Boshara (2015, 46) says, "there is a growing body of evidence that savings accounts and assets early in life lead to better outcomes later in life." When these findings are paired with the reality that "nearly half (43.9%) of [US] households—equivalent to 132.1 million people—do not have a basic personal safety net to prepare for emergencies or future needs, such as a child's college education or homeownership," there is need for concern, according to Jennifer Brooks and Kasey Wiedrich (2013, 3). This is troubling on a number of levels, but arguably the most important with respect to children is that there is a significant body of literature that suggests that the flourishing of children born into households with little or no wealth is impeded in many ways, not just financially, but across a whole range of behavioral and psychological indicators. For example, there is a positive association of household assets with children's educational outcomes, including high school graduation rates and staying in school, and this effect "is strongest for children of low-income households," Trina Williams Shanks et al. (2010, 1490) report. Research on adults has shown that asset holdings increase "a person's future orientation, which in turn brings about other attitudinal behavioral changes" (ibid.). Something similar may be going on in interactions between parents who hold assets and their children.

For example, "mothers who were homeowners or had savings of three thousand dollars or more had higher expectations for their children's educational attainment, even after controlling for maternal age, race, employment status, education, family structure, and child characteristics. In contrast, no significant effects were found between household income and maternal expectations (ibid., 1490–91). It is plausible that the parents of children with CSAs might engage in similar behavior and that such behavior may well change how the children themselves understand and experience their own education. Indeed, randomized controlled studies of this issue have begun to show that CSAs have these and other kinds of positive impacts on parents and their children (Sherraden et al. 2015).

Second, those working on public policies aimed at increasing savings and other kinds of assets in low-income households argue that hope about the future is one of the most powerful impacts of children's savings accounts. Importantly—and this is what makes a universal and progressive savings account policy so potentially transformative—it is the presence of assets that changes the way people *think*. As Michael Sherraden (1992, 155) puts it, "When assets are present, people begin to think in terms of assets. For example, if a young mother owns her own home, she begins to pay more attention to real estate values, property taxes, the cost of maintenance, and so forth. If she has a certificate of deposit, she is more likely to pay attention to interest rates and what make interest rates go up and down." Similarly, people who own stock are likely to pay more attention to stock prices and other investment options. Importantly, as Sherraden points out, "It is the assets themselves that create this effect (as opposed to educational programs or exhortations toward better values). Assets create a cognitive reality, a schema, because assets are concrete and consequential. All this can be said very simply: Assets matter and people know it, and therefore, when they have assets, they pay attention to them. If they do not have assets, they do not pay attention" (ibid.).

Third, while the level of income inequality in the United States is very high, wealth inequality is far greater. And the latter is particularly impacted by historical patterns of discrimination that have marked the United States since its inception. These structural injustices gave and continue to give advantages to whites and disadvantages to blacks, with devastating effects on the ability of African Americans to save and accumulate assets. Indeed, in the United States today, race is a stronger predictor of one's wealth holdings than is class. In 2016 the net worth of the typical non-college-educated white family was 40 percent higher than that of the typical college-educated black family, while the typical white family with a member holding a bachelor's degree or higher has a net worth that is nearly *seven times* that of the typical black family with a member holding a bachelor's degree or higher (Dettling et al. 2017). Because CSAs are conceived as universal (they are intended to be for all children) and progressive (children from income- and asset-poor households will receive greater amounts of funds for savings), they will necessarily help those with little, no, or negative savings (debt). Since households that fit that description are over-represented by African Americans, CSAs are likely to provide greater benefits to them than to others.

Fourth, the development of, and advocacy for, CSAs can be understood as a response to changing realities in the economy as a whole. For much of the twentieth century, according to Sherraden (2018, 36) it was assumed that labor income was sufficient to "support the well-being of most households," including adequate savings levels. That assumption "is increasingly tenuous" (ibid.). Globalization and information-age technologies have combined to exert downward pressure on wages (Sitaraman 2017) and create less stable job markets (ibid., 35).[13] The instability in job markets includes not just greater "turnover" in labor markets but also less dependable income flows from employment (i.e., varied hours from week to week or day to day). Unsurprisingly, a "disproportionate share of low-income and moderate-income families face [income] volatility. Meanwhile, better-off households not only earn more, but they are also much more likely to have steady earnings," write Jonathan Morduch and R. Schneider (2017, 34). The combination of relatively low income and unpredictable income flows makes it very difficult to set aside savings. CSAs are one means of addressing this changing reality.

Finally, because most CSAs are constructed to be both universal and progressive, they have the potential to create pathways to greater economic, social, and political participation in society. Put another way, they have the potential to move people from the economic, social, and political margins to the center of public life. In this way CSAs and other universal and progressive asset-building policies could facilitate what the

US Catholic Bishops have described as "justice as participation." As they put it, "Justice demands that social institutions be ordered in a way that guarantees all persons the ability to participate actively in the economic, political, and cultural life of society" (USCCB 1986, 78).[14] But whereas the bishops and much of the Catholic social justice tradition have tended to equate economic participation with wage labor, it is not at all clear (for reasons mentioned above) that wage labor is going to be sufficient to enable many households to save at levels that are adequate to secure what is necessary for human well-being.

CONCLUSION: BEGINNING AT THE BEGINNING AND THE HOPEFUL PROMISE OF CSAS

The breadth and depth of financial strain experienced by so many US households suggests a need to rethink who the poor are. It is no longer adequate—if it ever was—to conceptualize those in America who are poor as some distant *other* at the margins of society. The reality is that most people in the United States will experience poverty at some point in their lifetimes, and so, too, will "most Americans turn to public assistance at least once during adulthood," writes the sociologist Mark Rank (2003, 41). It is for this reason that Rank describes the experience of poverty in America as "mainstream," the rule rather than the exception (Rank 2013). As he points out, some "40 percent of Americans between the ages of 25 and 60 experience at least one year below the official poverty line during that period," and nearly "half of American children will live in households that use food stamps for some period of time." More dramatically, Rank wrote that "if we add in related conditions like welfare use, near-poverty and unemployment, four out of five Americans will encounter one or more of these events" in their lifetimes (ibid.). Poverty in the United States, it seems clear, is not "an issue of *them*" but is instead "an issue of *us*" (ibid., my emphasis).

CSAs acknowledge that wealth accumulation happens over time; therefore, it is important to begin at the beginning, not only with individual effort but also with social policies that will promote and support such effort. CSAs also recognize the challenges of adopting an orientation toward the future if immediate demands for survival are all that is in view.

As noted earlier, both the presence of assets and the process of developing them help to create an orientation toward the future and the freedom to plan and to dream. They have the potential to provide a foundation for hope for all of us. As Michael Sherraden (1992, 155) says, "Assets are hope in concrete form," acknowledging the reality that hope is integral to a flourishing life, as is material well-being. The degree of wealth inequality in the United States has led Richard Reeves (2017) to characterize those who are beneficiaries of this inequality as dream hoarders. CSAs are a vehicle for potentially expanding that dream in some small way to all.

NOTES

1. See, for example, Pope Leo XIII's *Rerum Novarum* (*RN*; 1891), in which, echoing Locke, Leo suggests that a person's labor is mixed with what it produces, and so it is theirs: "Now, when man thus turns the activity of his mind and the strength of his body toward procuring the fruits of nature, by such act he makes his own that portion of nature's field which he cultivates—that portion on which he leaves, as it were, the impress of his personality; and it cannot but be just that he should possess that portion as his very own, and have a right to hold it without any one being justified in violating that right" (*RN* 9).

2. "Basic justice calls for more than providing help to the poor and other vulnerable members of society. It recognizes the priority of policies and programs that support family life and enhance economic participation through employment and widespread ownership of property" (USCCB 1986, 91).

3. Martin Luther King, Jr., "Speech at Fourth Annual AFL-CIO Annual Convention," December 11, 1961.

4. Although, arguably, the tradition to which CST is heir makes this claim in stronger terms than does the CA. Cf., for example, St. Ambrose: "You are not making a gift of what is yours to the poor man, but you are giving him back what is his. You have been appropriating things that are meant to be for the common use of everyone. The earth belongs to everyone, not to the rich" (St. Ambrose, quoted by De Nabute, chap. 12, n. 53, cited by Pope Paul VI in *Populorum Progressio* 23).

5. I will use the term "wealth" more or less interchangeably with "assets" and "savings." As used here, the terms refer primarily to some kind of savings account, but it could also describe property ownership (including homeownership) and stock ownership.

6. "But man is by nature a social and political animal, who lives in a community [*multitudine vivens*]: more so, indeed, than all other animals; and natural necessity shows why this is so. For other animals are furnished by nature with food, with a covering of hair, and with the means of defence, such as teeth, horns or at any rate speed in flight. But man is supplied with none of these things by nature. Rather, in place of all of them reason was given to him, by which he might be able to provide all things for himself, by the work of his own hands. One man, however, is not able to equip himself with all these things, for one man cannot live a self-sufficient life. It is therefore natural for man to live in fellowship with many others" (Aquinas 2002, 5–6).

7. I have written about this elsewhere. See, for example, Bailey (2010), especially chapters 1 and 4.

8. Rothwell, Ottusch, and Finders (2019) use a standard definition of "asset poverty," which is an inability to sustain one's household for three months with no income. It should be noted, however, that the definition and measurement of asset poverty is far from settled. For an excellent discussion of the challenges and complexity of defining and measuring assets in a public policy context, see Nam, Huang, and Sherraden (2008).

9. Reeves is particularly dismayed by this, since he moved from the United Kingdom to the United States in part because he found the class-based system there morally repugnant.

10. In 2016 "the bottom half of [US] families ranked by household wealth ... own[ed] only 1%" of the total wealth in the United States (Kent, Rickets, and Boshara 2019).

11. Elliott and Lewis also point out that an unfortunate side effect of many income-based poverty policies is that they often require persons to spend down what few assets they have before they can qualify for income support (food stamps, housing subsidies, and so on). The effect of this is to make their financial situation more precarious.

12. "Human rights are the minimum conditions for life in community" (USCCB 1986, 17).

13. In the United States, from "1979 to 2008, 100% of the growth in income went to the top 10% of Americans. During this period, the income for the bottom 90% actually declined." By contrast, in the years between 1949 and 1979, "most income growth went to the bottom 90%" (Sitaraman 2017, 227 and 377).

14. Cf. the 1971 World Synod of Catholic Bishops' *Justice in the World*: "Participation is a right which is to be applied in the economic and in the social and political field" (no. 18).

WORKS CITED

Aquinas, Thomas. 1981 (circa 1265–1274). *Summa Theologica.* Translated by Fathers of the English Dominican Province. Notre Dame, IN: Ave Maria Press.

———. 2002 (circa 1266 CE). *On Kingship.* In *St. Thomas Aquinas: Political Writings*, edited by R. W. Dyson. Cambridge: Cambridge University Press.

Aristotle. 1980 (circa 335 BCE). *Nicomachean Ethics.* Revised edition. Translated by W. D. Ross. Oxford: Oxford University Press.

Bailey, James P. 2010. *Rethinking Poverty: Income, Assets, and the Catholic Social Justice Tradition.* Notre Dame, IN: University of Notre Dame Press.

Benedict XVI. 2009. *Caritas in Veritate: On Integral Development in Charity and Truth.* Encyclical. https://www.vatican.va/content/benedict-xvi/en/encyclicals/documents/hf_ben-xvi_enc_20090629_caritas-in-veritate.html.

Board of Governors of the Federal Reserve Bank. 2014. *Report on the Economic Well-being of U.S. Households in 2013.* Washington, DC: Federal Reserve Bank. https://www.federalreserve.gov/econresdata/2013-report-economic-well-being-us-households-201407.pdf.

Boshara, Ray. 2015. "The Future of Building Wealth: Can Financial Capability Overcome Demographic Destiny?" In *What It's Worth: Strengthening the Financial Future of Families, Communities, and the Nation.* San Francisco: Federal Reserve Bank of San Francisco and the Corporation for Enterprise Development.

Brooks, Jennifer, and Kasey Wiedrich. 2013. *Living on the Edge: Financial Insecurity and Possibilities to Rebuild Prosperity in America.* Washington, DC: Corporation for Enterprise Development.

Dettling, Lisa J., Joanne Hsu, Lindsay Jacobs, Kebin Moore, and Jeffrey P. Thompson. 2017. "Recent Trends in Wealth-Holding by Race and Ethnicity: Evidence from the Survey of Consumer Finances." In *FEDS Notes.* Washington, DC: Board of Governors of the Federal Reserve System. https://doi.org/10.17016/2380-7172.2083.

Elliott, William, and Melinda Lewis. 2018. *Making Education Work for the Poor: The Potential of Children's Savings Accounts.* Oxford: Oxford University Press.

Francis. 2013. *Evangelii Gaudium: The Joy of the Gospel.* Apostolic exhortation. http://www.vatican.va/content/francesco/en/apost_exhortations/documents/papa-francesco_esortazione-ap_20131124_evangelii-gaudium.html.

———. 2020. *Fratelli Tutti: On Fraternity and Social Friendship*. Encyclical. http://www.vatican.va/content/francesco/en/encyclicals/documents/papa -francesco_20201003_enciclica-fratelli-tutti.html.

Institute for Research on Poverty. 2021. "How Is Poverty Measured?" University of Wisconsin–Madison, Madison, WI. https://www.irp.wisc.edu /resources/how-is-poverty-measured.

Kent, Ana Hernández, Lowell Rickets, and Ray Boshara. 2019. *What Wealth Inequality in America Looks Like: Facts and Figures*. St. Louis: Federal Reserve Bank of St. Louis. https://www.stlouisfed.org/open-vault/2019/august /wealth-inequality-in-america-facts-figures#:~:text=Income%20allows %20a%20family%20to,card%20debt%20and%20student%20loans.

Kim, Youngmi, Jin Huang, Michael Sherraden, and Margaret Clancy. 2017. "Child Development Accounts, Parental Savings, and Parental Educational Expectations: A Path Model." *Child Youth Services Review* 79: 20–28.

King Jr., Martin Luther. 1961. "Speech at the Fourth Annual AFL-CIO Annual Convention." http://umdlabor.weebly.com/uploads/2/9/3/9 /29397087/speech_transcript.pdf.

Leo XIII. 1891. *Rerum Novarum: On Capital and Labor*. Encyclical. https:// www.vatican.va/content/leo-xiii/en/encyclicals/documents/hf_l-xiii_enc _15051891_rerum-novarum.html.

Lerman, Robert I., and Signe-Mary McKernan. 2008. "Benefits and Consequences of Holding Assets." In *Asset Building and Low-Income Families*, edited by Signe-Mary McKernan and Michael Sherraden. Washington, DC: Urban Institute Press. 195–206.

Levin, Ezra, Jeremie Greer, and Ida Rademacher. 2014. *From Upside Down to Right-Side Up: Redeploying $540 Billion in Federal Spending to Help All Families Save, Invest, and Build Wealth*. Washington, DC: Corporation for Enterprise Development. https://prosperitynow.org/sites/default/files /resources/Upside_Down_to_Right-Side_Up_2014.pdf.

Morduch, Jonathan, and R. Schneider. 2017. *The Financial Diaries: How Americans Cope in a World of Uncertainty*. Princeton, NJ: Princeton University Press.

Nam, Yunju, Jin Huang, and Michael Sherraden. 2008. *Assets, Poverty, and Public Policy: Challenges in Definition and Measurement*. St. Louis: Center for Social Development/Washington University in St. Louis.

Nieves, Emanuel, and Dedrick Asante-Muhammad. 2018. *Running in Place: Why the Racial Wealth Divide Keeps Black and Latino Families from Achieving Economic Security*. Washington, DC: Prosperity Now. https://prosperitynow .org/files/resources/Running_in_Place_FINAL_3.2018.pdf.

Oliver, Melvin, and Thomas Shapiro. 1995. *Black Wealth/White Wealth: A New Perspective on Racial Inequality.* New York: Routledge.

Paul VI. 1967. *Populorum Progressio: On the Development of Peoples.* Encyclical. https://www.vatican.va/content/paul-vi/en/encyclicals/documents/hf_p-vi_enc_26031967_populorum.html.

Putnam, Robert. 2015. *Our Kids: The American Dream in Crisis.* New York: Simon and Schuster.

Rank, Mark. 2003. "As American as Apple Pie: Poverty and Welfare." *Contents* 2, no. 3: 41 49.

———. 2013. "Poverty in America Is Mainstream." *New York Times*, November 2. https://opinionator.blogs.nytimes.com/2013/11/02/poverty-in-america-is-mainstream.

Reeves, Richard V. 2017. *Dream Hoarders: How the American Upper Middle Class Is Leaving Everyone Else in the Dust, Why That Is a Problem, and What to Do about It.* Washington, DC: Brookings Institution.

Rothwell, David W., Timothy Ottusch, and Jennifer K. Finders. 2019. "Asset Poverty Among Children: A Cross-National Study of Poverty Risk." *Children and Youth Services Review* 96: 409–19.

Scanlon, Edward, and Deborah Page-Adams. 2001. "Effects of Asset Holding on Neighborhoods, Families, and Children: A Review of the Research." In *Building Assets: A Report on the Asset-Development and IDA Field*, edited by Ray Boshara. Washington, DC: Corporation for Enterprise Development, 25–50.

Sen, Amartya. 1992. *Inequality Reexamined.* Cambridge, MA: Harvard University Press.

Shanks, Trina Williams, Youngmi Kim, Vernon Loke, and Mesmin Destin. 2010. "Assets and Child Well-being in Developed Countries." *Children and Youth Services Review* 32: 1466–90.

Sherraden, Michael. 1992. *Assets and the Poor: A New American Welfare Policy.* Armonk, NY: M. E. Sharpe.

———. 2018. "Asset Building as Social Investment." *Journal of Sociology and Welfare* 45, no. 4: 35–54.

Sherraden, Michael, M. Clancy, Y. Nam, J. Huang, Y. Kim, S. G. Beverly, L. R. Mason, N. E Wikoff, M. Schreiner, and J. Q. Purnell. 2015. "Universal Accounts at Birth: Building Knowledge to Inform Policy." *Journal of the Society for Social Work and Research* 6, no. 4: 541–64.

Shobe, Marcia, and Deborah Page-Adams. 2001. "Assets, Future Orientation and Well-being: Exploring and Extending Sherraden's Framework." *Journal of Sociology and Social Welfare* 28, no. 3: 109-27.

Sitaraman, Ganesh. 2017. *The Crisis of the Middle-Class Constitution*. New York: Knopf.

US Conference of Catholic Bishops (USCCB). 1986. *Economic Justice for All: Pastoral Letter on Catholic Social Teaching and the U.S. Economy*. https://www.usccb.org/upload/economic_justice_for_all.pdf.

Vatican Council II. 1965. *Gaudium et Spes: Pastoral Constitution on the Church in the Modern World*. https://www.vatican.va/archive/hist_councils/ii_vatican_council/documents/vat-ii_const_19651207_gaudium-et-spes_en.html.

Wolff, Edward N. 2017. "Household Wealth Trends in the United States, 1962–2016." Working Paper 24085, National Bureau of Economic Research, Cambridge, MA. http://www.nber.org/papers/w24085.

World Synod of Catholic Bishops. 1971. *Justice in the World*. Vatican City: World Synod of Catholic Bishops. https://christusliberat.org/journal/wp-content/uploads/2017/10/Justicia-in-Mundo.pdf.

Zhan, Min. 2006. "Assets, Parental Expectations and Involvement, and Children's Educational Performance." *Children and Youth Services Review* 28, no. 8: 961–75.

TWELVE

A Preferential Option for the Poor and Solidarity in Practice

A Salzburg Initiative to Combat Child Poverty in Romania

Helmut P. Gaisbauer

ABSTRACT

In this chapter I analyze an initiative to combat child poverty in Romania as a notable case of a preferential option for the poor, thus as a living example of the application of Catholic Social Teaching (CST). It is based on a theoretical approach that applies the capability approach (CA) to child poverty and thus focuses on the negative effects of capability deprivation on the personal development of children. This theoretical work is embedded in an interpretive concept of the preferential option for the poor with four analytical dimensions, the practically decisive of which is long-lasting commitment.

This was particularly important to the Christian organizers of the project against child poverty in Dumbrăveni, Romania, who came from Salzburg, Austria, as a secure growth perspective for children affected by poverty.

INTRODUCTION

In this chapter I explore the challenges and obstacles that stand in the way of development and growth. I focus on an aid project in Romania, an endeavor concerned with the capability-building of children in deep poverty. To begin, I describe the inception of a day care center in Dumbrăveni, Romania—LIFT,[1] that embodies the key principles of Catholic Social Teaching (CST), particularly an option for the poor based on solidarity. I then go on to theorize on capability- and capacity-building in child poverty contexts and offer examples of how LIFT aims to assist children in developing and growing under adverse circumstances. Finally, I highlight the dedication of key persons, initiators, and professionals under the premise of a CST option for the poor. The whole venture is comprehensively oriented toward development, growth, and commitment and represents a living case of CST in action.

CST AS A CONTEXT AND A SOURCE: AN OPTION FOR THE MIGRANT POOR IN SALZBURG AND BEYOND

Since the beginning of the new millennium, there has been an alarming rise in the number of impoverished families from former Communist states living on the streets in Western cities. A significant proportion of these families are of Romani origin; the Romani are an ethnic minority that found itself forced out beyond the margins of society after the collapse of state-directed economies in Central and Southeastern Europe.

The sudden and dramatic increase in migrant beggars received a mixed reception in Salzburg (as it did elsewhere), with highly emotional responses from both sides of this new equation. Scandalous reports in the media fanned the flames of an already heated discussion. "Migrant poverty" issues not only found their way into the local election campaign for the new lord mayor of Salzburg but also played a leading role in national polls. Interestingly, it was the conservative party that relied on traditionally Catholic voters who proclaimed that Salzburg's status as a city of beggars was absolutely unacceptable and adopted a zero-tolerance approach to the problem by proposing to reintroduce a clamp-down on all begging in the city.

It was amid this social and political upheaval that, in 2014, a civil rights group finally took a stand to represent and further the interests of this ethnic minority; finally, an option for the poor, rooted in CST, was being seriously sought.

An Option for the Poor: "Giving Poverty a Place—A Platform for the Migrant Poor"

An organized group of dedicated individuals with Christian charity-work experience (in Caritas Salzburg, Diakoniewerk der Evangelischen Kirche, and Stift St. Peter), took up the challenge of identifying the measures that would need to be adopted. Toward the end of 2013, talks began among Caritas Salzburg, the social service ministry of the Catholic Church; the Benedictine Abbey of St. Peter; the local Roma Association, Phurdo[2]; the Archdiocese of Salzburg; and other institutions and organizations active in the field. The objective was to concentrate efforts on tackling the plight of the so-called Notreisende ("immigrants in adversity") in a humane and organized manner. In early 2014 Armut hat Platz—Plattform für ArmutsmigrantInnen (Giving Poverty a Place—Platform for the Migrant Poor) was officially founded under the auspices of several charitable organizations, with a number of prominent figures and celebrities offering their support to act on behalf of the victims.

This project serves as a fresh example of CST in action. All three core communities and organizations—Caritas, Diakoniewerk, and the St. Peter Benedictine monastery—stood up for a preferential option for the alien poor. All three have set out on a journey of lasting commitment and pro-poor action, and all three have been brought together in encounter.

Two founding members expressed their reasons for setting up the initiative as follows: "People suffering poverty due to extreme adverse conditions need our help and as aliens, migrants, they must be enabled to access the things all human beings require for their basic needs. Emergency aid is not enough; they need an in situ environment in which they can experience positive face to face encounter" (Dines and König 2015, 212). Precepts such as these became the cornerstones of an initiative that was intent on going further than "just" providing aid and assistance: from the outset those involved dedicated themselves to showing real care and concern for these victims of adversity and deprivation. Their dedication set a benchmark for caring for the poor and needy in crisis and shone as a modern-day embodiment of CST.

Most of the work was done in Salzburg. I will now discuss what this work looks like and the impact it has had (and continues to have) on those hit by poverty. For our purposes, I will focus on an activity in Romania that is addressing the deep poverty afflicting a group of Romani children. What does this "option for the poor" as a vision for the future in CST mean for this particular vulnerable group, who are periodically begging on the streets of Salzburg? And what kind of commitments follow from that?

In an inspiring introductory chapter to *Humanities and Option for the Poor*, Clemens Sedmak highlights four key elements of a preferential option for the poor: First, it is an option that sets priorities. Second, it is an option that is both a voluntary and a lasting decision—an option distinguishes itself from a one-off decision in its binding character and in its acceptance of obligations and commitments; in a word, it differs in its lastingness. Third, an option for the poor is an option for a fellow human being; it is a decision taken both for the benefit of and on behalf of a third party. Fourth, an option for the poor has a clear target group: it is aimed at the poor, although this, in turn, leads us to ask who the poor are—are they all the same, and, if not, how do they differ (Sedmak 2005, 13)?

These core principles of an "option for the poor" help us to gauge and assess the motives and objectives and the cause and effect of the platform Armut hat Platz—Plattform für ArmutsmigrantInnen. How well they promote the interests of the poor is exemplified in the operation that is the focus of this contribution: the day care center LIFT in Dumbrăveni, Romania.

An Option for the Alien Poor

Many organizations and figures involved in "poor relief" (as it is some-times described) are not novices—they have considerable experience in the field of poverty alleviation. One such organization is Caritas, which is active in the Archdiocese of Salzburg. In every new situation they need to know who the poor are, which isn't always as simple to figure out as it might sound. In the case of migrant beggars forced to leave their homes under duress, it is not obvious and becomes a complicated question to answer. As this is an entirely new situation in relatively wealthy Austria, the whole set of circumstances demands a rethinking of previous notions and precepts of poverty.

From a socio-political point of view these Romani migrants are the "alien poor," and they are therefore expected to find aid elsewhere—per-haps where they come from. Likewise, in the eyes of the general public this is a problem that has nothing to do with them and should certainly not make demands on "their" local resources and municipal services (Waldron 2009, 161). We have a situation, therefore, in which the local and resident poor can rely on the support and solidarity of both the gen-eral public and social services, even in emergencies, but when it comes to individuals from the new EU member states of Romania, Bulgaria, Slo-vakia, and Hungary that support is withheld. In fact, rather than viewing these individuals as victims of poverty, authorities claimed to be plagued by bands of gypsies engaged in organized begging, branding them as members of a "beggars' mafia" with highly suspicious motives. It does not need to be pointed out that the pejorative undertones at work here are more than harmless undercurrents and, therefore, a key goal in setting up the platform Giving Poverty a Place was to challenge unwarranted bad press and malicious trolling attitudes and to offer truths, facts, and figures in their stead. The primary objective was to expel the notion of the migrant poor as monsters from another planet and to reveal "these aliens" as human beings, "just like you and me." They needed to be portrayed for what they were—people in dire need of help and support, forced to beg on the streets.

The name of the platform was important—it had to get the mes-sage across immediately by highlighting the plight of the human beings affected rather than focusing on the work that would be involved. In a society bombarded with hackneyed phrases and sentimental notions of stereotypical help, the name had to be instantly recognizable, without being confused with any dubious websites making unsolicited demands on human kindness. The focus also shifted from the idea of collecting money for "poor people" to concentrating on a reasonable, favorable option for a particular section of society and, in the process, underscoring a core notion of solidarity that lay at the heart of the initiative. Only by expressing solidarity can a society accommodate the poor and needy. Here we have people, victims, who must be allowed to be seen and make their cases known. They should be allowed to hope that life has more to offer than they have now. They should not be discriminated against or excluded from society just because they were born in the wrong part of Europe—ethically speaking, they have as much right as any "victims" in need of help and emergency aid (Dines and König 2015, 213).

The creation of this platform was a conscious and deliberate attempt to offer a dignified reception to this migrant minority in Salzburg. The aim is for these people to be recognized as people in need, as people who have been disappointed and let down in their human hopes and desires, and for them to be seen as human beings with feelings, personalities, and identities like everyone else. The goal is to change public opinion and the political discourse that currently prevents these people from being viewed as anything other than "migrant beggars" or people who don't fit into society. These are labels that are incredibly difficult to get rid of, labels that have been assigned to a group of people through no fault of their own. These objectives are vital in establishing the third core tenet of CST—an option for the poor as an option for someone—a real, specific person—who for now is unfortunately a migrant beggar.

An Option for Someone: Advocacy

From the beginning, this platform adopted an advocacy role, an important aspect of all social and charitable institutions. This option for advocacy of an ethnic minority from one of Austria's poorest post-communist neighbors is also an option to lobby on behalf of these people—an option that is the bedrock of CST thinking: in the words of Johannes Dines and Michael König (2015, 214), "to protect the rights and human dignity of this minority begging on the streets of Salzburg."

Its charter includes the following objectives with regard to advocacy:

- Commitment to a dignified perception and reception of these people in the City of Salzburg, together with an acquired sense of the real needs of this particular target group.
- Compiling and distributing information to raise awareness of the needs of this minority group and to promote accountability among policy-makers and a keener sense of responsibility in politics in general.
- Including the local population in all awareness-raising strategies to support a deeper and more objective perception and understanding of the living conditions of this sector of society. (Ibid., 214–15)

The contexts in which these options can be applied underline the flexible nature of advocacy, which could well be an option for the poor. In this particular case it is the quality of advocacy, especially at the political level, that makes a difference. A starkly polarized environment leaves little, if any, space for discourse or negotiation. A calm and rational approach was needed, which proved to be essential for purging the debate of political scare-mongering and replacing it with a pragmatic and objective discourse. At the same time, it was important that political figures not be incriminated in any way; this would have been counterproductive. Despite this rational approach, there were nevertheless moments when tensions were near to the breaking point—talking about raising awareness of the plight of these people and arguing for the rights they were being denied led to emotive discussions, to say the least. Beggars were sometimes physically removed from a public space they were "taking up," often without warning. Also, the boundaries of the areas in which they were prohibited to beg would be shifted overnight, which they were immediately expected to be aware of and comply with or risk facing hefty fines.

Another level of advocacy is PR work and getting as many people as possible involved in on-the-ground aid; these could include volunteers, social care institutions, self-help groups, and more. Such co-workers will keep the chain reaction of advocacy going, making it more valued as a solution tool. The advocacy of the platform is invaluable—those at the heart of platform activity quickly realized that the more volunteers who are brought on board, the better it is for creating a positive humanitarian energy field that can be coordinated and mobilized as necessary (ibid., 215–17).

Such advocacy is not purely a lobbying exercise. It is deeply rooted in supportive aid such as providing access to basic health and welfare services, bed and board, encounter and exchange, and advisory and empowering roles; all are equally important and as such are valuable in platform activities, even if they only lighten the load of an "alien" living in "exile" circumstances.

Option as Lasting Commitment

A third dimension of platform work in a preferential option for the poor involves the volunteers and the capability-building effort needed to break the cycle of poverty for a group of children from the Romani community in Dumbrăveni, Romania. The option we are looking at here is the nature of the long-term commitment of those willing to be part of the platform and project and those responsible for financing and promoting the day care center in Romania.

This notion of long-term commitment comes into focus if we look at the options of help and aid available to those wishing to be actively involved. Migrants arriving in Salzburg need a lot of help, which requires the commitments of many people with a host of skills and capabilities. The biggest challenge is the acquisition of accommodations—accessing basic shelter, out of the rain and cold. The level of charitable willingness on the part of key political players is low, and therefore, finding decent lodgings and clean beds for the night for alien vagrants is a huge task. It was not until the late Autumn of 2016 that purpose-built or converted emergency shelters became available, made possible by aid and support from the city and district councils of Salzburg. The first shelter to be opened was St. Francis, which has fifty beds (for men only).

But a shelter also needs to be supervised and managed, and the costs of this would be unmanageable were it not for voluntary help. Such voluntary help must be reliably long-term, requiring commitments from volunteers. This need for voluntary commitment is directly linked to investment costs—converting and refurbishing a building to provide basic lodgings for individuals is expensive, and real estate does not come cheap in Salzburg. Such costs must be justified to make public spending viable. That any such conversion and refurbishment took place at all is due to a lot of single-minded lobbying in political circles and to remaining stubbornly firm, but fair, in negotiations on behalf of the Roma—in other words, demonstrating "effective advocacy." The whole project, from "beginning to bed," took almost two years of hard work, and even though running costs must be reviewed and reset annually, recent years show that there is enough willing and long-term commitment to keep it going.

Finally, the day care project in Romania, initiated and operated by the platform, also requires—and depends upon—long-term commitment in this option for the poor. Four key organizations supporting the platform have decided to set up aid and support for the children of one Romanian village near the place that a large majority of the migrants come from. This LIFT project is primarily aimed at enabling children to receive a proper school education.

LIFT starts at the roots by building a daily routine for children in Romani and non-Romani families—regular warm meals and supervised after-school care so that children are not left to roam (and become used to roaming) the streets. Unlike many other Roma projects, LIFT has been created to run and have an impact for a number of years, not months, which was a key factor in securing financial backing. Its overall aim is to deeply impact the lives of a few individual children and to make a real difference by accompanying them in their daily lives over several years. The motive, of course, is self-evident—education is vital to a child's development, especially in breaking out of the vicious spiral of poverty. If the LIFT project is to succeed, organizations that have pledged financial support need to have a guarantee that there is a significant enough commitment to support it over a long period of time.

Members of the public, too, have a role to play in this project if this fight against poverty is to be a sustainable one. Public support and sentiment need to be stimulated, and to foster this the main regional newspaper in Salzburg has entered a media partnership with the LIFT project. Journalists and reporters have visited the village to see the project in action—what they report, in turn, informs and influences public opinion. The hope with the LIFT project is that it will become a shining example of good practice and go on to encourage the development of similar projects to follow its example.

In summary, we can see that the way the platform is set up, run, and managed underpins the core tenets of the CST ethos and, as such, has a significant impact on an option for the poor. A preferential option means prioritizing other options and asks for long-lasting commitment. All three of the communities and organizations involved stood up for a preferential option for the alien poor. All three have set out on a journey, all three have been brought together in encounter; and all three, in their effort to transform, are being transformed in that they must all take a stand and be in favor of an option that is both tangible and visible. All three of the communities and organizations have their own personalities and identities but are, collectively, leaders of representative organizations. Adopting an option for the poor has an impact on the way others (outsiders) see and judge an organization; it has an impact on the identity of that organization and its agents working on the ground; and it has an impact on the way the organization sees itself, which, in turn, influences the way it works.

The day care center, LIFT, is a special case that impressively shows and represents this impact. A good deal of courage, commitment, and vision is needed to put a project in place that addresses the causes of poverty (especially child poverty) and secures the finances for a necessary long-lasting commitment. Child poverty is an evil that requires long-term efforts in capability-building and alleviating the obstacles to personal growth and development. Romani children in poverty (in Romania, as well as elsewhere) face conditions that prevent them from developing their potential and breaking the vicious cycle of poverty. They are the victims of terrible educational injustice. LIFT tries to compensate for these adverse educational conditions and to alleviate the poverty of Romani children in Dumbrăveni. It is a special case of long-lasting commitment closely aligned with the core tenets of a preferential option for the poor.

THEORY: CHILD POVERTY, CAPABILITY DEPRIVATION, AND EDUCATIONAL INJUSTICE

Any preferential option of the poor understands poverty as a moral evil in at least two ways. According to Peter Townsend's seminal conceptualization, poverty means to "lack the resources to obtain the types of diet,

participate in the activities and have the living conditions and ameni-
ties which are customary, or are at least widely encouraged or approved,
in the societies to which they belong" (Townsend 1979, 31). Townsend
describes this as a state of deprivation. The poor are deprived of something they should have command of—the resources to live lives worth
living. The reasons for deprivation are mostly societal ones and are typically beyond the influence of those affected. Deprivation describes a state
of reduced (or entirely absent) well-being. This constitutes a moral evil.
Besides that, poverty also narrows the spectrum of possibilities for the
individual affected, and hence has a negative impact on the poor person's
future life. This constitutes another moral evil. In the worst case, it can
be described as a state of neglected (positive) future (Gaisbauer and Sedmak 2014). In other words, poverty is also a state of reduced (or entirely
absent) well-becoming. Poverty is the moral evil of depriving a person of
both their well-being and their well-becoming. It is important to underline that people do not live in isolation—poverty is, hence, always also
a crisis of family or social life. Thus, well-being and well-becoming are
embedded in a social web, and adverse circumstances affect individuals,
their families, and those close to them.

A two-dimensional conceptualization of poverty can help to outline
the effects of poverty over a particular period of a person's life. If multiple
periods of a person's life are examined, it provides an opportunity for
analyzing and exploring various aspects of child poverty (Duncan, Ziol-
Guest, and Kalil 2010). For a moral or normative perspective on child
poverty, it is important to bring together these two dimensions—the
being and the becoming aspects of childhood. Attempts to combat child
poverty have to operate within a special tension between a present- and
a future-centered perspective on children's lives (Schweiger and Graf
2015, 10–11).

A just society that avoids the moral evil of child poverty is one in
which "each and every child develops and achieves functionings and
capabilities that are necessary for their well-being and well-becoming"
(ibid., 18). Such a premise rests on an objective understanding of well-
being—rather than subjective notions of welfare, happiness, or satisfaction—and is expressed in the conceptual language of the CA. The
ethical obligation of a society is to provide all children with the full
range of capabilities and functionings necessary to reach comprehensive

well-being. Well-being, as an actual state of being well, should also allow for development and growth, that is, well-becoming, the change from one state of being to a state of well-being (Schweiger and Graf 2015, 18). Understood that way, well-being and well-becoming combine to become what Gottfried Schweiger and Gunter Graf (2015, 17–18) refer to as a multidimensional concept encompassing "a wide range of important features of children's lives: health, education, social inclusion and participation, access to material goods and shelter and the like." This concept goes far beyond ideas of subjective welfare and involves discussions about society and livelihood that are necessary to make children feel well and develop wellness, as well as enabling them to lead good lives as adolescents and grown-ups.

According to Mario Biggeri and Santosh Mehrotra (2011), capability theory proposes the following fourteen capabilities required for child well-being and well-becoming:

1. Life and physical health: being able to be born, be physically healthy and enjoy a life of normal length.
2. Love and care: being able to love and be loved by those who care, and to be protected.
3. Mental well-being: being able to be mentally healthy.
4. Bodily integrity and safety: being safe from violence of any sort.
5. Social relations: being able to be part of social networks and to give and receive social support.
6. Participation: being able to participate in and have a fair share of influence, and being able to receive objective information.
7. Education: having opportunities to be educated.
8. Freedom from economic and noneconomic exploitation: being able to be protected from economic and noneconomic exploitation.
9. Shelter and environment: being able to have shelter and to live in a healthy, safe, and pleasant environment.
10. Leisure activities: being able to engage in leisure activities.
11. Respect: being respected and treated with dignity.
12. Religion and identity: being able to choose to live according to a religion or an identity, or to choose not to do so.

13. Time autonomy: being able to exercise autonomy in allocating one's time.
14. Mobility: being able to move freely. (Biggeri and Mehrotra 2011, 51)

Lists like this offer a valuable heuristic by including all normatively important dimensions or features of well-being and well-becoming, but it is far from clear how to transform it into an instrument to capture or measure child poverty (ibid.), or to prescribe who exactly is responsible for combating this moral evil (Schweiger and Graf 2015). At least four important arguments explain why "capabilitarian" conceptual language might be especially helpful for understanding child poverty. First, there are at least two kinds of capabilities: the skills, powers, or capacities of an individual, such as the ability to speak, and opportunities afforded by an environment or society, such as the right to free expression (Gardner 2015, 69). As seen here, capabilities combine the individual and the social—a feature that is important to grasp in order to comprehend the two-fold reality of well-being and well-becoming, which sees children highly dependent on others as well as on their environments (Schweiger and Graf 2015, 9). Second, the individual capabilities, that is, skills, powers, or capacities of a person (or child), are in themselves dynamic and continue to develop. These capabilities are the main focus of educational efforts and hence are of crucial importance for a theory of development and growth. They also unlock the constraints of poverty, thereby allowing for growth in personality and the development of cognitive and social skills (Gardner 2015, 70). Third, the CA incorporates these concepts into a theoretical framework that asserts that the freedom to achieve well-being should be understood in terms of a person's capabilities—that is, their real opportunities to do and be what they have reason to value (Robeyns 2011). Doubtlessly, there are many suitable approaches to analyzing educational processes, human development, or personal growth. Fourth and finally, a capabilitarian approach fits into our reasoning because of its position in the "means-end debate" in accounts of social justice. In contrast to theories inspired by Peter Townsend, the CA holds that it is better to focus on the ends rather than the means because people differ in their ability to convert means into valuable opportunities or outcomes (Sen 1992, 26–28). Since ends are what ultimately matter when thinking about well-being and quality of life, means can work as reliable proxies of people's opportunities to achieve those ends only if they all have the same capacities or powers to convert those means into equal capability sets (Robeyns 2011). This is not the case in the context of a socially marginalized community, as seen in our case study. Here, the deficient individual, social and environmental conversion factors, and the accompanying vulnerabilities, lead to poor schooling and extremely high drop-out rates, which are the focus of the academic and social-practical interest of this contribution.

Let us summarize the points thus far: (1) Poverty is essentially a twofold phenomenon—an actual state and a reduced future potential. (2) Poverty can, therefore, be seen as a deprivation of well-being and well-becoming. (3) Child poverty brings a special tension into actual well-being and future well-becoming, with present ill-being as a two-fold evil: it deprives poor children of flourishing lives in the present and hinders them when they are attempting to exercise and develop their capacities, resulting in negative future outcomes (Macleod 2010). (4) Well-being is understood as more than subjective welfare or happiness and is considered an objective state encompassing a wide range of significant features, such as health, education, shelter, and so on. (5) Objective well-being of children is congruent with a conceptualization of capabilities from a child's perspective (Bagattini 2014, 175). (6) Capabilities are individual skills, powers, and capacities, as well as socially or environmentally afforded opportunities. The individual "part" or "dimension" of a capability can be developed deliberately (through cultivation or education), or it can be developed through unconscious learning from experience, and it can profit from a beneficial social and physical environment (Gardner 2015, 71). (7) By contrast, adverse social and environmental circumstances—often factors or causes of ill-being or poverty—slow down or hinder such individual development and personal growth, which, in turn, can either negatively affect well-becoming or perpetuate poverty. (8) Individual capacities develop throughout the human lifespan, but that process of development is especially rapid during childhood (ibid., 68). The cultivation of a particular set of skills, powers, and capacities is the primary goal of formal education. This simple goal is blind to adverse individual, social, and environmental conversion factors that affect those from socially excluded populations or groups, leaving them "vulnerable" to institutional incapacity or structural stumbling blocks. Adverse conversion factors, therefore, "attack" or diminish certain capabilities. The landscape of adverse conversion factors is the factual reality of educational injustice that precludes vulnerable and socially excluded groups from realizing the capability "education" (Biggeri and Mahrotra 2011, 51).

THE SOCIAL PRACTICE OF CAPABILITY-BUILDING: THE DAY CARE CENTER LIFT IN DUMBRĂVENI

The day care center studied, LIFT, in Dumbrăveni, is not formally based on a theoretical framework but instead inspired by values, norms, and the founders' professional knowledge of social work, with backgrounds in CST and inspired by a preferential option for the poor. Still, the normative assumptions and goals of the project can be construed as an endeavor to compensate for educational injustice and to cultivate capacities and capability-building in line with the principal tenets of the CA. Moreover, we argue that such an approach to combating child poverty is also in line with Catholic ideas of integral human development (Maritain 1973) and the core CST principle of human dignity (Sedmak 2017).

The LIFT Approach

As Daniela Palk et al. (2015) report, the project's goals were to address the issues that are likely to keep most Romani children in Dumbrăveni (and elsewhere) trapped in consistent poverty. They write:

> Dumbrăveni is a rural town at the periphery of Sibiu County with a lot of out-migration and strong social inequality. 15% of the inhabitants have a Romani background, which is considerably higher than the Romanian average. This community struggles with a multitude of problems and meets strong prejudice, discrimination and social exclusion. Children from this community do not have sustainable access to education and consequently to jobs for trained workers. The Centre . . . aims at enhancing the children's social and educational capacities and at empowering them to develop their own perspectives and

goals. It does so by providing educational support and social work. One main goal is to prevent children from dropping out of school in the first years; children get help through educational assistance and socio-cultural learning. Healthy diet, structures and rituals as well as individual and group coaching make them gather positive experiences of well-being, recognition and self-efficacy. (2015, 2)

This general analysis led the project initiators to a more specific definition of the issues: "(1) Children from poor and socially excluded (Romani) families face discrimination in school due to socio-cultural obstacles. (2) Their parents often lack basic education. (3) Ill-educated teenagers, often analphabets, do not have access to training or jobs for trained persons in Romania. (4) In Romania, Romani people meet strong prejudices and discrimination, and are often socially excluded" (ibid., 3).

Translated into capabilitarian conceptual language, points 1 to 4 describe the issues as deprivation of the capability "education." Education is an important factor in the well-being of children and a crucial capability in well-becoming. It is especially important for combating persistent poverty (and future poverty) on the level of the child. In this context, the poverty and social exclusion of Romani families result in children's diminished access to education, poor schooling, and high drop-out rates from as early as primary school. Since school is compulsory in Romania, and public schools are open and potentially accessible to all children in Dumbrăveni, educational injustice does not lie in the formal exclusion of certain groups of children from free and compulsory schooling; rather, it lies in the adverse conversion factors that amount to serious obstacles for the afflicted children and prevent them from living up to their educational potential. The project initiators rightly use the terms "discrimination" and "prejudices," "socio-cultural obstacles," and "limited social and educational capacities." Adverse conversion factors are mostly structural but also affect the vulnerable or those who are excluded on an individual level. Adverse conversion factors are in a way the negative currency of social exclusion and discrimination. It is at this point that the conceptual language of capability appears to reveal its heuristic value: the deprivation of educational capability is the effect of structural discrimination, social prejudices, poverty, poor parenting, and the transmissive effects of the poor education of parents, and so on, which, in turn, affect individual children, resulting in poor educational capacities or social skills, poor health, and more. The children afflicted by poverty are at the intersection of different adverse processes and environmental influences that hinder them from living up to their educational and personal potential. This deprivation of educational capability is embedded in a complex web of deprivation of several capabilities. This web of deprivation can here be focused by the heuristic lenses of educational injustice.

Social work that attempts to assist some of the children afflicted by persistent poverty and educational injustice needs to address various issues in this web of deprivation. Based on the evaluation cited above, the project managers of LIFT defined nine programmatic goals for the center's effort to combat child poverty in the long run:

1. Roma participation in the development of the project (empowerment).
2. Reduction of prejudice and xenophobia by diversity management.
3. Resonance and recognition for children and adolescents from Roma families; promotion of self-efficacy.
4. Regular participation keeps the children grounded in an alternative daily life.
5. Children gain knowledge through coaching in homework and studying in groups. This provides them with a sense of achievement.
6. Accommodation of the children to basic cultural norms and good habits.
7. A warm meal for every child safeguards healthy diet, helps the families and contributes to a beneficial group identity.
8. Enhancing vocational knowledge and future perspectives in work through education.
9. Enhancing the respect to and valuation of education in poverty-stricken families through counselling and mentoring. (Ibid., 3–6)

This list confirms that the center's main goals (5 and 8) boil down to the best possible education for the children in poverty it serves. Setting such a goal impressively reflects the long-lasting commitment of the Salzburg platform. It is underpinned by the inspiring vocation for a CST option for the poor; it boldly dedicates personal and financial resources to a restricted field of action based on the belief of doing the right thing.

The benchmarks for such best possible education in cases of strong deprivation of educational capability are incredibly low. De facto benchmarks are to avert early school drop-out and to prevent very low levels of reading, writing, and mathematical skills (i.e., preventing analphabetism), to increase daily school attendance, and to extend the number of (successful) years of schooling in the regular school beyond three, four, or five years. For achieving goal 5, the list resembles a range of secondary goals or dimensions that address different adverse conversion factors of the bad school performance of the center's target population. Goals 3, 4, 6, and 7 concentrate on strengthening individual capacities, skills, and powers, enabling personal development and growth. Goals 1, 2, and 9 aim to address matters of collective empowerment and anti-discriminatory practice at the community level.

To summarize, the goals show a balanced and hands-on approach with regard to counter-educational injustice and the overall web of deprivation. This approach focuses on personal development and growth—it cultivates skills, powers, and capacities in the children, but also addresses structural obstacles by empowering Romani families and combating prejudices and social exclusion.[3]

Some LIFT Results

LIFT was scientifically evaluated in 2017 by the Centre for Ethics and Poverty Research at the University of Salzburg. The first report creates a comprehensive picture of the adverse environment the children live in (Gaisbauer 2019). It also analyzes how the children experience the facilities, how regularly they take part in activities—a proxy for regularity of school attendance—and, the most difficult to measure and observe, whether they grow in personality, skills, and capacities.

The report shows that most of the children experience the day care center as a safe harbor that allows them to play and learn without stress. The most important factor is the personal one: the female social workers built close relationships with the children, which the children deeply appreciated (ibid., 14). The small staff of four female social workers truly embody the vocation of an option for these impoverished children (and their families), which is an approach that goes far beyond that of ordinary professional social workers. The children report significant recognition by the social workers and do see their interest in caring for them; the supportive environment and routine experience allow for stable relationships that help them to gain self-confidence (ibid., 15). By witnessing the routine of a shared meal at lunchtime, an external observer gains a clear sense of the impressive quality of child care at this center: the atmosphere is relaxed, the children are well behaved; help to prepare the table and organize the dishes; say a short prayer; and then enjoy a tasty meal—all indicators of healthy well-being. The achievement of this shared well-being becomes even more significant when one considers that at least half of the households that the children come from do not have tables for shared meals (Gaisbauer 2019, 16).

A major success of the first three years of the LIFT program has been the consolidation of a group of around twenty children, which saw all the children regularly attending the program and even improved the regularity of their school attendance. It is again worth pointing out that these children live in acute poverty, experience profound illiteracy, suffer extreme social marginalization, and are victims of severe stigmatization in a small town of fewer than ten thousand inhabitants (ibid., 17).

Classmates generally rate the children's participation in the day care center program as positive. Only one child has reported hearing that they come to the center only for the food. By contrast, several classmates find participation good and report that some are actively interested in the program. This evaluative report confirms how well-regarded the institution is, an opinion echoed by parents and school directors alike, and a finding that was by no means a foregone conclusion, as the center's work is operated with "lobby" money from abroad and dedicated to the least respected children and parents in the town (ibid., 27).

Improving basic school skills and capacities requires a lot of work and effort. The main reasons for poor schooling, lack of regular attendance, and high drop-out rates are the structural segregation and discrimination encountered by Romani children in the school system. Other reasons include the negative combination of material and institutional interests among the municipality, the school, and the impoverished parents. Taken altogether, this analysis reveals the many obstacles and challenges the day care center faces (ibid., 33).

Also positive is the benefit that the day care center provides for the children, which is unmistakable. The report shows that the children have made significant progress in terms of developing good behaviors, healthy eating habits, and hygiene. They have become noticeably calmer and more relaxed and seem to be benefiting from having a warm, safe, and stimulating "substitute part-time home" in the LIFT day care center (ibid., 37). These results were complemented by a second evaluative report that focused on stress, stress resistance, and the stress-managing capacities of children and their parents (Gaisbauer 2020). The lockdown of schools and public life over the course of the COVID-19-pandemic in 2020 and 2021 exacerbated the causes and amplified the consequences of child poverty in Romania and left this population in an even greater state of vulnerability. This situation further heightened the importance of LIFT, which helped the children to access online learning tools and dissuaded them from dropping out of school.

CONCLUSION: ACTION SPEAKS LOUDER THAN WORDS

The evaluative reports were well received by the managers of the LIFT program in Dumbrăveni and Salzburg, as they clearly outlined the obstacles and challenges that need to be addressed in order to offer a long-lasting commitment to both the impoverished children in Dumbrăveni and the staff who care for them. Capability- and capacity-building in socially adverse environments of profound child poverty and social exclusion call for a bold action plan and dedicated commitment. It needs a real option for the poor. This has never been more true than in the current crisis brought about by the recent pandemic. LIFT in Dumbrăveni represents a living enactment of the fine CST tradition. It truly binds together many different contexts and people into one common good. The important point is this: actions speak louder than words.

NOTES

1. "LIFT" stands for Lernen, Integration, Förderung, Tagesstruktur (Learning, Integration, Advancement, Daily Routines) as well as for a lift/elevator.

2. This Romani word means "bridge."

3. Most of the capabilities on Biggeri's list are covered by the LIFT approach.

WORKS CITED

Bagattini, Alexander. 2014. "Child Well-being: A Philosophical Perspective." In *Handbook of Child Well-Being: Theory, Indicators, Measures and Policies*, edited by Asher Ben-Arieh, Ferran Casas, Ivar Frønes, and Jill E. Korbin. Dordrecht: Springer, 163–86.

Biggeri, Mario, and Santosh Mehrotra. 2011. "Child Poverty as Capability Deprivation: How to Choose Domains of Child Well-being and Poverty." In *Children and the Capability Approach*, edited by Mario Biggeri, Jérôme Ballet, and Flavio Comim. Basingstoke, UK: Palgrave Macmillan, 46–75.

Dines, Johannes, and Michael König. 2015. "'Armut hat Platz': Zivilge-sellschaftliches Engagement in einem polarisierten gesellschaftlichen Diskurs." In *Betteln fordert heraus*, edited by Johannes Dines, Helmut P. Gaisbauer, Michael König, et al. Vienna: Mandelbaum, 211–27.

Duncan, Greg J., Kathleen M. Ziol-Guest, and Ariel Kalil, eds., 2010. "Early-Childhood Poverty and Adult Attainment, Behavior, and Health." *Child Development* 81, no. 1: 306–25.

Gaisbauer, Helmut P. 2019. *Value Dumbraveni: Erster Zwischenbericht*. Salzburg: Centre for Ethics and Poverty Research, University of Salzburg.

———. 2020. *Value Dumbraveni: Zweiter Zwischenbericht*. Salzburg: Centre for Ethics and Poverty Research, University of Salzburg.

Gaisbauer, Helmut P., and Clemens Sedmak. 2014. "Neglected Futures: Considering Overlooked Poverty in Europe." *European Journal of Futures Research* 57, no. 2: 1–8.

Gardner, Bill. 2015. "The Developmental Capability Model of Child Well-being." In *The Well-Being of Children*, edited by Gottfried Schweiger and Gunter Graf. Berlin: De Gruyter Open, 68–83.

Macleod, Colin. 2010. "Primary Goods, Capabilities and Children." In *Measuring Justice—Primary Goods and Capabilities*, edited by Harry Brighouse and Ingrid Robeyns. Cambridge: Cambridge University Press, 174–92.

Maritain, Jacques. 1973 (1968). *Integral Humanism* [Humanisme Intégral]: *Temporal and Spiritual Problems of a New Christendom*. Reprint of the edition published in New York in 1968. Notre Dame, IN: University of Notre Dame Press.

Palk, Daniela, et al. 2015. *Projekt LIFT Tagesbetreuung für Kinder aus sozial benachteiligten Familien in Dumbraveni: Jahresbericht 2015*. Gallneukirchen, Austria: Diakoniewerk Gallneukirchen.

Robeyns, Ingrid. 2011. "The Capability Approach." In *The Stanford Encyclopedia of Philosophy*, edited by Edward Zalta. http://plato.stanford.edu/archives/sum2011/entries/capability-approach/.

Schweiger, Gottfried, and Gunter Graf. 2015. *A Philosophical Examination of Social Justice and Child Poverty*. London: Palgrave Macmillan.

Sedmak, Clemens. 2005. "Introduction: Commitments and an 'Option for the Poor.'" In *Humanities and Option for the Poor*, edited by Magdalena Holztrattner and Clemens Sedmak. Vienna: LIT, 9–22.

———. 2017. *"Die Würde des Menschen ist unantastbar": Zur Anwendung der Katholischen Soziallehre*. Regensburg: Friedrich Pustet.

Sen, Amartya. 1992. *Inequality Reexamined*. Cambridge, MA: Harvard University Press.

Townsend, Peter. 1979. *Poverty in the United Kingdom: A Survey of Household Resources and Standards of Living*. Berkeley: University of California Press.

Waldron, Jeremy. 2009. "Community and Property—For Those Who Have Neither." *Theoretical Inquiries in Law* 10, no. 1: 161–92.

THIRTEEN

Combining the Capability Approach and Catholic Social Teaching to Promote Integral Human Development

Séverine Deneulin and Augusto Zampini-Davies

ABSTRACT

*In this chapter we advance a methodology that combines the capability approach (CA) and Catholic Social Teaching (CST) so as to better respond to the "cry of the poor and of the earth" (*Laudato Si';* Francis 2015, 49). We follow CST's inductive three-stage methodology of "see-judge-act" and combine each stage with the CA, using illustrative examples from Latin American informal settlements and the Amazon basin. We then sketch key features of such a combined methodology, which could inform analysis and social action in other contexts to promote integral human development. In the first stage, we argue that CST places a stronger focus on "listening" and on our relationship to the earth, while the CA provides more conceptual and practical tools for social evaluation. In the second* *stage, while the CA provides a comparative framework for "judging" situations and for uncovering the institutions that constrain or facilitate the conditions for people to develop integrally as humans, CST emphasizes the importance of a culture of encounter and goes further into the relation between how people relate to each other and how institutions function. Finally, in the "acting" stage, the CA offers a greater analysis of the role of collective action in addressing unjust situations, while CST provides a greater focus on love as a motivation for action and greater emphasis on the relation between personal and structural change.*

INTRODUCTION

As highlighted in the introduction to this volume and in all contributions to it, Amartya Sen's emphasis on freedom in its dual aspect of well-being and agency—but always with reference to justice—struck a chord with the Catholic social tradition and its teachings (CST). Putting the freedom of the children of God at the core of socio-economic development is a central concern for both. In that regard, the capability approach (CA) is a natural ally to the Pastoral Constitution of the Catholic Church in the Modern World of the Second Vatican Council, *Gaudium et Spes*, and its aspirations for making "the joys and the hopes, the griefs and the anxieties of the men of this age, especially those who are poor or in any way afflicted" (Vatican Council II 1965, 1), the joys, hopes, and concerns of the Church.

Though the CA and CST may be natural allies in their motivation to address situations of injustice, and to challenge and transform the structures that violate human dignity and prevent women and men from living flourishing human lives, they do share some different point of emphasis, as many contributors to this volume have highlighted. In this chapter we bring together the methodologies that the CA and CST employ to remedy injustices and explore how the strengths and weaknesses of each can be overcome by combining their respective methodologies. We focus on Amartya Sen's writings and conceptualization of the idea of justice, as its indeterminacy and its withholding of explicit philosophical commitments make it particularly open to combination with

CST and its philosophical and theological commitments (see especially the chapter by Amy Daughton).

To respond to situations in which human dignity has been violated, CST proposes an inductive approach based on a three-stage methodology known as "see-judge-act." This approach has been made especially visible in Pope Francis's encyclical *Laudato Si'*, published in 2015. It starts with the "seeing" of reality, especially through the eyes of those who are suffering (the poor and the earth); "judging" such reality through the light of the Christian tradition in dialogue with others; and proposing lines of "action" to respond accordingly—for example, policy regulation, economic reforms, education, and spirituality. Similarly, to respond to situations of poverty and human suffering, the CA proposes a three-stage methodology that could be called "assess-reason-act." It starts with assessing the reality of people's lives in the functioning/capability space, evaluating what people are able to be and do, or not, in given circumstances. It then submits that evaluation to public reasoning processes to identify what needs to be remedied, what needs to change. It leaves it to social actors involved in the public reasoning process to decide which course of action would be best to take.

In this chapter we detail further each of the three stages of these respective methodologies and explore how CST and the CA can enrich each other, hoping that future researchers and social actors can adopt, and adapt, this CST-CA combined methodology in their respective contexts. In order to link our methodological argument with concrete realities of injustice and suffering, we will use illustrative examples, most of them drawn from Latin America's informal settlements and the Amazon region.[1]

SEEING (AND LISTENING): ASSESSING POVERTY IN THE CAPABILITY SPACE AND IN OUR RELATIONSHIP WITH THE EARTH

The methodology of Catholic Social Teaching (CST) for addressing situations of injustice in the world is the triple movement of seeing-judging-acting. Because of its deep biblical roots, this method developed throughout centuries before being officially recognized in an encyclical by Pope John XXIII, *Mater et Magistra*, published in 1961

(Zampini-Davies 2014). One foundational biblical text for the method is the parable of the Good Samaritan (Luke 10:25–37), a powerful and inspiring narrative that helps us be attentive to and read the reality surrounding us, to judge it beyond our religious or any other ideological boundaries, and to follow long-term lines of action that can best respond to the social problems involved and transform people's lives. Pope Francis discusses the parable at length in his encyclical *Fratelli Tutti* (2020a).

The text tells us that when a priest and a Levite, both liturgical officials, "saw" a wounded man lying half-dead along the road on their way to Jericho, each passed by on the opposite side. Unlike them, a Samaritan, a member of a group hated by the Jews, after "seeing" the victim, approached him, poured oil and wine over his wounds, and bandaged them. Then he lifted the man onto his own animal, took him to an inn, and cared for him. Furthermore, when he had to leave, he gave instructions to the innkeeper to look after him, paid him for his services, and promised to pay any further expenses on his return, which in modern language is like issuing a letter of credit.

A main difference between the Samaritan and the liturgical officials is the way their "sight" affected their judgment and actions. In the case of the priest and the Levite, "seeing" the half-dead man on the road did not affect their view of the world. Their deductive theology, in which liturgical commitments were uncontested first priorities (they might have been concerned with becoming impure by touching the wounded person), prevented them from reacting to a clear injustice that appeared in front of their eyes. Unlike them, when "seeing" the same situation, the Samaritan was moved by compassion,[2] which in the Gospel of Luke is a specific characteristic of God.[3] Thus, the parable implies that this compassionate and inclusive way of seeing reflects our likeness to God. The unknown Samaritan, a socio-religious rival of those who were listening to the story, becomes paradoxically the one who behaves as a neighbor,[4] seeing with compassion the wounded and defenseless man, judging the situation with solidarity, and acting with justice. Indeed, by behaving as a neighbor, he has done, as the Evangelist Luke says, "what is right and good," which is the correct response to the question that had triggered the parable. Behaving as a good neighbor to people who are even strangers or enemies, moving beyond our own limited vision of what is right and good, is, according to the Christian tradition, one of the main human attributes.

From a methodological perspective, this well known Christian parable proposes that the starting point of socio-ethical reflection and social action is seeing the suffering of others with empathy (Zampini-Davies 2014). Not surprisingly, in the capability approach (CA), empathy is a basic social emotion that enables us to foster a more just society (Sen 1977). The parable also tells us that it is not necessarily the religious authorities or social leaders who "see" rightly—the one who saw and acted rightly was neither the Levite nor the priest, but a Samaritan, a good citizen from a different religious tradition. Indeed, responding to a situation of suffering is not a task limited to social leaders and those who occupy a privileged position in society but a universal responsibility. In *The Idea of Justice*, Sen (2009, 171–72) refers to the parable of the Good Samaritan to discuss our responsibilities for responding to situations of suffering and to illustrate his argument that our responsibilities toward others, in concrete situations of need, cannot be circumscribed by nationality or membership in other groups.

A central characteristic of the "seeing" stage of CST is that it takes its standpoint from the perspectives of those who live in situations of poverty and disadvantage—of which the person lying wounded in a ditch is a paradigmatic example. However, as Nebel (2014) asked: "Which poor actually?" While the preferential option for the poor lies at the heart of CST, it does not provide a way to identify the poor. Using the income poverty measure has long been the main method for assessing poverty but has considerable limitations (Alkire, Foster, and Seth 2015; Sen 1983; Stewart, Saith, and Harriss-White 2007). For example, a resident of an informal settlement on the outskirts of any big city, such as Buenos Aires, may have an income above the national poverty line yet be unable to go out at night because of fearing drug gangs or to get proper treatment in a public hospital (Mitchell and Macció 2018). Yet the dimensions of health and violence cannot be excluded from poverty measures. Similarly, measuring well-being or poverty in the Amazon rainforest in terms of income would not make sense if people do not use money as a means of exchanging goods. The capability to live in the land of their ancestors—and to live well or enjoy "good living" (*buen vivir*), would be a much more important dimension for assessing poverty. As

Pope Francis writes in his apostolic exhortation *Querida Amazonia*, published in February 2020: "The indigenous peoples of the Amazon Region express the authentic quality of life as 'good living.' This involves personal, familial, communal and cosmic harmony and finds expression in a communitarian approach to existence, the ability to find joy and fulfilment in an austere and simple life, and a responsible care of nature that preserves resources for future generations" (Francis 2020b, 71).[5]

The CA offers tools for better identifying who are the poor we need to see, since it offers a methodology for identifying those who live in poverty using information about people's capabilities instead of simply their incomes. This method has informed the design of multidimensional poverty indexes worldwide. One of those is the Global Multidimensional Poverty Index computed by the Oxford Poverty and Human Development Initiative (OPHI), which measures poverty in three dimensions—health, education, and standard of living—using a mix of ten indicators. A person is poor if she is deprived in at least one dimension (OPHI 2021). The difference between measuring poverty in terms of income and in terms of capability deprivation can be significant. In Pakistan, for example, the number of people living in multidimensional poverty is nearly ten times higher than the number of people living in income poverty (on less than $1.90/day) (OPHI 2020). It comes as no surprise, therefore, that many governments are also developing their own multidimensional poverty measures with dimensions more adapted to their national context, such as the Chilean multidimensional poverty index, which includes the capability of being part of social networks (MPPN 2021).

As explained in the introduction to this volume, the CA is an open-ended framework. Sen has deliberately left undefined the type of information needed to "see" and assess states of affairs. The decision on which human functionings/capabilities are valuable and should constitute the informational basis for the "seeing" needs to be decided in a given context. For example, in his application of the CA to evaluate a government housing program in informal settlements in Brazil, Frediani (2015) uses the capability to extend one's house. Because the program ignored this capability, it failed. The government provided pre-fabricated houses that started to crack when people began to build extensions for their extended families. Therefore, people started to rent out their new houses and went back to living in the shacks that they could indeed extend. Similarly, in their CA evaluation of a housing program in Argentina, Mitchell, Macció, and Fages (2019) use measures of the quality of sleep, privacy, security, health, and inter-personal relationships to evaluate the impact of an emergency housing program. In another evaluation of poverty in the informal settlements in Buenos Aires, Mitchell and Macció (2018) have used indicators of housing, health, education, decent and secure employment, and safety. Their study revealed that more than half of the households in informal settlements live in overcrowded dwellings compared to those living in other areas of the city, which affects their sleep. Moreover, many of their houses are damp and unventilated, accentuating respiratory diseases. Given that most of them have no access to health insurance and depend entirely on overloaded and limited health centers that lack medical specialists, they have a limited capability to live healthy lives. Likewise, living in environments where the possibilities of physical exercise, such as walking, are limited due to inadequate pavements and lack of security increases their ill health. Moreover, crime and violence, often related to the drug trade, affect not only residents' bodily integrity but also other dimensions of their lives, such as attending school or participating in civil society organizations.

We can see how the CA enriches CST's preferential option for the poor, especially by interconnecting different dimensions of life (capabilities) and offering more accurate poverty assessment. To tackle poverty, we need to know who the poor are, and this is not limited to those experiencing income poverty. Still, if we are to consider the interconnections of capabilities, we cannot exclude the relational (communal) and the spiritual dimensions. Here is where CST can, in turn, further the CA's poverty/well-being assessments. For CST, as Pope Francis puts it in *Laudato Si'* (*LS*), "everything is interconnected" (*LS* 70): the body and the soul of an individual; people of different personalities, nationalities, and cultures among themselves; humanity with the rest of creation; all ecosystems among themselves; and all creation with the Creator. This means that, although the main reference of poverty is the material one, there are other poverties as well, such as "relational" or "spiritual poverty," as explained in the introduction to this volume. Yet all these types of poverty are interrelated; hence, the need to address them together. Back in 1967, in the encyclical *Populorum Progressio* (*PP*), Pope Paul VI made a specific reference to the link between the spiritual poverty of some—"those who are crushed under the weight of their own self-love" or "abuse of ownership or the improper exercise of power"—and the material poverty of others (*PP* 21). In other words, individualism and an excess of wealth and power are not conducive to poverty reduction since they are actually causing poverty—spiritual for the rich, material for the poor. Conversely, good relationships and a strong sense of life in a faith community can offer greater hope for change. In a study of a faith community in an informal settlement in Buenos Aires (Suárez 2020), residents have expressed how the presence of a church, with its many social activities, is a sign of hope for the neighborhood. The fact that the church provides a range of services—like school support, nutrition programs, or a clothes bank—is no doubt valuable for their material well-being but is also key to enhancing their ability (or even capability) to hope for a better future. The church presence is a sign that life can improve and that the situation of violence and social desolation they see around them can actually be transformed.

Given this relational dimension of humanity, the "seeing" stage is also about "listening." For the CA, there is an undisputable link between individuals' dignity, their freedom, and a more just (or less unjust) society (Sen 2009), for which listening to people's voices is primordial. This connection, ultimately, comes down to our concrete relationships and the way we approach our differences. However, the CA does not much (or very much) develop the connection between human relationships and our bond with nature, something to which CST can contribute, as Clemens Sedmak's chapter in this volume explained. Based on biblical theology and on previous papal and episcopal documents, in *Laudato Si'* Pope Francis makes it clear that "nature cannot be regarded as something separate from ourselves or as a mere setting in which we live. We are part of nature, included in it and thus in constant interaction with it" (*LS* 139). Therefore, for CST, a particular model of development rooted in the idea of people as separate from the environment and having control over it also makes them act as dominators or colonizers, either of the earth or of other people, which causes the earth or the dominated people to cry out (*LS* 49). Listening to the cry of the poor is inextricably linked to listening to the cry of the earth.

To illustrate our argument, we would like to refer to the Amazon region and the Church's Synod of the Amazon, which took place in

Rome in October 2019. It was a month-long gathering of Amazonian bishops, indigenous leaders, and experts to address how the Church can respond to the new challenges the Amazon region and its population are facing. The Amazon Synod was the offspring of *Laudato Si'*, meaning a concrete expression of new paths for development, ecology, and the Church (Deneulin 2021). For the Synod, in addition to the seeing, the "listening" was omnipresent: two years of preparation preceded it, during which more than eighty thousand people from approximately 350 Amazonian communities had been consulted. The diagnosis was crystal clear: the degradation of people's lives and the degradation of ecosystems go hand in hand, especially in this region, on whose health, species, and ecosystems the planetary equilibrium depends (Francis 2020b, 48–49). Despite this and the biome's splendor and immense beauty,

> The Amazon today is a wounded and deformed beauty, a place of suffering and violence. Attacks on nature have consequences for people's lives ... appropriation and privatization of natural goods, such as water itself; legal logging concessions and illegal logging; predatory hunting and fishing; unsustainable mega-projects (hydroelectric and forest concessions, massive logging, monocultivation, highways, waterways, railways, and mining and oil projects); pollution caused by extractive industries and city garbage dumps; and, above all, climate change. These are real threats with serious social consequences: pollution-related diseases, drug trafficking, illegal armed groups, alcoholism, violence against women, sexual exploitation, human trafficking and smuggling, organ traffic, sex tourism, the loss of original culture and identity (language, customs and spiritual practices), criminalization and assassination of leaders and defenders of the territory. Behind all this are dominant economic and political interests, with the complicity of some government officials and some indigenous authorities. The victims are the most vulnerable: children, youth, women and our sister mother earth. (Synod of Bishops 2019, 10)

This reflects how, for CST, social and ecological issues can neither be separated from nor ignore the questions of justice, which will help us "to hear both the cry of the earth and the cry of the poor" (*LS* 49). In Pope Francis's words in his apostolic exhortation following the Synod and titled *Querida Amazonia* (*Beloved Amazon*): "The colonizing interests that have continued to expand—legally and illegally—the timber and mining industries . . . are provoking a cry that rises up to heaven," both from the forest and from cities (Francis 2020b, 9–10). But it is precisely due to these cries of nature and of people that we have the opportunity to listen to the incarnated word of God and to recover the mission he "has entrusted to us all: the protection of our common home" (Francis 2020b, 19). Listening to people's protest, so present in the CA, can and must also include listening to the earth's protest.

One could argue that the cries of a particular territory and its people are a local issue. However, "the cry of the Amazon region reaches everyone because the conquest and exploitation of resources . . . has today reached the point of threatening the environment's hospitable aspect: the environment as 'resource' risks threatening the environment as 'home'" (Francis 2020b, 48). This injustice should provoke a healthy indignation: "We need to feel outrage, as Moses did (cf. Ex 11:8), as Jesus did (cf. Mk 3:5), as God does in the face of injustice (cf. Am 2:4–8; 5:7–12; Ps 106:40). It is not good for us to become inured to evil; it is not good when our social consciousness is dulled before "an exploitation that is leaving destruction and even death" (Francis 2020b, 15).

This is not foreign to the CA, for which there could be a righteous anger for the right reasons, an anger coming from a sense of actual injustice, a reasonable movement or emotion toward the desire to reduce injustices (Sen 2009). The addition CST proposes is the outrage due to ecological destruction and the deep motivation coming from spiritual values that enhances freedom—or people's capabilities: "If God calls us to listen both to the cry of the poor and that of the earth, then for us [Christians], the cry of the Amazon region to the Creator is similar to the cry of God's people in Egypt (cf. book of Exodus, chapter 3, verse 7). It is a cry of slavery and abandonment pleading for freedom" (Francis 2020b, 52). This cry or call moves us toward an integral conversion (ibid., 56) "to respond to this heartrending plea" (ibid., 57), and thus bring more justice and freedom to the world (see the chapters in this volume by Guillermo Otano Jiménez and by Clemens Sedmak for further discussions on integral conversion).

This vivid "seeing" and "listening to" the Amazon and its people allowed one to discern some dimensions of poverty that concur with those of the CA, which would phrase them as deprivations in the following capabilities: to enjoy beauty; cultivate food; fish and hunt; drink, cook, and wash; live a healthy life; exercise practical reason and form a life plan; be protected from harm and experience bodily integrity; express one's culture; listen to the spirits in the forest (Gosh 2021, 205–16; Kopenawa and Albert 2013); and avoid a premature death. In short, an evaluation of the situation of the Amazon, from a mere CA perspective, would enable one to *see* which capabilities people are deprived of. But if enriched with CST, the evaluation could be extended to what is happening to "our sister mother earth," thus reaching out beyond the social sciences to disciplines such as hydrology, geology, plant sciences, zoology, biology, and others. It could also enrich the CA by pointing out that poverty also has a spiritual dimension and that lack of love—for the vulnerable and the earth—is also an important dimension, as the next section elaborates. And it could enrich the "see-judge-act" method by pointing out that the cries have to do with economic and political interests, hence providing a basis for the "judging" stage.

JUDGING (WITH THE POOR FIRST): COMPARING AND ANALYZING CAPABILITIES AND INSTITUTIONS, AND GOING INTO THE ANTHROPOLOGICAL ROOTS

The CA's method for judging states of affairs is to offer a comparative evaluation of capabilities and an analysis of which institutions lie underneath different social outcomes. For example, why are life expectancy and health achievements higher in the Indian state of Kerala than in the state of Bihar? Often differences in the capabilities of people to live long and healthy lives depend on the quality of political institutions and on people's ability to set up political organizations with which they can advance their political claims and, eventually, change government spending priorities. In the case of Kerala (Drèze and Sen 2013), the low-caste, who have been able to get politically organized, can orient public spending toward investment in primary health care and thus demand greater accountability and citizen scrutiny of public spending, leading to less corruption. In short, the CA demands what Drèze and Sen (2002, 20) call "an institutionally integrated approach" to *judge* states of affairs.

The expansion of people's capabilities cannot occur without the presence of key institutions such as markets, public services, a judiciary, political parties, media, social norms, and so on. As Sen (1999, 142) puts it, "Our opportunities and prospects depend crucially on what institutions exist and how they function." Analyzing institutions, therefore, is fundamental to know if we are progressing toward a freer, fairer, and more sustainable society.

In *The Idea of Justice*, Sen (2009) argues against labeling institutions as just or unjust as such. He proposes, instead, to judge them according to how they function and, more importantly, how their activities affect people's lives. For instance, to analyze how to advance greater equity in health, Sen (2015) compares the health attainments in Rwanda, Thailand, Bangladesh, and of some states of India (Kerala, Himachal Pradesh, and Tamil Nadu). It is interesting to note that Sen starts this comparison with the story of Buddha, who "was moved in particular by *seeing* the penalties of ill health—by the sight of mortality (a dead body being taken to cremation), morbidity (a person severely afflicted by illness), and disability (a person reduced and ravaged by unaided old age)" (emphasis ours). He then examines which health policy decisions have been taken in those countries, considering their own political and economic contexts. Through this comparison he concludes that improved health outcomes can be achieved, despite limited economic resources, when there is a public commitment to invest in universal primary health care and when those without access to private health insurance are politically well represented. The CA institutional comparison, thus, helps us judge states of affairs in a more integrated way than if we do it merely from a purely economic perspective or from our own standpoint, vision, or ideology.

This also applies when comparing different capabilities of people in the same territory, in this case a city. For instance, why does a person born in one urban neighborhood have fewer opportunities to live a healthy life, to have formal and secure employment, or to have the ability to go out safely in the streets at night than a person born a few miles away? The city of Buenos Aires, for example, which generates a third of Argentina's total economic output, is a striking story of worlds apart within the same city (Mitchell and Macció 2018). More than half of the inhabitants of informal settlements there live in overcrowded housing, compared to fewer than a tenth elsewhere in the city. This overcrowding has a particular effect on children, who have little room to play, let alone to have tables to do their school homework. There is a similar stark divide on health and employment. According to the data collected by Mitchell and Macció (2018), the percentage of families in informal settlements who have no working members is double that of the rest of the city, as is the percentage of families in which no family member has a formal job. This level of informality can have a large negative impact on a person and on a family's ability to plan their future.

The aim of this institutional comparison is, first, to judge different levels of capability achievements in different parts of the same city and, second, to generate a public discussion about the extent to which institutions are conducive to improving people's lives. For example, why is the school drop-out rate much higher in informal settlements despite the fact that secondary education is compulsory? Does the presence of educational institutions in the midst of informal settlements reduce school drop-out rates? Why is it more difficult for people who live in informal settlements to have formal employment than people who live elsewhere in the city, despite having similar educational qualifications? From studies that sought to answer these questions it emerged that the presence of non-state institutions, especially Catholic parishes, plays a crucial role in providing safe, secure, and stable spaces for children to do their homework and play or participate in extra-curricular activities (Mitchell 2016). Research also highlights that one key factor leading to unequal capabilities between youth from the informal settlements and youth from the rest of the city is the prejudice and stigma about informal settlements' residents—for example, ideas that they are "lazy" or "thieves" (Lépore and Simpson 2018; Mitchell, Del Monte, and Deneulin 2018), which contributes to youths' low self-esteem and lack of aspirations for better futures. Another factor is the lack of physical connectivity and public transport availability, which increases their sense of non-belonging, of being in a world apart from that of the city. This means that public transportation, as an institution, needs to improve if we are to help tackle education or employment inequality in the same city. It also means that public policies should be put in place so as to address social stigma, because otherwise urban inequality will perpetuate. Rather than pointlessly analyzing prima facie if public transportation in a given city is just or not, or if public policies are actually inclusive or not, the

CA permits us to judge social reality by linking capability expansion or deprivation with how institutions function. This sounds like a good tool for judging the inextricable bond that, for the CST, exists between "the health of a society's institutions" and "the quality of human life" and of "the environment" (*LS* 142).

Still, while the CA provides accurate tools for comparing situations and judging how well institutions function in terms of enhancing people's capabilities, CST offers other resources that can complement those tools—thus delve deeper into "judging" states of affairs. One is evaluation through the lens of the excluded, marginalized, or oppressed. In fact, this is not foreign to the CA, for which it is central to put the lives of the marginalized at the core of public reasoning and public policy. So much so that Drèze and Sen (2013), in their analysis of economic development policy in India, note that the lives of the poor are seldom the subject of discussion in the media, and this influences the outcomes of elections and policy priorities. But for CST, the lack of awareness of problems affecting the excluded is due, to a great extent, to the lack of what Pope Francis, in his exhortation *Evangelii Gaudium* (*EG*; 2013) and encyclical *Fratelli Tutti* (*FT*; 2020b), calls a "culture of encounter" (*EG* 220; *FT* 215–21 and the chapter by Ilaria Schnyder von Wartensee and Elizabeth Hlabse in this volume). It is a point he also makes in *Laudato Si'*:

> Many professionals, opinion makers, communications media and centers of power, being located in affluent urban areas, are re- moved from the poor, with little direct contact with their problems. They live and reason from the comfortable position of a high level of development and a quality of life well beyond the reach of the majority of the world's population. This lack of physical contact and encounter, encouraged at times by the disintegration of our cities, can lead to a numbing of conscience and to tendentious analyses which neglect parts of reality. (*LS* 49)

In other words, the evaluation or judging of a state of affairs must start from the perspective of the poor, for which a culture of encounter is needed, one that may counter the "culture of prosperity" that deadens us (*EG* 45), one that can recognize the immense value of the "culture of the lowly" (*EG* 124). To put it bluntly, the "see-judge-act" method is about putting people's experiences at the heart of the Church's teaching (Deneulin and Zampini-Davies 2016, 113–14). If the sources of CST were purely based on previous papal documents or statements, then the experiences of the poor would rarely be taken into account. But when experience is placed at the forefront of the method, people's struggles to live better lives provide substance to the teaching and its methodology, including the judging stage. Normally, Catholic theologians will try to enlighten the discernment (judging) in the light of the Gospel and the tradition of the Church. What Pope Francis clarifies in *Laudato Si'*, however, is that this "light" is also about people's wisdom, especially that of people who are considered the last ones. In his apostolic exhortation *Querida Amazonia* he strongly argues that any social dialogue needs to start "with the poor," who

> are not just another party to be won over, or merely another individual seated at a table of equals. They are our principal dialogue partners, those from whom we have the most to learn, to whom we need to listen out of duty of justice, and from whom we must ask permission before presenting our proposals. Their words, their hopes and their fears should be the most authoritative voice at any table of dialogue. (Francis 2020b, 26)

In the Amazon region, for example, the great imbalance of power between colonizing economic elites and indigenous peoples—hence the absence of the aforementioned dialogue, has caused great suffering to communities and to the forest, and has also enriched wealthy nations while impoverishing the already poor (Francis 2020b, 13). Colonization is still happening, albeit under a new guise (ibid., 16). In order to overcome it, the last ones have to be first, and the ones from the peripheries have to be our central concern when judging social, economic, and political institutions. A culture of encounter that privileges their wisdom in caring for the land is needed if we are to promote a new inclusive and sustainable social and economic system.[6] Their judgment as to how "to contemplate" and "love" the territory, and "not simply analyze it" or "use it" (ibid., 55), will aid us all in having proper "public reasoning processes"—to put it in the language of the CA—from which capability expansion and ecological care can ensue. The possibility of indigenous people bringing to the global fore their ancestral wisdom could enable a combination of such wisdom with contemporary technical knowledge in order to, for instance, create a "sustainable management of the land while also preserving the lifestyle" and values of its inhabitants (ibid., 51). This is central to indigenous peoples' wisdom, as for them, "the forest is not a resource to be exploited; it is a being, or various beings, with which we have to relate" (ibid., 42).

No wonder Pope Francis, in *Laudato Si'*, emphasizes the link between the way we treat each other—especially the poor and nature, which is among the most abandoned and maltreated of our poor—and social progress and ecological care. For him, the root of the socio-ecological crisis underpinning the symptoms of global inequality, climate change, and biodiversity loss is especially the following: the myth of perennial progress, the prevailing technocratic paradigm, the globalization of indifference, the lack of political will, and the consumerist lifestyle that goes together with a throwaway culture. But *Laudato Si'* goes even deeper than this social judgment by emphasizing its anthropological origins (or original sin), that is, the misunderstanding of our role in society and within creation, what scientists call modern anthropocentrism (*LS* 115–36). This is a third important addition to the judgment stage that the CA alongside CST can provide: it is not enough to analyze and compare people's capabilities and institutions or to ensure that the judgment of the poor is at the center of public discussions. It is also necessary to address the roots of socio-ecological problems through a deep relational-anthropological analysis.

Given the power of biblical narratives, which "prove meaningful in every age" to open new horizons of understanding (*LS* 199), *Laudato Si'* brings the light of the story of creation (Genesis, chapters 1–3) to judge the way we are relating to others and to the world (*LS* 65). As it explains, "Human life is grounded in three fundamental and closely intertwined relationships: with God, with our neighbor and with the earth itself . . . relationships [that] have been broken, both outwardly and within us," which is a sin (*LS* 66). To replace the harmony of these relationships, it is therefore vital to acknowledge the fact that "we are not God" (*LS* 67), nor are we "lords and masters" of the earth (*LS* 2). Any Christian teaching that has encouraged the unbridled exploitation of nature is therefore a misinterpretation of the role of humans on earth, of the Bible, and of the tradition of the Church.

In acknowledging the fundamental role of relationships for human flourishing, Sen highlights the importance of some relational attitudes—such as sympathy or the ability to see the world from another person's perspectives—and the need for public reasoning processes in order to deal with people's different views (Drèze and Sen 2013; Sen 2009). But he does not discuss how the way we exercise our freedom affects these relationships. Yet for CST, human freedom is not limitless (see the chapter by Lori Keleher in this volume), and its misunderstanding and misuse—as in ignoring anything higher than ourselves—usually generate despotic actions toward others and nature (*LS* 6), undermining our relational life. Although it is true that we need "a legal framework that can set clear boundaries and ensure the protection of ecosystems" and the poor (*LS* 53), personal and collective virtues are also needed to recalibrate freedom for the good of individuals, communities, and the earth. For CST's relational anthropology, freedom is always open to ambivalence, since good will for cooperation and trust goes *pari passu* with selfishness, betrayal, and what is known as "sin," that is the capacity to do wrong and cause harm to ourselves and others and to our social, economic, political, and all other sorts of relationships. Moreover, individual wrongdoings fomented by a misuse of freedom are also connected to, or influenced by, structures of society that hinder human flourishing (Deneulin and Zampini-Davies 2016, 2020).

This is why the notion of "limits" is key, as Pope Francis emphasizes in *Laudato Si'*. Limits are not merely those at the individual level (e.g., how many holiday homes a rich person needs in order to exercise the capability to rest), but also those of collective power, especially of certain groups (Robeyns 2017, 2019). As Pope Francis argues, "Our freedom fades when it is handed over to the blind forces of the unconscious, of immediate needs, of self-interest, and of violence. . . . We stand naked and exposed in the face of our ever-increasing power, lacking the wherewithal to control it. We have certain superficial mechanisms, but we cannot claim to have a sound ethics, a culture and spirituality genuinely capable of setting limits and teaching clear-minded self-restraint" (*LS* 105). This self-limitation is needed more than ever in times of the dominant "technocratic paradigm" that, paradoxically, limits our freedom, diminishes our creativity, and jeopardizes our capacity to make genuine decisions (*LS* 108) toward a healthier, more human, social, and integral way of living (*LS* 112). CST, however, offers a hopeful perspective and, like the CA, takes the view that humans are oriented toward exercising their freedom (or agency) for the good of others: "Human beings, while capable of the worst, are also capable of rising above themselves, choosing again what is good, and making a new start, despite their mental and social conditioning . . . and to embark on new paths to authentic freedom" (*LS* 205). In other words, human beings are capable of profound change, of conversion. But the conversion needed in the face of an unprecedented socio-ecological crisis is a radical and comprehensive one, an urgent and bold "cultural revolution" (*LS* 114) that can change the way we relate to each other and the earth, a "new universal solidarity" (*LS* 14) that can counter a development model that is exploitative and sees nature and others as a means to further one's own ends.

In short, the "judging" of reality needs to "touch us deeply" (*LS* 15) so as to move us to action. The public "reasoning-judgment" process must also be a true encounter with the poor, whose voices can open our hearts and minds and create spaces for integration (*LS* 149). Such public debate requires patience, self-discipline, and generosity (*LS* 201), where particular interests or ideologies do not prejudice the common good (*LS* 188). The "judging" stage also needs to be open to something beyond us (humans), open to the intercommunicating systems of the earth, so that we can discern countless forms of relationship and participation (*LS* 79). This, for people of faith, also comprises an openness to God's transcendence and grace, which always prompts us to change our ways, to turn our hearts to God, to act differently, and to restore broken relationships with other people and creatures, and with the Creator. This path toward life-altering transformation, or conversion, is what our final section will address.

ACTING: TAKING ACTION COLLECTIVELY, A CONVERSION AT ALL LEVELS

The concept of agency, as the power of action one has to make decisions about one's life and exercise one's responsibility toward others, even at the cost of one's own well-being, is key for the CA. An indigenous person in the Amazon who resists illegal logging and campaigns to protect the forest and indigenous rights may risk her own life. However, while so doing, she exercises and strengthens her agency (in Sen's sense of the word). But identifying which agency-driven actions a person should take to have the life she values and to improve social institutions is not that straightforward. In the context of informal settlements in Buenos Aires, what actions are more conducive to the residents' walking safely in the streets, having healthy lives, or having access to decent and secure jobs? To improve safety, should one take action first toward improving urban mobility or toward addressing drug consumption and youth unemployment? Similar questions arise in the context of the Amazon region. What actions should we take to stop deforestation and the dispossession of indigenous peoples from their land? Should European countries ban imports of goods that cannot be certified as having been legally sourced? Should Americans or Europeans try to reduce beef and soy consumption? Which actions are better to protect the capabilities of indigenous peoples to live according to their cultures? The CA does not offer insights to these questions beyond offering an analysis of how capabilities interconnect. It leaves people to decide how to act on the basis of that information.[7] In his works, and especially those co-authored with Jean Drèze, Sen makes ample use of examples about the crucial role of "public action" to change the way institutions function and to orient them toward providing the conditions necessary for human flourishing.

Public action, understood as the direct efforts undertaken by the public at large to improve their lives, can take a multiplicity of forms. Sen believes that the specific forms of public action are best determined through processes of public reasoning, which should be inclusive of all voices, especially those of the most marginalized, as discussed in the "Judging" section. In informal settlements, it can take the form of local residents' coming together to establish a communal kitchen and provide better nutrition for children, to establish a library and after-school support, or to organize activities for teenagers to keep them away from street gangs (Mitchell 2016). Or it can take the form of direct participation with local state authorities to decide on public spending and priorities, such as whether to secure safer gas and electricity connections first or to prioritize the creation of more green and recreational spaces for children. In the Amazon region, public action can take the form of indigenous peoples' forming representative organizations and international networks to ensure that their human rights and rights to self-determination are respected.

Despite stressing the role of public reasoning and public action to transform societies (see the chapter by Guillermo Otano Jiménez in this volume), the CA does not much emphasize the role of personal transformation. As alluded to above, CST judges situations not only from the perspective of institutional shortcomings but also from the perspective of personal shortcomings, contributing to stressing the link between institutions and people. Institutions change and are better oriented toward the flourishing of people if people change, too. This is why CST calls for both personal *and* structural change. In the context of informal settlements in Buenos Aires (and in most big cities), it is as much about personal transformation to overcome stigma and prejudice as it is about the creation of public spaces where different residents of the city can mix and encounter each other. In the context of the destruction of the Amazon region (and of the earth), it is only that combination of personal and structural transformation that could lead us to a "cultural revolution" (*LS* 114) in which the unrestrained agency for extraction of the earth's minerals, destruction of forests for the sake of cattle grazing, and the like can be converted into agency for the care of people and the planet. In fact, says Pope Francis, "The ecological crisis is also a summons to profound interior conversion ... or change of heart. ... Nevertheless, ... social problems must be addressed by community networks and not simply by the sum of individual good deeds. ... The ecological conversion needed to bring about lasting change is also a community conversion" (*LS* 217–19).

In order to help each other and our communities to start a journey (or process) toward an ongoing radical ecological conversion at all levels of society, we need not only to "see," "discern," and recognize what thwarts our relationships (as discussed in the previous section). We also need to "stop doing" what damages them and "start doing" something that can strengthen them. At the political level, this would imply that we need to convert from short-termism, corruption, sterile and excluding dialogues, and the protection of elite interests so as to promote a long-term vision and the participation of all, especially the poor. Pope Francis reports from the voices of the poor in the Amazon region that they view corruption as "a culture that poisons the state and its institutions, permeating all social strata, including the indigenous communities. We are talking about a true moral scourge; as a result, there is a loss of confidence in institutions and their representatives, which totally discredits politics and social organizations" (Francis 2020b, 24). He also poignantly illustrates the lack of political participation of "the last ones" in the Amazon region with a poem:

The timber merchants have members of parliament
while our Amazonia has no one to defend her. . . .
They exiled the parrots and the monkeys. . . .
The chestnut harvests will never be the same. (Ibid., 9)

Political change, thus, requires the conversion of political leaders, who will need to design new public infrastructure and planning, new regulations for international trade and global finance, new trade agreements and tax policies, new subsidies to promote a greener and just people-centered economy, new norms on technological innovation and security, and so on. Those policy decisions will not come out of the blue. They will come from political dialogue and public action, as Sen rightly argues. But according to Pope Francis, policy changes also need far-sighted and open policy-makers "capable of reforming and coordinating institutions, promoting best practices and overcoming undue pressure and bureaucratic inertia" (*LS* 181). For that, policy-makers need to be far-sighted enough to see beyond immediate political needs (*LS* 197), wise enough to understand global as well as local problems (*LS* 180), brave enough to challenge and resist becoming subject to the economy or to an efficiency-driven paradigm of technocracy (*LS* 189), honest enough to promote transparent political processes (*LS* 182), determined enough to break the perverse logic of corruption, and open enough to seek honest dialogue and international, enforceable agreements (*LS* 173). This does not mean that political change necessarily begins with individual policy-makers' conversions; political pressure from below is necessary, too. What we are highlighting here, however, is the vital role of personal change when addressing institutional change, a dimension often forgotten in many policy forums.

At the economic level, we need to convert from an economy that dominates and kills to recover an economy that serves and promotes well-being. We need to say, personally and collectively, as Pope Francis urges us to do in *Evangelii Gaudium*: "No to an economy of exclusion. . . . No to the new idolatry of money. . . . No to a financial system which rules rather than serves. . . . No to the inequality which spawns violence" (*EG* 53–60). Moreover, we need to start calling by their names, in our public dialogues for action, "businesses, national or international, which harm the Amazon and fail to respect the right of the original peoples to the land and its boundaries, and to self-determination and prior consent," both unjust and criminal (Francis 2020b, 14). And of course, we need to design a new development model that can say "Yes" to caring for people and the environment. Still, even if we have proper public reasoning processes, we will not be able to promote such a change if we do not acknowledge the harm the current economy is inflicting. For CST, there is no possible conversion without acknowledging the sin. For example, we have not yet assimilated "the lessons of the global financial crisis" (*LS* 109), which have made it even more difficult for residents of informal settlements in Buenos Aires (and many other places) to get decent and secure work. Likewise, we have not yet assimilated the lessons from the exploitation and colonization, at all costs, of rain forests such as the Amazon, which "has been presented as an enormous empty space to be filled, a source of raw resources to be developed, a wild expanse to be domesticated" (Francis 2020b, 12). Acknowledging what has caused harm, at both the personal and collective levels, is a first necessary step for conversion. As the final document of the Amazon Synod urges us to ask ourselves: "We may not be able to modify the destructive model of extractivist development immediately, but we do need to know and make clear where we stand, whose side we are on, what perspective we assume" (Francis 2020b, 70). Acknowledgment or *recognition* of the sin or harm we inflict on others and the earth enables *repentance*, which provides the basis for *repairing*. The "acting" stage, therefore, must include the acts necessary to repair, for example, the damage inflicted on the Amazon and to people's health by oil and mining explorations. Likewise, cities like Buenos Aires must think about how to repair the capability deprivation of informal settlement dwellers due to, for instance, the lack of public investment in infrastructure. And these repairing actions must come from both personal agents (individuals or particular companies or groups that have either inflicted damage or directly benefited from such damage) and from society at large.

At the cultural level, we need to move away from an individualistic, utilitarian, and technocratic approach to a communal wisdom approach, from a culture of domination toward a culture of respect, love, and care. If someone behaves as a lord and master of the land and has "not learned to stop and admire something beautiful," writes Pope Francis, "we should not be surprised if he or she treats everything as an object to be used and abused without scruple" (2020b, 56). Such a culture of domination has profound effects on the land and on the lives of the people whose lives are intertwined with the land. The destruction of the Amazon forest goes hand in hand with the destruction of the cultures of its people. And as he highlights in *Laudato Si'*, "The disappearance of a culture can be just as serious, or even more serious, than the disappearance of a species of plant or animal" (*LS* 145). Therefore, cultural colonization is also something we need to convert from. The multiple cultures of the Amazon—as varied as the biodiversity of the territory—have a particular wisdom that the world cannot afford to lose. Such lack of a culture of love and care is as damaging in Buenos Aires or in any big city as it is in the Amazon. This is reflected, among other ways, in a lack of public investment in informal settlements, leaving these spaces with a minimal state presence and rudimentary public services and leaving its residents struggling to find, for example, decent and secure work (Mitchell and Macció 2018). As Pope Francis has noted, informal-sector workers who live in informal settlements not only are "exploited" but also are "left-overs" of an economic system that does not need them and sees them as "consumer goods to be used and then discarded" (*EG* 53).

That is why today we need a deep cultural shift, as Naomi Klein writes, "from a culture of endless taking [from the earth and from others] to a culture of caretaking; caring for the planet, and for one another" (2019, 197), or a culture of fraternity and of seeing "brothers and sisters all" as Pope Francis discusses at length in *Fratelli Tutti*. One possible trigger for this cultural change, as the pope contends, is an interior and communal conversion that can help us "enter into communion with the forest" (or nature), in which "our voices will easily blend with its own and become a prayer: as we rest in the shade of an ancient eucalyptus, our prayer for light joins in the song of the eternal foliage" (Francis 2020a, 56). This is a "personal conversion, which entails the recognition of our errors, sins, faults and failures, and leads to heartfelt repentance and desire to change" (ibid., 218). Yet, as mentioned before, this conversion starts with examining our lives and acknowledging "the ways in which we have harmed God's creation" and other people, "through our actions and our failure to act" (*LS* 218). Without such an examination and recognition, without begging for forgiveness from those we have harmed, and without commitment to repair the damage we have caused, there is no possible change.

As we can see, to promote such a holistic conversion of our politics, our economies, and our cultures, public debates and direct political actions are necessary, as the CA points out, but these are not enough. We also need personal conversion of leaders who can debate and design new policies and a new economy, capable of recognizing the value of each culture, "the value of everything" (Mazzucato 2018). Moreover, we also need to acknowledge that the world needs a "radical change," a change often accompanied by strong resistance at many levels, at the national and global levels, as well as at our own personal, family, and community levels. Indeed, a radical change implies a transformation of the way we live, work, and produce, the way we trade and consume, and the way we dispose of things. And this necessarily brings about the usual psychological resistance implied in any difficult change, and, more importantly, resistance from those controlling and benefiting from a development model (and an entire global culture) that is too dependent on extracting minerals and fossil fuels from the earth and on the exploitation of people's labor and nature. To change this, we need something more than comparing social outcomes and institutional processes, more than public dialogue and direct interventions, and more than acknowledging our personal and collective wrongdoings. To change *radically* we need to go deep down into our roots (as the Latin word *radix* for "root" suggests), especially the cultural and spiritual ones.

Anthropological research (Moran 2017; Rappaport 1979) tells us that motivation for a radical change does not come merely from an economic logic of costs and benefits, or even from the scientific logic of research and knowledge. Rather, motivation for radical change comes from a combination of sources connected more with the meaning of life and with the celebration of rituals, particularly religious ones. Emilio F. Moran (2017, 169) argues that rituals, indeed, have played a crucial role in our evolution as "social beings," because through them, individuals in human communities became "as one" in common purpose, and "through participation in ritual they were socialised into the value of the common good ... of sharing." Because they operate in a higher order of meanings that are not necessarily based on discursive reasoning, these rituals help people convert from an individual-oriented framework toward a community-oriented value framework, from analyzing their behavior from a merely pragmatic point of view toward a more holistic and existential one. For example, for residents of informal settlement in Buenos Aires, Catholic rituals can help foster a sense of belonging and solidarity with the wider neighborhood in which the ritual is celebrated (Suárez 2020). Perhaps even clearer is the influence of rituals in the Amazon region, since they are totally in tune with Mother Earth and natural cycles, helping the residents to perceive existentially their bond with nature and prompting their care for it. In short, religious rituals can help transition the much-needed journey of radical transformation. They provide the motivation for change and for engaging our agency with our deep relational selves, namely love for God's creation and for our neighbors. Also, religious rituals can trigger a deep and long-lasting change, one that comes from our hearts, not only from our minds. The language of love, contemplation, and poetry, indeed, can "help free us from the technocratic and consumerist paradigm that destroys nature and robs us of a truly dignified existence" (Francis 2020b, 46).

CONCLUSION: JOINING FORCES FOR RADICAL TRANSFORMATION

Focusing on the "see-judge-act" methodology of CST, in this chapter we have examined how the CA and CST can best work together to address social and environmental challenges such as urban social exclusion and inequality and the destruction of the Amazon ecosystems and their residents. We have argued that the CA can strengthen CST's preferential option for the poor by providing some conceptual tools for identifying those who live in situations of poverty. In turn, CST makes a stronger connection between poverty and environmental degradation and adds to the evaluation of states of affairs a stronger affective component. It is not only about "seeing" who lives in poverty but also about "listening" to their suffering and letting oneself be moved by them. We have also argued that the CA helps CST to make a connection between what happens to people's lives and the institutions within which they live. In turn, CST goes deeper into the anthropological roots of how well institutions function and whether they are serving the lives of people and ecosystems. It makes a stronger association between personal attitudes and institutional functioning. If individuals are manifesting a lack of love and care and have an attitude of domination and exploitation toward others and nature, so will their economic, social, political, or cultural institutions. Finally, we have argued that the CA stresses the importance of public action in its different forms to bring about the transformation of institutions needed to protect ecosystems and promote human flourishing. In turn, CST, and spiritual traditions more widely, provide further resources for motivating personal and structural change for a more inclusive and sustainable world, more food for the long and difficult journey of integral and radical conversion. We hope that the combined methodology of CST and the CA sketched in this chapter can contribute to, and hasten, this transformative journey toward integral human development, toward the flourishing of each person and the whole person, and this includes the flourishing of all ecosystems with which humans are intimately bound.

NOTES

1. These illustrative contexts have been chosen because one (informal settlements) informed Pope Francis's ministry prior to his election to the papacy, and the other (the Amazon region) is the context in which *Laudato Si'* has first been implemented at the ecclesial level with the Amazon Synod. Both authors of this chapter have also worked in these contexts.

2. The Greek original term is *esplanchnisthē*, from the verb *splanchnizomai*, to be moved from the entrails and to express this emotion through external actions.

3. The Gospel of Luke uses the same word when Jesus "sees" the grieving widow of Nain (chapter 7, verse 13) and when the father "sees his son returning home" (chapter 15, verse 20).

4. The Greek word is *plēsion*, which is a friend or close relative.

5. For how belonging to the land is essential to indigenous peoples and how the loss of that connection is affecting their health and lives, see Survival International (2007). To be in contact with a territory in order to have an enriching life is not limited to indigenous people. As the climate activist Naomi Klein (2019, 124–28) explains, because the terrain on which climate changes are taking place is intensely local, only those closely connected to their ecosystem can notice the differences. Still, our urbanized, industrialized, and technological way of living undermines such a connection with our own local environment, impeding us from loving it and thus from caring for it. It is therefore no wonder that Pope Francis highlights the need for contemplation of nature and reconnection with it if we are to care for our common home (Francis 2020a, 55).

6. Indigenous peoples care for nearly 22 percent of the Earth's surface, representing 80 percent of the planet's remaining biodiversity (UNESCO 2021).

7. Wolff and De-Shalit (2013) talk of "fertile capabilities" as those capabilities that most enhance others and of "corrosive disadvantages" as those capabilities whose lack most undermines others.

WORKS CITED

Alkire, Sabina, James E. Foster, and Suman Seth. 2015. *Multidimensional Poverty Measurement and Analysis*. Oxford: Oxford University Press.

Deneulin, Séverine. 2021. "Religion and Development: Integral Ecology and the Catholic Church Amazon Synod." *Third World Quarterly* 42, no. 10: 2282–99.

Deneulin, Séverine, and Augusto Zampini-Davies. 2016. "Theology and Development as Capability Expansion." *HTS Theological Studies* 72, no. 1. https://hts.org.za/index.php/HTS/article/view/3230.

———. 2020. "Religion and the Capability Approach." In *The Cambridge Handbook of the Capability Approach*, edited by Siddiq Osmani, Mozaffar Qizilbash, and Enrica Chiappero-Martinetti. Cambridge: Cambridge University Press, 686–705.

Drèze, Jean, and A. Sen. 2002. *India: Development and Participation*. Delhi: Oxford University Press.

———. 2013. *India: An Uncertain Glory*. London: Allen Lane.

Francis. 2013. *Evangelii Gaudium: The Joy of the Gospel*. Apostolic exhortation. http://www.vatican.va/content/francesco/en/apost_exhortations /documents/papa-francesco_esortazione-ap_20131124_evangelii-gaudium .html.

———. 2015. *Laudato Si': On the Care for Our Common Home*. Encyclical. http://www.vatican.va/content/francesco/en/encyclicals/documents/papa -francesco_20150524_enciclica-laudato-si.html.

———. 2020a. *Fratelli Tutti: On Fraternity and Social Friendship*. Encyclical. http://www.vatican.va/content/francesco/en/encyclicals/documents/papa -francesco_20201003_enciclica-fratelli-tutti.html.

———. 2020b. *Querida Amazonia*. Apostolic exhortation. http://www.vatican .va/content/francesco/en/apost_exhortations/documents/papa-francesco _esortazione-ap_20200202_querida-amazonia.html.

Frediani, Alex. 2015. "Space and Capabilities: Approaching Informal Settlements." In *The City in Urban Poverty*, edited by C. Lemanski and C. Marx. Cambridge: Cambridge University Press, 64–84.

Gosh, Amitav. 2021. *The Nutmeg's Curse: Parables for a Planet in Crisis*. Chicago: University of Chicago Press.

John XXIII. 1961. *Mater et Magistra*. Encyclical. http://www.vatican.va /content/john-xxiii/en/encyclicals/documents/hf_j-xxiii_enc_15051961 _mater.html.

Klein, Naomi. 2019. *On Fire: The Burning Case for a Green New Deal*. London: Allen Lane.

Kopenawa, Davi, and Bruce Albert. 2013. *The Falling Sky: Words of a Yanomami Shaman*. Cambridge, MA: Harvard University Press.

Lépore, Eduardo, and Simca Simpson. 2018. "Concentrated Poverty and Neighbourhood Effects: Youth Marginalisation in Buenos Aires' Informal Settlements." *Oxford Development Studies* 46, no. 1: 28–44.

Mazzucato, Mariana. 2018. *The Value of Everything: Making and Taking in the Global Economy*. London: Penguin.

Mitchell, Ann. 2016. "Civil Society Organizations in the Informal Settlements of Buenos Aires: Service Providers and Forces for Change." *Voluntas* 27, no. 1: 37–60.

Mitchell, Ann, and Jimena Macció. 2018. "Same City, Worlds Apart: Multidimensional Poverty and Residential Segregation in Buenos Aires." *Anales de la Asociación Argentina de Economía Política*. https://repositorio.uca.edu .ar/bitstream/123456789/9376/1/same-city-worlds-apart.pdf.

Mitchell, Ann, Pablo Del Monte, and Séverine Deneulin. 2018. "School Completion in Urban Latin America: The Voices of Young People from an Informal Settlement." *Oxford Development Studies* 46, no. 1: 45–56.

Mitchell, Ann, Jimena Macció, and Diego Marino Fages. 2019. "The Effects of Emergency Housing on Wellbeing: Evidence from Argentina's Informal Settlements." *European Journal of Development Research* 31: 504–29.

Moran, Emilio F. 2017. *People and Nature: An Introduction to Human Ecology Relations.* 2nd edition. Chichester, UK: Willey-Blackwell.

Multidimensional Poverty Peer Network (MPPN). 2021. *Chile: National Multidimensional Poverty Index.* https://mppn.org/paises_participantes/chile/#T1.

Nebel, Mathias. 2014. "Servir les Pauvres ; Oui, mais Dites-Moi : 'Quels Pauvres au Juste?'" *Revue d'Ethique et de Théologie Morale* 2, no. 279: 3–56.

Oxford Poverty and Human Development Initiative (OPHI). 2020. *Global MPI Country Briefing 2020: Pakistan.* https://ophi.org.uk/wp-content/uploads/CB_PAK_2020.pdf.

———. 2021. *The Global Multidimensional Poverty Index.* https://ophi.org.uk/publications/mpi-methodological-notes.

Paul VI. 1967. *Populorum Progressio.* Encyclical. https://www.vatican.va/content/paul-vi/en/encyclicals/documents/hf_p-vi_enc_26031967_populorum.html.

Rappaport, Roy. 1979. *Ecology, Meaning, and Religion.* Richmond, VA: North Atlantic Books.

Robeyns, Ingrid. 2017. "Freedom and Responsibility: Sustainable Prosperity through a Capability Lens." Centre for the Understanding of Sustainable Prosperity, University of Surrey, Surrey, UK. https://www.cusp.ac.uk/themes/m/m1-4.

———. 2019. "What, If Anything, Is Wrong with Extreme Wealth?" *Journal of Human Development and Capabilities* 20, no. 3: 251–66.

Sen, Amartya. 1977. "Rational Fools: A Critique of the Behavioural Foundations of Economic Theory." *Philosophy and Public Affairs* 6, no. 4: 317–44.

———. 1983. "Poor, Relatively Speaking." *Oxford Economic Papers* 35, no. 2: 153–69.

———. 1999. *Development as Freedom.* Oxford: Oxford University Press.

———. 2009. *The Idea of Justice.* London: Allen Lane.

———. 2015. "Universal Healthcare: The Affordable Dream." https://www.theguardian.com/society/2015/jan/06/-sp-universal-healthcare-the-affordable-dream-amartya-sen.

Stewart, Frances, Ruhi Saith, and Barbara Harriss-White. 2007. *Defining Poverty in the Developing World.* Basingstoke, UK: Palgrave Macmillan.

Suárez, Ana Lourdes, ed. 2020. *La Comunidad Virgen de la Asunción: Signo de Esperanza.* Buenos Aires: Ediciones Guadalupe.

Survival International. 2007. *Progress Can Kill: How Imposed Development Destroys the Health of Tribal Peoples.* https://www.survivalinternational.org/progresscankill.

Synod of Bishops, Special Assembly for the Pan-Amazonian Region. 2019. *The Amazon: New Paths for the Church and for an Integral Ecology—Final Document*. The Vatican, October 26. http://www.vatican.va/roman_curia /synod/documents/rc_synod_doc_20191026_sinodo-amazzonia_en.html.

United Nations Educational, Scientific and Cultural Organization (UNESCO). 2021. *Indigeneous Peoples*. https://en.unesco.org/indigenous-peoples.

Vatican Council II. 1965. *Gaudium et Spes*. https://www.vatican.va/archive /hist_councils/ii_vatican_council/documents/vat-ii_const_19651207 _gaudium-et-spes_en.html.

Wolff, Jonathan, and Avner De-Shalit. 2013. *Disadvantage*. Oxford: Oxford University Press. Second Edition.

Zampini-Davies, Augusto. 2014. *Amartya Sen's Capability Approach and Catholic Social Teaching in Dialogue: An Alliance for Freedom and Justice?* Doctoral thesis, University of Roehampton, London. https://pure.roehampton.ac .uk/ws/portalfiles/portal/338258/PhD_Thesis_A_Zampini_electronic _version.pdf.

Conclusion

Clemens Sedmak and Séverine Deneulin

A couple of hours' drive outside of Uganda's capital, Kampala, in the Kasana-Luweero Diocese, a pioneering agricultural training initiative, the Bethany Land Institute, was set up in 2012.[1] The seed of the initiative pre-dates the publication of Pope Francis's *Laudato Si'* (*LS*; 2015), but the encyclical subsequently gave it a further impetus and roadmap. The mission of the initiative is the formation of leaders who are committed and equipped to transform rural communities in Uganda. During a two-year residential training program, the students—called caretakers when entering the program—are *formed* in the principles of integral ecology, such as learning to contemplate and "stop and admire something beautiful" (*LS* 215) and taught various sets of capabilities, such as that of managing accounts. This passage from *Laudato Si'* best summarizes why the initiative has been set up and its aims: "Ecological culture cannot be reduced to a series of urgent and partial responses to the immediate problems of pollution, environmental decay and the depletion of natural resources. There needs to be a distinctive way of looking at things, a way of thinking, policies, an educational programme, a lifestyle and a spirituality which together generate resistance to the assault of the technocratic paradigm" (*LS* 111).

This passage also contains many insights about the relationship between the Catholic Social Teaching (CST), a part of the Catholic tradition, and the capability approach (CA). The current socio-ecological crisis requires a spiritual dimension and a "way of seeing," but also a set of appropriate capabilities (a "way of doing") cultivated through educational processes. The avoidance of a "technocratic paradigm" also requires "meta-capabilities," that is, second-order capabilities that help practitioners order and realize first-order capabilities. The Bethany Land Institute intends, therefore, not only to teach but also to "form." Thus, a CST-inspired approach and a commitment to (first-order and second-order) capabilities come together.

Moreover, the Bethany Land Institute initiative also points to another relationship between CST and the CA, namely, that a commitment to the most marginalized comes together with a commitment to the earth. The three major challenges in rural Uganda that the institute aims to address (deforestation, food insecurity, and poverty) clearly demonstrate *Laudato Si's* thesis that "we are faced not with two separate crises, one environmental and the other social, but rather with one complex crisis which is both social and environmental" (*LS* 139). The region faces mass deforestation and resulting topsoil cover depletion as a direct consequence of unsustainable rural practices—such as the cutting of trees for firewood or digging of marshes for brick-making—which are given free range by the Ugandan government in the absence of sustainable environmental policies. A rapidly growing population and continuously changing rain patterns due to climate change only exacerbate the issue, making the land increasingly arid and unproductive and triggering a food insecurity crisis across the country. Families often resort to extending their property boundaries to compensate for the land's sterility. This, in turn, has ignited widespread land disputes between neighbors.

The lack of viable economic options in rural Uganda has therefore not only an impoverishing but also a dehumanizing effect on its inhabitants, who have only their ever-deteriorating land as a source of labor and profit but are ill equipped to manage this land in a way that ensures their economic survival, preserves their self-worth, and guarantees social peace. Young people become especially demoralized by the scarcity of economic prospects in the countryside, and migrating to Kampala for work seems the only option they have.

In *Laudato Si'* Pope Francis views labor, following earlier Catholic social teachings on labor, especially Pope John Paul II's encyclical *Laborem Exercens*, published in 1981, not only as a source of sustenance, but also as "a path to growth, human development and personal fulfilment" (*LS* 128). Further inspired by this encyclical, the Bethany Land Institute intends to develop capabilities in the areas of (a) agriculture, forestry, and care for creation, (b) finances and marketing, and (c) leadership and empowerment.

As mentioned above, the institute goes beyond these first-order capabilities to form future rural leaders in some meta-capabilities, for a "way of doing" is inextricably linked to a "way of seeing." Among these meta-capabilities, the current strategic plan of the institute highlights the ability to respect and honor human dignity, to express nobility in the care of creation, to work hard, to have a sense of self-esteem, to manifest a spirit of service, to express gratitude, and to demonstrate tenderness.

These meta-capabilities can be grasped under the ethical concept of "virtues" as dispositions to act in a certain way. Therefore, they translate into a strengthening of the agency of individuals, in the CA sense of the word, but give it an orientation or sense of direction—or, one could say, a *telos*. In this sense, the Bethany Land Institute connects an investment in agency expansion with a commitment to building up the inner life. The initiative works with regular prayer times and liturgies. This is a point that may be worth mentioning: prayer is key to the inner life in a Christian understanding, but it cannot be properly described in terms of the CA concept of agency. Carmelite Sister Ruth Burrows puts this well when she writes: "Almost always when we talk about prayer, we are thinking of something we do and, from that standpoint, questions, problems, confusion, discouragement, illusions multiply. For me, it is of fundamental importance to correct this view. Our Christian knowledge assures us that prayer is essentially what God does, how God addresses us, looks at us" (Burrows 2006, 1).

This is a dimension that the CA cannot easily grasp with the categories it has to offer. This is not a statement about the limits of the CA but an indication that the CA and CST have different histories and have been developed for different purposes. The point of this book has been to explore what both accounts have to contribute to an understanding of human development and integral ecology.

This book has been an experiment. It has been an attempt to facilitate a dialogue between the CA and CST. It has to be noted that the dialogue has been an encounter between clearly different partners. On the one hand, the CA has its roots in development economics and philosophy, has a far-reaching policy impact, and gathers a diverse community of scholars from different disciplines and backgrounds. On the other hand, CST has a long historical and institutional embeddedness, a faith foundation, and it faces the challenge to move to a more diverse authorship of its normative documents.

There is, however, a lot of common ground between the two approaches. Both are committed to social transformation (as Guillermo Otano Jiménez examines in his chapter), and both invite collaboration between practitioners and scholars. Both are based on commitments to values such as human dignity and human freedom. Both contain critical reflections on the notion of development or progress, and both operate on the level of global ethics with the potential of influencing local contexts. Both ask the question of what it means to live meaningfully, based on "the deep recognition of the social character of human flourishing" (as Joshua Schulz observes in his chapter), and both are based on an understanding of the necessary material aspects of well-being (as James Bailey points out in his chapter). Both focus on aspects of agency and human initiative, and both see individuals as relational beings. The CST-based "preferential option for the poor" and the CA-based understanding of poverty as capability deprivation reach common ground on the practical level, as Helmut Gaisbauer's chapter has illustrated. Séverine Deneulin and Augusto Zampini-Davies' chapter has shown how the "see (listen)-judge-act" method can be fruitfully applied using the CA, whereas the latter can help CST make connections between institutions and their impact on people's lives.

However, there are also significant differences that set the CA and CST apart and make them distinct. The fruitfulness of the dialogue is partly owed to these differences. One fundamental difference lies in their genealogy. The CA may be rooted in an encounter with reality, such as Amartya Sen's experience of a famine in his childhood. CST is rooted in the encounter with Jesus Christ, an encounter that changes every aspect of life. In the light of the contributions of this book, we highlight three main areas of difference between the CA and CST that have emerged from the chapters.

The first area of difference is their respective understandings of *freedom*. As Lori Keleher points out in her chapter, freedom is at the core of the CA; all capabilities are freedoms. Freedom is also at the core of

CST, but only a subset of our capabilities are considered to be freedoms. Keleher suggests using the term "authentic freedom" to talk about this subset. "Authentic freedom, or the freedom to be and act as we ought, is the freedom to be and act in accordance with dignity" (105). In this context, another important difference emerges. Within CST, Keleher observes that "we fail to achieve the perfectionist goal of acting in accordance with dignity when we lack an internal state or attitude of love" (107). Within the CA, freedom can be defined in terms of agency, as the capacity to act (or not to act) as we choose or prefer, without external compulsion or restraint. This understanding of freedom is connected to choices about courses of action and external obstacles. In contrast, in the understanding of CST, as the Bethany Land Institute initiative illustrates, there is an important inner dimension of freedom. Acting and internal dispositions go together. The second paragraph of the "Instruction on Certain Aspects of the Theology of Liberation," which the Congregation for the Doctrine of the Faith (CDF) published in 1984, exemplifies this inner dimension of freedom in CST: "Liberation is first and foremost liberation from the radical slavery of sin. Its end and its goal is the freedom of the children of God, which is the gift of grace. As a logical consequence, it calls for freedom from many different kinds of slavery in the cultural, economic, social, and political spheres, all of which derive ultimately from sin, and so often prevent people from living in a manner befitting their dignity" (CDF 1984).

This is a statement about the primacy of the inner dimension of freedom. This does not exclude agency-based ways to understand freedom in the Catholic tradition,[2] but there is a clear understanding of the priority of the inner life and the order of salvation. Pope Leo XIII, for example, in his letter *In Plurismis*, which he wrote in 1888 to the bishops of Brazil about the abolition of slavery, defends the freedom of the human person on the grounds of a theological anthropology and condemned the institution of slavery (saying that "the system . . . is wholly opposed to that which was originally ordained by God and by nature"), but he clarifies that "the worst slavery . . . is the slavery of sin" (Leo XIII 1888, 2–3). This language points to inner constraints and an understanding of a lack of freedom based on truth, as the title of the 2009 encyclical by Pope Benedict XVI (*Caritas in Veritate*, or Charity in Truth) points out. The way truth's claims are articulated also points to a difference between

CST and CA; more about this point below. The inner dimension of freedom has to do with the Christian idea of interiority, as developed by St. Augustine in his *Confessions* (Taylor 1989). The human person has an inner life. CST clearly emphasizes this inner dimension of the human person, as Ilaria Schnyder von Wartensee and Elizabeth Hlabse have shown in their chapter. The inner life is connected to an understanding of the soul in the Christian tradition (Tyler 2016, 9–26). Our inner core as humans is understood to be shaped by our experiences and the dynamics within the soul. The idea of the soul is integral to the Catholic tradition, as is discussed at length in the *Catechism of the Catholic Church* (*CCC* 990, 992, 997, 1703, 1705, 1711), even though the idea can be found in Greek and medieval philosophy, in psychology (Kraus 2018), and in Kant's moral philosophy. The discourse on the soul and interiority pushes the CA, in a certain sense, out of its intellectual comfort zone, to borrow from the expression of Clemens Sedmak's chapter.

Another nuance of the different understandings of freedom found in the CA and CST is in relation to the community dimension of freedom. Meghan J. Clark's contribution to this book made it clear that CST, in contrast to the CA, has a stronger connection to community and a connection to love. She summarizes her reflections on CST with this statement: "CST is distinct from the CA because it is teleological by nature—the human flourishing it aspires to is not only one of expanding substantive freedoms but also seeks the common good marked by solidarity. While there is a sense of solidarity implicit in Sen's emphasis on participation, justice, and responsibility for others, my claim is that CST goes further, defining solidarity as a virtue" (203).

This leads us to a second area of difference, and fruitful dialogue, between the CA and CST, their understanding of *community* and *the public*. Let us start with their understanding of the public: there is a difference in the way both think about public and democratic discourse. The CA's insistence on public justification and public discourse cannot be realized in the same way in CST given its position and role within the Catholic Magisterium. The latter makes strong truth claims based on an understanding of the authority of the Church. In all CST-based discourses, then, there is a strong connection to truth that is not primarily negotiated or emerging in a discourse. The normative sources that the CA and CST work with are clearly different. The main normative source of the CA is a democratic discourse, while the main normative sources for CST are the tradition(s) of the Church and Sacred Scripture, as described in the Vatican Council II document *Dei Verbum* (1965), interpreted by the Magisterium of the Church, even though an analysis of "the signs of the times" (and experience) plays an important role. Truth claims emerging from a democratic discourse are relative to a particular discursive community and subject to change; truth claims based on the Catholic sources are more rigid in nature—but they are also more mystical. To quote Anna Rowlands (2021, 5): "CST's origin and end are ultimately contemplative and mystical. They are rooted in a truth and a relation that is revealed as, and in, gift and encounter with what and who is other than ourselves and can only partly be known."

Additionally, this book has also illuminated CST's struggle with inclusiveness: Katie Dunne points out in her chapter that "CST's conception of integral human development . . . fails . . . to adequately address the demands of gender justice and the realities of women's experiences" (149). CST, she writes, "is woefully deficient in its lack of gender awareness and inclusivity" (164). Public and inclusive discourse is a strength of the CA, but not much present in CST. However, CST may be stronger in its understanding of the role of virtues in public institutions, given its attention to people's inner lives, as highlighted above. CST makes a stronger association between personal attitudes and institutional functioning. It holds that sustainable reforms need conversion of hearts. For good reasons, Pope Francis uses the term "ecological conversion" in *Laudato Si'* (*LS* 216–21). Then there are the differing ways of understanding community and the common good. In CST community is valued as an expression of the order of creation (as the Book of Genesis 2:18 states: "It is not good that the man should be alone") and even as an expression of divine nature (the triune God). Community is valued at a deep level. This does not come as naturally to the CA. Meghan Clark observes that "Sen is himself rather apprehensive about any further statements about the role of community in general . . . communities remain instrumental realities" (229). In Clemens Sedmak's chapter he tries to show that there is a similar challenge with regard to nature (not to reduce it to a "natural resource"). CST, it seems, can more easily see both community and nature as valuable in themselves; every living entity, whether human or non-human, has intrinsic value. There is a risk in the CA, with its commitment to each person as an end, of seeing community and nature as means and resources for the flourishing of the individual human person, a position that does not concur with the idea of integral ecology, as Cathriona Russell shows in her chapter.

A third area of difference is in understandings of *anthropology*. CST works with a theological anthropology, as Amy Daughton and Dana Bates have pointed out in their chapters, an anthropology based on the idea of *imago Dei*, understood in a Trinitarian way. The idea of self-relating concerns will have different connotations in the CA and in CST, the latter being more skeptical of them as foundations for a person's agency. It is easier for CST to accommodate the idea of interdependence beyond free choices of connections. Human beings are communal beings. This is not based on observations, but on a certain understanding of metaphysics. Joshua Schulz observes that the CST account of dignity and community is "metaphysical and theological" (131).

Within CST, the human person is seen as a communal being created out of love and for love. Whereas the CA may see "freedom" as its most important normative concept, CST suggests that it is "love," as Pope Benedict XVI developed in his encyclical *Deus Caritas Est*, published in 2005. God's love for the human person is the basis for dignity and life; God's love for creation is the basis for the imperative to respect the human person and creation. The role of love (encounter) has also been emphasized in the chapter by Ilaria Schnyder von Wartensee and Elizabeth Hlabse.

An important element of Christian anthropology is its sensitivity to an end goal, or telos. There is a final destination for the human person, and it is the responsibility of theology to ask these first and last questions. One way of interpreting the CA is the idea that the realization of one's values is the end goal and capabilities the means to achieve it. Sen writes, "Individual advantage is judged in the capability approach by a person's capability to do things he or she has reason to value. A person's advantage in terms of opportunities is judged to be lower than that of another if she has less capability—less real opportunity—to achieve those things that she has reason to value" (Sen 2009, 231). The CA does not have an eschatological horizon that makes us think about "the ultimate" and this life as the penultimate, beyond, one could argue, including a "capability to hope" as something a person has reason to value. However, this is very much part of the CST way of approaching reality.

With these questions of the ultimate, the CA reaches its limits, which are the limits of philosophy and economics. The ideas of the spiritual and the transcendent are integral aspects of anthropology in CST and are connected to the ultimate. In the words of *Populorum Progressio* (*PP*), published by Pope Paul VI in 1967: "United with the life-giving Christ, a person's life is newly enhanced; it acquires a transcendent humanism which surpasses its nature and bestows new fullness of life. This is the highest goal of human self-fulfillment" (*PP* 16). Talking about the last questions and maybe even the horizon opened up by mysticism makes us reach the limits of philosophy and the limits of the CA.

In this book we have intended to show the fruitfulness of the dialogue and the potential for mutual enrichment. The differences between the CA and CST may lead to disagreements, for example, with regard to the justification of normative claims and the sources of moral obligations, the place of freedom and autonomy in a wider understanding of the ethics of the good life, and the ontology of the person. There is clearly also enrichment, since the two are different and can thus challenge each other.

Since the CA and CST operate from different points of departure and with different comprehensive commitments, there may also be a challenge of recognizing the limits of a dialogue between the two. Such a dialogue may need not only the ability to understand, but also the ability to (respectfully) not understand (Gurevitch 1989). This is the ability to accept differences without losing respect for the other position and the willingness to learn without developing the need to appropriate the other position.

A fruitful dialogue between CST and the CA seems important since both approaches constitute important communities that intend to be forces for the good in a world troubled by injustice, poverty, war, and ecological destruction. It is timely to join hands in the effort to respond to these challenges with an integral understanding of development in mind. As we write this conclusion, Russia has invaded Ukraine and Ukrainians are mobilizing to defend their freedom, which is being taken away from them by the orders of an autocratic and criminal president whom Russian citizens risk their lives to oppose. This is yet another lesson on how precious freedom is—both the external freedom of agency and self-determination and the inner freedom that guides a person to truth and life, away from lies and destruction.

NOTES

1. The initiative has been mainly spearheaded by Emmanuel Katongole, a professor of theology and peace studies at the University of Notre Dame and a priest from the Archdiocese of Kampala (Bethany Land Institute, n.d.).

2. The *Catechism of the Catholic Church* (*CCC*), published by John Paul II in 1992, characterizes "freedom" as "the power, rooted in reason and will, to act or not to act, to do this or that, and so to perform deliberate actions on one's own responsibility" (*CCC* 1731).

WORKS CITED

Benedict XVI. 2005. *Deus Caritas Est.* Encyclical. https://www.vatican .va/content/benedict-xvi/en/encyclicals/documents/hf_ben-xvi_enc _20051225_deus-caritas-est.html.

———. 2009. *Caritas in Veritate: On Integral Human Development in Charity in Truth.* Encyclical. https://www.vatican.va/content/benedict-xvi/en /encyclicals/documents/hf_ben-xvi_enc_20090629_caritas-in-veritate .html.

Bethany Land Institute. No date. "Our Story." https://bethanylandinstitute .org/our-team.

Burrows, Ruth. 2006. *Essence of Prayer.* London: Bloomsbury.

Catechism of the Catholic Church (*CCC*). 1992. Vatican City: Libra Editrice Vaticana. https://www.vatican.va/archive/ENG0015/_INDEX.HTM.

Congregation for the Doctrine of the Faith (CDF). 1984. *Instruction on Certain Aspects of the "Theology of Liberation."* https://www.vatican.va/roman _curia/congregations/cfaith/documents/rc_con_cfaith_doc_19840806 _theology-liberation_en.html.

Francis. 2015. *Laudato Si': On Care for Our Common Home.* Encyclical. https:// www.vatican.va/content/dam/francesco/pdf/encyclicals/documents/papa -francesco_20150524_enciclica-laudato-si_en.pdf.

Gurevitch, Zali D. 1989. "The Power of Not Understanding: The Meeting of Conflicting Identities." *Journal of Applied Behavioral Sciences* 25, no. 2: 161–73.

John Paul II. 1981. *Laborem Exercens.* Encyclical. https://www.vatican.va /content/john-paul-ii/en/encyclicals/documents/hf_jp-ii_enc_14091981 _laborem-exercens.html.

Kraus, Katharina. 2018. "The Soul as the 'Guiding Idea' of Psychology: Kant on Scientific Psychology, Systematicity, and the Idea of the Soul." *Studies in History and Philosophy of Science* 71: 77–88.

Leo XIII. 1888. *In Plurismis: On the Abolition of Slavery.* Encyclical. https://www.vatican.va/content/leo-xiii/en/encyclicals/documents/hf_l-xiii_enc_05051888_in-plurimis.html.

Paul VI. 1967. *Populorum Progressio* (*PP: On the Development of Peoples.* Encyclical. https://www.vatican.va/content/paul-vi/en/encyclicals/documents/hf_p-vi_enc_26031967_populorum.html.

Rowlands, Anna. 2021. *Towards a Politics of Communion: Catholic Social Teaching in Dark Times.* London: T&T Clark.

Sen, Amartya. 2009. *The Idea of Justice.* London: Allen Lane.

Taylor, Charles. 1989. *Sources of the Self.* Cambridge, MA: Harvard University Press.

Tyler, Peter. 2016. *The Pursuit of the Soul: Psychoanalysis, Soul-Making and the Christian Tradition.* London: T&T Clark.

Vatican Council II. 1965. *Dei Verbum: Dogmatic Constitution on Divine Revelation.* https://www.vatican.va/archive/hist_councils/ii_vatican_council/documents/vat-ii_const_19651118_dei-verbum_en.html.

James P. Bailey is an associate professor and chair of the Department of Theology at Duquesne University in Pittsburgh, Pennsylvania. He holds an MA in religion from Yale University and a PhD in theological ethics from Boston College. He is the author of *Rethinking Poverty: Income, Assets, and the Catholic Social Justice Tradition*, published by the University of Notre Dame Press.

Dana Bates is the executive director and co-founder of New Horizons Foundation, which seeks to inspire youth to lead and produce social change through innovating and sustaining models of experiential education in Romania. He has a degree in philosophy from Gordon College in Wenham, Massachusetts, and a master's of divinity from Gordon Conwell Seminary in Hamilton, Massachusetts. He has a PhD from the University of Middlesex in London, and his dissertation was titled "The Glory of God Is Humanity Fully Alive: Exploring Eastern Orthodoxy as a Resource for Human Development in Conversation with the Capability Approach." Based in the Jiu Valley in Romania, he leads the Semester Abroad Program for Northwestern College in Orange City, Iowa, and Gordon College in Wenham, Massachusetts.

Meghan J. Clark is an associate professor of moral theology in the Department of Theology and Religious Studies, St. John's University in New York. She is the author of *The Vision of Catholic Social Thought: The Virtue of Solidarity and the Praxis of Human Rights* (Fortress, 2014). In 2015 she was a Fulbright Scholar at Hekima University College in Nairobi, Kenya, and she has conducted fieldwork in Kenya, Ethiopia, and Tanzania examining the development work of the Daughters of Charity.

In 2018 she was a visiting residential research fellow at the Centre for Catholic Studies at the University of Durham, UK.

Amy Daughton is an associate professor in practical theology in the Department of Theology and Religion at the University of Birmingham in the United Kingdom, where she is also currently the head of department and director of the doctoral program in practical theology. Her research is situated at the intersections of theology, politics, and practice and is ultimately concerned with questions of the moral life and the contributions of theology in a plural society. Significant recent publications include work on Paul Ricoeur and intercultural hermeneutics in conversation with Thomas Aquinas in *With and For Others*, and she co-edited the *T&T Clark Reader in Political Theology*.

Séverine Deneulin is the director of international development at the Laudato Si' Research Institute in Campion Hall at the University of Oxford and an associate fellow in international development in the Oxford Department of International Development. She has been a visiting fellow at the Kellogg Institute for International Studies at the University of Notre Dame. Prior to the founding of the Laudato Si' Research Institute, she was an associate professor in international development in the Department of Social and Policy Sciences at the University of Bath in the United Kingdom.

Katie Dunne is a lecturer in religious education at St. Angela's College, Sligo, a college of the National University of Ireland in Galway. She holds a PhD in theology alongside MTh and BATh degrees from St. Patrick's Pontifical University in Maynooth, Ireland. Prior to joining the faculty at St. Angela's College, she was an assistant professor in theology in the School of Religion at Trinity College in Dublin.

Helmut P. Gaisbauer has been a senior scientist at the Centre for Ethics and Poverty Research at the University of Salzburg since 2011. One of his long-term research projects validates the efforts of combatting child poverty in Romania organized by faith-based organizations in Salzburg. He holds a doctorate in political science from Salzburg University and the Salzburg Centre for European Union Studies. He has published extensively on poverty and social exclusion in Europe.

Elizabeth Hlabse is the director of the Program on Faith and Mental Health at the McGrath Institute for Church Life of the University of Notre Dame. A licensed mental health therapist, she supports persons therapeutically through an integrative, neural-developmental lens that attends to the intersection of spirituality and psychology. She holds an MS from Divine Mercy University in Sterling, Virginia, and completed postgraduate studies in Christian ethics at the University of Oxford.

Lori Keleher is a full professor in the Department of Philosophy at New Mexico State University. She is the president of the International Development Ethics Association and a fellow of the Human Development and Capability Association, director of policy at the Center for Values in International Development, and co-lead editor of the *Journal of Global Ethics*. She co-edited with Jay Drydyk *The Routledge Handbook of Development Ethics* (Routledge, 2019); with Stacy Kosko, *Agency and Democracy in Development Ethics* (Cambridge University Press, 2019); and with Des Gasper, *Lebret and the Projects of Économie Humaine, Integral Human Development, and Development Ethics*, a special issue of the *Journal of Global Ethics* (2021).

Guillermo Otano Jiménez works as an advocacy officer at the Alboan Foundation, a Jesuit NGO in Spain. He is also the coordinator of Justice in Mining, a Global Ignatian Advocacy Network (GIAN) created by the Society of Jesus that gathers together the Jesuit social centers, NGOs, and universities seeking to discern and promote socio-environmental justice in conflicts related to mining. He has a BSc and a PhD in sociology from the Public University of Navarre. As a researcher, he has focused on the capability approach and the analysis of social changes and the link between religion and development.

Cathriona Russell teaches ethics, theology, and hermeneutics in the School of Religion, Theology and Peace Studies at Trinity College Dublin. She has a PhD and a BA in theology and ethics from Trinity College and a BSc and MSc in agricultural science from University College Dublin. Her teaching, research, and publications focus on environmental theology and philosophy; technology, development, and medical and research ethics; and creation theologies in cosmology, anthropology, and hermeneutics. She is an avid plant collector and vegetable gardener with a special interest in the manuscripts of the Chester Beatty Library in Dublin and the urban environments of her native city.

Ilaria Schnyder von Wartensee is the director of IN-WONDER LLC, an experiential learning program on human flourishing. From 2014 to 2022, she served as the Ford Family Research Assistant Professor at the Kellogg Institute for International Studies at the University of Notre Dame. Her main research interests are international development and the study of migration, with a particular focus on the dignity of people and their integral human development. A native of Switzerland, she graduated in international relations from the Graduate Institute in Geneva and holds an MSc in anthropology and development from the London School of Economics and a PhD in international law and economics from Bocconi University in Milan.

Joshua Schulz earned a PhD from Marquette University in Milwaukee and is presently an associate professor of philosophy at DeSales University in Center Valley, Pennsylvania. Working in the Aristotelian-Thomistic tradition, he has published widely in moral philosophy on issues concerning personhood, political liberalism, medical ethics, and artificial intelligence. He also serves as co-chair of the Ethics Committee and as a clinical ethics consultant for the Lehigh Valley Hospital Network in Pennsylvania.

Clemens Sedmak is a professor of social ethics and the director of the Nanovic Institute for European Studies at the University of Notre Dame. He is also the co-director of the Center for Ethics and Poverty Research at the University of Salzburg. He has co-edited, with Paolo Carozza, *The Practice of Human Development and Dignity* (for the University of Notre Dame Press).

Augusto Zampini-Davies is a priest and moral theologian of the Diocese of San Isidro, Buenos Aires. He served as adjunct secretary of the Dicastery for Promoting Integral Human Development at the Vatican and as the head of the Vatican COVID-19 Commission, as well as an expert advisor to the 2019 Synod of the Amazon. He has also worked as theological advisor to the Catholic Fund for Overseas Development (CAFOD) in the United Kingdom and as an assistant priest and lecturer in social ethics in England and Argentina. He has a PhD in theology from the University of Roehampton in London, an MSc in international development from the University of Bath in the United Kingdom, and a licentiate degree in moral theology from the Universidad del Salvador, Argentina. Prior to becoming a priest, he worked as a lawyer in Argentina.

INDEX